W9-BUH-088

FIGURE SKATING

FIGURE

SKATING

A HISTORY

James R. Hines

UNIVERSITY OF ILLINOIS PRESS • URBANA AND CHICAGO

WORLD FIGURE SKATING MUSEUM AND HALL OF FAME • COLORADO SPRINGS

SALINE DISTRICT LIBRARY
555 N. Maple Road
Saline, MI 48176

MAR 2006

Published by the University of Illinois Press and the

World Figure Skating Museum and Hall of Fame

© 2006 by the Board of Trustees of the University of Illinois

All rights reserved

Manufactured in China

Library of Congress Cataloging-in-Publication Data

Hines, James R. (James Robert), 1937–

Figure skating : a history / James R. Hines.

p.   cm.

Includes bibliographical references and index.

ISBN-13: 978-0-252-07286-4 (ISBN-10: - 13 paper : alk. paper)

ISBN-10: 0-252-07286-3 (ISBN-10: - 10 paper : alk. paper)

1. Figure skating—History.

I. World Figure Skating Museum and Hall of Fame.

II. Title.

GV850.4.H56   2006

796.91'2'09—dc22   2005009419

TO THE MEMORY OF MY MOTHER, IMOGENE MARY DUNN HINES

CONTENTS

ACKNOWLEDGMENTS

During the years I worked on *Figure Skating: A History* many individuals and organizations provided encouragement and assistance. Tara Hurt, Readers Services Coordinator of the Thomas J. Dodd Research Center at the University of Connecticut, provided valuable material. The Special Collection of skating books there is especially rich for the nineteenth and early twentieth centuries. Sharon O'Brien, a reference librarian at the Troy Public Library in New York, did a significant amount of research on Jackson Haines, saving me a trip to Troy. Giovanna Robbiani at the International Skating Union furnished an abundance of material and answered many questions, as did Mary Gastner and Carole Shulman at the Professional Skaters Association. Ivan Basnicki and Julie Green, archivists at Skate Canada, provided information on Canadian skaters. Brian Alexander, director; Beth Davis, curator; and Karen Cover, archivist, at the World Figure Skating Museum and Hall of Fame in Colorado Springs have been immeasurably helpful by providing material and answering questions throughout the course of the project. Dennis Bird of England, long a skating historian, responded to multiple inquiries and shared valuable information, especially on English-style skating. The staff of the Captain John Smith Library at my own institution, Christopher Newport University, has responded repeatedly to my needs, particularly Cathryn Doyle, director of the Library; Amy Boykin, reference librarian; and Leslie Condra, interlibrary loan librarian. Two deans, Christine Ramirez-Smith and Douglas Gordon, as well as a department chairperson, L. Barron Wood Jr., generously supported the project.

Most important as an advisor, colleague, mentor, and friend has been Benjamin T. Wright, an honorary member and the historian of the International Skating Union, a former member and chair of the ISU Figure Skating Technical Committee, and an honorary World Championship referee. He is also an honorary member and senior past president of the United States Figure Skating Association and the author of many articles and several books on figure skating. He has generously responded to numerous questions, read the manuscript, made helpful suggestions, and provided introductions to persons in the skating community who themselves have contributed in a myriad of ways.

Others have helped in ways too numerous to mention individually. They are included here in alphabetical order: Tenley Albright, Donna Atwood, Lynn Benson, Cecilia Colledge, Tom Collins, Karen Burr De-Jung, Andrea Dohany, John Fahey, Pat Gale, John Hoaglund, Lars Jansson, Carol Heiss Jenkins, Junko Hiramatsu, Pete Jones, Caryn Kadavy, Kate Keller, David Kirby, Adrienne S. Lamm, Shane Leasure, David and Rita Lowery, Ronald Ludington, Dale Mitch, Jeffrey Perrier, Christie Allan-Piper, Valerie Powell, Jirina Ribbins, F. Rossoukhi, Rhea Schwartz, Helen Smith, Barbara Standke, Bob Thickman, Don Watson, Margaret White, Debbi Wilkes, and Mary Louise Wright. To all of them I offer my sincere appreciation. Each shares in the ultimate success of this book.

Special acknowledgment and appreciation is expressed to providers of 226 pictures employed throughout the book and in its "Picture Gallery of World and Olympic Figure Skating Champions." Most are from the extensive collection at the World Figure Skating Museum and Hall of Fame in Colorado Springs. Those for many of the more recent skaters are from photographers Michelle and Paul Harvath. Other providers include Tom Collins Enterprises, Inc., the Currier and Ives Foundation, the Broadmoor, Frank J. Zamboni Company, the McCord Museum of Canadian History, George S. Rossano, Jyrki Kostermaa, Michelle Wojdyla, Lois Yuen, J. Barry Mittan, Alexandre Fadeev, Barbara Wagner, Courtney Jones, Paul Thomas, and Rhea Schwartz. For the pictures included throughout the text, sources are acknowledged with the pictures. For pictures in the gallery, sources are acknowledged collectively at the beginning of that section. Figure skating is a performing art, and pictures depict artistry when words prove inadequate. To all who have provided pictures I am deeply grateful because they have allowed me to more completely report the history of figure skating.

Finally, I thank all persons at the University of Illinois Press who have assisted in the production of this book.

INTRODUCTION

The sports world was stunned in 1993 when tennis star Monica Selles was stabbed by a fan of her competitor Steffi Graf. Less than a year later, figure skating star Nancy Kerrigan was temporarily disabled in a brutal attack that implicated her competitor Tonya Harding. Sports, professional and amateur, were suffering from the misdeeds of persons outside and within their own ranks. The tragedy of violence seemed unavoidable.

Public interest in figure skating had been growing steadily for more than a half century, but following the Kerrigan-Harding incident it exploded. The short program at the Olympic Games, just two months after the attack, was viewed by a television audience of forty-five million households; for about four years afterward, fans could not get enough figure skating. Televised events, amateur and professional, saturated the airwaves to meet public demand. That could not be sustained, and by 1998 the bubble had burst. Public interest in figure skating settled quickly to a level similar to that of a decade earlier, but during that heightened period a much broader public gained appreciation for the world's most beautiful sport.

That event is now fading from memory, but changes resulting from it, directly and indirectly, will continue to affect figure skating for years to come. Most significant has been the huge monetary value of television contracts to the sport's governing organizations and the reciprocal demands placed on those organizations by the media. Lucrative opportunities for skaters resulted as well, causing some of the most gifted competitors to turn professional (termed ineligible) immediately after winning major titles. Responding to the loss of eligible skaters, governing organizations in an effort to keep skaters competing have made it advantageous to remain eligible by awarding prize money in many events and relaxing long-standing rules relative to income-generating activities. Indeed, eligible skaters today can often make more money than ineligible skaters.

Figure skating is unique among sports. Its balance of artistry and athleticism permeates its history. For many years the artistry of tracing figures on the ice ruled supreme, but as the sport became competitive and more athletic, maintaining a balance between artistry and athleticism posed fascinating, sometimes difficult problems. Subjective judging, a necessity for evaluating artistry, has spawned controversies, some legitimate and some not. The pairs competition at the Salt Lake City Olympic Games in 2002 provides a well-known example. Such controversies provide fascinating history, but more important, they often lead to significant changes in the sport, as did the one at Salt Lake City.

My involvement with skating dates from the 1950s, but like many I was caught up in the media hype following the attack on Kerrigan. I sought out and read the small number of serious books that have been written about figure skating and soon realized that an up-to-date history of the sport was sorely needed. That rekindled interest coupled with my training and curiosity as a historian led to the decision to write a comprehensive history of the sport.

To be sure, a number of books on various aspects of figure skating describe enthusiastically the sport as practiced from its formative years to the present; until recently, most have dealt primarily with skating technique. The earliest and most important of them provide starting points for major chapters of the text. Robert Jones's *The Art of Skating* (1772), the first in any language, sets the stage for the evolution of skating in nineteenth-century England. Jean Garcin's *Le vrai patineur* (The true skater, 1813) describes a much different style of skating practiced in France following the Revolution. Yet another style evolved in Austria, described in detail by three skaters from the Vienna Skating Club, Demeter Diamantidi, Carl von Korper, and Max Wirth, authors of *Spuren auf dem Eise* (Tracings on the Ice, 1881), the most extensive technical book ever written on the sport. Other important books are mentioned throughout the text.

Biographies or autobiographies, such as Sonja Henie's *Wings on My Feet* (1940), remain rare until well after World War II, but since the mid-1970s, their number has grown dramatically, clearly a result of public interest in elite skaters generated by television coverage of major competitions. Many of them are intended for young readers and fall into the category of juvenile literature.

Scholarly works are limited. The only previous history of the sport, Nigel Brown's groundbreaking *Ice Skating, a History* (1959) is excellent but badly out of date and has not been available for many years. Most important are histories of three of skating's oldest governing organizations, two by Benjamin T. Wright, *Skating in America*, written for the seventy-fifth anniversary of the United States Figure Skating Association, and *Skating around the World, 1892–1992*, written for the centennial of the International Skating

Union, and one by Dennis Bird, *Our Skating Heritage,* written for the centennial of the National Ice Skating Association of the United Kingdom. A few long-established skating clubs have also published histories, the most extensive being *Hundert Jahre Wiener Eislauf-Verein,* written for the centennial of the club in Vienna, Austria.

Young people entering the sport, their parents, skaters who have advanced significantly in the competitive structure, coaches, and millions of fans had no place to turn for a history of the sport for which they have so much interest and enthusiasm. In the broader arena of sports history, figure skating needs to be better represented among sports whose history is better known. My purpose has been to fill the critical need for those who love the sport while contributing to the body of literature on sports history. Beginning with its roots in Nordic mythology and continuing through the 2002 skating season, *Figure Skating: A History* identifies persons, places, organizations, and events that have shaped figure skating and molded it into the popular sport it has become.

Skating as a mode of transportation is at least three thousand years old, probably much more. Travel across the frozen landscape is recorded in the oldest Nordic myths, primarily as a necessity for the hunt. Skating as a recreational activity goes back at least eight hundred years, undoubtedly more. One of the earliest documents we have is a fascinating description of skating in London dating from the twelfth century. Skating as a sport is at least two hundred years old, almost certainly more. Records of specific races date from the eighteenth century. Organized competitive skating, however, in its three most important branches—speed skating, ice hockey, and figure skating—under the control of international governing organizations is just over a century old. This book describes one of those branches, figure skating. Although its roots are traced back to the ancient world of mythology, the real birth of figure skating occurred in Stuart England. From then to the present, its intriguing story is recounted.

From simple figures traced on frozen ponds by gentlemen nearly four hundred years ago to difficult competitive programs executed on artificial ice by elite competitors today, the narrative describes figure skating's evolution into one of today's most popular sports. It is divided historically into three major parts separated by the world wars. Appendices list medal winners for skating's most important international competitions: the World Championships, the European Championships, the Four Continents Championships, the North American Championships, and the Olympic Games. A picture gallery includes all World and Olympic champions. Professional figure skating, totally a product of the twentieth century, is covered in two separate chapters.

The birthplace of figure skating is England, following the return of Charles II in 1660. For two hundred years it remained exclusively a recreational activity, and still in the mid-nineteenth century members of the London Skating Club opposed adamantly anything suggesting competition, even proficiency tests. Skating was an activity for gentlemen fascinated by the tracings they could leave on the ice. Combined skating, the sophisticated tracing of geometric figures by groups of skaters, was considered the highest form of skating art, and it dominated the sport for nearly a half century, becoming known as the English style of skating.

In the eighteenth century England's influence was felt on the Continent and in the New World, but in the nineteenth century national characteristics gradually developed in those places. The Austrians were more progressive than the British, but there, too, members of the Vienna Skating Club viewed skating totally as a recreational activity. They took dance to the ice in the late 1860s, but fascination with tracing figures remained preeminent. *Spuren auf dem Eise* reveals in its title what was considered to be most important. The Viennese style of skating, later to become the International style, provides a direct link to modern free skating.

French skaters approached skating specifically as an artistic endeavor. They viewed body position as more important than tracings left on the ice. *Le vrai patineur* emphasized the grace that can be achieved through body position, reflecting the French fascination with ballet. Garcin's book was dedicated to the premier dancer at the Imperial Academy of Music. The French style remained insular throughout most of the nineteenth century, while technical advancements occurred in other places, especially England and Austria.

Across the Atlantic, skating in Canada and the United States mirrored at first developments in England, but as the nineteenth century progressed a distinctively American style evolved, one fundamentally different from that practiced in England. North American skaters placed emphasis on difficult one-foot figures such as letters and numbers and two-foot figures called grapevines. The British did not consider such "antics" good skating. Those figures could not be accomplished with the rigid body position employed for combined skating. Thus, each skating center developed and fostered its own unique style. The evolution of three dominant styles—the British, the American, and the Continental—prevalent in the late nineteenth century are described in separate chapters.

Competitive figure skating, local at first, dates from the mid-nineteenth century in most countries. It became international later in the century, and problems surfaced almost immediately as skaters trained in their own national styles competed against skaters trained in other styles. Competitions often included events requiring different styles to be skated, but they were fundamentally so different that skaters could excel in one event and flounder in another. Responsible judging was difficult to achieve. The need for one universal style with prescribed judging criteria was clear. The International Skating Union (ISU), established in 1892, adopted the two-event competition of compulsory figures and free skating that reigned supreme for nearly a century, and the first World Championship was held at St. Petersburg, Russia, in 1896.

Nineteen World Championships were held before the outbreak of World War I. Only men competed at first, but competitions were added for ladies in 1906 and pairs in

1908. Unlike today, the number of competitors was typically small, sometimes not enough to award all the medals. Twice, the gold medalists were the only competitors. The number of countries that entered skaters was likewise small, a total of just nine through the period. Swedish skaters dominated, claiming a third of the gold medals awarded. Ulrich Salchow, the most famous of them, has been immortalized by the jump he invented and that bears his name. But all the prewar skaters were pioneers; they laid the foundation on which the sport has grown ever since. With them, the first part of the narrative is brought to a close.

World Championships were not held for seven years owing to the war. When competition resumed in 1922, the ISU was thirty years old, and skaters no longer had ties to the earlier national styles. They competed in the only style they knew. The years between the wars were ones of development, as free skating evolved rapidly and became technically more demanding. Compulsory figures retained a strong link to the past; free skating was the wave of the future. Spins became faster, with more revolutions. One thinks immediately of Sonja Henie's extraordinary spins, which can still be viewed in her Hollywood films. World Champion Cecilia Colledge of Great Britain invented and introduced the camel spin, the third basic spin position and a requirement in short programs today. While spins became increasingly spectacular, jumping made even greater strides. Jumping, viewed negatively through most of the nineteenth century, was incorporated in some but not all prewar free-skating programs. Between the wars, extensive experimentation occurred as jumping achieved importance equal to that of spinning. By the end of the period, the modern repertoire of jumps had evolved, and many were being doubled.

Pair skating likewise experienced remarkable advancements between the wars as daring lifts, death spirals, side-by-side jumps, and pair spins became a part of competitive programs. Before the war, pair skating was closer to ice dancing, but by the late 1920s spectacular new elements were being introduced by a growing number of outstanding pairs, including Andrée and Pierre Brunet from France, Emilia Rotter and László Szollás from Hungary, and Maxi Herber and Ernst Baier from Germany. They won collectively twelve World and three Olympic titles.

Ice dancing also realized tremendous development, especially in England where talented ice dancers participated in national competitions. They had inherited only a small number of dances from the prewar era, leading them to invent new ones, many of which are still being done. Ice dancing was not contested internationally until the 1950s, but during the 1930s it evolved into a popular, highly competitive discipline at the national level.

The years between the wars proved to be among figure skating's most important. All disciplines flowered and became technically more demanding in the process. Skaters from Canada and the United States competed in ISU competitions now held on both sides of the Atlantic. Although the technical demands of free skating would increase after the war, it was the generation of talented, gifted, and enthusiastic skaters between the wars who molded figure skating into the guise we recognize and appreciate today.

Professional figure skating dates from the early twentieth century. In 1914 Charlotte Oelschlagel, the first great show skater, headlined a group of women from Germany who performed in highly successful shows at the New York Hippodrome. Charlotte, as she was known in the United States, was also the first skater to appear on the silver screen. Professional skaters from the early years of the century performed anywhere an ice surface of any size could be provided as they took figure skating to the public in cities large and small. By the late 1930s, major companies were touring successfully in the United States and elsewhere. The Ice Follies, Henie's Hollywood Ice Review, and Ice Capades all date from the years just before the United States entered the war. Contemporaneously, Hollywood took skating to an ever wider audience through a series of highly successful films featuring Sonja Henie, capitalizing on her reputation as the world's greatest figure skater.

Figure skating since World War II, the third major period in this history, is primarily the story of practitioners who have carried forward the now well-established sport and reached the top of the medal stand in international competition, constantly stretching the limits of athleticism and the boundaries of artistry as they have done so. They are the athlete/artists who an appreciative public has admired and cheered on as they pursued relentlessly their quests to be the best in the world. Owing to an ever-increasing number of competitors and the ever-expanding technical demands placed on them, reaching the top of the medal stand has become more difficult, and staying there is much less common. There are, for example, just fourteen lady World champions from the forty-one competitions held through 1960 but twenty-six from the next forty-one held through 2002. Even more revealing is the difference in the number of repeat champions. Only four of the earlier champions failed to repeat, but since 1960 seventeen have failed to repeat.

In the early days of competition, before World War I, training was limited to the availability of natural ice. As artificial ice became more widely available in the years between the wars, year-round training became possible, but the extensive training that elite skaters undergo today is a product of more recent years. In addition to working with their coaches, skaters study ballet, do off-ice physical conditioning, and work with skating choreographers. Without such extensive ancillary training they would find it difficult to incorporate athletically difficult elements into artistically pleasing programs and to compete successfully at the international level. In addition, top skaters employ costume designers, makeup artists, and hair stylists in order to present themselves in the best light possible and to achieve competitive advantage. Some have consulted sports psychologists to help handle the tremendous pressure of competition.

In former times, competitors typically maintained full-time jobs while training on a part-time basis. Those of college age continued studying full time while they competed. Although training since World War II has required an ever-increasing time commitment, skaters in the 1950s and 1960s still found it possible to matriculate while competing. Dick Button, Tenley Albright, Hayes and David Jenkins, Manfred Schnelldorfer, and Alain Calmat provide excellent examples. They won World titles while earning degrees as full-time students. Today that seems impossible. Tonia Kwiatkowski and Matt Savoy are recent graduates who attended college while competing. They earned spots on World teams but did not medal. World Champion Michelle Kwan was determined to attend college while competing but found that to be impossible. Olympic gold medalist Sarah Hughes matriculated in 2003, electing not to compete while in college

This book is about skaters, especially the 148 World and Olympic champions from 1896 through 2002. Their successes and their failures are identified; their contributions are celebrated. Other skaters are included, provided they meet a criterion credited to commentator Dick Button: "They left the sport better because they were in it." The narrative through the postwar period progresses generally by decades. It emphasizes major issues, some short-lived but others extending over longer periods, that are identified with the skaters most directly affected. General concerns of the ISU are addressed throughout. From the 1950s, a section is devoted to "Judges, Judging, and Controversy," and from the 1960s a section reports on "Skating and the Cold War." Later sections include "ISU Concerns of the Seventies" and "The ISU Turns One Hundred."

Skating's disciplines are treated separately in each chapter, with emphasis on those undergoing significant change, such as ice dancing becoming a world sport in the 1950s, pair skating becoming more romantic with the beginning of the Soviet dynasty in the 1960s, and singles skating wrestling with the value placed on compulsory figures in the 1970s. This organization allows readers interested in particular subjects to go directly to them.

The coverage provided to individual skaters is determined by their competitive success and contributions to the sport. Some entries are as short as a few sentences, whereas others are far more extensive. Wolfgang Schwarz, the 1968 Olympic gold medalist, won no other major title and thus receives only a brief mention. Scott Hamilton and Kurt Browning, two of the most popular skaters in recent times, however, won a combined eight World titles and enjoyed brilliant professional careers afterward. They share a section entitled "Two Matinee Idols." Some skaters important to the sport never won a World or Olympic title but have met the "Button criterion." They include Janet Lynn, Toller Cranston, and Surya Bonaly.

The single most important change in competitive figure skating since World War II has been the gradual reduction in importance of compulsory figures and their ultimate discontinuance from competition. Reductions in the number of figures prepared and skated and their relative scoring values are described. Skaters who benefited or suffered from them are identified. Jeannette Altwegg and Trixi Schuba are World and Olympic champions who were masters of compulsory figures and benefited from their relative value in competition; others such as Janet Lynn, Denise Biellmann, and Midori Ito were masterful free skaters who suffered from their inability to perfect compulsory figures. Major sections covering this important topic include "Ladies and the Compulsory Figures" and "The Total Elimination of Compulsory Figures."

Figure skating as a sport is unique in that it incorporates elements of the performing arts, is interpretive, and is done to music. As a result, it must be judged subjectively, opening the evaluation to abuse and dishonesty. From the earliest days of local competitions in the nineteenth century to the Olympic Games and World Championships in 2002, figure skating has been plagued with judging problems and controversies, and it is safe to assume that problems will occur in the future. It must be acknowledged, however, that throughout its history the ISU has dealt decisively and effectively with this inherent problem. The most celebrated judging controversies are described as yet another component of skating's exciting history.

Outstanding black skaters have appeared since the 1970s, and in 1986 Debi Thomas, an American, became the first and only one to win a World title. Two years later the "Battle of the Carmens" provided one of several highlights at the Calgary Olympic Games as Thomas and Katarina Witt both skated to music from Bizet's opera. A section entitled "The Advent of Black Skaters" identifies social problems suffered by blacks in the United States that carried over into the skating world. Although the number of elite black skaters remains small, an increasing number of young people of all races are now entering the sport, and that bodes well for the future.

Owing to the theatrical nature of figure skating, there is great public interest in individual skaters, primarily those who reach celebrity status as either amateurs or professionals. Their personal lives are always of interest to fans but are of somewhat less importance to a general history of the sport. Biographical information has necessarily been held to a minimum, but for many skaters, biographies geared toward their fans are readily available. Yet some skaters transcend the normal bounds of competition and directly influence the sport positively or negatively. Their contributions are identified. On the positive side, there have been marvelous role models such as Peggy Fleming, Dorothy Hamill, and Michelle Kwan, skaters who have inspired many young people to take up the sport and to emulate them. On the negative side, one thinks immediately of Tonya Harding, who through her misdeeds brought figure skating to the fore, actually increasing its popularity as a spectator sport. Much of the change that has occurred since 1994 can be attributed directly to the attack on Nancy Kerrigan.

Skating today is sometimes considered a "ladies sport," and some facts support that view. More young girls than boys take up figure skating, and inherent problems result from that gender imbalance. Those who want to compete in pairs or ice dancing often have difficulty finding partners. Synchronized skating, the sport's newest internationally contested discipline, was conceived specifically as a ladies' sport, possibly a factor in its popularity and phenomenal success. This view has become an issue in figure skating today, but it is a recent development, one that did not exist and was not an issue in the early history of the sport. In fact, the opposite was the case. Participation by women was evolutionary and is addressed throughout the narrative.

Women donned skates in the eighteenth century, but that was more the exception than the norm. Figure skating was a male-dominated sport throughout most of the nineteenth century. Only gradually were women allowed to join skating clubs. By the 1890s that was changing, as evidenced by the popularity of hand-in-hand skating and the craze for waltzing on ice. They became active and equal participants. As the twentieth century dawned they not only participated recreationally, but they also competed. In 1906 Madge Syers became the first lady World champion. Twenty-one years later, Sonja Henie, the sport's most decorated singles skater, won her first World title. Between the wars, women's participation in competitive figure skating grew to equal that of men.

The perception of figure skating being a ladies' sport, especially in the United States, is a product of the post–World War II era, one that has become most prevalent since the 1960s. The advent of televised skating events has been a major influence and contributing factor because figure skating is a sport that appeals especially to a female viewing audience. Many mothers take their daughters to ice rinks and enter them into group lessons.

This perception is real and has validity on many levels, but it is not obvious when one places the emphasis on skaters who reach the elite level of competition. More girls than boys take up the sport and compete at the developmental levels, but that differential moderates as skaters move ahead in the competitive structure. An approximately equal number of women and men qualify to compete at major competitions. Because emphasis in this book is placed on skaters who compete on the international stage, specifically World and Olympic champions, the issue of figure skating as primarily a ladies' sport becomes less significant.

Although it is acknowledged that today females are most often referred to as women, in the sport of figure skating, from the eighteenth century to the present, the term *ladies* has been employed for young novice skaters through the oldest adult skaters. It was a subject of discussion at an ISU Congress, the result of which was confirmation that in figure skating there are only men and ladies. In an attempt to be historically accurate, the term *ladies* has been used extensively throughout this text.

Social and cultural issues are always of interest because they affect the sport directly. For example, Madge Syers, "Skating's First Feminist," entered the "all male" World Championship in 1902. She could not be stopped because there was no rule to prevent it. The importance of that event cannot be overstated. It led to the establishment of the first World Championship for ladies four years later, and the impact of gender on the development of figure skating has been ongoing. Other more recent social issues such as ethnicity and sexuality deserve further study, but for practical reasons I have treated them only tangentially. The nature of a survey-type history is to provide a foundation from which others can investigate such specialized areas, and it is hoped that this book will inspire future scholars to undertake those studies.

The spelling of proper names has occasionally presented a challenge because variant spellings exist in official documents. In the case of Russian and other Slavic languages that sometimes results from transliteration employing the Cyrillic alphabet. I have attempted to achieve consistency while employing logical spellings or those most frequently found. For medal winners in ISU championships before 1992, the spellings employed are those printed in *Results: Figure Skating Championships, 1968–1991*. Many skaters compete using the nicknames by which they are commonly known. In those cases, a given name is provided, with the nickname in parenthesis at the first or most important mention. Otherwise the nickname is used.

Some organizations, competitions, and skating terminology have undergone name changes. To avoid confusion, in a few cases one name is employed throughout the book. These are clarified by endnotes acknowledging the changes. The International Skating Union (ISU), for example, was officially the Internationale Eislauf-Vereingung (IEV) until 1948. After describing its formation in 1892 as the IEV, the acronym *ISU* is used consistently.

Some skating titles have been shortened for stylistic considerations and ease in reading. I have reduced "lady World champion" to "World champion" when the gender is clear. National titles include the names of the respective countries, such as "U.S. lady figure skating champion." Those titles are reduced to "national champion" when the gender and country are clear.

I have employed various criteria to avoid the national bias of an American writing a history of international skating. One is to include all skaters who have won World or Olympic titles. Other skaters as well as writers, coaches, and officials are included if they had a definable impact on the sport and left it better because of their involvement. Thus, no attempt has been made to name every important person or skater. That would be impossible. Those included in the early years, before the advent of World and Olympic competition, are writers, organizers, and practitioners who clearly influenced the sport.

Figure skating, like all sports, is constantly evolving, with new records being set every year. This history covers skating through the 2002 season. Inevitably, some statistics will be superseded and former records broken before publication. At the end of the 2002 season, for example, no skater had completed a triple Axel Paulsen jump in ladies' competition since Midori Ito did so at the Olympic Games in 1992. That is no longer true. Early in the 2003 season two skaters, Japan's Yukari Nakano and Russia's Ludmila Melinda, completed the jumps less than thirty minutes apart at Skate America.

The appendices and "Picture Gallery of World and Olympic Figure Skating Champions" have been updated through 2005. Owing to major changes in the judging system adopted by the ISU at the 2004 Congress, a result of the controversy following the pairs' competition at the 2002 Olympic Winter Games, an Epilogue covers the contentious debate that occurred within the skating community and among fans relative to those changes.

ABBREVIATIONS

AAUC	Amateur Athletic Union of Canada
ASAC	Amateur Skating Association of Canada
ASC	American Skating Congress
CAS	Court of Arbitration for Sport
CBE	Commander of the Order of the British Empire
CFSA	Canadian Figure Skating Association
FISA	International University Sports Federation
FSD	Figure Skating Department (of the ASAC)
IEV	Internationale Eislauf-Vereingung
IOC	International Olympic Committee
ISU	International Skating Union
IPSA	International Professional Skaters Association
ISUofA	International Skating Union of America
MBE	Member of the Order of the British Empire
NASA	National Amateur Skating Association
NCAA	National Collegiate Athletic Association
NSA	National Skating Association of the United Kingdom
OBE	Officer of the Order of the British Empire
PSGA	Professional Skaters Guild of America
USFSA	United States Figure Skating Association
WSF	World Skating Federation

PART ONE

Skating to World War I

ONE

Skating before Figures

SKATING on artificial ice in indoor rinks is today a year-round recreational activity enjoyed by people of all ages and abilities as well as a sport both amateur and professional that enjoys unprecedented popularity. But throughout most of its history, ice skating has been an activity limited to short seasons and possible only in countries where lakes, ponds, canals, or other bodies of water provide frozen surfaces on which skaters could enjoy the challenge and excitement of gliding across natural ice.

In the ancient world, long before skating became a recreational activity or a sport, those same frozen surfaces provided a different kind of challenge. Passage over them was a necessity for survival during harsh winter months. Snowshoes, skis, skates, and sledges evolved early as practical means of travel over the frozen landscape. But whether as a means of transportation in ancient times or as a recreational activity in the modern world, skating outdoors has always provided practitioners with an exhilarating experience of rapid movement, with cool winter air blowing on their faces. Brian Boitano expressed it well following the filming of *Water Fountain* in Alaska when he said, "Skating on the lake in Alaska was probably one of my dreams come true. I can truthfully say that . . . it was the closest I've come to being so touched that I cried in a skating performance."[1]

Today, competitive skating is done indoors under controlled conditions, certainly an advantage in the highly competitive world of figure skating. No longer must skaters concern themselves with the hazards of natural ice, with adjustments for wind conditions affecting all aspects of their programs, or with the biting cold temperatures that can adversely affect performance, but those hazards were reality and part of the challenge for competitive skaters until 1966, when the last major outdoor figure skating competition, the World Championships, was held at Davos, Switzerland.[2] It is unlikely that any contemporary skater would choose to return to those former conditions, but something was lost when skating moved indoors. Many former skaters fondly remember competing on outdoor ice. "What I loved most was the sheer joy of skating, natural ice that gave jumps their spring, flowing movements, and deep edges, vibrant skies, and glorious mountains, all of which lifted my spirits," reminisced Olympic champion Dick Button in 1990.[3]

Skating has developed into three disciplines, speed skating, ice hockey, and figure skating, all of which are practiced both on ice skates and roller skates. Indeed, the histories of skating on blades and rollers have parallel developments. Ice skating has a longer history and is today more popular, particularly at the competitive and professional level, but at times skating on rollers, first developed in the nineteenth century, has been as popular as skating on blades. Roller skates were invented to provide year-round skating in the days before artificial ice, and their popularity surpassed all expectations. The public filled roller rinks, and some early skaters competed successfully in both arenas. This history, however, deals only with figure skating on blades.

MYTHOLOGY AND THE EARLIEST SKATERS

A history of figure skating must begin with myths from Scandinavian countries, stories that provide the earliest accounts of movement on ice in the ancient world and tell us about skating's earliest practitioners. Although none were committed to writing before the twelfth century, they recount stories from much earlier times. Some may date back as far as the Scandinavian Bronze Age, which lasted for more than a thousand years, beginning about 1600 B.C., but because no written sources survive from that period, we must rely on archeological evidence for our somewhat limited knowledge. Identifiable gods and goddesses associated with skating appear early, but their history remains obscure until the period of migration, beginning about 300 A.D.

Written sources for northern myths are by two Christian writers, Saxo Grammaticus, a twelfth-century Dane, and Snorri Sturluson, a thirteenth-century Icelander. They recount stories that had long been in oral tradition. It is from Snorri, a brilliant poet, historian, and politician whose *Prose Edda* dates from about 1220, that we gain most of our knowledge about the gods themselves. Saxo preserved many tales in his lengthy history of

Denmark. A third important source, not discovered until the seventeenth century, is the anonymous manuscript *Codex Regius,* commonly referred to as the "Poetic Edda."

In that ancient mythological world, skating was not a recreational activity but a practical means of movement over ice and snow during the long Scandinavian winters, a necessity for travel and hunting. The implements employed were not ice skates in the modern sense. Most were closer in use and construction to snowshoes or skis. Animal bones or blocks of wood were fastened to the traveler's feet, and staffs or poles were employed to push themselves across the ice or snow.

We know little of skating's most ancient practitioner Ull, the god of snowshoes, of the shield, of the bow, of hunting, and for a time of security and law. He was reported to be fair to look at and a mighty hunter. His importance in the world of the gods is acknowledged by all scholars. The meaning of his name is debated, but one leading theory suggests that it relates to glory or brilliance. On his snowshoes, Ull represented the brilliance of the winter sky. In one account, he crossed the sea on a magic bone, clearly referring to the earliest kind of ice skates. Skating across lakes would have been an appropriate activity for an important deity of the North. As a chief god, Ull appears frequently in myths, but his eminence is most clear from one specifically about him. Saxo tells us that Ull replaced Odin, who as a chief god had been disgraced by disguising himself as a woman in order to beget an avenger. Ull reigned in Odin's absence for ten years, even taking his name, but the gods eventually took pity on Odin and restored him to power. Ull fled to Sweden, where he was killed by the Danes.

Also important is Skadl, the goddess of snowshoes. Snorri reports that she traveled on snowshoes, used a bow, and hunted animals. She was probably also a goddess of winter and thus of darkness and death. What is confirmed by the myths is that in the ancient world movement over ice or snow was necessary for survival, and primitive forms of skates, snowshoes, and sledges were used for that purpose. But by the time these myths were recounted in the twelfth and thirteenth centuries, skating had become a recreational activity and a sport in England and probably elsewhere.

THE EARLIEST SKATES

Skates are known to have been in use more than three thousand years ago. Made from the leg bones of large animals, including horses, deer, and sheep, they were filed and shaped to create a smooth surface throughout their length. They were not sharpened, thus having no edge like a modern skate. Holes were drilled in the bones so straps could be employed for fastening them to the skater's shoes. Bone skates have been found in various European countries, including Denmark, England, Holland, Norway, and Sweden, and are on display in many museums.

These primitive skates facilitated movement quickly and efficiently across ice. Both feet were kept on the surface, and poles were used for pushing. Because the bones were not sharpened, skaters could neither push off nor maintain forward motion in the modern way. This was proven by an experiment undertaken in the 1890s by G. Herbert Fowler, a member of the London Skating Club, who constructed a pair of bone skates modeled exactly on a pair from the Guildhall Museum and confirmed by skating on them that it was not possible to "strike off" using the side of the bone. He did discover that it was possible to propel himself forward using the toe of the bone, which could bite the ice, but historical evidence suggests that staffs or poles were always employed for propulsion until the development of the bladed skate.[4]

Bone skates date back at least three thousand years, but other bone and stone implements were in use as much as ten thousand years ago in the same areas of Europe associated with the earliest skates. It seems probable that when hunting implements were being made, arrows were being shaped, and bone was being crafted into various tools, man would have discovered that by tying bones to his feet he could move efficiently across the ice, aiding in the hunt. Thus, the use of skates could have begun thousands of years earlier than can presently be documented.

The earliest known iron skates date from about 200 A.D. They were not sharpened but were strips of iron that functioned in the same manner as bone. The early iron runners may seem to have been an improvement, but they did not replace bone. Peasants would not have had the means of securing iron; bone was free. Iron runners provided no apparent advancement and probably no advantage to the art of skating. Skates continued to be made of bone throughout most of the Middle Ages, but sometime before the fourteenth century the Dutch revolutionized skating by employing sharpened steel blades. With that development, skating began its evolution into those sports associated with it today.

AN EARLY ACCOUNT OF RECREATIONAL SKATING

Although skating served first as a means of travel, at an early date it must have served also as a recreational activity, particularly among young people. Animal bones were readily available to anyone who would take the time to shape them into a pair of skates. Recreational skating, that is, skating just for fun or as a game, could easily date back many centuries, but the earliest descriptive account, written by William Fitz Stephen, dates from 1180. Fitz Stephen's extensive description of Norman London includes a major section devoted to various games and sports, arranged seasonally, beginning with those practiced during Carnival. Games and sports played by young men not yet vested with the belt of knighthood were always combative and often incorporated lances and shields. Skating was no exception. On Sundays and feast days the public would turn out in large numbers to watch and cheer on the youths who participated.

Skating is the last sport mentioned because the winter season precedes Carnival. To many, skating was simply sliding across the ice, but it became a game when those with the greatest skill and best balance tied bones to their feet and moved with great speed, pushing themselves along with steel-pointed poles. Fitz Stephen's account confirms that skating in twelfth-century London was both a recreational activity and a sport:

> When the great marsh that washes the Northern walls of the city is frozen, dense throngs of youths go forth to disport themselves upon the ice. Some gathering speed by a run, glide sidelong, with feet set well apart over a vast space of ice. Others make themselves seats of ice like millstones and are dragged along by a number who run before them holding hands. Sometimes they slip owing to the greatness of their speed and fall, every one of them, upon their faces. Others there are, more skilled to sport upon the ice, who fit to their feet the shinbones of beasts, lashing them between their ankles, and with iron-shod poles in their hands they strike ever and anon against the ice and are borne along swift as a bird in flight or a bolt shot from a mangonel. But sometimes two by agreement run one against the other from a great distance and, raising their poles, strike one another. One or both fall, not without bodily harm, since on falling they are borne a long way in opposite directions by the force of their own motion; and whenever the ice touches the head, it scrapes and skins it entirely. Often he that falls breaks shin or arm, if he fall upon it. But youth is an age greedy of renown, yearning for victory, and exercises itself in mimic battles that it may bear itself more boldly in true combats.[5]

SKATING AS A TOOL OF WARFARE

Skates became a practical tool of warfare four centuries later. In 1572, during the Dutch revolt against Spain and the reign of terror suffered under the ruthless Duke of Alva, King Philip II's chief minister to the Netherlands, the Dutch fleet was trapped in frozen water at Amsterdam. Attacking from land across the frozen sea, Spanish soldiers were forced to retreat when they discovered that the Dutch had chopped a mote around the ships. As the Spaniards retreated, Dutch musketeers on bladed skates surprised them by moving with the mobility skates provided. They routed and massacred their attackers, who wore clogs with spikes that provided stability but not quickness on the ice. Alva reportedly ordered seven thousand pairs of skates for his own troops, but no other known battle on skates ever occurred.

THE DUTCH ROLL

The Dutch success in routing the Spanish resulted from maneuverability possible with bladed skates. It is not clear when bladed skates first appeared, but it was before the fourteenth century in the Netherlands. Countries further north were not as conducive to ice skating because frozen lakes there were often covered with thick blankets of snow, suitable for sledging, skiing, and snowshoeing but not for skating on blades. The Netherlands, however, experienced long spells of cold weather and much less snow. Numerous canals that provided primary routes of trade and communication from town to town remained frozen for extended periods during the winter months. With less snow, canals could easily be maintained for travel by skaters, and the Dutch employed skates for winter travel.

The introduction of sharpened blades changed the course of skating. Able to grip the ice, skaters no longer needed poles to push themselves along. They could use the edges of their bladed skates to push off as is done today, and continuous motion from foot to foot must have followed almost immediately. Discarding the poles had a practical side as well. The arms became free to carry items as skaters traveled from town to town. More important to the history of figure skating was the discovery of edges. At first skaters pushed and glided in a manner similar to what they had previously done with poles, but they must have soon discovered that by leaning to the left and right they could maintain a continuous and flowing motion that was both practical and artistic. The resulting edges, probably inside at first, provided great speed and physical beauty. This continuous movement, known as the Dutch roll, was clearly defined by the sixteenth century, but iconographic evidence supports skating on edges at least a century earlier. A famous late-fifteenth-century woodcut of St. Lydwina's accident shows a skater approaching her who appears to be skating on an inside edge.[6]

The Dutch developed edges, inside and outside, the first figure skating moves and the basis of all figure skating. Compulsory figures and, with specific exceptions, virtually all free skating and dance moves are done on edges. Similar movement was just as necessary for the development of speed skating, and it was in speed skating, not figure skating, that the Dutch excelled during the ensuing centuries. The English became the first dominant force in figure skating, beginning with the introduction of the Dutch roll in the mid seventeenth century and continuing with figures derived from it, figures that would eventually give the sport its name.

SKATING'S PATRON SAINT

It is appropriate to conclude this first chapter with a brief description of figure skating's patron saint, the virgin Lydwina of Schiedam. Lydwina is remembered for a life of suffering that resulted from a skating accident. Born on Palm Sunday 1380, she was the only daughter in a poor family of nine children. By age fifteen she had become a vivacious and beautiful young lady. During the winter of 1395–96, while skating with friends on a frozen canal, Lydwina collided with another skater and broke a rib as she fell to the ice. Although she received the best medical care available, she never recovered. In fact, she grew steadily worse, not just in the short term but throughout her life, which lasted

The Accident to Saint Lidwina (1396)

Johannes Brugman's fifteenth-century woodcut *The Accident to St. Lidwina*. (World Figure Skating Museum and Hall of Fame)

nearly thirty-eight more years. She died on Holy Tuesday in the year 1433. Within a year after the accident she suffered unexpected reactions as spasms of pain convulsed and contorted her body and she lost almost all muscular control of her limbs. Symptoms of various diseases appeared, and she was permanently bedridden. None of her former beauty remained.

Lydwina was ministered to by a priest from the local church, Father John Pot, who urged her to think always of the suffering of the lord and to relate her suffering to his. Constantly meditating on the Passion, she grew to believe that God had called on her to be a victim for the sins of others. About 1407 she began to have mystical visions, communing with God, various saints, and her guardian angel. Unable to eat solid foods, she subsisted on a liquid diet, and for the last seven years of her life she rarely slept. After her death a hospital was built on the site of the home where she had spent her years of suffering.

Modern knowledge of Lydwina comes from two early biographers, one her cousin,

John Gerlac, and another by no less a writer than Thomas à Kempis. Although she is referred to as Saint Lydwina, she has never been officially canonized by the Church, but in 1890 her cult was formally confirmed by Pope Leo XIII. That year marked the beginning of a decisive decade of international importance in the history of figure skating. A major international competition was held in St. Petersburg, Russia, in 1890, The first European Championship was held in 1891, the International Skating Union was founded in 1892, and the first World Championship was held in 1896. It is appropriate that the cult of the remarkable Lydwina was recognized at the time figure skating entered its modern and international period.

TWO

England: The Birthplace of Figure Skating

ELIZABETH I, the last of the great Tudor monarchs, died in 1603, and the English throne passed to James VI of Scotland, the first of the Stuart monarchs. More than a half century of economic problems, political turmoil, and civil war followed. Charles I, James's successor, was beheaded in 1649 following the infamous Rump Parliament, causing the Stuarts to flee the country during the decade of Oliver Cromwell's protectorate.

When the monarchy was restored in 1660, two years after Cromwell's death, Charles II returned home triumphantly, and optimism prevailed as the populace anticipated a return to England's former splendor and greatness, a time of peace and prosperity like they had known under their beloved Queen Elizabeth. As Samuel Pepys observed, "The whole design is broken, and every man begins to be merry and full of hope." Recreational activity and sports, including ice skating, were part of that merriment. Pepys continued, "Over the Parke where first in my life, it became a great frost, [I] did see people sliding with their skeets, which is a very pretty art."[1]

It was not just the populace. The royal family was skating as well. While in Holland, Charles's illegitimate son, James, the Duke of Monmouth, reportedly taught English country dancing to ladies of the Dutch court and in turn learned from them how to execute the Dutch roll, a skill he did not forget upon returning to England. Pepys confirms his ability, reporting that the future James II "would go slide upon his scates," and "he slides very well."[2] James was sliding on steel-bladed skates, as the words *scheets* or *scates* used at that time referred specifically to bladed skates like those used by the Dutch. The words *scatch* or *yce bone* referred to the primitive bone skates still widely in use among the populace.

Skating in mid-seventeenth century England had retained the popularity described by Fitz Stephen five centuries earlier but had advanced no further. Skating in the Netherlands, however, had advanced significantly, resulting from the invention of bladed skates and the discovery of the Dutch roll. Holland was the birthplace of modern skating, but it was in speed skating that the Dutch were to excel. The early development of figure skating occurred in England.

THE FIRST SKATING BOOK

In 1772, a century after the Restoration, Robert Jones (d. 1772), an early devotee of figure skating, published a short treatise entitled *The Art of Skating,* "founded on certain principles deduced from many years experience by which that noble exercise is now reduced to an art and may be taught and learned by a regular method with both ease and safety." It may not have been the first book on skating, but earlier ones have not survived. Jones's treatise provides the first and only description of skating technique in the eighteenth century and provides a point of departure for understanding the rapid development that was to occur in the nineteenth century. Skating in the eighteenth century was viewed by many as an activity suitable only for men, but Jones felt differently. He saw "no reason why the ladies are to be excluded. To object to it as not being hitherto practised is the effect of prejudice and confined ideas," he wrote, and humorously continued that while skating "a lady may indulge in a *tête-à-tête* with an acquaintance without provoking the jealousy of her husband."[3]

Bladed skates had transformed the sport, but standardization of skate design was still a century and a half away. Skating books through the nineteenth century debate ad infinitum skate design, especially the merits of various methods for fastening them to the boots. Fastening with straps as well as clamps was employed, but for most skaters Jones recommended straps at both the heel and instep.[4] He warned against overtightening straps, which would cause poor circulation, and addressed problems resulting from strings and straps stretching and breaking. In the Netherlands, low, straight blades served well the needs of speed skating, but for figure skating Jones recommended curved blades that had no more than about two inches touching the ice. That reduced friction and, more important, allowed sharper turns. He also called for increased blade height, which allowed deeper edges.

Subtitled *Plain Skating and Graceful Rolling,* the first part of Jones's treatise addresses fundamentals, including inside and outside edges, rolling, running, and stopping. Inside edges, although not considered desirable or pretty, were used, sometimes as a rest from continuous skating on the more elegant outside edges. Good skaters purposely avoided inside edges, although Jones noted, as do later writers, that they are more natural, easier, and therefore especially appropriate for beginners. Owing to the all-to-frequent short skating seasons in England, it sometimes took three or four winters for a skater to master the coveted outside edges, but once mastered they provided the epitome of graceful skating.

Spread eagles, a basic connecting move between elements in free skating today, are described on both inside and outside edges. The feet are pointed in opposite directions, but, unlike today, the legs are bent at the knees. Jones called the difficult outside spread eagle a dangerous figure that could be accomplished only by the most advanced skaters.

Speed, required for the more difficult figures, was obtained by running, and Jones described in detail the correct technique. Short steps were taken, with the toes pointed outward as much as possible. For each step the heel was to hit the ice first on an inside edge and in a manner similar to "stomping on the ground," and the arms were used "as in running on the ground."

The ability to stop quickly was critical because skaters often crowded the ice. Three methods are described. One could lean back on the rear ends of the blades, causing them to dig into the ice. Although practical because blades did not extend fully under the heel of the boot as they do today, that was not considered desirable. A second method was similar to the hockey stop of today in which both feet are quickly turned ninety degrees to the direction of travel. Finally, highly proficient skaters could jump into a stop, landing with both feet parallel and turned as far as possible to either the right or left.

After fundamentals were learned, skaters could develop the "more masterly parts of the art." Five advanced figures are described with large color plates showing the correct posture for three of them, the Mercury position, rolling, and the fencing position. Rolling, considered an advanced figure, was simply forward movement on long but not particularly deep outside edges. Eighteenth-century style required a slightly bent skating leg and a clearly bent free leg. Arms were crossed in front. The body was held upright, with the skater looking in the direction of travel.

The spiral, an arabesque on skates and perhaps the most artistic figure of the day, was done only on outside edges. Jones called for a bent skating leg with the body leaning well forward, but the position did not approach the modern spiral in which the body is characteristically parallel to the ice, with a straight skating leg and the free leg in a high extension. The spiral position was held until momentum was lost, and then the skater resumed an upright position. The figure was completed with a stroke to an outside edge on the opposite foot.

The Mercury Position   *Rolling*   *The Fencing Position*

Published by Hodgson & Co 10 Newgate Street.

The flying Mercury position, rolling, and the fencing position, as shown in a fold-out from Robert Jones's *The Art of Skating* (1772), illustrating skating positions employed in eighteenth-century England.

The flying Mercury, the showiest figure of the time, was distinguished by the body position employed while performing it. Jones's plate shows the skating leg to be straight and the free leg bent. One arm is at the side; the other is extended slightly higher than the head, with the index finger pointed. A two-foot spin of two or three revolutions provided an optional but artistic conclusion to the figure.

Jones described skating backward as a "whimsical movement" that is neither necessary nor pleasant. He felt obliged to "lay down the plainest instructions for it" because skaters were attempting it. Backward skating was required, however, to complete Jones's last described figure, a heart on one leg. It was a basic three turn from an outside edge at the midpoint of the figure with the inside edge held until a complete heart had been traced.

Jones's only example of combined skating, that is, more than one person skating in consort, is the salutation, a figure that remained popular well into the nineteenth century. It is a simple figure eight in which two skaters begin close to and facing each other. They trace opposite lobes of the eight on right outside edges. As they return to the point of beginning, called the center, they trace the opposite lobes on left outside edges.

Other movements and figures were known and practiced, but Jones dismissed them collectively as "neither graceful nor pleasing." Thus, his limited body of figures represents the basic and accepted repertoire of figures in eighteenth-century England. The treatise received several additional printings with revisions and remained available until the mid-nineteenth century, demonstrating its importance as well as the fact that little technical advancement occurred for more than a half century after it first appeared.[5]

THE FIRST SKATING CLUB

Skating popularity spread throughout the British Isles during the eighteenth century.[6] Although England, specifically London, can be called the birthplace of figure skating, the Irish were skating, as were the Scots; skating history was made in Edinburgh, where the world's first skating club was founded. The actual date is in dispute, but an 1865 publication of unknown authorship, *The Edinburgh Skating Club,* reported the club to be "upwards of two hundred years old." Frequent references have been made to a note indicating that the club did not meet in 1642 "on account of the melancholy and disturbed state of the country."[7] Historians believe the date should have been 1742, although that presumes two errors, the indicated date and the two hundred–year life span. Scotland was in a disturbed state in 1642, but that predates the Restoration and any documentation of figure skating in the British Isles. The club could date from later in the seventeenth century, sometime after the Restoration, but was probably not formed before the second quarter of the eighteenth century, and there are no records of its activities before the late eighteenth century.

The earliest extant minutes date from 1778, and from that time the club prospered. By the mid-nineteenth century, a hundred years after its probable founding, the club's primary objective was "to enable the members to skate together in consort," a clear reference to combined skating. Lord Henry Cockburn, a member since 1801, was perhaps the first person to call figure skating "poetry in motion." As an analogy, he observed that "a well-matched pair of horses in harness keep perfect time, step well together, and work harmoniously in concert, so each movement of the skaters opposite each other should exactly correspond, each beginning and completing his respective circle, or portion of a circle, at precisely the same moment."[8] Cockburn has described perfectly the developing, all-encompassing goal of combined skating that became the raison d'être for figure skating after mid-century.

Every figure described in the Edinburgh Skating Club's "Program of Figures" is either specifically a combined figure or one that can be done by multiple skaters. Interlocking figure eights are the most important. They are arranged so that one lobe of each eight is common to all and serves as a central circle. Various permutations of half and whole circles create the figures skated. Discussed separately are five figures requiring backward skating, which can be done singly or in consort. All begin forward and employ three turns to get on backward edges. Apart from the realm of serious skating, several unique figures are described, including sixes, the worm, the crossing, and the wild goose. The worm, for example, was a follow-the-leader figure done by any number of skaters, "the more the better." Its name was derived from the deep curves, always outside edges, set by the leader. Although not in physical contact, the skaters were no more than two feet apart.

Admission to the Edinburgh Skating Club was by election following a petition from the candidate supported by recommendations of two members, but one blackball resulted in denial. Women were not allowed and could not participate with men in combined skating. A skating test required candidates for membership to skate complete circles on both feet, presumably outside edges, and to jump over hats placed on top of each other, first one, then two, and finally three. Membership was an honor requiring skill and artistry in the sport. Pins signifying membership were worn proudly, and failure to wear one's pin while skating resulted in a fine. The club's official skate maker was Archibald Young, whose "club skates" were described as "remarkably comfortable, neat in appearance, and suitable for skating in figures where the skaters are brought into very close contact," important because combined figures required skaters to pass "so close to each other as almost to rub shoulders."[9]

The rapidly developing sport of figure skating needed organization and leadership that could guide and mold it into an artistic and eventually competitive discipline. National and international regulatory bodies were still many years in the future, but skating clubs, which proliferated during the nineteenth century, provided critical leadership. Scotland remained a bastion of figure skating. Its second club, the Glasgow Skating Club, was formed in 1830. Candidates there had to demonstrate proficiency in forward skating, backward cross rolls, and three turns on both legs before earning the privilege of wearing a silver pin denoting membership. The club's most famous member was George Anderson, the second important British writer on the sport.

GEORGE ANDERSON, ALIAS "CYCLOS"

As skating grew in popularity during the nineteenth century so did the number of books about it, and early authors described enthusiastically the status of their sport. All were tutorials describing figures and requisite technique in great detail. Most came from England, although authors in other countries, including France, Germany, and the United States, added to the list. One of the earliest and most important is George Anderson's *The Art of Skating,* dating from 1852 and published under the pen name Cyclos.[10] Anderson, for many years president of the Glasgow Skating Club, justified his work by stating that Robert Jones's book was "erroneous in many respects and deficient in others."[11]

Before addressing skating technique, Anderson devoted fully half of his book to the state of skating in mid-century England and its place in that society. Like William Fitz Stephen seven centuries earlier, he first surveyed sports practiced seasonally throughout the year, beginning with those played in the spring. Addressing criticism still heard today, that skating is an effeminate sport, Anderson responded boldly, saying that those critics "must be of somewhat deficient mental calibre." He called them "the rough diamonds of the world."[12] Skating to Anderson was a sophisticated pastime for gentlemen to cultivate with elegance.

Lamenting short skating seasons that so often plagued the British Isles, Anderson assured readers that those all-too-rare skating opportunities were never missed, and extended cold spells were joyously received everywhere. In London, "when the Thames has been frozen over, a fair was always held on its surface, which lasted with the ice." But Londoners usually looked to alternate sites such as the pond at Hyde Park, which froze quickly and more frequently. "When that is well frozen," Anderson reported, "the scene is a very animated one, the crowd being so dense, as to preclude much fancy skating."[13] Members of the London Skating Club, then in existence for more than twenty years, would not have missed an opportunity to trace figures for their own delight as well as for the less skilled skaters who watched in amazement.

"In Scotland," Anderson confessed, "notwithstanding our national vanity, we must, I fear, acknowledge our inferiority in skating." In Glasgow there was "less skating than in any town in the kingdom of near its size," but, he continued proudly, "these few [skaters] form the centre of a very flourishing skating club." Turning to Edinburgh, he noted that at ponds in that city "there is a large sprinkling of ladies, and one or two of them you see with skates on, and performing very well too, generally much better than the cavalier on whose arm they affect to lean."[14]

Devoting an entire chapter to the perennial problem of skate design and calling the ordinary skate an "imperfect implement," Anderson addressed problems with the wood, methods of fastening, and the blades. The wood to which blades were affixed too often did not sufficiently follow the shape of the foot, which resulted in shifting. The problems of fastening with straps remained critical. Anderson never wore boot skates, but because they had been available for at least sixty years and had not enjoyed much popularity he surmised that there must be "some strong objection" to them. A practical concern arguing against boot skates was what to do with shoes worn to the pond. Theft was clearly a problem.

The skate of choice in Glasgow was the "club skate," which Anderson called "superior to any other in principle." It featured wooden stock made right and left to properly match the soles of boots. Its blade was rounded in the front rather than having a fancy prow, which, Anderson joked, "our grandfathers esteemed necessary elegancies." In a major improvement facilitating backward skating, the blade now extended back completely under the heel and was rounded slightly to avoid a sharp point. The height of the blade was about an inch, allowing a skater to lean adequately on an edge. The radius of curve for the blade was much debated. One writer of the period called for a radius of two feet, which Anderson deemed excessive. The arc, he felt, should be slight and not a true curve with the ends of the blades not less than a eighth of an inch nor more than a quarter of an inch above the ice.[15]

This basic skate design is attributed to Henry Boswell of Oxford, an outstanding skater of the 1830s. Inherent difficulties encountered in skating backward resulted from the blade ending abruptly and not extending completely under the heel. Skaters had to lean forward on the blade when skating backward to avoid having it catch on impediments in the ice. To overcome that problem Boswell curved the blade up, front and back, extended it past the heel, and removed the embellishing prow from the front. That was in 1836, and the design proved so practical that it became standard for the remainder of the century.

Addressing his book to beginners as well as advanced skaters, Anderson covered fundamentals thoroughly. The perils of skating, including the perennial danger of thin ice, are identified, and beginners are warned that "a jolly good tumble now and then may be considered an inevitable necessity."[16] He took strong exception to the body positions described by Jones relative to the skating leg and arms. We arrive here at the most telling characteristics of the developing English style of skating, a straight and locked skating leg and arms down at the sides rather than crossed in front.

After dealing with forward skating, Anderson discussed figures requiring backward skating, which include the Q figure, the flying Mercury, and the shamrock. Most important is the Q figure, which in various forms was to become an important part of a skater's repertoire for the remainder of the century. The basic Q begins on an outside forward edge, with a change to an inside forward edge on the same foot, a serpentine motion, after which a three turn is followed by a complete circle on an outside backward edge. The letter Q is traced on the ice. The flying Mercury, a forward figure in Jones's treatise, is now skated backward. The shamrock, called a "beautiful figure," consists of three circles, each about two-thirds completed. Considered difficult, this one-foot figure requires two three turns. Anderson emphasized the importance of learning double and triple three turns for this and other basic figure eight patterns.

Two combined figures, the salutation and the satellite, conclude Anderson's repertoire. To the salutation, already described by Jones, the satellite is added. It can be done by any number of skaters. They begin equidistant apart on a circle about nine feet in diameter. Marking their spot with a ball or orange, they skate on an outside edge around the circle to the mark set by the skater behind them. They then skate a complete circle, the satellite, on the opposite foot outside the tracing circle. This procedure is continued until all skaters have done the satellite at each mark.

Although more difficult and more sophisticated figures were on the horizon, the most important figures—eights, threes, and Qs—provided a clearly defined basis for figure skating at mid-century. Tremendous progress had been made in just one generation, and the impetus for that progress came from serious skaters who were members of a growing number of skating clubs.

THE LONDON SKATING CLUB

Skaters crowded London's frozen ponds as the popularity of skating soared at mid-century. Serious skaters practiced figures diligently until they could do them perfectly, but a much larger number of skaters took to the ice for the sheer pleasure and challenge of gliding across its surface. They enjoyed watching more experienced skaters, but most had no illusions of attaining such a high level of skill. The advancement of the sport for pleasure and as an art was phenomenal. In 1869, just seventeen years after Anderson's treatise, Henry Eugene Vandervell (1824–1908), the "Father of English Figure Skating," collaborated with a younger colleague, T. Maxwell Witham, to publish the monumental *System of Figure Skating.* Praising Anderson's book as the only one "worthy of the art" yet published, they proceeded to describe new innovations in skating technique as well as "club figures," a term referring specifically to those fostered by the London Skating Club.

The London Skating Club, founded in 1830, provided the impetus for major advancement in figure skating. Although officially named the London Skating Club, members proudly referred to it as the "Skating Club."[17] Among them were the most accomplished skaters of the day, and a badge of membership signifying skating sophistication was worn proudly. At the time Vandervell and Witham published their book the club numbered about 130 members, primarily persons of noble rank, members of the clergy, and professional people. A skating test was not prerequisite to membership, but an unwritten rule limited it to those well skilled in the art of figuring. Vandervell promoted the establishment of a series of tests and badges for members, believing they "would create just emulation" and tend to elevate the art, but strong resistance to that concept existed for many years.[18] Club members considered themselves amateurs. Tests, they thought, would lead to professionalism, which would surely lead to gambling, a blemish in most sports. The thought of that inevitable threat horrified club members.

The club erected a marquee on the banks of the Serpentine at a point called the Long Water. It was such a popular skating spot that club members were "well-bruised all over" from throngs of people, nonmembers who enjoyed skating and delighted in watching the skilled members skate their figures. Although crowds were a nuisance, Vandervell confessed that "we are not altogether free from vanity . . . many of us preferring to perform with crowds to admire [us], even though our admirers are sadly in our way."[19]

The London Skating Club remained the dominant force in skating for the remainder of the century. There, the English style evolved. It reflected the austerity of the Victorian era, but even before Prince Albert's death in 1861 ushered in strict Victorian attitudes, figure skating in England was becoming sophisticated, rigid, and highly stylized.

Participation was increasing. Vandervell's penultimate chapter, a "Chapter for the ladies," was included because "within the last few years the girls of England have been taking to skating in considerable numbers." Dealing with what he viewed as feminine perils, Vandervell warned that ladies should not skate in the "tremendously high heels at present in vogue." Wearing a large chignon he felt was desirable because it provided a "buffer or fender to save the back of the head from the painful effects of an unlucky tumble." Long dresses were not seen as a hindrance to skating, but, Vandervell mused, "should we find [ladies] wearing a dress rather short we should smilingly approve."[20]

Although never having known of its use, Vandervell described a suggestion made some years previous that "as a support to ladies learning skating" they might use "a kind of basket-work crinoline or petticoat, and therefore of a bell-shape, tightly strapped round the waist, and reaching within a few inches of the ice. With this it would certainly appear impossible to fall." But, he continued, the "natural support," also "the most agreeable, if not quite perhaps the best aid, is for the young lady to be supported by the arms, or by the elbows, or hands, either by two or a single gentleman."[21]

NEW TURNS AND FIGURES

Before turning his attention to combined figures, Vandervell, like his predecessors, covered basic skating technique. Series of three turns were given special names as difficulty increased according to the number of turns accomplished. The half double required two turns, and the double three required three. "To skate a double three to perfection," Vandervell wrote, "an immense amount of hard practice is necessary." Skaters were instructed to employ large circles, eight yards or more in diameter, and strive for great velocity. No special name was given for series of four or six turns, but five was called a triple three and seven a quadruple three. The ability to manage a large number of three turns enhanced a skater's reputation. There were reports of more than twenty, although the authors had doubts because they had never accomplished more than fourteen on the right foot or twelve on the left. Multiple three turns continued to be a challenge for

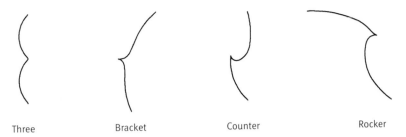

| Three | Bracket | Counter | Rocker |

The four possible one-foot turns—three, bracket, counter, and rocker—can be done from forward to backward or backward to forward beginning on an inside or an outside edge. The three turn and bracket have an obligatory change of edge as the skater remains on the same circle. The rocker and counter retain the same edge as the skater changes circles. (Pete Jones)

many years.[22] Douglas Adams, writing in 1890, said, "I have seen a good skater make as many as twenty-four turns or more on one foot."[23]

More important to the history of figure skating was the development of other one-foot turns. Only the three turn, with its ninety-year history dating back to Jones's heart-shaped figure, was known before about 1860. Its limiting factor was the obligatory change of edge. Vandervell experimented with a turn in which the same edge could be retained, resulting in the rocking turn, a name derived from the sensation he felt while skating it. Described as being "so difficult that only the most skillful skaters would have a chance of accomplishing it," he devoted ten pages to describing it.[24] Within a decade its name changed to "counter," that used today.

The bracket, first done by Witham on roller skates, predated Vandervell's rocking turn but was reportedly not done on ice skates until sometime later. The bracket, like the three turn, includes a change of edge. Its difficulty results from the body's rotation, which is opposite to that of the circle being traced. The last one-foot turn was a collaborative effort of Montague Sneade Monier-Williams (1860–1931) and Winter Randall Pidgeon (1860–1926). Working with Vandervell's rocking turn (counter), they experimented with rotation in the direction of a three turn but retaining the same edge. Called initially a three-quarter turn, it became known as the rocker by 1892 when Monier-Williams published his book *Figure Skating*. This completed the evolution of all possible one-foot turns.

The history of two-foot turns is more difficult to document because changing from one foot to the other was viewed for many years as simple stroking. Two basic turns are possible, one in which a skater stays on the original circle and retains the same edge and the other in which a skater changes circles and switches edges, outside to inside or vice versa. The turns were employed long before modern terminology appeared in writing. Because the names are Native American, one would presume they originated in

North America, and the first mention I have found is in a *New York Times* article of 1880 that identifies the Mohawk as a two-foot turn on the same circle.[25] George Meagher, a Canadian writing twenty years later, describes the Mohawk by name but not the Choctaw, which changes circles. In his second book, published in 1919, Meagher confirms that the Mohawk originated in North America but still makes no mention of the Choctaw. The history of this terminology is complicated by the fact that in England Monier-Williams described the turns by their Indian names in 1892, twelve years after the *New York Times* article and eight years before Meagher's first book.[26] This raises significant questions regarding the derivation of the names. The term *Mohawk* was probably first used in North America, but concrete evidence to support such a presumption for *Choctaw* is lacking. It is possible that Monier-Williams or someone else in England matched one Indian name, Mohawk, with another, Choctaw, in order to create consistent terminology for similar types of moves.

Vandervell devoted an entire chapter to loops and Q figures, some of which he deemed "excessively difficult." Emphasizing the now equal importance of inside edges, he warned that if they have not been "properly learnt, it will be quite useless to attempt carrying out . . . the evolutions treated."[27] Loops, introduced here for the first time, were not placed on the long axis of a figure eight, as would be done later in compulsory figures. They were individual figures.

The Q figure can begin on an inside or an outside edge, backward or forward. When it begins on the circle rather than the tail of the figure it is called a reverse Q. (Pete Jones)

George Anderson described only the basic Q figure, which begins on an outside edge at the tail of the figure. Vandervell expanded the repertoire to include eight possibilities. The basic figure can begin on any of the four edges, and the direction of skating the figure can be reversed. When the circle is skated first, the figure is called a reverse Q. There are also Q figures in altered form, most of which no longer look like the letter *Q*. They simply employ a serpentine line and a three turn. Spectacles, a connection of two Q figures that trace the shape of eye glasses, was for many years a popular figure. It, along with united shamrocks and united roses, were the most commonly employed extensions of the basic Q figures.

Vandervell's final chapter, "Nondescript Figures," is a "collection of curious movements." He left the decision of whether to learn them "to the judgement, good taste, and pleasure of the skater." Some are as mundane as variations on serpentine lines; others are more unique. The Canadian figure, accomplished "by swinging the legs alternately to the front in a kind of circular walk forwards," is totally out of keeping with the developing English style. One paragraph is devoted to jumping, which is called "a perilous feat." Vandervell recommends that all skaters learn to jump but not because of its elegance because "it is ugly in the extreme." He was speaking of jumps "completely off the ice of any height the skater can attain to." Jumping was considered useful only "to clear obstacles that are frequently met with on the ice."[28]

COMBINED SKATING

The wave of the future in England was combined skating. Jones described the salutation, and Anderson added the satellite. Vandervell devoted an entire chapter to combined skating, providing the first detailed description of what was to become the highest level of the skater's art as practiced by members of the London Skating Club. In less than a generation there had been an explosion in its popularity, and it was to dominate skating in England for the remainder of the century. Combined skating is of profound historical significance because it represents an important dimension of the sport. Skating in consort ultimately manifested itself in multiple disciplines, including ice dancing, pairs, and synchronized skating. Four was considered an ideal number for combined skating, with skaters stationed opposite each other on an outer circle, but any number from two to seven could participate. When there were five or seven skaters, the "odd man," according to Vandervell, held "a post of honor." Later writers preferred "simultaneous skating," where skaters were not opposite each other but arranged equidistance apart on the outer circle. Henry Cecil Lowther, an authority on combined skating, considered simultaneous skating "more satisfactory" when there is a non-paired person because it avoided a "lopsided appearance."[29]

Each combined figure began at a center marked by a ball or an orange placed on the ice. Skaters approached the center from points on the circumference of an outer circle on left outside edges, always keeping the center ball outside their arc. Each successive pair, or each skater in the case of simultaneous skating, left the outer circle slightly later to avoid a collision at the center. As the center was approached, the leader called the first figure of the set to be skated. From the center, skaters moved in opposite directions, all doing the same figure, collectively creating intricate and symmetrical designs. Each time they returned to the center a new figure was called, and the process continued until a dismissal call sent the skaters back to the outer circle. A group of consecutive figures was called a set, originally a reel or quadrille, and could contain any number of figures. Unique terminology evolved and was employed by the caller, who guided skaters through sometimes complex variations of otherwise basic figures.

Good technique and care were required to ensure that tracings and speed were the same for each skater, a necessity in avoiding collisions as well as maintaining perfect geometric proportions. Emphasis was placed on unison and formation, not interaction. Physical contact was not a part of combined skating, and skaters were not gender-specific. For many years it was primarily men who participated.

Combined skating represented the English style for half a century. Later British

A Combined Figure Being Skated on Wimbledon Lake in 1891, the frontispiece in Monier-Williams, Pidgeon, and Dryden's *Figure Skating Simple and Combined,* shows the rigid body position employed in the English style. The ball marks the center of the figure.

writers devoted entire books to the practice and devised exceedingly difficult sets of figures. Lowther ended *Combined Figure Skating* with a section entitled "Difficult Calls for Advanced Skaters," because "first-class skaters require something more to put them on their mettle, and, as their number is happily increasing year by year, calls requiring a higher standard of proficiency should eventually be in more frequent demand."[30]

HAND-IN-HAND SKATING

One other movement in English skating, although important for only a short period, must be mentioned. Hand-in-hand skating, which developed rapidly during the last decade of the century, provided a major step toward ice dancing. Writing in 1896, Capt. J. H. Thompson, a member of the figure skating committee of the National Skating Association, attributed the popularity of hand-in-hand skating partially to the "improvement which has taken place in the skating of the lady members of some of the leading clubs."[31] Another important and practical reason was an increasing number of artificial-ice rinks that had small skating surfaces. They were not conducive to static combined skating in which four skaters effectively dominated a large patch of ice, characteristically about 625 square feet. Hand-in-hand skating usually employed continuous movement

The side-by-side position with two hands joined as illustrated in Norcliffe Thompson and F. Laura Cannan's *Hand-in-Hand Figure Skating* (1896).

around a rink, similar to skating in an open session today. Many hand-in-hand figures were designed specifically for rink skating.

Norcliffe G. Thompson, the major source on hand-in-hand figure skating, describes 106 figures, arranged according to difficulty. All but a few are suitable for rink skating. Those few, called local figures, include sixteen figure eights, two circular patterns, and one oval pattern, all of which repeat but do not move around a rink. The other eighty-seven, called progressive figures, can be repeated around a rink of any size. Two progressive figures are specifically for three skaters. Sketches show one lady with two men.

Basic positions in hand-in-hand skating were called side by side; echelon, a side-by-side position in which one partner skates slightly behind the other; face to face; and vis-a-vis, a face-to-face position in which the partners skate sideways. All are basic positions employed in ice dancing today. Seven hand positions are described, three in which only one hand is joined and four in which both hands are joined. A technique required for hand-in-hand skating is passing, in which one partner moves to the opposite side of the other. Typically, the lady crosses in front of the man. If their hands remain joined, it is called a lock pass.

including figure skating under its jurisdiction, but the idea was rejected. Digby reports, "It was considered whether the promotion and encouragement of figure skating should not be included in its objects, but it was agreed that it would be better not to attempt too much at first, and besides figure skating stood in a somewhat different position to speed skating, for skating clubs had long existed for the former, whilst for the latter no organization existed. . . . It was felt by some [that] . . . the skating clubs might deem it presumption on their part. And it was agreed to devote all the early energies of the Association to placing speed skating on a broad and firm basis and wait for overtures from the figure skaters."[38]

Those overtures came quickly. In late 1880, less than two years after its founding, the NSA ratified a proposal for the inclusion of figure skating as a department of the association, a proposal supported enthusiastically by England's most distinguished figure skating personalities, including Anderson, Vandervell, and Monier-Williams. An ice figure committee was established, and Vandervell served as its chair until his death in 1908. Proficiency tests were adopted, and, as Vandervell had predicted a decade earlier, they stimulated great interest among skaters. Within two years, ninety-two bronze, sixteen silver, and seven gold medals had been awarded. One gold medal was earned by Lily Cheetham, a talented skater who could inscribe her name, Lily, on the ice. She also wrote the chapter on ladies' skating in Douglas Adams's book *Skating*.

For more than two centuries England was the undisputed leader in the evolution of figure skating. No one country at any time has been so important to the development of the sport. In a litany of firsts Great Britain can boast of creating the first skating club, the first book on skating, and organizing the first national governing organization. In England, the basic figures, eights, threes, and Qs were developed, and there combined skating evolved and was promoted as an art form. Skilled practitioners such as Anderson, Vandervell, Monier-Williams, and others published books on the state of the sport, providing detailed descriptions of skating technique. The English style was rigid and austere, reflecting the mood of Victorian England. Serious figure skating was a discipline indulged in by men of means, those who could afford to be members of exclusive clubs. Most important, England gave the sport its name, figure skating.

THREE

Skating in the New World

BONE skates as a practical solution for travel across frozen landscapes were discovered independently in various parts of the world. French trappers who worked in eastern North America learned from the Iroquois Indians the practice of tying bones to their feet to traverse frozen rivers. Thus, in North America as in Europe and Asia, skating on bones must have existed for thousands of years. Bladed skates, however, were probably unknown in the New World before the eighteenth century, perhaps introduced by British officers stationed in Nova Scotia following its seizure from the French in 1713. The Pilgrims had arrived from the Netherlands, the birthplace of skating on blades, nearly a century earlier, but skating was the kind of recreational activity against which pietists rebelled. The serious and devout colonists would have viewed skating as a waste of time. They were concerned with survival. In addition, cargo space on the tiny ships that crossed the Atlantic was at a premium. It is unlikely that it would have been devoted to something as frivolous as ice skates.

By the mid-eighteenth century, however, skating was practiced along the East Coast whenever ice was available. Philadelphia, then a bustling city of fifteen thousand, became skating's first important center and could boast of competent figure skaters. Benjamin West (1738–1820), destined to become one of America's most famous painters, was also America's first skater of renown. Col. William Howe, a British commander stationed in Philadelphia, became a close friend and skating companion of the talented West. Years later he recounted the difficulty of the Philadelphia salute he learned from West. It was a combined figure similar to Robert Jones's salutation in which two skaters approach each other on outside edges.

West sought his fortune in Europe. After spending two years in Italy he took up residence in London, where he relished the opportunity of again donning skates. That winter, 1763–64, was unusually cold, providing a welcomed long skating season. Not having brought his skates, West rented a pair at St. James's Park, where he glided through a crowd of skaters who were fascinated by this stranger's talent. Observing his skill, a gentleman addressed him: "I perceive Sir you are a stranger and do not perhaps know that there are much better places than this for the exercise of skating. The Serpentine River in Hyde Park is far superior, and the Basin in Kensington Gardens still more preferable. Here only the populace assemble. On the Serpentine, the company, although better, is also promiscuous. But the persons who frequent the Basin in the Gardens are generally of the rank of gentlemen, and you will be less annoyed among them than at either of the other two places."[1]

West, not averse to skating in "better company," purchased a pair of skates the following day and at Kensington Gardens demonstrated his Philadelphia style of skating to the gentlemen skating there. The idea of a competent skater from the Colonies was a novelty to Londoners, and it is significant that West, who had learned to skate and had developed his technique in America, was able to impress skaters in England, the birthplace of figure skating. He continued to skate throughout his long career in London, although less frequently in later years. William Dunlap, one of his students at the Royal Academy, recalled skating with West two decades later. He was, Dunlap said, "the best, though not the most active, then on the ice."[2]

There is much evidence of skating activity throughout the Colonies in the years before the American Revolution. It was a recreational activity, with racing being especially popular, but as a discipline little is known about it. Figures were skated, some brought directly from England and others created in America. There was even impromptu dancing on skates. The *Maryland Gazette* reported in 1765, that "a very merry set of gentlemen [in Annapolis] had a commodious tent erected on the ice between the town and Greenbury's Point, where they had an elegant dinner . . . and in the afternoon diverted themselves with dancing of reels, on skates."[3] Colonial newspapers offer other amusing vignettes. In Boston, it was reported in 1731 that the "warehouse of Mr. Joshua Winslow . . . was broke open and there was stolen about thirty pair of mens Spanish silk stockens . . . and a pair of skates."[4] And in Philadelphia in 1748, twenty shillings were offered as a reward for a runaway belonging to David Lindsay. He had absconded with "a fiddle and a pair of skates."[5]

SKATING CLUBS

The late eighteenth century was a turbulent time as Colonists fought for and gained independence, and the early nineteenth century was a time of economic devastation as the United States and Canada suffered from the effects of the War of 1812. But throughout those years, cold weather and frozen lakes were greeted enthusiastically by skaters seeking diversion from political, military, and economic problems. As the economy improved after 1820, skating throughout North America experienced significant growth, paralleling that in England. People were skating in cities, towns, and in the countryside.

St. John, New Brunswick, a picturesque little town located on the north side of the Bay of Fundy, was the home of the first known skating club in North America. Formed in 1833, it followed by just three years the London Skating Club. Progressive compared to Old World clubs, it included women among its members decades ahead of such acceptance in England and Scotland. Other clubs may have been formed throughout Canada and the United States during the first half of the century, but no records of them have been discovered before 1849.

Skating meanwhile became increasingly popular, spurred by the economic recovery. By mid-century, newspapers reported enthusiastically on skating ponds, their condition, and the throngs of people frequenting them.[6] In Montreal, it was reported in January 1866 that "skating mania" gripped the country: "The skating mania increases daily. . . . With the weather of Saturday and yesterday, the skating mania rose to fever heat. In the early part of Saturday afternoon, almost every second person, young or old, seen in any of the leading thoroughfares, was possessed of 'a pair of irons' and hurrying along towards the rinks on the river. Again yesterday afternoon the number was very great."[7]

The Skating Club of the City and County of Philadelphia, founded in 1849, was the first in the United States. Twelve years later it joined forces with the local humane society and incorporated as the Philadelphia Skating Club and Humane Society. A large clubhouse on the Schuylkill River served as its meeting place. Still maintaining its full title, the Philadelphia Skating Club and Humane Society became a charter member of the United States Figure Skating Association (USFSA) in 1921.

Its constitution, adopted in 1850, stated that "the object of the Association shall be instruction and improvement in the art of skating, the cultivation of a friendly feeling in all who participate in the amusement, and the efficient use of proper apparatus for the rescue of persons breaking through the ice."[8] Skating was a perilous activity, one dealt with by many nineteenth-century writers. Enthusiasm to get on ice that was much too thin led to accidents, sometimes drownings. Club members were required to carry a reel of rope while skating to assist with rescues. Failure to do so resulted in a hefty one-dollar fine. The committee on rules approved a model that could be purchased for 18¾ cents. Made of hard wood, it was about five inches long and contained about fifty feet of cord.

Most mishaps ended with successful rescues. Although records were not kept, a writer in 1895 estimated that club members had saved between eight and nine hundred people.

A skating test was not prerequisite to membership. The by-laws provided only that "every member shall have a right to scrutinize freely the character of a candidate for membership."[9] Women must have been scrutinized most thoroughly because the 1864 membership list includes only sixteen, eleven of whom were single, out of a total membership of 261. Skating attire may have been important at first, as it was in England. It has been reported that the Philadelphia club required uniformity of dress until 1865, with men wearing top hats, swallow-tailed coats, pantaloons, and white ties, but the 1864 by-laws make no mention of a dress code. The club badge was a small silver skate worn on the left breast of the coat. Not wearing it resulted in a separate fine for each offense.

Skating clubs were soon established in other cities and even small towns. Some survived no more than a season because strong leadership, a large membership, and financial support were required for sustainability, but all clubs, even those that failed to survive, advanced the cause of skating. Unlike in England, where clubs catered to aristocratic and professional classes, people of lesser wealth were encouraged to join American clubs; dues were kept low to make participation possible. One commentator noted in 1868 that "it is a sad fact that luxurious living induces disinclination to exercise, and it is not, therefore, to the wealthier class of our cities that we may look for representatives in our skating clubs."[10]

Major skating centers in addition to Philadelphia included Boston and New York. The Skating Club of Boston, incorporated in 1912, also became a charter member of the US-FSA. Among its early members was A. Winsor Weld, father of Theresa Weld (Blanchard), America's first Olympic medalist. Other members included World competitors Nathaniel W. Niles and Sherwin Badger and writer George H. Browne. Fourteen years before the founding of the club in Boston, a club was established just across the Charles River in Cambridge. Browne, a resident of Cambridge, was an original member, and he, like many serious skaters, held membership in both clubs. The Cambridge Skating Club, an outdoor facility, is still located on its original site. Included among its early members is one of America's most decorated skaters, Maribel Vinson.

Skating clubs existed in the New York area in the early 1860s, much earlier than in the Boston area. The Washington Skating Club in Brooklyn was among the first. The New York Skating Club, chartered in 1863 with an initial membership of 150, included dealers and manufacturers of skating equipment as well as skaters. It reportedly grew to three hundred members within two years. Located first at MacMillan's Pond, a year later it secured the exclusive use of Conservatory Lake in Central Park, and there a clubhouse was built. A program of figures developed by the club was adopted by the American Skating Congress and remained for many years the standard for competition in the United States. The club ceased to exist after 1870.

The Artists Skating Club, so named because of the large number of artists in its membership, was formed in 1916 by skaters who frequented the St. Nicholas Ice Rink, a popular skating site for more that twenty years. Two years later that facility closed, and the club moved to Iceland Rink and changed its name to the New York Skating Club. Members included such notables as Irving Brokaw, Henry Howe, and James Cruikshank. Like the Philadelphia and Boston clubs, it became one of seven charter members of the USFSA, and it remains today one of the most active.

THE SKATERS TEXT BOOK

Just four years after its founding in 1863, New York Skating Club member Edward F. Gill published America's first skating book, *The Skater's Manual,* which the *The New York Times* called "a neat little manual copiously illustrated and teaching . . . how to do it gracefully."[11] Gill's book was eclipsed the following year by the larger and more comprehensive *Skater's Text Book* by Frank Swift and Marvin Clark.[12] Dedicated to "The Skaters of America," Swift and Clark covered thoroughly the state of skating in the United States, including skating history, equipment, basic movements, fancy skating, combined skating, special figures, clubs and organizations, roller skating, and even skating poetry.

Through copious descriptions of carriage, fundamental differences between the English style and the developing American style become clear. In America, the knee of the skating leg was to be slightly bent, and that was an "absolute rule." Nothing, the authors said, "so effectually destroys the beauty and gracefulness of movement as stiffness of the limbs." Arms were to hang naturally to the side, and elbows were to be slightly bent. The authors stated emotionally that "skaters ruin all the grace which they naturally possessed by spasmodic clutching of the fingers, continual swinging of the arms, bending the arms at a right angle, holding the arms out from the body, or spreading the fingers, until the three Graces must have wept in anguish and hidden their faces in vexation."[13]

"Fancy skating," a term first used by George Anderson in *The Art of Skating,* referred at that time to almost any figure other than basic edges forward or backward. Swift and Clark include specifically spread eagles, serpentines, three turns, grapevines, loops, ringlets, spins, waltz steps, and toe steps.

Grapevines, which may have developed first in Canada, are the most important North American contribution to figure skating. Their uniqueness resulted from having both feet on the ice throughout the figure. Repeating patterns were usually done in a straight line but could in some cases be done around a large circle as well. Although many variations were created during the remainder of the century, Swift and Clark described only the basic grapevine, which they termed the "acme" of fancy skating.

Loops, which later became the basic element in three groups of compulsory figures

were at this time done in a chainlike series. Ringlets were similar to loops except that the circles were perfectly round. Loops
were oval-shaped, and spins were understood to be upright.
The Jackson Haines spin was considered a special figure. Eight
one-foot and six two-foot spins are described. One-foot spins
included those forward and backward, on inside and outside
edges, and on either foot. Two-foot spins were divided into
plain and cross-foot varieties.

Although Jackson Haines was already dancing on skates,
and it was done in France even earlier, dancing with a partner
had not yet evolved in England or North America. Swift and
Clark describe "waltz steps" generically as "any movement in
which the skater goes perpetually around and keeps time to
the music of the waltz." This is one of the earliest mentions
of skating to music. Noteworthy is the reference to "skater"
in the singular. The most beautiful dance, they said, was "the
ordinary German waltz, which is executed the same as in dancing upon the floor."[14] Toe dancing is mentioned as well, but no
description is provided.

By century's end, the term *fancy skating,* although still
including some basic figures, tended to connote specifically
moves that left complex tracings on the ice, including those
difficult to accomplish in a graceful manner and thus con-

The basic grapevine is a
two-foot figure probably
first skated in Canada.
Complex variations
evolved in the late nine-
teenth century. (Pete
Jones)

trary to basic precepts of British skating. Writing in 1900, George Meagher, a Canadian,
provided diagrams of figures he included in fancy skating: one- and two-foot figures,
including numbers, letters of the alphabet, abstract designs, and grapevines. What
separates them from the special figures that a decade earlier had become a separate
discipline in Europe is that they are less often closed or geometric designs. Another
term used at the time for any one-foot figure, closed or open, was *continuous skating,*
described as that in which "the skater moves entirely upon one foot, never allowing the
balance foot to touch the ice."[15]

Swift and Clark, like their British counterparts, considered combined skating the
highest level of a skater's art, but their requisite figures are fundamentally different from
those of Vandervell and Witham, whose book was published a year later in England.
Most significant is the fact that physical contact is involved. Swift and Clark's combined
figures begin with pairs of skaters holding hands. It is presumed that combined skating
was not gender-specific, but in the description of one figure, the rose, a series of figure
eights done by groups of four to sixteen skaters, ladies stand on the outside line of a

circle, gentlemen standing inside.[16] The authors also describe three specialized combined figures specifically for two skaters in hand-in-hand positions. They are collectively referred to as "field steps," meaning that they were not done within prescribed bounds. For two of them, the flying scud and the Mercury, skaters face each other and reverse their skating direction, employing three turns. We have here the rudiments of waltzing on ice. In the third, the bishop eight, skaters are side by side and disengage hands only as they perform three turns. The figure ends with side-by-side pirouettes.

Swift and Clark provide also an early definition of specialties, defining them as "movements identified with individual skaters, as performed only by that individual, or one in which a skater specially excels, or one which he executes better than any other step he can perform."[17] Specialties of thirteen well-known skaters are included. Jackson Haines's sit spin, called a "one-foot spin, peculiar," is described as a combination spin: "while revolving, stooping so low that his balance leg must necessarily be perfectly horizontal to clear the ice, then rising gradually and finishing the spin upon his toe."[18]

NEW YORK'S SKATING VENUES

Philadelphia was still the largest American city at the beginning of the nineteenth century, but New York was growing rapidly. With the opening of the Erie Canal in 1825 it surpassed Philadelphia, developed into the country's largest commercial center, and became its most important cultural center as well. Numerous ponds and lakes were available for skating, and newspapers reported annually on the facilities, including sizes, quality of the ice, and amenities available. Lighting, music, and restaurants enhanced the popularity of the larger ones. Venues were available throughout the city as well as in Brooklyn, Hoboken, Jersey City, and Staten Island. Most charged an admission fee, but some were free. All were crowded. Skating in the United States as in Canada had escalated in popularity over a short period of time. An 1865 editorial in *The New York Times* noted that "twelve years ago skating was confined almost exclusively to urchins who boasted but of one skate for each pair of feet, while their ponds were mainly the frozen gutters in the alleys or back streets."[19]

By 1865 New York's ponds were crowded with thousands of skaters. A large ball was hoisted over the Central Park Skating Pond, indicating when the ice was in fair condition and skating was permitted, although ideal conditions were not always a prerequisite, especially for an enthusiastic public at the beginning of a skating season. Other signals included a white pennant raised when the ice was safe to walk on and a red pennant when it was very dangerous. Accidents did occur, and preventative actions were taken. Describing venues available that year, *The New York Times* reported that "new ponds will not be over four feet in depth, so that there is but small chance of drowning should

Central Park Winter/The Skating Pond (1862) by the American lithographers Currier and Ives shows the popularity of skating in New York after mid-century. The white flag atop the building indicates that the ice is safe to walk on. (the Currier and Ives Foundation)

anyone break through." Equipment was available "to rescue any stray unfortunate who may perchance go under," and "fires . . . [were] . . . kept in all the cottages near the lakes for the convenience of those who may get a 'ducking' or succumb to king frost."[20]

IMPROVEMENTS IN SKATE DESIGN

With skating's exploding popularity, Yankee ingenuity soon invaded the sport. Intricate figuring of the developing American school necessitated skates being attached rigidly to boots. Neither the concept nor the solution were new. The British had experimented with skates that clamped to the boots and with boot skates as early as the late eighteenth century, but skaters there continued to prefer fastenings with straps. Henry Boswell significantly improved skate design in 1837 by lengthening the blades, which lessened the perils of backward skating, but the blades were still mounted to heavy wooden stock and strapped to boots. Americans developed and perfected all-metal skates, which were much lighter, and clamped them rigidly to their boots. Those were tremendous improvements.

The Skater's Text Book provides a general chronology of skate types in use before the American-designed Acme skates. First, there were ones of German manufacture with a "beautiful twist" of several loops on the prow, ending with a brass knob. Straps were wound around the feet to hold them in place, and sticks were used to "tighten them to an excruciating degree." Next came English-designed skates with the prow cut off level with the sole of the boot and a wide fastening strap across the instep. "Rockers," the term for London club skates, followed. Boot skates were seen but only occasionally.

As early as 1697, Czar Peter the Great, while in the Netherlands, had made for his own use a pair of skates that had blades fastened permanently to the boots, but contemporary skaters viewed such antics as frivolity among the nobility. Boot skates were available in England a century later and were advertised in Canada in 1862, but nowhere did they receive significant acceptance until being used by Jackson Haines. Some continental skaters then took notice, but boot skates as a standard are a product of the twentieth century. Herbert Yglesias, writing in 1905, was the first to state emphatically that "the skate must be screwed permanently to the boot; any other mode of fastening is useless."[21]

In the meantime two North American improvements revolutionized skate design. In 1848 Edward V. Bushnell, a charter member and the first treasurer of the Philadelphia Skating Club, eliminated wood stocks and replaced them with metal, producing a lighter and stronger skate. In 1854 John Forbes of Dartmouth, Nova Scotia, designed a metal plate that clamped to the boot utilizing a spring fastener, which provided rigidity and ease of mounting. Forbes's design was employed by the Acme Skate Company, and the term *Acme skates* was often used for all skates of this type, regardless of the manufacturer. Swift and Clark championed New York club skates, which were all steel and clamped to the boots. Perfection had been achieved, they said: "To American mechanics for their invention . . . the skating fraternity of the whole world are under eternal obligations."[22] Height, thickness, radius, and length of blades were still matters of personal taste and much discussion, but the hated straps had been discarded.

SKATING RINKS

The skating season in Philadelphia averaged fifteen to twenty days annually. In years when the Schuylkill River did not freeze across, smaller ponds throughout the city provided skating opportunities. Canadians enjoyed much longer skating seasons, but frequent snowfall resulted in the sometimes daily irritation of clearing snow from the ice before skating could begin. It is not surprising that a solution would be sought, and the answer was covered rinks. They were originally open on all sides because their sole purpose was to keep snow off the ice. The first, built in Quebec City in 1852, opened with much pomp and ceremony. Called an "ice rink," it gave birth to the term still employed for skating venues. The rink featured a skating surface of sixty by 120 feet and was lighted by gas lights, which made safe evening skating an added benefit.

The novelty of skating in a covered and lighted facility further enhanced the sport's growing popularity, but in spite of its success Quebec City's ice rink remained the only such facility for the remainder of the decade. During the 1860s, rinks were built in other Canadian cities. Montreal's first, the Montreal Skating Club, opened in 1860, and just a year later it was enclosed and heated. Montreal was also the first city to support multiple rinks. The Victoria Rink, opened in 1862, was described as the largest and most extravagant in the city. It boasted a skating surface of 100 by 250 feet. Toronto, Hamilton, St. John's, Sarnia, and Brantford soon built ice rinks as well, several of which, like the one in Montreal, were named for Queen Victoria. The provinces followed suit. The Horticultural Gardens in Halifax, Nova Scotia, opened in 1863, and the Victoria Rink in St. John, Newfoundland, opened in 1865.

The unprecedented popularity of recreational skating supported these extravagant covered rinks throughout Canada, but traditional skating ponds were far more numerous. In Toronto they included the Royal, West End, Toronto, Yorkville, Maria Street, and Military among others. Major cities in the United States also supported multiple but uncovered skating venues. Those in New York and its environs included Central Park Pond, Fifth Avenue Pond, Capitoline Skating Lake, Nassau Pond, Chichester's Pond, Sylvan Lake, Hercules Pond, Morris Canal, and Silver Lake.

People of all ages in Canada and the United States had discovered skating, and newspaper accounts tell of skaters numbering in the thousands. *The New York Times* noted that on Christmas Day of 1878 five thousand persons were turned away at Prospect Park because of poor ice conditions, but six thousand skated at Capitoline Grounds and another three thousand at Union Grounds. Skating became fashionable during the 1860s, and its popularity mushroomed in the 1870s.

With this growing popularity, competitions, called by various names, including contests, races, and tournaments, occurred with increasing frequency. Races were the most popular, but they often included closing events of figure and fancy skating. Most were local or regional, with participants coming primarily from a sponsoring club. Time, travel costs, and a lack of established rules affected participation in and the success of many early competitions but not the enthusiasm of skaters who wanted to compete. A "Grand Tournament" in figure skating was held at Montreal in February 1875. Invitations were extended to "sister clubs," requesting their support, but only the Halifax club responded. Still, the event was deemed "a most brilliant affair." An audience of two thousand was on hand for the ladies' and boys' events in the afternoon, and it increased to three thousand for the men's event in the evening. The men skated twenty-seven figures each and then showed their skill in fancy skating "of whatever kind they fancied most." The prize was awarded to W. Barnston, who was said to have been "steady and powerful all through."[23]

THE AMERICAN SKATING KING

Jackson Haines (1840–75), skating's first superstar, set sail for Europe in 1864. He was twenty-four years of age. An itinerant actor, dancer, skater, and entertainer, Haines had not made a name for himself in his native country. He touted himself as the "champion of America," a title he reportedly won at a competition in Troy, New York, in 1864, but there is no indication in local newspapers that such a competition occurred.

Haines was born and spent his childhood in New York City, one of five children. His grandfather was a hat manufacturer, and his father was employed by Park and Tilford, a department store. A trade was not a consideration for the young Haines because the call of the theater was too strong. From early childhood the boy yearned for the stage. Leaving home as a teenager, he pursued an entertainment career, possibly working first as a

Jackson Haines, "the American Skating King" and father of the Viennese style, was figure skating's first international figure. (World Figure Skating Museum and Hall of Fame)

ballet master in Philadelphia. From there he took dance to the ice. He worked diligently, concentrating on body position, which he felt was more important than tracing intricate figures. In appearance, Haines was said to have been small but muscular. During the war years he probably toured throughout the North as a dancer and entertainer, but in 1864, following a skating exhibition in Toronto, he departed for Europe, never to return to his homeland.

Haines first stop was England, which proved to be disappointing. English skaters, with their Victorian attitudes and growing devotion to combined skating, viewed Haines's style as fancy skating, a term used in a derogative sense to describe his pirouettes and dancing on ice. But Haines was not to be dissuaded. For several years he traversed the Continent, skating in various cities of Europe, and his performances were received with interest, sometimes enthusiasm. It was a style not seen before. In Vienna especially, his skating touched the pulse of the populace. Advertisements for an exhibition there in 1865 billed him as "the celebrated American ice dancer," a description confirmed by his program, which included a march, a waltz, a mazurka, and a quadrille. Success was immediate, and Vienna became Haines's home for a short time. There he taught the next generation of skaters, those destined to become the leaders and developers of a new style of skating.

Haines, skating's first international figure, is the father of the Viennese school, which later gave birth to the international style of skating. His background in acting, dancing, and entertaining all influenced his persona on the ice. He arrived in Vienna, the musical city with its love of dance, especially the waltz, and enhanced the parameters by dancing on ice. The American in Europe had introduced a new style of skating, and his contribution is perhaps the most significant of any individual in the history of the sport.

Three free-skating moves have sometimes been attributed to Haines: the sit spin, the spread eagle, and the arabesque. Most important is the sit spin, which legend says he spent nine years perfecting. One of three basic spin positions, it remains an important part of most free-skating programs. The spread eagle and the arabesque, however, had been known for a long time and are not attributable to Haines. Robert Jones described the spread eagle in 1772, Jean Garcin lauded it in 1813, and George Anderson described it negatively in 1852. Arabesque positions likewise date to the eighteenth century. Spirals were described by Jones, but they were not important figures in nineteenth-century England because the forward-leaning position was totally out of keeping with the developing English style of skating. The spiral became an important figure in Vienna later in the century, following Haines's trips.

Boot skates were not yet the choice of skaters, but Haines employed them. The blades were connected to steel plates that were in turn fastened to the boots by screws.

Described as strong, reliable, and elegant, his skates were similar to skates of today but without toe picks. Although not adopted widely during Haines's lifetime, the basic design was to become standard early in the new century.

Documentable information on Haines's life and activities is limited, although much legend about him has evolved, especially during the early twentieth century.[24] Circumstances surrounding his death remain clouded. Although a sister had spent a year with him in Europe, no relatives were there at the time of his death. Haines was buried in a churchyard at Gamla-Karleby, Finland, following his untimely death there on June 23, 1875, possibly a result of pneumonia. He was thirty-five. The Rotary Club of Gamla-Karleby later provided a tombstone engraved with a passage from Ecclesiastes: "For there is no work, nor device, nor knowledge, nor wisdom, in the grave, wither thou goest." The club noted on an accompanying plaque "in remembrance of the American skating king." Haines was an original inductee into the World Figure Skating Hall of Fame, which was established in 1976, a century after his death.

THE CANADIAN FIGURE SKATING ASSOCIATION

Haines performed in Montreal in early 1864, shortly before departing for Europe. Three-year-old Louis Rubenstein (1861–1931), destined to become a fine skater himself and leave his mark on the sport, was reportedly in the audience. Haines is said to have been his inspiration and that at age sixteen Rubenstein traveled to Vienna to coach with him, but that is legend, not fact.[25] Had that occurred, it would have been in 1877, two years after Haines's death. There is no evidence that Rubenstein studied skating in Vienna or with Haines, but the Rubenstein family was well-off financially and did provide the means for their talented son to devote his energies to skating throughout his teens and twenties. He won the Championship of Montreal in 1878, and other successes followed throughout the Canadian provinces. He competed in New York as the champion of Montreal at the National Amateur Skating Association Championship in 1887. Another Canadian, T. H. Robinson, champion of Toronto, won the competition, and J. B. Storey, champion of America, was second. Rubenstein returned a year later and won.

Rubenstein was the first North American figure skater to compete abroad. Traveling to St. Petersburg, Russia, in 1890, he skated in an international competition occasioned by the twenty-fifth anniversary of the St. Petersburg Skating Club. Sporting a pair of skates presented as a gift by the U.S. firm of Barney and Berry, his name engraved "handsomely" on the blades, Rubenstein traced his figures, a star, a figure eight on one foot, loops, and ringlets and won that portion of the competition. Two other events, special figures and specialties, were required. They were won by Alexei Lebedev of Russia, who received the gold medal. Rubenstein won what he viewed as most important.

Louis Rubenstein, champion of Canada and an international competitor. (McCord Museum of Canadian History, Montreal)

To him, special figures and specialties represented "a tendency to acrobatic work, which would not be recognized as fine skating in Canada." Although controversy resulted, Rubenstein reacted philosophically. "I would like to have won everything," he said. "But I won what the skating association sent me to do and am satisfied."[26]

As the popularity of skating grew during the late nineteenth century increasing numbers of skaters wanted to compete, and competitions became more frequent. Clubs challenged other clubs in neighboring cities and beyond, sometimes across national borders, but serious inconsistencies resulted from the lack of established standards and rules. In figure skating, judging was especially controversial, as judges, often totally unqualified, functioned without prescribed criteria. Popularity played a role in some decisions, and coaches sometimes judged their own students. Problems increased as the number of competitions grew and the skill level improved. National organizations that could set standards were sorely needed.

Although the National Skating Association was well established in England, and similar organizations existed or were being formed in other countries, there was in 1890 no international organization to oversee skating contests. Rules and procedures varied greatly, and in figure skating the problems multiplied owing to differences in national styles, English, continental, and American. Judges had difficulty comparing objectively the different styles. Rubenstein, a competitor in Canada, the United States, and Europe, understood; indeed, he had experienced the problem.

Two years before traveling to St. Petersburg, Rubenstein participated in a meeting at Montreal called specifically to deal with problems of inconsistency at the national level. It included representatives from skating clubs throughout Canada. From that meeting the Amateur Skating Association of Canada (ASAC) was formed. At its first meeting, rules governing competitions were established, and amateur status, nearly identical to that of Britain's NSA, was granted to one who "has never competed with or against a professional for any prize, and who has never taught, pursued, or assisted in the practice of athletic exercises as a means of obtaining a livelihood."[27]

Skating titles not given by national organizations could have little meaning because titles bearing the same name were probably awarded by different clubs at their respective competitions. Jackson Haines has been credited with being the champion of America. Perhaps he was, but the competition was not held in Troy, New York, as legend states and probably not under the auspices of a national association. Thus, ASAC fulfilled a need and just two months after its founding held the first official Canadian National Championships for speed and figure skating. Greater interest in speed skating was clear when the figure skating event had to be postponed to gain a minimum number of participants; six days later Rubenstein won the gold medal. From 1889 through 1892 figure skating events were planned each year, all of which had to be postponed or canceled owing to a lack of entrants. The importance of ASAC lies not in the number of participants, which would increase with the next generation of skaters, but rather in the governance of skating competitions by a recognized regulatory body.

Sports organizations in Canada were under the umbrella of the Amateur Athletic Union of Canada (AAUC). ASAC was granted membership, but problems soon developed over continuously debated but established AAUC policies on amateur status, which ASAC apparently did not follow strictly. Membership was terminated in 1907 by the parent body. Internal disagreement, primarily between speed skaters and figure skaters, also plagued ASAC. Participation in competitive figure skating was increasing, and some events required elimination rounds. Ottawa had become the figure skating capital of Canada, and clubs there and elsewhere grew to resent ASAC's strong emphasis on speed skating.

The solution adopted was the establishment of a figure skating department (FSD) within ASAC, which allowed figure skaters to control their own destiny. By that time, World War I was less than a year away. Competitions were canceled, but the FSD, led by Rubenstein, accomplished much during the war years. Test standards were established, judges were appointed, and training programs were developed. Canada entered the postwar era organized and hopeful of developing world-class figure skaters. The name Canadian Figure Skating Association (CFSA) was adopted in 1939 and subsequently changed to Skate Canada in 2000. Rubenstein was honored in 1984 with election to the World Figure Skating Hall of Fame for his work on behalf of skating in Canada as well as for his outstanding competitive career.

FIGURE SKATING ORGANIZATIONS IN THE UNITED STATES

In the United States as in Canada the number of skating clubs increased steadily after 1860. Unlike their counterparts in England, where club members viewed skating as a gentlemen's sport, in America effort was made to attract persons of all social and economic levels. Modest membership fees allowed some clubs to become quite large. As a result, the number of inter-club competitions increased, creating the need for a governing body. In 1868 a call was issued for delegates from throughout the United States and Canada to establish rules for figure skating. At a meeting held in February of that year in Allegheny City, Pennsylvania, the American Skating Congress (ASC) was established. A constitution and by-laws were adopted, as was a program of figures that included basic edges, serpentines, figure eights, loops, ringlets, and grapevines.[28]

At its first sponsored competition, held that season, a gold and diamond medal reportedly valued at $500 was awarded. The ASC survived for at least three seasons because a congress was held in 1871 in New York City, where delegates from skating clubs throughout the United States and Canada were in attendance. It is not known how long the ASC continued, but it appears to have been a healthy organization on its third anniversary. Additional annual or triennial meetings may have been held in other cities. America's next governing body for skating was fifteen years in the future.

Although the actual date of its organizational meeting is unknown, the National Skating Association held its first competition at Hoboken, New Jersey, in February 1886. Gold, silver, and bronze medals were awarded in five speed events and in figure skating. Poor ice conditions marred the racing events. "The two hundred pounds of [A. J.] Queckberner were entirely too much for the fragile ice, and after a couple of laps he crunched through the ice like a ferry boat. He was followed by S. D. Lee, who caught his

The Championship Jewel.

The Champion Jewel, designed by Messrs. Hervey and Johnson, was first awarded in February 1868 at a tourney held following the American Skating Congress in Alleghany, Pennsylvania. (Frank Swift, *The Skaters Textbook* [1868])

foot in the hole, turning a half somersault, which left him with his head in the mud and his glistening extremities in the air."[29] The figure skating event was postponed.

Proof of amateur status was required to enter that first competition, and by the next season the word *amateur* was added to the organization's name, yet another indication of the perplexing problem of amateur versus professional status, primarily in speed skating.[30] The now renamed National Amateur Skating Association (NASA) took amateur status seriously and enforced it. Stephen O'Brien, winner of the 220–yard race in 1888, was disqualified and required to relinquish his title after it was learned that he had previously skated in Canada for a portion of the gate receipts.

Ice conditions were ideal for NASA's competition in 1887. Figure skating was an evening event held at the Hoboken Ice Rink, which was lighted with Chinese lanterns and electric lights. A local brass band provided music. The competition lasted until midnight as each contestant skated twenty-five figures. The specific figures skated are unknown, but those required in a similar Canadian competition were published in *The New York Times:*

> The figure skating will consist in addition to specialties, of plain skating, forward and backward; the outside and inside edge, both ways; threes, inside and outside forward to inside and outside backward, and the reverse; rocking turns on the same principle; spins, outside and inside, forward and backward, on flat of skates and crossfoot and pyramid; plain eight, four styles; double eight in the same fashion; eight with loops and threes; grapevine, single and double; scissors; Philadelphia single and double; crosscut or anvil, outside and inside, forward and reverse; pivot figures and locomotive steps.[31]

Skaters could also include up to ten specialties, but they had to be entirely different from the required figures. Points were awarded for each figure, weighted according to difficulty.

NASA served an important role in the history of American figure skating, overseeing competitions in the United States for two decades until its demise in 1905. Fortunately, the now well-established Championships of America continued until 1909 under the auspices of the New York Skating Club. The reason for NASA's demise is not clear, but its function needed to be filled. To meet that need the International Skating Union of America (ISUofA) was founded in 1907, just two years after NASA folded. It included five regional organizations, two from Canada and three from the United States. Although its competitions were open to skaters from both countries, it was the direct predecessor of the USFSA.

In fourteen years the ISUofA sponsored just four competitions, one before and three after the war, all of which were held in the United States. They were notable because skaters who would succeed internationally after the war competed in them. Two Americans deserve special mention. At three of the four competitions, the senior ladies' champion was Theresa Weld (Blanchard) (1893–1978), who won America's first Olympic medal in figure skating, bronze at Antwerp in 1920. The junior ladies' champion in 1921 was Beatrix Loughran (1900–1975), who won the silver medal at the Winter Games at Chamonix in 1924 and the bronze medal at the World Championships that same year.

The ISUofA held its last figure skating championships in February 1921. Two weeks earlier, a proposal had been submitted by Paul Armitage, chair of its figure skating committee, calling for figure skating in America to be governed by a United States Figure Skating Association with sole authority for that branch of the sport but under the umbrella of the ISUofA.[32] The proposal was adopted unanimously, and seven clubs became charter members. All but one are still members.[33]

THE AMERICAN STYLE

The rigidly fastened skates of American design allowed skaters to create, ornament, and refine numerous intricate figures on the ice, and the ability to accomplish those difficult maneuvers was the ultimate challenge for serious American skaters. Two categories of special figures existed, grapevines and complex one-foot designs. Grapevines, which probably originated in Canada, are the most American of all figures. Their uniqueness results from both feet remaining on the ice through the duration of the figure, doing the same basic moves but not in unison. The constant crossing of the feet creates interesting chainlike designs. Expressing enthusiasm for them, one writer colorfully said "to watch two cunning feet executing them, winding in and out in all directions, leaving upon the ice the most beautiful designs . . . is a skating delight."[34] One-foot figures included closed designs, but Americans had a greater fascination for open designs such as letters and numbers.

The English viewed the American school of skating with derision. These stunts had no place in the true art of figure skating. For the British, beauty stemmed from combined skating performed with rigid body position, unison among the skaters, and smoothness of motion. Bent legs, abrupt movements, and body contortions associated with grapevines and special figures were the absolute antithesis of the art they loved. Canadians and Americans viewed the manner of execution as important but always secondary. Beauty of design was paramount.

As the nineteenth century drew to a close, as specialized books on skating were being published, and as more international events were being held, the established schools of skating, English, American, and continental, could not coexist. Change had to occur. When George A. Meagher, Rubenstein's contemporary, published his *Lessons in Skating* in 1900, it received acclaim from Algernon Henry Grosvenor, a committee member of the London Skating Club. Acknowledging national differences, Meagher included a chapter entitled "Skating in England" that was written by no less an expert than Montague Monier-Williams. "There are only two styles of figure skating" Monier-Williams wrote, "the British and the non-British." Uniformity of style is a requirement he said, as "the ultimate aim of most English figure skaters is combination skating."[35] The critical essentials of combined skating were uprightness of carriage, straightness of the skating leg, positioning of the free leg behind the skating leg, and facing in the direction of motion. A straight skating leg, the most telling characteristic of the English style, separated the British from the non-British. Intricate American figures, by contrast, required a bent skating leg. Responding to Monier-Williams, Meagher wrote, "In justice to our own style of skating, I can but still preach against the straight knee," and "unconvinced that we Canadians and Americans are wrong, the only alternative now, so far as I can see, is to agree to disagree."[36]

Meagher's book is a veritable compendium of skating in North America at century's end. There are sections on basic figures, one- and two-foot turns, grapevines, fancy figures, and combined skating. One- and two-foot spins, called buzzing movements, are described in various positions, forward and backward. The Jackson Haines spin is called a bowsprit. Jumps of a half and a full revolution are described, but one called the "cleanest and most perfect jump" is unlike any done today. Skating forward with the feet close together on the flats of the skates, a full revolution is done in the air with a landing on the flats of the skates. A half-revolution jump, called today the waltz jump and done as a first step toward learning the Axel Paulsen jump, is described but not yet named. The spread eagle jump is of one revolution, beginning and ending in a spread eagle position. One is reminded of Peggy Fleming's double Axel Paulsen jump, beginning and ending in a spread eagle position and done in 1968, the year of her Olympic gold medal.

All figures described by Swift and Clark thirty-two years earlier were repeated in Meagher's book, but others were added, the most important being Q figures. The grasshopper, mentioned for the first time here, is a simple move now called "shoot the duck" in which the skating leg is bent to put the skater in a sitting position, with the free leg extended fully in front and parallel to the ice. When skaters in this position swing their arms up and behind and are pushed by a second skater, the figure is called a wheelbarrow.

The number of combined figures Meagher included more than doubles those described by Swift and Clark, but the discipline was changing. Combined skating in America by 1900 had become synonymous with hand-in-hand skating and was increasing in popularity. Nearly all figures performed singly could be performed in combination, that is, hand in hand, although Meager reports that "of this fact few skaters seem to be aware."[37] In Canada, combined figures were often performed to music, a practice Meagher indicates was seldom seen abroad.

Meagher's *Lessons in Skating,* published exactly at the turn of the century, represents the culmination of the American style. Meagher, a competitor in Europe as well as in North America, was cognizant of the differences between skating styles on both sides of the Atlantic but one does not sense any effort to reconcile them. During the next decade the new international style invaded North America, and Meagher's second book, published in 1919, a year after the war, reflects somewhat that change but not without resistance. He was a conservative of the old school, the American style, and has left the best description of that style at the zenith of its development.

FOUR

Skating on the Continent

THE Duke of York's eldest daughter, Princess Mary, moved to Holland in 1677, having married the Dutch prince, William of Orange. A visit by her cousin, the Duke of Monmouth, in 1685 included an afternoon of skating.[1] Among those present was the French ambassador, who, scandalized by what he saw, recounted that now famous event in a dispatch to Louis XIV: "Twas a very extraordinary thing to see the Princess of Orange clad in petticoats shorter than are generally worn by ladies so strictly decorous, those tucked up half-way to her waist, and with iron pattens on her feet learning to slide sometimes poised on one leg sometimes on another."[2]

We do not know exactly when figure skating was introduced into France, but the wording of the ambassador's communique referring to iron pattens on Mary's feet suggests that skating on bladed skates, as practiced in the Netherlands and England, had not yet crossed the channel into France. Sometime during the next century, well before the Revolution, figure skating did arrive there, and it became a popular winter activity spurred at least in part by acceptance at the court of Louis XVI, who reigned from 1774 to 1792. As in England, an aristocratic society had the financial means and free time to participate in skating at a sophisticated and artistic level, but the larger French populace was surely sliding on the ice or skating on bone skates as they did in England and probably had been doing so for centuries. For the French aristocracy, skating became a fashionable pastime, but unlike their English counterparts who put emphasis on methodical technique and precision, the French stressed grace and elegance.

THE DELIGHTS OF SKATING IN FRANCE

Robert Jones's entire repertoire of figures was known in France, but the style was different. Even the names of the figures changed. In England, artistic grace tended to be considered effeminate. Skating was a sport for men, and its beauty resulted from execution in an athletic style. In France, the love of ballet carried over into skating, and its beauty resulted from body position and grace of execution, as in dance. In England, skating remained for many years a male-dominated sport; in France, women may have donned skates at an earlier date, possibly influenced, at least in the late eighteenth century, by Marie Antoinette's participation. In both countries, skating was enjoyed by practitioners as well as spectators. Where there was skating there was an audience, and contemporary descriptions recount the inconvenience and nuisance of people who crowded the ice, some on skates, some not, interfering with those more skilled.

When figure skating crossed the English Channel the known figures, those described by Jones, were learned and enjoyed, but the repertoire expanded. In the post-revolutionary era a French style evolved that included figures not known in England. Artistically, French skaters surpassed the English, and it was in the realm of artistry that they excelled. At the forefront of this development were the Gilets Rouges, an elite group of skaters whose credo was artistic sophistication.

The most famous of the Gilets Rouges was Jean Garcin, an outspoken proponent of artistic skating. His legacy lives in his monumental book of 1813, *Le vrai patineur* (The True Skater), the first skating book in French. Garcin provides a comprehensive picture of skating in the years just after the French Revolution, one much different from that Jones described forty years earlier and still being practiced in England. Jones's emphasis was on correct technique within a limited body of figures. To Garcin, technique was important but artistic expression was preeminent. He subtitled his book *How to Skate with Grace* and dedicated it to Geneviève Gosselin (1791–1818), the premier dancer at the Imperial Academy of Music in Paris. Skating in France represented the love of ballet carried onto the ice as an art of graceful expression.

An extensive preface in *Le vrai patineur* describes the state of skating in France, where, as in England, skating seasons were eagerly awaited:

Yes, citizens silent when water is unfrozen,
When hard ice finally covers it:

Friends, let us take advantage of the transparent surface
As an open road to the throne of Neptune.[3]

Like most nineteenth-century writers on skating, Garcin's initial chapters cover practical considerations, including skate design and methods of fastening them to the boots. Then, before addressing technique and a repertoire of figures, Garcin devotes entire chapters to the positioning of the arms and hands, not for balance or control but specifically for their expressive qualities. Poise and grace, the artistry associated with ballet, preceded technique. Seven full-page plates show correct carriage of the body and the uniform dress of the Gilets Rouges. At least one arm was always to be above the head. The palms of the hands were usually up, with the fingers curved and separated from the thumbs. Neatly fitting waistcoats and tight-fitting leotards, like those used in ballet, were shown. A hat was worn, either mortarboards or berets. A low skate blade put the boot close to the ice, suggesting that edges must have been relatively shallow. Large curved prows ornamented the fronts of the skates, and blades stopped well short of the backs of the heels.

Garcin begins his treatment of skating technique by stressing the usefulness of all edges, inside and outside, backward and forward and then describes a series of circle-eight figures still a part of skating today. Jones had viewed inside edges as suitable primarily for beginners and called skating backward unpleasant and unnecessary. That attitude was changing in England, but it was in France that skaters first appreciated the equal beauty of all edges and approached skating backward as artistry, not trickery. Skating backward was, perhaps, the most important advancement in the history of figure skating since the discovery of the Dutch roll five centuries earlier.

After describing all edges, Garcin deals with running, stopping, and spinning. Running was employed to begin figures, and the technique was exactly that described by Jones. Stopping was a different matter. Grace and poise were paramount in bringing figures to artistic conclusions. Abrupt stops, like those described by Jones, were to be avoided except when "danger is imminent." Although not yet given its modern name, Garcin preferred the more graceful T stop, which he described as "beautiful, easiest, and quickest to learn."[4]

The chapter on spins is especially helpful in understanding and appreciating French artistry. Continuous motion through a figure and a beautiful pose at its terminus were prime considerations in achieving the desired grace and poise. Spins employed to conclude a figure were called pirouettes; those employed within a figure, including three turns, were called *crochets* (hooks). Pirouettes of two or three revolutions, usually on two feet, provided graceful conclusions to figures as forward motion ceased and the skater struck the final pose. This displayed both skill and artistry, of which Garcin approved enthusiastically. Some skaters, however, were experimenting with crochets of multiple revolutions at interim spots within figures. Of this Garcin disapproved adamantly. Simple crochets done on one foot did not halt forward motion, and, he wrote, "I admit sincerely that the simple crochet where the half revolution is placed to connect one step to another is indispensable and at the same time gracious as much as the others [those of multiple revolutions] are useless and disagreeable."[5]

Garcin describes more than thirty figures, many of which have fanciful names. The *révérence* (bow) is a spread eagle performed on either an inside or an outside edge. An extensive description, longer than that for any figure, suggests its importance as well as its difficulty. It was considered especially useful in getting onto an inside backward edge. Unlike spread eagles of today, done with straight legs, Garcin's sketch shows the knees bent, the forward one significantly more so than the trailing one.

Among Garcin's various figure-eight patterns, *le courtisan* (the courtier), an outside forward three, is the most important historically. Jones had employed a three turn in his heart-shaped figure. Garcin incorporated it in a figure eight requiring a step back to the forward edge. Owing to the required changes of edge and feet, Garcin instructs, "as to the position of the body, it should be developed graciously: the head held high, the

Révérence en ligne directe,

"Reverence," the spread eagle figure as pictured in Jean Garcin's *Le vrai patineur* (1813). The skater is wearing the uniform dress of the Gilets Rouges.

eyes attentive to the direction of movement, the arms free but comfortably positioned, allowing free movement of the shoulders with each turn of the head."[6]

Among Garcin's most interesting figures is the *pas d'Apollon,* called the "most perilous" of all steps. From a *révérence* position, the skater raised one foot and made a small jump to the other, ending on a backward edge. "The most difficult [figure] known without exception" was *l'ecrevisse* (the crayfish), a figure eight done on two feet, the change of circle accomplished by a twist of the hips. This may seem out of character with artistic Garcinian ideals, and that was clearly on Garcin's mind when he wrote, "It is certainly not to be less gracious than other figures."[7] Garcin, as always, insists on correct body position with arms placed properly on the hips. L'ecrevisse was an early predecessor of many challenging two-foot figures, particularly grapevines, that became important later in the century.

The *valse* was composed of two steps on a small circle separated by a double pirouette. It could be repeated multiple times, either on a figure-eight pattern or on a circle for skaters "not afraid of dizziness." Acknowledging his edict against pirouettes in the middle of figures, Garcin rules that in this case it is gracious, and devotes half of his description to justifying it. The valse, which could be done by two skaters in the form of shadow skating, provides the earliest mention of movement associated with ice dancing and pair skating.

Garcin ends his comprehensive treatise, like Jones, by telling readers that he has described only the most important figures. Skaters who had accomplished them would be able to do others being skated in France and elsewhere. He muses about attempts he has heard about in other places of skaters scribing their names on the ice, a feat he calls "extraordinary" but not possible to accomplish with grace.[8] This is the first mention of special figures, that yet unnamed branch of skating so important later in the century as well as the criticism and primary reason for their ultimate demise, the difficulty of skating them gracefully.

Sumptuous and colorful ballet had flourished at the royal court in France since the late sixteenth century. For more than two hundred years, stage entertainment, including ballet, theater, and opera, pervaded all aspects of cultured French society. Not surprisingly, the grace associated with ballet, and the drama associated with theater, carried over as the French developed a love of skating. From England, they learned figures and how to do them correctly. To them they added the beauty of ballet. The French expanded the sport and made it an art form, but its style tended to remain insular.

VIENNA AND THE CONTINENTAL STYLE

English skating during the mid-nineteenth century evolved into a technically sophisticated style of austerity and rigidity. French skating experienced little further development but retained its style of grace and fluidity. As the century progressed, the styles did not converge. They moved further apart. In England, skating reflected Victorian attitudes. Practitioners traced their figures with absolute accuracy, and combined skating was done with the precision of a military drill team. Skating was viewed as a sport and science but not as an art in the balletic sense. It is not surprising that Jackson Haines did not impress the English when he skated there in 1864 because not until the 1890s did British skaters begin to consider foreign styles anything other than effeminate and affected.

Skating's next great impetus occurred in Austria, specifically, Vienna. Figure skating there at mid-century showed influences from both the English and French styles. Haines provided the catalyst for change, and it is appropriate that he is called the "Father of the Viennese style." Vienna welcomed Haines with open arms. He arrived there in 1865 and presented a show the likes of which skaters there had not seen before. Haines danced on the ice to music, and Vienna, the music capital of Europe, was awe-inspired.

In the Romantic Era music moved from the court into the concert hall, from an art of the aristocracy to an art of the public. It was the era of virtuosos, star performers, and matinee idols. Violinist Niccolò Paganini in the 1820s and pianist Franz Liszt in the 1830s being the two most famous. Skating to music, which could be enjoyed by the public as spectators and by skaters as participants, could not avoid similar popularity.

Haines became skating's first matinee idol. His tours of northern and central Europe took his artistry to a public ready for the spectacular. It was a graceful art but one not free of theatrics. Haines was trained in ballet, but he was also an entertainer. He could skate gracefully, but he could also skate on stilts. Now famous, he was received as an international figure, sometimes with great enthusiasm.

When Haines returned to Vienna in 1870, just three years after the Wiener Eislauf-Verein (Vienna Skating Club) was founded, club members were developing the kind of skating he had introduced five years earlier. It was the antithesis of combined skating then coming into full flower in England. It was as romantic as the English style was classic. How long Haines remained in Vienna following his appearances there in 1865 and 1870 is unknown, but during those intervals he taught the next generation of skaters. They included Leopold Frey, winner of the Great International Skating Tournament in 1882; Franz Balazzi, who partnered with Haines in shows; and Demeter Diamantidi, Carl von Korper, and Max Wirth, who wrote *Spuren auf dem Eise* (Tracings on the Ice), a monumental publication describing the state of skating in Vienna in 1881. The book includes 413 figures practiced by members of the Vienna Skating Club as well as detailed descriptions of the style of skating associated with the now well-established Viennese School. Of tremendous importance, a second, expanded, edition appeared in 1892 on the eve of the International Skating Congress held that same year. It documents figure skating on the Continent at that decisive juncture in its history.

SPUREN AUF DEM EISE

Spuren auf dem Eise, like Garcin's *Le vrai patineur* seventy years earlier, begins by describing poetically the excitement felt with the impending first ice of the season. When
it arrived, thousands of skaters donned their skates, glided across the frozen surface,
and enjoyed the bright reflections from the shimmering ice. But Viennese skaters did
not just slide across the ice or practice figures. Haines had shown them that skating was
much more, and by the time *Spuren auf dem Eise* was published, skaters were dancing
on ice to music as well as connecting figures in a way that would ultimately lead to modern free-skating programs. It was the emerging international style.

The authors could not get past page two of their introduction before discussing
dancing on ice. Although sometimes done with groups of four skaters, it was not British
combined skating. The groups were always two couples, not just four skaters. They were
waltzing, not creating the geometric formations of combined skating. The Viennese, who
danced their way through the nineteenth century, took dance to the ice, where musical
interpretation offered seemingly endless possibilities. Skating was to them an art meant
to participate in and also to watch. Carnivals staged by the Vienna Skating Club were gala
events attended by thousands of spectators. In spite of that, skating was viewed as a
sport. "Next to riding and hunting, next to fencing and gymnastics, swimming and mountain climbing, figure skating is considered to be the healthiest and happiest exercise."[9]

The preface to the first edition of *Spuren auf dem Eise* lists nineteen members of
the Vienna Skating Club who, directly or indirectly, influenced the writing of the book.
Although most are now obscure, others are still well known, including Josef and Franz
Belazzi, Franz Biberhofer, Leopold Frey, Theodore Langer, and Ernst von Stein.

Like most earlier books, equipment, including skates, boots, and appropriate cloth-
ing, is among the first topics covered. The next chapter, "To the Theory of Skating," is
especially enlightening. Before learning to push off, stop, and do basic edges, emphasis
is placed on body position, but not for beauty, poise, and grace as described in Garcin's
book. That was important, but the emphasis in *Spuren auf dem Eise* was placed on the
physical advantages of power and athleticism for which arms and legs could be used.
The skating leg was bent, the free leg was poised elegantly behind, and the arms were
held up in an artistic way, but most important, the limbs were employed to assist in the
execution of turns.

An elaborate system of figures follows, the most extensive ever compiled in any
language. Beginning with basic edges and progressing generally by degree of difficulty,
they are arranged by logical groupings such as pirouettes, dance steps, and special
figures. The authors provide diagrams as well as written descriptions for this complete
spectrum of figures, which includes the repertory of compulsory figures soon to be adopted by the International Skating Union. Many special figures are included. Among the

more unusual are a boomerang, a buffalo horn, a tulip, a mill wheel, and a circular saw. Throughout the history of special figures, various shaped stars were particularly popular. Those in *Spuren auf dem Eise,* cataloged by the names of their inventors, include the Engelmann star, the Hügel star, and the Schmidt star. Free-skating moves include inside and outside spirals done singly and in combination. Spins are described on inside and outside edges, forward and backward, on both feet, and in combination. There are one-foot, two-foot, and cross-foot spins; all are upright except for the Jackson Haines spin. Jumping, although mentioned briefly by previous writers, had not yet become an important part of figure skating. The otherwise mammoth book devotes just two pages to brief explanations of three jumps: a high jump, a long jump, and a half-turn jump.

Dancing on skates, which suggests skating rhythmically to music, evolved during the quarter century following Haines's arrival in Vienna. The expanded 1892 edition of *Spuren auf dem Eise* provides a comprehensive list of dances then in the repertoire of the Vienna Skating Club. There are four marches, nine waltzes, three mazurkas, and an additional dance, *das Hupferl* (the hop), without specific rhythmic indication. Only the Schöller march, later known as the ten-step, remains on the list of test dances today, albeit with a repeated sequence of steps making it the fourteen-step. The *Amerikanscher walzer* bears the name of a contemporary test dance but is totally different. Many dances carry the names of their inventors. Haines is credited with a waltz and a mazurka, and Eduard Engelmann Jr., European champion in 1892 and 1894, is credited with two waltzes. The importance is not with specific dances, however, because most are no longer done, but with the Viennese contribution of carrying social dancing to the ice. The dances described in *Spuren auf dem Eise* could be done by mixed couples. Their execution tended to imitate a rather static ballroom type of dancing, often with both feet remaining on the ice. The possibilities that flow across the ice could provide were about to be fully discovered.

Spuren auf dem Eise is far more than just a compendium of figures. It represents the style of skating that evolved in Vienna in the generation after Jackson Haines's departure. Known first as the Viennese style, it was to become the international style, the direct predecessor of skating as we know it today.[10] Reflecting so directly on Haines's influence, it represents the greatest tribute to the "American Skating King."

SKATING IN THE SWISS ALPS

In the 1870s, skating styles were generally nationalistic in scope. All stemmed from basic figures developed in eighteenth-century England and then transmitted to the European and North America continents, but cultural differences in those places led to stylistic divergency as national development took place. Before successful international competition could be possible, those differences had to be reconciled. The International

Skating Union, founded in 1892, was the body that would ultimately effect that reconciliation, although compromise was to be more implied than real. Ultimately, there was a triumph of the international style over the English and American styles, a process that occurred over two decades. It began during the 1870s with a significant increase in communication and interaction between skaters of different nationalities, particularly those from Austria, England, Germany, and Russia. Much of this occurred at winter resorts in Switzerland.

Increasing numbers of skaters, men and women, were participating in the sport, and with the often short skating seasons in much of the skating world it is not surprising that devotees with the means to do so would seek winter vacation spots that could provide opportunities to practice their sport. They discovered the Swiss Alps. Three to four months of skating were assured, and the stunning mountain scenery offered added appeal. By the end of the century Switzerland boasted numerous resorts that offered multiple sports activities. Those most important to the history of figure skating were among the first developed, Davos and St. Moritz.

Davos, established originally as a sanatarium for persons with consumption, is located in a valley at an elevation of 5,100 feet. It provides an excellent balance of long skating seasons, much sun, and natural protection from strong winds. There are reports of skating there by the Dutch, Germans, and Russians as early as the 1860s. The Hotel Belvedere opened an ice rink in 1877 that was dominated by British skaters and became known as the English rink. A second rink soon opened, primarily to accommodate German and Russian skaters, and in 1880 the Davos Skating Club was formed, with membership numbering more than two hundred from throughout the skating world. There, members shared ideas and witnessed other national styles, and converts to the developing international style were made. George Browne, who was to become the principal promoter of the international style in the United States, was converted during a sabbatical leave at Davos.

In the 1870s, a decade after skating was first reported at Davos, skaters from England traveled to St. Moritz, a mountainside resort. The Engadine Hotel at that time was not equipped for winter residence, but by special arrangement it was opened for that purpose. There people skated on the lake it overlooked. At an elevation of 6,900 feet, winter lasts well into March, which assures a four-month skating season. Annual pilgrimages began, and, like Davos, St. Moritz became a major skating center. There too, skaters from many countries met and learned from each other.

Davos and St. Moritz became skating capitals and later served as sites for international competition. Davos has been the site for eleven World Championships in figure skating, sometimes for just one discipline. Pairs' and ladies' competitions before World War II were often held at different locations from the men's competitions. Only Vienna has hosted as many World Championships. St. Moritz has twice been the site for the

Olympic Winter Games, in 1928 and 1948. Only Innsbruck in Austria and Lake Placid in the United States have equaled that number.

INTERNATIONAL COMPETITIONS

Figure skating competitions were held with increasing frequency throughout the second half of the nineteenth century. Initially, they were local or regional, often just closing events to speed skating contests. Postponements and cancellations were sometimes necessary, owing to an insufficient number of skaters, but those early competitions generated interest in the sport as an ever-increasing number of figure skaters gained proficiency and sought opportunities to compete. By the 1880s, major competitions were being staged throughout the skating world.

The first important international competition was sponsored by the Vienna Skating Club in 1882. Billed as the "Great International Skating Tournament," it attracted many elite skaters.[11] Haines's student, Leopold Frey, won the event. Fellow club member

Leopold Frey, a student of Jackson Haines and winner of the Great International Skating Tournament in 1882. (World Figure Skating Museum and Hall of Fame)

Eduard Engelmann Jr., later to became the first European champion, placed second. Axel Paulsen (1856–1938) of Norway placed third. In addition to compulsory figures, contestants offered special figures. Frey connected an outside spread eagle to a backward outside eight and terminated with a sit spin, showing the influence of his teacher. Engelmann incorporated pirouettes in an interesting figure of three turns. Paulsen introduced the jump that still bears his name and is now a required element in short programs for both men and ladies.

Theodore Langer was fourth. For his special figure he created an intricate four-point star. That was said to have created a dilemma for judges who had to compare the static but very difficult one-foot closed figure with the flow of basic free-skating moves offered by Frey, Engelmann, and Paulsen. Although Langer placed fourth, it cannot be presumed, as some writers have suggested, that the judges favored free-skating moves over special figures. All four skaters were among the best of their day, so the results themselves fail to prove that judges preferred one style over the other or that they let personal preference influence their decisions over quality of the skating.

Axel Paulsen, inventor of the most difficult jump in figure skating. (World Figue Skating Museum and Hall of Fame)

Other offerings included a complex figure connecting edge jumps with threes, loops, and counters by Franz Biberhofer and a beautifully skated loop star with four points by Ernst von Stein. They, too, represented both types of skating. Biberhofer's offering was basic free skating; Stein's offering was a one-foot closed figure. These two popular but totally different types of skating were soon divided into separate categories: free-skating moves, sometimes called specialties, and special figures. Coupled with compulsory figures, competitions to World War I and beyond included one or any combination of the three disciplines.

By the late 1880s international competitions were being held almost annually, with several in St. Petersburg, Russia. The 1890 event was sponsored by the Neva Skating Association, predecessor of the St. Petersburg Skating Club. Participants were leading skaters of the day, including Rudolf Sundgrén of Sweden, Karl Kaiser and Willi Dienstl of Austria, Alexei Lebedev of Russia, John Catani of Finland, and Louis Rubenstein of Canada. The winner was Lebedev, a master of special figures and winner of many previous competitions. After his competitive career he coached the last generation of Russian skaters before the Bolshevik Revolution in 1918 effectively ended that country's long tradition of outstanding figure skating. Not until the 1960s would Russian skaters again become serious competitors on the international scene.

Controversy following the St. Petersburg competition resulted not from the judging but from the styles of skating employed. Skaters were required to demonstrate skill in the three disciplines, diagrams (compulsory figures), special figures, and specialties, all of which counted equally. Lebedev won the special figures and specialties events. Special gold medals were awarded to Rubenstein, who won the diagrams, and to Catani for the general high quality of his skating. Learning that Rubenstein had received a gold medal, the *Montreal Gazette* incorrectly declared him to be the "champion figure skater of the world," a statment that had to be retracted.[12]

The controversy posed the broader question of international versus English and American styles. "Diagram skating," the term employed for compulsory figures, was basic to all styles. Specialties, figures including jumps and spins, were the wave of the future, the evolving international style. Special figures, popular in the Scandinavian countries and elsewhere, were placed in the balance. The Russians had included all three types of competitive skating and evaluated them equally. Fairness can not be brought into question, and it is noteworthy that the top four skaters represented as many countries, Russia, Canada, Sweden, and Austria. Successful and meaningful international competition in the future would require agreement on a style of skating that all could accept. That was soon to come.

SPECIAL FIGURES

Special figures were intended to be unique, complex, and difficult. They were usually designed by and associated with individual skaters, and many winning designs were published in books from the period. Judging was based on degree of difficulty and artistic result. Although their popularity soared in the 1890s, their genesis is much earlier. It lies in England and Canada. Spectacles, a one-foot open figure first popular in England, was described by Vandervell in 1869, and the earliest grapevine, a two-foot figure, probably originated in Canada at about the same time. The interesting tracings that these figures left on the ice, and the skill required to accomplish them, provided the appeal they held for skaters. As increasingly complex designs evolved during the 1870s, the ability to perform them with rigid carriage of the body was no longer possible and thus contrary to basic precepts associated with combined skating. British skaters contributed nothing further to the discipline. Skaters in North America and northern Europe, Scandinavia, and Russia especially were less enamored with combined skating. They thrived on the challenges special figures provided and expanded significantly the complexity of artistic designs.

Special figures were not large and required only a few basic moves. One-foot turns and loops were fundamental. Other moves associated specifically with them include crosscuts, sometimes called anvils, and beaks, both of which may be of Canadian origin. Crosscuts require three changes of direction. From an abrupt halt on any edge, the skater moves away from the edge for a short distance, often in a straight line and on the flat of the skate. After another abrupt stop, a mirror to the original edge is skated in the opposite direction. Beaks require an abrupt stop and a pull-back of the tracing foot just a few degrees off the original circle, with no change in body position.

A music treble-clef sign was skated by Lebedev in 1893, but by that time most special figures were closed and geometrically balanced designs. These complex one-foot figures, which their adherents saw as the future of figure skating, remained an important part of competition throughout the prewar years and were included as an official event at the 1908 Olympic Games. Nicolai Panin of Russia won the gold medal.[13]

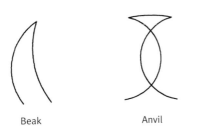

Beak   Anvil

Beaks and anvils are essential to many special figures. (Pete Jones)

Although they required a good command of basic figures and a great sense of balance, the manner in which they had to be executed was characteristically jerky, with the skater looking down almost continuously. The major criticism against special figures was that little concern could be given to body position, grace, or elegance. Although this clearly influenced their demise after the war, the perception was a paradox. Edgar Syers, a champion of the international style, reported in 1913 that even the most difficult special figures could be executed with precision and grace. Panin, he tells us, was "mathematically precise in his tracings, and his positions and movements were never in the least awkward or jerky." He continued, saying that Panin skated with his "body and head erect [and] he found it only necessary to glance occasionally at the maze of curves and turns which his skate described with such consummate ease."[14]

Skating styles were thus expanding and changing rapidly during the late nineteenth century, but they no longer remained localized. Developments in one country soon influenced those in another. Even in England, with its diehard conservative combined skaters, special figures were recognized, at least for their difficulty. As Monier-Williams, Pidgeon, and Dryden wrote in 1892, "There is a large class of small figures which are performed upon one foot, and which, owing to the energetic action of the unemployed leg, and strange contortions of the body they seem to necessitate, have earned for themselves the generic name of 'kickers.' They . . . are exceedingly difficult to learn, and apparently impossible, with our present knowledge, to skate gracefully." The authors elected not to describe them because they "so often proved themselves to be absolutely destructive to the good form of those who practise them."[15] English skaters remained committed to combined skating with all its rigidity, whereas skaters on the Continent were developing flowing free-skating programs. Special figures were foreign to both styles.

Owing to the evolution of skating styles and techniques, the terminology employed is itself confusing. "Special figures" was initially employed as a broad term used to represent anything other than the most basic figures of the day. Thus, figures such as continuous loops or ringlets, circular movement in a confined space, crosscuts, and grapevines were all termed special figures, as were future free-skating moves such as

Back and Three Star

Hügel Star

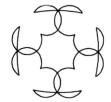
Swedish Crosscut Star

Engelmann Star

Various shaped stars were among the most popular special figures. The beak and three star was first done by World Champion Henning Grenander. The Hügel star was first done by three-time World Champion Gustave Hügel. The Swedish crosscut star is one of the easier ones. Its original designer is unknown. The Engelmann star was first done by three-time European Champion Eduard Engelmann Jr. (Pete Jones)

spins, spread eagles, and jumps. When done on one foot, figures such as spectacles, the term *continuous skating* was sometimes employed. Fancy skating is a much older term and not, as has sometimes been said, an offshoot of continuous skating. Originally, "fancy skating" referred to anything other than basic edging, but by the waning years of the century it suggested difficult one- and two-foot figures, including objects such as letters, leaves with veins, and fish with fins. The terms *fancy skating* and *continuous skating* disappeared with the century. Afterward, the terms *compulsory figures* and *free skating* were used in their modern sense. The term *special figures* continued and was used in the narrower sense of unique, typically closed, designs often associated with a particular skater.

THE INTERNATIONAL SKATING UNION

By the 1890s many local clubs and a few regional and national organizations existed. Most important was the National Skating Association, which had been established specifically to develop standards for competitive speed skating in England. Recognizing a broader need, as early as 1879 it called for the establishment of an international council to oversee contests between countries. That did not happen quickly, but thirteen years later, July 1892, sixteen delegates from six countries—Austria, Germany, Great Britain, Hungary, the Netherlands, and Sweden—attended a three-day congress in Scheveningen, the Netherlands, to form an international organization. Letters of interest were received from Norway, Russia, and the United States, countries unable to send delegates. The resulting Internationale Eislauf-Vereingung (International Skating Union) was sanctioned to govern both speed skating and figure skating.[16] It was a pioneer sports organization, the first international governing body for a winter sport. Only the International Rowing Federation, founded that same year, claims an earlier organizational date. The International Olympic Committee (IOC) was formed two years later, in 1894.

Initial emphasis was placed on speed skating, and in 1893 the first World Championship under the auspices of the new federation took place in Amsterdam. Four distances were skated, and in order to be named champion of the world a skater had to win three of them. That honor went to Jaap Eden of the Netherlands.

In 1895 a committee was appointed to recommend rules for figure skating and select compulsory figures for championships. The first World Championship, called the Championship of the Internationale Eislauf-Vereingung (IEV), was held in 1896. There was only a men's event and with four competitors. Gilbert Fuchs of Germany became the first World champion; other contestants included Gustav Hügel of Austria, Georg Sanders of Russia, and Nicolai Poduskov of Russia. The era of world competition in figure skating under an international governing body had arrived.

FIVE

The End of an Era

FIGURE skating made great advancements during the 1870s and 1880s. In England, combined skating reached a high level of perfection. On the Continent, the connection of figures provided the seminal beginning of modern free skating. In the Scandinavian countries, special figures became ever more intricate. Although these styles tended to remain regional in scope, communication through books, competitions, and fellowship at the winter resorts in Switzerland created a broad awareness of them, and some mixing of the styles would seem to have been inevitable. Unfortunately, they were fundamentally so different that any logical mixing of them was not possible. Ultimately, there had to be universal acceptance of one style rather than the creation of a new hybrid style.

International competitions in the 1880s accelerated the need for change, and the establishment of the International Skating Union (ISU) in 1892 provided a structure capable of effecting that change. The primary challenge for the union was to formulate a universal style from disparate national styles and to guide future development of the sport in a manner that would assure meaningful and sustainable international competition. In historical perspective, the result was logical. Combined skating was not a competitive genre. Special figures, although part of international competition at the time, were soon to disappear. Basic figures fundamental to all styles and free skating were left, and they became for nearly a century the two parts of international competition. Basic figures, now called compulsory figures, were given greater scoring value, and perhaps that can be viewed as some consolation to conservative British skaters.

EUROPEAN AND WORLD CHAMPIONSHIPS

Change through the 1890s was dramatic. The first European Championship was held in 1891; the ISU was founded in 1892, and the first World Championship was held in 1896. The European Championships, although not continuous, remain the oldest international figure skating competition. Eighteen months before the founding of the ISU, the first was held in Hamburg under the auspices of the German and Austrian Skating Association. For five years the European Championships functioned primarily as regional events. They were held twice each in Germany and Austria and once in Hungary, then a part of the Austro-Hungarian Empire. All but two of the competitors came from those three countries.

One of figure skating's most celebrated judging controversies occurred at the 1893 Championship. The Berlin Skating Club, host for the event, named Henning Grenander of Sweden as champion. The German and Austrian Skating Association, the sponsoring organization, named the defending champion, Eduard Engelmann Jr. of Austria, as champion. The problem resulted from different interpretations of scoring rules. Grenander won by point count, 1,988 to 1,987, unless one took into consideration half-points, in which case there was a tie at 1,988 points. Compulsory figures served as the tie breaker, and Engelmann won that portion. The ISU ultimately annulled the competition, but the *Results in Figure Skating,* published on the occasion of the union's seventy-fifth anniversary, lists Engelmann as winner.[1] A note indicates that "the European Championships for 1893 had been invalidated by the 1895 Congress."

Willem J. H. Mulier of the Netherlands, an all-around sportsman and author of several books on sports, served from 1892 to 1895 as the ISU's first president; Ary Prins of Germany/Austria was secretary. The Berlin controversy taxed their leadership to the point that they were unable to organize the Congress scheduled for 1894. Prins resigned, and Mulier announced his intention to step down at the end of his term. The future of the young organization seemed precarious, but, fortunately, Viktor G. Balck of Sweden, a member of the founding committee, was elected president by a mail vote of the original members. His leadership proved to be decisive. Serving for three decades, he guided the young organization through its formative years. He was also a charter member of the International Olympic Committee.

At the 1895 Congress, in addition to annulling the 1893 European Championship, ISU members voted to establish an annual World Championship and scheduled the first for the following February. The European Championships were subsequently canceled but reinstated in 1898. Realization that World Championships would eventually be held in North America and habitual concern over cancellations owing to uncooperative weather, a scenario that occurred for the European Championships of 1902 and 1903, were contributing factors leading to the desirability of holding both competitions. Since 1898 they have been annual events under the auspices of the ISU.

After their reinstatement sites for the European Championships were widely distributed. Trondheim, Norway, hosted the 1898 competition, the furthest north that any European or World Championship has been held. Scheduled for Amsterdam in 1902 and 1903, both had to be canceled for lack of ice. Other sites included the former host cities Berlin, Budapest, and Vienna, as well as Bonn, Davos, Oslo, St. Petersburg, Stockholm, and Warsaw. Fifteen European Championships were held in ten cities between 1898 and the outbreak of World War I.

The era of World competition arrived in 1896, but not until after World War I did skaters from North America participate. The cost of travel, and the time required, made competing in Europe an activity possible only for the wealthy or those who might obtain sponsorship. Louis Rubenstein is the only North American known to have participated in a major figure skating competition abroad other than the 1908 Olympic Games before the war. Surprisingly, only six British men competed in the thirty-nine European and World competitions held before the war, none of them more than once. All placed last or next to last. One might presume that continuing devotion to English-style skating may have contributed to the small number of entries and poor showings in the earlier competitions, but that theory is not valid for later years. With the advent of ladies' events in 1906 and pairs' events in 1908, British skaters competed most years, and much more successfully than the men. Madge Syers was the first lady World champion, and Phyllis and James Johnson were twice the World Pair Champions. Events for ladies and pairs were not offered at the European Championships until 1930.

EARLY WORLD CHAMPIONS

International competitions in the quarter century before World War I attracted skaters whose names are legendary in the history of the sport: Gilbert Fuchs of Germany, Gustav Hügel of Austria, and Ulrich Salchow of Sweden. Gilbert Fuchs (b. 1871) was figure skating's first World champion. His long and distinguished career began a year earlier with a third-place finish at the 1895 European Championship. Balancing a medical education with skating, Fuchs competed in but did not win four European and World competitions during the next nine years. He reclaimed the World title in 1906 but again was unable to defend it. Fuchs's career record over fifteen years, competing in just ten European and World Championships, includes two World titles plus five second-place and three third-place finishes. He also won an international competition for special figures held at Munich in 1903. Fuchs is remembered as a technician and especially strong in compulsory figures. His skating success resulted, he said, from "critical analysis" as he strove to bring various skating moves to perfection. His article "Theory of Skating," published in Brokaw's *The Art of Skating,* expands on the importance of the free leg previously emphasized in *Spuren auf dem Eise* and describes in detail the correct execution of one-foot turns. His book *Theorie und Praxis des Kunstlaufes am Eise* (Theory and Practice of Figure Skating on Ice), published sixteen years later, provides a valuable resource for skating technique practiced on the eve of World War I.

Gustav Hügel (1876–1954) was the second World champion. His impressive career was shorter than that of Fuchs, lasting just ten years, but he competed many more times. From 1894 through 1900 he missed only one European Championship and never a World Championship. In his final effort, the European Championship of 1901, he defeated both Fuchs and Salchow, a significant win because it was the only time all three competed in the same competition. Hügel's record includes one European and three World titles. He never placed lower than second. At an international competition for spe-

Gilbert Fuchs, Gustave Hügel, Georg Sanders, and Nicolai Poduskov (left to right) were the only four competitors at the first World Championship in 1896. (Irving Brokaw, *The Art of Skating* [1926])

cial figures held contemporaneously with the 1896 World Championship, Hügel received the gold medal.

Ulrich Salchow (1877–1949) was the most legendary of the early champions. He was Danish by birth, but his family moved to Sweden when he was still young, and he became that country's junior champion. Salchow first entered the World Championships in 1897 and placed second behind Hügel. He became the European champion a year later. He again placed second to Hügel at the World Championships in 1899 and 1900, but their roles reversed at the European Championships. Salchow's competitive record at twenty-four European and World Championships between 1897 and 1913 includes an impressive twenty gold medals. The other four medals, three silver and one bronze, came early in his career, years when Fuchs and Hügel were still competing. Salchow was also the gold medalist at the Olympic Games in 1908, the first to include skating events. In his only postwar effort, the Olympic Games in 1920, he placed second in the compulsory figures behind another legend of the sport, Gillis Grafström, and a respectable fourth overall. He was forty-one years of age.

Salchow was a master of compulsory figures, and, like Fuchs and Hügel, his special figures were also strong. He placed second at the Panschin Memorial Competition in Special Figures held in St. Petersburg in 1908. Although free skating was viewed as his weakest discipline, Salchow is most remembered for the jump that bears his name and remains part of most free-skating programs. It requires a takeoff from a backward inside edge and a landing on a backward outside edge on the same circle. Although one of the simpler jumps, it is one of the most beautiful.

Salchow was not only one of the great skaters of his generation and the inventor of an important jump, he continued to influence the sport administratively, serving as president of the ISU from 1925 to 1937. During his presidency, World competitions were twice held abroad, first in New York in 1930 and then in Montreal in 1932; the number of skaters competing in ISU-sponsored events increased significantly; judging was refined; and rules for ice dancing were adopted. Disputes at the 1937 Congress, including disagreement over a minimum-age rule for competitors, resulted in his bid for reelection being defeated, but Salchow and his predecessor, Viktor Balck, led the ISU through forty-two years of growth and into a strong and respected organization. Salchow was honored in 1976 as one of twenty initial inductees into the World Figure Skating Hall of Fame.

Fuchs, Hügel, and Salchow, all born within two years of each other, represent the strong quality of figure skating in the early years of world competition. Collectively, they were World champions every year less one for sixteen years. Outstanding in compulsory figures and free skating, they all won medals for special figures as well. They competed against each other from 1895 through 1909, but only once, the European Championship in 1901, did all three compete in the same competition. The order of medals was Hügel,

Ulrich Salchow, ten-time World champion and the first Olympic gold medalist. (World Figure Skating Museum and Hall of Fame)

Fuchs, and Salchow. In their years of head-to-head competition each of the three defeated the others at least once, which means, of course, that each was defeated by the others at least once. They were the most talented and complete skaters of their day and provided the sport with its first great rivalry.

Other successful skaters who competed before the war include Henning Grenander

(1874–1958) of Sweden, who in 1898 defeated Hügel and Fuchs to become the World champion. Fritz Kachler of Austria succeeded Salchow as World champion in 1912, winning twice.[2] Gösta Sandahl of Sweden defeated Kachler in 1914 to become the last prewar World champion. Bronze and silver medalists during the prewar years included Georg Sanders and Nicolai Panin of Russia, remembered primarily for their skill in special figures; Edgar Syers of England, Bror Meyer of Sweden, and Willy Böckl of Austria, all of whom wrote important books on figure skating; Per Thorén of Sweden and Werner Rittberger of Germany, whose names are associated with the half-loop and loop jumps; and Max Bohatsch of Austria, who may have invented one version of an important dance.

PAIR SKATING BEFORE THE WAR

Pair skating came to the fore about the turn of the century and in 1908 became a competitive discipline in World and Olympic competition. Several factors influenced its development, including the popularity of hand-in-hand skating beginning in the late 1880s and the crazelike fascination with ice dancing beginning in the mid-1890s. Pair skating in its infancy consisted primarily of couples executing basic figures and free-skating moves side by side, often hand in hand, and connecting them with dance steps. Modern terminology would call these technical elements and connecting steps, but modern elements such as lifts, pair spins, and throw jumps were still many years in the future. The most important free-skating moves done by pairs at this time were long, flowing spirals, forward or backward, with one or two hands joined. Spins were included by the better skaters, primarily as conclusions to their programs. Skating basic figures well was paramount. Connecting them with dance steps provided continuity.

The first pair champions were the unbeatable Anna Hübler (b. 1885) and Heinrich Burger (b. 1881) of Germany.[3] Their skating careers collectively included few outings. Hübler never competed as a singles skater in international competition, but Burger competed twice at the European Championships and four times at the World Championships, collecting one bronze and three silver medals. Their appearances as a pair included the World Championships in 1908 and 1910 and the Olympics in 1908, all of which they won. They were recognized for their strength and speed, always skating in perfect time with the music.

A British husband and wife pair, Phyllis (1886–1967) and James Johnson (1874–1921), challenged Hübler and Burger at the three competitions, always to second- or third-place finishes. The Johnsons were World champions twice, 1909 and 1912. They reappeared after the war at the Antwerp Olympic Games and placed third. James Johnson never competed in singles events at the international level, but Phyllis Johnson com-

Ludowika Eilers and Walter Jakobsson won their first World pair title in 1911 representing two countries, Germany and Finland. Following their marriage that year they represented Finland and won two additional World titles, one before and one after the war. An Olympic title was added in 1920. (World Figure Skating Museum and Hall of Fame)

plimented the 1912 pairs title with the first of three successive singles efforts. She was third that year and second and third in succeeding years.

Another prewar pair warrants special mention. Their remarkable career spanned a quarter century, including competitions before and after the war. Ludowika Eilers (1884–1970) of Germany and Walter Jakobsson (1882–1957) of Finland first skated at the World Championships in 1910, placing second behind Hübler and Burger. Competing every year through 1923, they were three times the World champions and four times silver medalists, and they won Olympic gold at Antwerp in 1920. At their last World title he was fourteen days short of his forty-first birthday, and she was thirty-eight. Before their marriage in 1911 they represented their respective countries, a procedure then possible under ISU rules. Afterward, they represented Finland. Eilers competed also in singles events early in her career but with no great success.

One other successful pair skater began her career before the war. Helene Engelmann (b. 1898) competed with Karl Mejstrik (b. 1895). They were World champions in 1913 and silver medalists in 1914. After the war Engelmann partnered with Alfred Berger and won gold medals at two World Championships and at the 1924 Olympic Games.

ENTHUSIASTIC WRITERS

Books by contemporaries of the early champions, men who themselves were skaters, allow us to glean much understanding of the sport's development at that decisive time in its history. They did not win major skating titles, but their exuberant love of the sport is reflected in their prose. Most important are Irving Brokaw of the United States and Bror Meyer of Sweden, but there are others. Douglas Adams's popular little book *Skating* was published in 1890. Adams, a member of the London Skating Club, the Wimbledon Skating Club, and the National Skating Association, competed at the European Championship of 1905 held at Bonn, the only entrant not from Germany or Austria. He placed last in a unanimous decision. Adams begins by acknowledging his devotion to the British tradition of Vandervell and Witham, but like other contemporary British authors he shows an inquisitive interest in other styles. He was one of four Englishmen asked to demonstrate combined skating during a competition at Stockholm in 1889. What he learned there was a revelation, and that led him to devote an entire chapter to differences between English and Swedish skating styles. Adams was amazed at the power achieved by Swedish skaters and concluded correctly that it was "gained by the swing of the unemployed leg."[4] Equally fascinated by the intricacies of special figures offered at that competition, Adams included sketches of those skated by the winners, Rudolf Sungrèn, Ivar Hult, and John Catani. He also described grapevines and other two-foot figures but ignored free-skating moves, of which he may have been less aware.

Adams's book portrays the state of skating in England on the eve of one of its most important decades. Combined skating still reigned supreme. Although some skaters were enjoying the challenge of some two-foot figures, special figures were still an anomaly in England. Adams recognized the tremendous skill they required but dismissed them as not possible to accomplish with the English style of skating.

In the decade after Adams's book the international style challenged the deep-rooted English style. The two most important protagonists for change were Herbert Yglesias (1867–1949) and Edgar Syers (1863–1946), both of whom were active, office-holding members of the NSA. Yglesias had long been a respected judge. Syers received a bronze medal behind Hügel and Salchow at the 1899 World Championship and with his wife won a bronze medal in pairs at the London Olympic Games in 1908. Yglesias, a lawyer, published *Figure Skating* in 1905, basing his book on the rapidly evolving international style. The volume was so successful that it warranted five editions and remained available through 1940. Syers served as joint general secretary of the NSA, a position of great influence, and as an advocate for the international style was instrumental in luring the 1898 World Championship to London. His most important book, coauthored with his wife, Madge, is *The Art of Skating (International Style),* published in 1913.

Irving Brokaw (1869–1939), the champion of America in 1906, did not compete in the European or World Championships but did represent the United States at the London Olympic Games in 1908. He placed sixth. It was at St. Moritz a year later that he completed his first book, and it was there that he became totally converted to the international style. Brokaw left his mark on skating through four books, all bearing the same title, *The Art of Skating*.[5] For the first book, published in 1910, he sought the expertise of leading skaters for several chapters, including Georg Sanders of Russia for special figures, Phyllis and James Johnson of England for pair skating, and Gilbert Fuchs of Germany for an essay entitled "Theory of Skating." Brokaw's purpose in writing the book was to present "the rules and regulations of the International Skating Union and to give instruction in the clearest and simplest manner."[6]

Another American active during that period, and equally committed to the international style, was George Henry Browne (1857–1931), a Harvard University graduate and headmaster of the Browne and Nichols School in Cambridge, Massachusetts.[7] Browne spent the winter of 1902–3 on a sabbatical in Davos, where he, too, was converted to the international style. After returning to Boston he arranged for a demonstration of it with Brokaw, Karl Zenger, and Frank Bacon as featured skaters.[8] Browne had described the strict English style and the slightly more relaxed American style in two earlier books, a time when he was less familiar with the evolving international style, but his later books, especially *The New Skating, International Style*, dating from 1910, the same year as Brokaw's *Art of Skating*, show his total conversion.

Bror Meyer (b. 1886), a competitor at the European and World Championships in 1906, wrote one of the most valuable books on figure skating. Although not published until three years after the war, *Skating with Bror Meyer* represents the state of skating at the end of the prewar era. Excellent diagrams support an element-by-element approach to free skating. Of special interest is his philosophy on content and construction of free-skating programs because it represents a starting point for the postwar generation of skaters. Free skating, he said, "should consist of movements and combinations which are original and characteristic of the skaters individually." He continued, "a competition program is judged by its contents and execution, but in my opinion, the skater must impress upon his mind that 'grace' is the highest essential."[9]

THE TRIUMPH OF THE INTERNATIONAL STYLE

Three distinct styles of skating evolved during the nineteenth century, and competent writers described and championed them all. The ISU adopted rules for competition in figure skating in 1897, and although they suggest compromise, in reality they represent a triumph of the international style, which was more readily accepted than might have been expected. Americans were converted under the leadership of Browne and Brokaw. Conversion was not as easily attained in England, where the national style was so deeply ingrained, but there, too, dominant personalities such as Yglesias and Syers prevailed as many skaters discarded the shackles of combined skating and adopted the international style.

National styles had resulted from different interests in England, North America, and on the Continent. For British skaters, satisfaction had been found in combined skating, which was totally noncompetitive. Their figures were complex and intricate, and strict form was required. The skating leg was kept absolutely straight, and there were no exceptions. The free leg was held close to, although not necessarily touching, the skating leg, with the toe pointed down and out.[10] The body and head were held erect. Shoulders were forced back and held stiff to avoid leaning forward. Arms were held down at the sides of the body, elbows turned in. Although viewed as excessively rigid by North American and continental skaters, that body position was ideally suited for combined skating.

In comparison, the American style can best be described by rules enunciated by Swift and Clark some thirty years earlier and reconfirmed by Browne in his book of 1900, *Handbook of Figure Skating*.[11] The body was held erect but yielding and generally square to the front. The head was carried upright, inclining slightly backward. Shoulders were kept slightly back of the breast and moderately low. Legs were not stiff, and the knee of the skating leg was bent slightly. The arms hung loosely at the side. George Meagher, a Canadian also writing in 1900, relaxed those rules somewhat by calling for a more natural position: "Allow the body to yield, yet it should be held naturally erect, and with the chest well expanded. All the members of the body should work in unison in an easy and pliable manner, with no stiffness. . . . The head . . . should fall into position naturally. . . . It should incline . . . in a graceful motion without apparent effort. . . . The shoulders should always be kept well back. . . . A pliability of form is absolutely necessary. . . . The unemployed leg . . . should never be held with the knee perfectly straight."[12]

The international style, called the continental style by the British, can not so easily be described by defining body position. *Spuren auf dem Eise* emphasized the technical advantage of using the arms and free leg for power more than for the aesthetic positioning of them. On the Continent by century's end, showmanship in free-skating moves held sway. The greatest concern was with beauty of movement, a general characteristic that dates from the time of Jean Garcin and the Gilets Rouges.

Although admittedly an oversimplification, one can categorize basic differences in national styles as interest in geometric formations on the ice by English skaters, interest in unique designs on the ice by North American skaters, and interest in movement across the ice by continental skaters. These differences were dealt with decisively at the ISU's 1897 Congress, and consensus was reached. Correct posture required:

> upright carriage, not bent at the hips, but without being stiff; strong bending of the knee or body to be only momentary. Head upright. Unemployed foot raised only a little from the

ice, not dragging behind, with the toe turned downward and backward, bent a tride [*sic*] at the knee, and generally held behind the employed foot; otherwise swinging freely, and assisting the movement, but not held far away. Arms, hanging down easily without swinging, may, like the employed foot, be used to assist the movement, but elbows or hands not to be raised far from the body, the latter never, if possible, above the waist. Fingers neither spread nor clinched. In general, everything violent, angular, or stiff in the action to be avoided; no endeavor to be violently expressed, but the impression is to be given that the execution of the figures requires no effort.[13]

Austria, Canada, Denmark, Finland, Germany, Great Britain, Holland, Norway, Russia, Sweden, and Switzerland sent delegates to the 1897 Congress. Thus, all national styles were represented, and compromise on body position is evident in the wording. The body will not bend at the hips but will not be stiff. The free leg will be held behind the skating leg and bent slightly at the knee but not far away. The arms will not swing but may be used to assist the movement.

This became the judging criteria for international competitions under ISU control that included just two events, compulsory figures and free skating. Separate competitions continued to be held for special figures but not under ISU sponsorship. It had been just a decade since combined skating reigned supreme in England as the most sophisticated and stylized type of skating in the country that could boast the beginning and development of the sport, but with the advent of regulated international competitions, combined skating was destined to become passé.

Madge and Edgar Syers introduced the international style to England, bringing Ulrich Salchow and Henning Grenander from Sweden to demonstrate it. Brokaw and Browne had done the same thing in America. In both England and America there were many converts. When skating resumed after the war, a new generation of skaters born after the founding of the ISU would carry the sport forward in one international style, the only style they knew.[14]

SKATING'S FIRST FEMINIST

Florence Madeline (Madge) Syers (1881–1917), a member of the London Skating Club and a strong advocate for the international style, was skating's first feminist. Born Florence Madeline Cave, she married Edgar Syers in 1900 and together they influenced figure skating profoundly in England and internationally. In their book *The Art of Skating (International Style),* published in 1913, they noted how rapidly the international style had progressed since its introduction in England. A fine skater, Madge Syers had the audacity to enter the 1902 World Championship held in London. Competitive skating was viewed as a male activity, and the notion that a woman would enter had not been considered.[15] There was no regulation prohibiting it, and, politically, because Madge and Edgar Syers were influential members of the NSA, there was no solution other than to let her compete. She placed second to the reigning champion, Ulrich Salchow.

The topic of women skating competitively was a major topic of discussion at the ISU's 1903 Congress, but no gender-specific legislation resulted. Continuing her one-woman crusade, Madge Syers entered the 1904 European Championship at Davos but owing to an injury had to withdraw after the compulsory figures. The topic of lady competitors appeared on the agenda for the 1905 Congress. Supported by strong lobbying from the NSA, a "ladies championship" was approved, although not quite with equal benefits. The World Championship remained the domain of men, whereas women could skate in an event called simply a championship of the IEV. Most years up to World War II the ladies' competition was held at a different time and place than the men's competition, but they could now compete against each other, limited only by any perceived lack of athletic prowess.

The first ladies' figure skating championship was held at Davos in 1906, and Madge Syers prevailed, suggesting that her success four years earlier had not been accidental. Five skaters from four countries competed that year, and all but one returned in 1907

Madge Syers, skating's first feminist, entered the presumed all-male World Championships in 1902 because there was no rule to prevent her doing so. She placed second to Ulrich Salchow. Four years later the ISU established a championship for ladies. (World Figure Skating Museum and Hall of Fame)

with the same results. Syers was again the champion. Second, third, and fourth places in both years went to Jenny Herz of Austria, Lily Kronberger of Hungary, and Elsa Rendschmidt of Germany. Syers added the first ladies' Olympic gold medal to her laurels in 1908 and with her husband entered the pairs event. They carried home bronze medals. Syers is the only champion to medal in two events at the same Olympics.

Madge Syers died of heart failure caused by acute endocarditis at thirty-five. Edgar Syers then ceased all involvement with the sport, but in the prewar years he and his wife had been among England's most active skating participants and strongest advocates for the international style. They published three books, were influential members of the London Skating Club and the NSA, and competed as well. Madge Syers was honored by election to the World Figure Skating Hall of Fame in 1981.

Two Hungarians followed Syers as prewar lady World champions, Lily Kronberger (1890–1974) for four years beginning in 1908, and Opika von Méray Horváth (ca. 1888–1977) for three years beginning in 1912. Kronberger, from a wealthy aristocratic family, was well known for her lavish costumes, but for her final competition in Vienna in 1911 she appeared with her own brass band as well and skated to "Pas des patineurs." There was more at stake than the fact that a wealthy woman wanted to skate to live music by a well-rehearsed band. Since the days of Jackson Haines, the role of music in skating had gradually grown in importance, but its function remained more background than substantive. Kronberger, an early advocate for appropriate music, was among the first to recognize its interpretive potential in free skating, saying, "It is first necessary to hear the music inwardly, then to interpret."[16] She was elected into the World Figure Skating Hall of Fame in 1997.

Opika von Méray Horváth began her brief international career with a silver medal behind Kronberger in 1911, the only time they competed against each other outside Hungary. After the former champion's retirement Horváth proved to be unbeatable for three years before World War I curtailed her skating. She was thirty-four when competition resumed after the war and no longer competed.

ARTIFICIAL ICE AND YEAR-ROUND SKATING

Madge Syers competed on indoor artificial ice at the 1902 World Championship held at the National Skating Palace in London. It was the first international competition skated on artificial ice. Ironically, that same year the European Championship, scheduled in Amsterdam, was canceled for lack of ice. This demonstrated conclusively a major advantage of artificial ice, but only a few venues existed. In addition, many skaters felt strongly that skating on natural ice was not only better but also a tradition that should be continued. The perils of skating on natural ice and coping with the elements remained for many years an integral part of the sport. It would be another sixty-five years before ISU rules would require all competitions to be held on artificial ice and in enclosed rinks.

There had been experiments with artificial-ice rinks in the 1870s, both in America and in England, but the first rink of importance, dating from 1876, was constructed in England by John Gamgee in Chelsea on the north bank of the Thames River. Its ice surface was small, twenty-four feet by forty feet, but it included a lavishly appointed gallery for spectators. Swiss Alpine scenery was painted on the walls, and bands are known to have played for skating on some occasions. It was a rink specifically for noblemen and gentlemen who gained membership by subscription, but other rinks soon opened for the general public and not just in London.

By the end of the century, many major cities, including Baltimore, Brussels, Munich, New York, Paris, and Philadelphia, boasted indoor artificial ice rinks that had large skating surfaces. Crowds of recreational skaters frequented the facilities, making it difficult for serious skaters to practice their figures and, in London, engage in combined skating. London's Prince's Skating Club was opened in 1896 specifically to combat that problem. It boasted a long, narrow skating surface, two hundred by fifty-two feet, exclusively for use by its members. There the elite of English skaters practiced combined skating without interference.

Not all artificial-ice rinks were enclosed. An open-air, artificial-ice rink was opened

The Chelsea Skating Rink, London's first artificial-ice rink. (World Figure Skating Museum and Hall of Fame)

in 1909 in Vienna by Eduard Engelmann Jr. Its success was such that three years later a much larger facility was opened on the site of the Vienna Skating Club, and yet a third opened before the war. Others followed in Prague and elsewhere. Artificial ice provided extended skating seasons and when rinks were enclosed allowed year-round skating. Increased ice time ultimately led to a higher-quality of skating realized after the war, the second period in this history of figure skating.

Artificial ice also provided opportunity for the sport to develop in warmer countries where skating had not previously been possible. Some eight thousand miles from the European skating capitals, Australia's first rink opened in Adelaide in 1904. Melbourne followed in 1906, and Sydney was just a year later. The National Ice Skating Association of Australia, founded in 1931, joined the ISU in 1932. Although skating was a popular recreational activity, no Australian skater competed at the World Championships until 1947, and participation was sporadic for another twenty-five years. Travel distance was a contributing factor. Australian skaters have competed every year since 1972, but none have been medal contenders. The World Championships have not yet been held in Australia, although the World Junior Championships have twice been held in Brisbane.

Skating reached South Africa with the opening of a rink in Johannesburg in 1909. The South African Ice Skating Association was founded in 1937, and membership in the ISU was granted in 1938. Rarely have South African skaters competed in World competition, limited in the post–World War II era partly by the cold war and apartheid, problems discussed later. South Africa remains the only country from that continent to hold membership in the ISU.

OLYMPIC SKATING

Fifteen hundred years after the Romans abolished Olympic competition, a tradition that had spanned twelve hundred years, the games were revived in 1896, owing largely to the efforts of Baron Pierre de Coubertin (1863–1937). Appropriately, they were held in Athens, Greece, and King George I officially opened the first modern Olympics, in which 311 athletes, all men, from thirteen countries participated. Twelve years later the games were held at London, where, owing to the availability of indoor artificial ice, figure skating became an Olympic sport. The games that year had originally been scheduled for Rome, but owing to costs associated with rebuilding following the volcanic eruption of Mt. Vesuvius the Italian government was unable to commit the necessary funding. London gladly accepted an eleventh-hour offer to host the games. That turn of events accelerated figure skating's prominence as it became the first and only winter sport contested at the games before World War I. It was a one-time event because artificial ice was not available in Stockholm, site of the games in 1912, and the games scheduled for Berlin in 1916 were canceled because of the war. When they were revived at Antwerp in

1920, artificial ice was available, and figure skating reappeared.[17] In 1924 the first separate Olympic Winter Games were held in Chamonix, France.

Events for men, ladies, and pairs were all contested at the London games, where twenty-one skaters from seven nations competed. Swedish men swept their events, with medals going to Ulrich Salchow, Richard Johansson, and Per Thorén. Madge Syers easily won the ladies' event, with Elsa Rendschmidt of Germany and Dorothy Greenhough-Smith of Great Britain winning the silver and bronze medals. Germany and England split the pairs medals. Anna Hübler and Heinrich Burger won the gold medals, and the English husband-and-wife pairs of Phyllis and James Johnson and Madge and Edgar Syers won the silver and bronze medals.

Special figures were included as a fourth event. Nicolai Panin of Russia won the gold medal. Two British skaters, Arthur Cumming and George Hall-Say, the only other competitors, claimed the silver and bronze medals. Representing a dying discipline, special figures were not contested at the Antwerp games twelve years later.

THE NORDIC GAMES

The Nordic Games held in Stockholm, Sweden, have sometimes been viewed as the direct predecessor of the Winter Olympics, primarily because they were quadrennial and included the same sports as the Winter Games, but Olympic figure skating events were never held in connection with the Nordic Games. The World Championships, however, maintained a close relationship to them for twenty-five years. The Nordic Games were established primarily for Scandinavian and Finnish athletes, but some sports, including figure skating, were open to athletes from other countries. Viktor Balck, president of the ISU from 1895 to 1925, has been called the "Father of the Nordic Games" and, not surprisingly, during his tenure ties existed between the ISU and the Nordic organization.

Because of Queen Victoria's death in 1901 the World Championship scheduled for London was moved to Stockholm and held simultaneously with the first Nordic Games. Four years later Stockholm was selected as the site for the World Championship, specifically so figure skating could again be held at the same time as the Nordic Games. A pattern was thereby established. By 1909 ladies' and pairs' events had become a part of the World Championships. That year the men and pairs competed in Stockholm, two weeks after the ladies had competed in Budapest. In 1913 the ladies and pairs competed in Stockholm, but the men competed in Vienna two weeks later. After the war, the Nordic Games moved to an even-year cycle spaced between the Olympic Games, and twice more World Championship events were held in connection with them, men and ladies in 1922 and ladies in 1926. The first separate Winter Olympics were held in 1924, Balck stepped down as ISU president in 1925, and after 1926 the ISU had no further connection with the Nordic Games.

One month after the assassination of Francis Ferdinand, Archduke of Austria, in Sarajevo on July 28, 1914, Europe was plunged into war. The bastions of figure skating—Austria, England, France, Germany, Hungary, and Russia—were among those nations pitted against one another in "the war to end wars." For the next seven years there were no ISU-sponsored championships, but if political events in the early years of the century had divided countries and thrust them into war, competitive events in those years brought skaters and skating countries together in a sense of comradery that could outlast the war. Skating recovered relatively quickly and expanded greatly after the war because its governing organization and its adopted, international style were solidly established before the assassin's bullet was fired. The Old World order was left behind as society and skating entered the modern world. Skating owes much to the pioneers who laid the foundation on which the sport has grown ever since.

PART TWO

Skating between the World Wars

SIX

Competitive Skating between the Wars

THE devastation of the world wars fought on European soil has twice placed a hiatus on the development of figure skating, causing cessations in European and World competitions for periods of seven years each. Each time, skating was able to survive the ravages of war and become a more competitive, more exciting, and more popular sport than it had been before. The seeds necessary for survival from World War I were sewn on fertile ground. Talented athletes from throughout the skating world had competed against one another, and supporting organizations, national and international, had been formed. Disparate ideas that had nationalized the sport through most of the nineteenth century were reconciled into a style that could survive and assure meaningful international competition. Nineteen World Championships for men, nine for ladies, and seven for pairs were held before the war. Stemming from that solid foundation, skating was able to rebound relatively quickly, grow in stature, and gradually take on a guise we can recognize and appreciate today.

The European and World Championships did not resume until 1922, although the Olympic Games were held two years earlier.[1] Hostilities ended in November 1918, but the devastating Treaty of Versailles was not signed until the following May. Its demands far exceeded Woodrow Wilson's "Fourteen Points" on which the defeated nations had counted, and in 1920 the concept of good sportsmanship associated with Olympic competition could not overshadow the general attitude of the victors. Invitations to participate at the Antwerp Games were not extended to the vanquished nations: Austria-Hungary, Bulgaria, Germany, and Turkey. Because Austria-Hungary and Germany were constituent members of the ISU, the federation declined to participate in either the planning or the conduct of the games although it did not attempt to keep skaters from participating. Figure skating events were overseen by the skating club in Antwerp, and ISU rules were followed. It was the second and last time figure skating was contested before separate Winter Games were held at Chamonix four years later.[2] Gold medals were won by Magda Mauroy-Julin of Sweden, Gillis Grafström of Sweden, and in pairs by Ludowika and Walter Jakobsson of Finland.

Special figures, which had been contested at the London Games in 1908, were not included at Antwerp. Grafström and other skaters kept the discipline alive in the 1920s, but this once popular branch of skating was soon to become a forgotten art. Postwar emphasis was placed on artistry associated with the international style in the more popular discipline of free skating, a discipline with a much longer history. Its roots date back to Jean Garcin and the Gilets Rouges. Beauty of design on the ice, so important to the proponents of special figures, gave way totally to the beauty of movement across the ice associated with free skating. The postwar generation perfected the ISU-established combination of meticulously skated compulsory figures and flowing free skating done to music, a combination that would survive for another seventy years.

The 1914 World Championships were held just five months before the assassination of the Austrian archduke created the spark that ignited simmering hostilities and ultimately claimed the lives of ten million soldiers. In its last prewar communication, dated December 21, 1914, the ISU announced that owing to the war in Europe in which nine constituent members were belligerents, no competitions would be held in the 1914–15 season.[3] It did, however, sanction competitions in countries not at war, specifically Switzerland and Norway.

The Treaty of Versailles marked the end of the war, but the rebuilding of Europe was a slow process hindered badly by the severity of the treaty and the resulting economic depression. In spite of this, the ISU was able to hold its first postwar congress in October 1921 and set dates for resumption of competition early the following year. The Union had survived the war with fifteen nations still members, and within a year participation in the European and World Championships equaled that of the prewar years. Expansion followed quickly. By the end of the 1920s, membership in the ISU had increased by more than 50 percent, with new members coming from East European countries, the Baltic states, Italy, the United States, and Japan.[4]

COMPULSORY FIGURES

Many nineteenth-century figures were open, meaning they could not be retraced. The terminus of an open figure is not connected to its beginning point. Q figures and grape-vines are examples. Closed figures that could be retraced were sometimes called continuous figures. By 1895 a set of compulsory figures, most often called "school figures," had evolved and been adopted by the ISU.[5] All were closed, either in the shape of an eight or a similar three-lobed figure, and could be retraced. In 1910, Irving Brokaw included them in *The Art of Skating* and numbered them as adopted by the ISU. Ten years earlier George Meagher had published a similar but less complete list without numbers in his *Lessons in Skating*.

Both authors referenced the ISU, which had begun adopting rules for figure skating in 1897. Figures were traced three times, and judging was based largely on the geometric perfection of the circles and accuracy of the retracings. The quality of the figures and their tracing together with carriage, form, and speed of execution was the goal, not the intricacy of unique designs that excited the skaters of special figures.

Compulsory figures were viewed as a means of developing technique necessary for elite free skaters. As scales are the material by which musicians develop the facile technique required to perform major compositions, so compulsory figures were viewed as the material by which skaters develop the facile technique required for free-skating programs. Forty-one figures were arranged numerically into twenty-three elementary and eighteen advanced figures. Although the numbering remains the same, the ordering no longer represents the earlier perceived degrees of difficulty. The USFSA included some advanced figures in its first test, whereas some elementary figures were placed as high as the fourth test. Skaters in the United States advanced through a series of nine tests as specified figures become progressively more difficult, but that is no longer true in most countries.[6] The ISU has abolished all tests in compulsory figures, but in the period under discussion, and for many years afterward they counted for such a large portion of the score in competition that skaters traditionally spent hours of daily practice perfecting them.

If figures in skating relate to scales in music, individual figures can be viewed as small etudes, each with its own particular technique to perfect while maintaining geometrically perfect circles. The names of the figures indicate the skating move or technique involved. Most employ specific one-foot turns not done in combination with other one-foot turns. Eight include loops without one-foot turns. One generic name variant has occurred since the early listings. Those figures requiring two tracings of a pattern to complete the figure before returning to the starting point have become known as paragraph figures. The former three-change-three, for example, is now called the paragraph three.

FREE SKATING BECOMES DEFINED

Owing to the separation in competition of compulsory figures and free skating one often thinks of the two disciplines as totally separate aspects of figure skating, but historically they are not. Free skating evolved from the connection of individual figures with dance steps. Spirals, spread eagles, jumps, and spins were originally individual figures, sometimes special figures, done separately. When Axel Paulsen first did his famous jump at the Great International Skating Tournament in 1882 it was offered as his special figure. Many figures date back to the late eighteenth and early nineteenth centuries. Free skating became the international style when multiple figures were connected in a continuous flowing program set to music. Pedagogy today follows that same historical development. A jump or spin is learned separately and then included in a free-skating program.

Important elements of free skating in the 1920s and 1930s, included spirals, jumps, spins, and dance steps. Spirals, first described by Robert Jones in the eighteenth century, were posed positions held by a skater leaning forward in an arabesque position. Willy Böckl, writing a century and a half later, described spirals as "extended edges taken with speed and with exaggerated posed positions."[7] The key words are *speed* and *posed*. In Jones's day, running steps were employed to gain as much speed as possible, after which the forward leaning position was held until all forward momentum was lost. Spirals were done on a forward outside edge, the pose being the most important aspect of the figure. In 150 years there had been little basic change, just expansion. Spirals are now done forward and backward, on outside and inside edges and frequently in sequence. Böckl provides six pictures of skaters in spiral positions, including Sonja Henie, Cecilia Colledge, and Karl Schäfer. The free leg is always parallel or at an obtuse angle to the ice, well extended and turned out. In only two pictures is the torso parallel to the ice, but the body is always well arched with the head upright. A spiral sequence is a required element in a lady's short program, and we immediately associate this element with the beautiful extension of skaters such as Michelle Kwan.

Spread eagles likewise date to Jones's treatise. They are two-foot figures in which the feet point in opposite directions with the legs stretched apart in a continuous straight line from the hips to the ankles, forming an inverted V relative to the ice.[8] Their popularity has continued unabated throughout the history of the sport, and skaters have continually included them in free-skating programs. They are among the first free-skating moves learned and are also among the showiest, especially when skaters connect inside and outside positions in long, flowing serpentine lines.

Grapevines were an important element in free skating before the war, and Brokaw in *The Art of Skating,* 1915, made clear his belief in their usefulness by including a history of them with an extensive list of various patterns. It is curious that he repeated this a decade later in his 1926 book because neither Meyer in *Skating with Bror Meyer,* 1921, nor Böckl in *Willy Böeckl on Figure Skating*, 1937, mention them. This was undoubtedly a holdover from the old American style. Brokaw was American, whereas Meyer and Böckl were European. Although grapevines may have occasionally been incorporated into free-skating programs of the 1920s, like special figures they became relegated to skating's storied past.

JUMPING AND SPINNING

Spirals and spread eagles date from Jones's treatise in the eighteenth century, and grapevines have a long history in the nineteenth century, but jumping was still not part of serious skating a century after Jones's treatise. Nineteenth-century writers discussed jumping but not seriously. They viewed jumps as acrobatic tricks, not as a part of a skater's art. Candidates for membership jumped over hats before being accepted into the Edinburgh Skating Club, and H. E. Vandervell recommended that all skaters learn to jump although jumping had no place whatsoever in English combined skating. Skaters on the Continent experimented with leaps from the ice during the last quarter of the century but not extensively. Axel Paulsen was being tremendously progressive when in 1882 he made skating history with his famous jump done as a special figure.

Jumps evolved in the postwar era. Many are related to corresponding compulsory figures, and their names refer to those figures. The loop jump is an example. There are also bracket jumps, counter jumps, and rocker jumps, all having the same rotational tendencies as the corresponding figures. Other jumps, including the Salchow and Axel Paulsen, take their names from the skaters who invented or popularized them.

Most jumps in the standard repertoire today were defined between the wars. Those were years of exploration for jumping, and even jumps that may never have been attempted were described. One writer, Pat Low of England, defined all jumps theoretically possible through an identification system of five variables: the approach edge, the rotation in the air relative to that of the approach edge, the number of revolutions in the air, whether the landing foot was the same as the take-off foot, and the relationship of the rotation in the air to that of the landing edge.[9] There were, Low theorized, eighty possible edge jumps up to one revolution, and that number doubled if the jumps were done on both feet. One can presume that most were tried, but only a few ultimately entered the standard repertoire. To this theoretical list of edge jumps can be added all possible toe-assisted jumps. Let's describe briefly some of the most important of them, ones that have survived and are done today.

The half-revolution waltz jump, a lead-up to the Axel Paulsen jump, is sometimes called, incorrectly, a three jump, but it does not reference that basic figure.[10] It is the first rotational jump that beginners learn. From a forward outside edge, a half revolution results in a landing on a backward outside edge on the opposite foot and on the same circle. Sometimes called the flying three or once-back, it could also be done from backward to forward, and Böckl lauded the effectiveness of performing two or three of them in succession.

The loop jump, a basic loop figure with a leap from the ice, has a takeoff from a backward outside edge with a landing on the same foot and same backward outside edge. The jump is attributed to Werner Rittberger of Germany, silver medalist at the World Championships three times, and in Europe it is called the Rittberger jump. The half-loop jump, perhaps the most misnamed jump in skating, is characteristically done today in combination with other jumps. It has a takeoff from a backward outside edge, as does a loop jump, but after a full revolution the landing is on a backward inside edge, on the opposite foot and same circle. In Europe it is often called the Thorén jump, named after World and Olympic bronze medalist Per Thorén of Sweden.

Among other jumps named for their inventors is the Salchow, which has a takeoff from a backward inside edge and a landing on a backward outside edge on the opposite foot and on the same circle. The Axel, still officially called the Axel Paulsen jump, has a takeoff from a forward outside edge and a landing on a backward outside edge on the opposite foot but on the same circle following one and a half revolutions in the air. Two formerly popular variations, now seen infrequently, are the inside Axel Paulsen, which has a takeoff from a forward inside edge and a landing on a backward outside edge on the same foot, first done by four-time World Champion and Olympic silver medalist Willy Böckl of Austria, and the one-foot Axel Paulsen, with a takeoff from a forward outside edge and a landing on a backward inside edge on the same foot, first done by World champion and Olympic silver medalist Cecilia Colledge of Great Britain.

Split jumps were as popular between the wars as they are today. They are toe-assisted jumps done on inside or outside edges with a half revolution from backward to forward. The goal is to raise the legs as nearly parallel to the ice as possible. Variations include the Russian split jump, with legs to the side in a basic V position, and the stag jump, not frequently done today, in which the forward leg is bent under with the thigh parallel to the ice.

Other toe-assisted jumps include the flip jump, sometimes called a toe Salchow, the toe loop, and the Lutz jump. The Lutz, the most difficult jump other than the Axel Paulsen, is approached on a backward outside edge, with rotation in the opposite direction and a landing on the opposite foot, circling in the opposite direction.[11]

Most jumps employed today are drawn from the repertoire that was evolving and being standardized between the wars. Although double jumps, specifically Salchows and loops, were known, it was the next generation, the postwar skaters, who pushed the envelope of jumping to extremes that skaters of the 1930s would not have thought possible. Skaters between the wars experimented with and developed a basic repertoire of jumps that has lasted. Skaters after World War II would increase the number of revolutions.

Although skaters in the 1920s remained timid about jumping relative to the athletic approach of today, some skaters of the 1930s are remembered for tremendously athletic jumps. World champion Felix Kaspar of Austria was reported to have had the highest and longest jumps ever seen. His Axel Paulsen jump was said to be four feet in height and twenty-five feet from takeoff to landing.[12] Loops and Salchows were being doubled by the most athletic skaters. Women as well as men included them in their programs, especially the women from Great Britain: Cecilia Colledge, Megan Taylor, and Daphne Walker.

Spinning also advanced greatly between the wars, as can be confirmed by viewing Sonja Henie's films from the late 1930s. Her jumps, most often simple waltz jumps, pale by comparison to today's athletic jumps, but her spins, often reaching forty or more revolutions, are usually well centered, fast, and as exciting to watch today as they were then.

Spinning, unlike jumping, was a graceful and appreciated aspect of skating throughout the entire nineteenth century. As early as 1813 Garcin recognized its beauty, especially when employed as an artistic conclusion to a figure, and still today most freeskating programs end with an exciting spin, often a scratch spin. A century after Garcin, Brokaw emphasized the importance of spinning in free-skating programs and expected advanced skaters to be able to execute one or more varieties equally well on either foot. Variety did not refer to positions, as might be understood today, but rather to changes of the employed feet. Included were single and double flat-foot spins, cross-foot spins, and two-foot whirls, described as "a series of ringlets where the tracings on the ice were made by the skater standing with toes pointed towards each other and spinning very rapidly."[13] One example is a flat-foot spin into a two-foot whirl, finishing with a cross-foot spin, all in an upright position.

By the late 1930s all three basic positions were employed: upright spins, sit spins, and camel spins. Skaters were expected to be able to spin in both directions, but as spins became more difficult and faster that skill gave way to spinning in one direction only. It is rare to see skaters spin in both directions, and it is always commendable when they develop the skill. John Curry's sit spins in both directions in his 1976 Olympic program are especially memorable.[14]

Toe spins, mentioned briefly by Brokaw, were described more fully by Bror Meyer, but they eventually outlived their usefulness. By the end of the period they had disappeared in favor of faster and more exciting multiple-revolution spins. The camel spin, originally called the parallel spin and at times the arabesque spin, was first done in the mid-1930s by World Champion Cecilia Colledge. The body and free leg are parallel to the ice, with the skating leg straight and locked.

DANCE STEPS

Dance steps were employed as connecting links in free-skating programs. From Meyer, writing in 1921, to Böckl, writing in 1938, emphasis is placed on their importance in the connection of flashy free-skating elements. Böckl states, "Of course the spectator likes good spins and jumps but the genuine artistry of a program is found in its linking dances and steps when the natural rhythm and skating ability of the skater holds sway."[15]

That statement has validity today. The public counts triple jumps and waits eagerly for clean quadruple jumps but does not fully appreciate the artistry displayed by skaters whose grace surpasses sheer athleticism. Peggy Fleming's interpretation of Johann Pachelbel's *Canon in D* fifteen years after she won her Olympic gold medal is but one memorable example.[16] The three-minute program included just three jumps, the most difficult being a single Axel Paulsen, but her balletic presentation transcended the need for more athleticism and demonstrated the consummate artistry associated with figure skating.

Free skating is a collection of jumps, spins, spirals, and other elements with appropriate connecting steps. Complex footwork is today a required element in short programs, but simple connecting steps between difficult elements have always been an important part of a balanced program. The approach in the period under consideration was to incorporate steps from ice dances, primarily the waltz and the ten-step. Advanced skaters could increase the difficulty by substituting more difficult turns such as brackets, counters, and rockers for the simpler three turns employed in the dances. Judges scrutinized their ability to incorporate all moves, simple or complex, in time with music. The meter made no difference as long as steps and turns were done on accented beats with rhythmic accuracy. Thus, the waltz pattern could be used for music in either duple or triple meter. Emphasis was not yet placed on musical interpretation because the purpose of a program was simply to present an exciting and artistic few minutes of figure skating. The music provided primarily a rhythmic background. An amusing story is told about World Champion Felix Kaspar, whose recording was damaged at a competition when left near a radiator. Unconcerned, he said, "No problem, just put a waltz on and I will be fine."[17]

Free-skating programs in competitions, carnivals, traveling ice shows, and motion pictures did much to popularize figure skating during the 1920s and 1930s. They provided audiences with exciting entertainment from talented skaters who demonstrated the beauty of movement on ice.

MEN CHAMPIONS

Thirteen men from six countries participated in the 1914 World Championships, the last before the war. Six of them returned after the war, including all the medalists. Three became postwar champions. Seven years of war neither dampened their spirits nor deterred their love for the sport. Gösta Sandahl of Sweden, World champion in 1914, claimed the bronze medal in his only postwar competition nine years later. Fritz Kachler of Austria, silver medalist in 1914, repeated in 1922 before becoming the World champion a year later. Willy Böckl of Austria, bronze medalist in 1914, returned and won one bronze and two silver medals before becoming a four-time World champion. Most successful of the returning skaters was Gillis Grafström, the first postwar World champion.

Grafström (1893–1938), an architect by profession, was the last in a long line of great Scandinavian skaters. At his first World Championship in 1914 he placed seventh, and after the war he built a reputation that led his contemporaries to consider him the greatest skater of all time. At Antwerp in 1920 he won his first of three consecutive Olympic gold medals, a record duplicated by only one other singles skater, Sonja Henie. In 1932, at age thirty-eight, he made a fourth Olympic bid, where, suffering from a leg injury, he settled for a silver medal behind Karl Schäfer.

Grafström entered competitions selectively, including just three widely spaced World Championships, 1922, 1924, and 1929, all of which he won. He is remembered not only for his forward inside spiral and flying sit spin, a move he invented, but also of importance to the history of figure skating, he was one of the last great practitioners of special figures. Off the ice his interest in art and sports led him to amass an extensive collection of skating memorabilia, now permanently housed at the World Figure Skating Museum in Colorado Springs. Grafström was one of the initial inductees into the World Figure Skating Hall of Fame.

Grafström, Kachler, and Böckl along with three younger skaters, Karl Schäfer, Felix Kaspar, and Graham Sharp, won all eighteen World Championships held between the wars. Grafström never competed in the European Championships, but the other five skaters, collectively, won all of those titles as well.

Fritz Kachler (d. 1973) enjoyed a competitive career that spanned fifteen years, including four before and four after the war. His appearances in three European and seven World Championships resulted in as many medals, five gold, four silver, and one bronze. Remaining active in the sport for many years, he served the ISU in various capacities, including two years as vice president for figure skating.

Wilhelm (Willy) Böckl (1896–1975) appeared on the international scene in 1913, skating in both the European and World Championships. By the end of the next season, the last before the war, he had garnered one silver and three bronze medals. When competi-

Gillis Grafström, three-time
Olympic gold medalist. (World
Figure Skating Museum and
Hall of Fame)

tion resumed in 1922 he earned six European titles, which were continuous except for
1924 when he did not compete. Following a bronze medal in 1922 and silver medals in
1923 and 1924, he became a four-time World champion. At the Olympic Games he was
twice the silver medalist behind Grafström. Böckl's free skating was especially strong,
and at the Chamonix Games he defeated Grafström in that portion of the competition.
He invented the inside Axel Paulsen jump, which he called the Böckl jump.

After retiring from competitive skating in 1928, Böckl, although trained as a structural
engineer, responded to an inquiry from the Skating Club of New York, which was seeking a professional instructor. He recommended himself, was selected, and served in that
capacity for many years. It was a time when American skaters were beginning to gain
respect on the international scene, and Böckl was able to influence a generation of them.
As a highly successful competitor turned instructor and equipped with the analytical
mind of an engineer he was well prepared to develop his pedagogical technique at a time
when skating was becoming more precise technically, and he left detailed descriptions
of both compulsory figures and free skating in *Willy Böeckl on Figure Skating*. It documents the state of skating as it evolved between the wars and remains one of the most

definitive sources on the subject. Böckl was inducted into the World Figure Skating Hall of Fame in 1977.

Karl Schäfer (1909–76), Austria's greatest star, was eight times the European champion, seven times the World champion, and twice the Olympic gold medalist. Only Salchow won more European and World titles, and only Grafström won more Olympic gold medals. Schäfer appeared on the national scene in 1927, placing second to Otto Preissecker at the Austrian Championships. The results were the same for another year, but following Preissecker's retirement Schäfer became and remained the national champion for eight years. Internationally, from 1930 until his retirement in 1936 he skated in every European, World, and Olympic competition and was never defeated.

Perhaps the most bizarre incident in the history of competitive figure skating occurred at the 1930 European Championships in Slovakia, which were sponsored by the Czechoslovakian association. Two irregularities occurred in the men's competition. First, the referee was not ISU-certified, but in addition the Yugoslavian judge, likewise not ISU-certified, was a replacement who served falsely under the name of a duly appointed judge without being detected until after the competition. The winner, who defeated Schäfer, was Josef Silva, a Czech whose three previous international competitions had all resulted in fifth-place finishes. Upon discovery of the irregularities, the ISU nullified the results and ordered the event to be reskated. Schäfer won easily. Silva did not compete, and his only later competition was at the World Championships the following year, where he placed twelfth out of thirteen.[18]

The multitalented Schäfer was also an Olympic swimmer and a competent musician. After retirement he was featured in carnivals and traveling ice shows in the United States and later taught skating on both sides of the Atlantic. Like Salchow and Grafström, Schäfer was a member of the original class of inductees into the World Figure Skating Hall of Fame.

Felix Kaspar (b. 1915) had a shorter career than his predecessors. He was three times the Austrian national champion and twice each the European and World champion. All except his first national title were in 1937 and 1938, years he won every competition entered. At the Olympic Games in 1936 he claimed the bronze medal, behind Schäfer and Ernst Baier. His retirement after the 1938 season was possibly a reaction to Germany's annexation of Austria because Austrian skaters in 1939 skated under the German banner. Kaspar embarked on a professional skating career in Australia and subsequently in the United States. He was elected to the World Figure Skating Hall of Fame in 1998.

With Kaspar's retirement the era of Austrian domination ended. Great Britain's Graham Sharp (1917–95), who had placed second to Kaspar for two years, was waiting in the wings. His career included eight national titles. He became the World champion in 1939, the last international competition before the war. After serving six years in the army, he won an additional British title in 1946 and could not resist the challenge of a second Olympic bid. Twelve years earlier he had placed fifth; at thirty-six he was able to place a respectable seventh in a new field of younger and more athletic postwar skaters.

Great Britain produced a generation of fine skaters during the 1930s. In addition to Sharp, the men included Jack Dunn (1917–38), later one of Sonja Henie's skating partners and a silver medalist at the World Championships in 1935, and Freddie Tomlins (1919–43), silver medalist behind Sharp at the 1939 European and World Championships. Tomlins died in service to the Royal Air Force. By the summer of 1940, owing to the severity of the Battle of Britain, all skating in England was effectively stopped for the duration of the war.

Among notable skaters from other countries was Ernst Baier of Germany, who collected two silver and two bronze medals at the World Championships and a silver medal at the 1936 Olympic Games. He is remembered primarily as Maxi Herber's pair partner.

German aggrandizement began with the annexation of Austria in 1938 where the amateur careers of a new generation of talented young skaters were dramatically affected by the war. Most promising was Edi Rada (b. 1922). He became the Austrian national champion in 1938 following Kaspar's retirement, a position he held through 1949 save for the one year in which he did not compete. The Austrian National Championships were held during the war years except in 1944 and 1945. Rada's postwar efforts resulted in a bronze and a gold medal at the European Championships, a bronze medal at the World Championships, and a bronze medal at the Olympic Games. Following retirement from competition he coached for many years in Canada. Among his students was Karen Magnussen, the 1972 Olympic silver medalist and 1973 World champion.

LADY CHAMPIONS

The slate of men after World War I included several prewar skaters. Women, however, began with an almost completely blank slate. Only Svea Norén (b. 1895) of Sweden, bronze medalist at the World Championships in 1913, returned. She won the silver medal at the Antwerp Olympic Games in 1920 and two additional medals, bronze in 1922 and silver in 1923, at the World Championships.[19] Two remarkable skaters dominated the sport after the war. Herma Szabo of Austria was a five-time World champion, beginning in 1922, before being bested in 1927 by Sonja Henie of Norway, who enjoyed a ten-year reign as one of figure skating's most colorful figures.

Szabo (1902–86) was an avant-garde individualist as well as a talented athlete. Shortening of skirts has sometimes been associated with Henie, but Szabo, ten years Henie's senior, was already wearing them by 1923, earlier than anyone else on the competitive scene. The caption for her picture in *100 Jahre Wiener Eislauf-Verein* (A Hundred Years of the Vienna Skating Club) states: "The dreadful baggy pants, that jump out of this picture at us, were in their day decidedly wicked," but the author notes that "no other figure skater up to this time comes close to approaching the string of successes of Herma Szabo."[20] She was known for her athleticism, and short skirts allowed a freedom not possible with the long skirts characteristic of that generation. In addition to her impressive career as a singles skater, Szabo excelled in pairs with her partner, Ludwig Wrede. They won World titles in 1925 and 1927. Szabo was the World champion in both disciplines in 1925, a feat not duplicated since. She was a master of compulsory figures as well as a dynamic free skater. One competitor from the Chamonix Olympic Games described her compulsory figures as "nearly equal to those of the best men" and years later stated that, owing to her strength, Szabo would have been able to do double jumps, a skill then years in the future for lady skaters.[21] Szabo was elected to the World Figure Skating Hall of Fame in 1982.

Austrian women, like the men, were highly successful between the wars and stood on the medal stand at every World competition less one from 1922 through 1934, collecting a total of fifteen medals. A ladies' event was implemented at the European

Herma Szabo, five-time World champion and the Olympic gold medalist in 1924. (World Figure Skating Museum and Hall of Fame)

Championships in 1930, and there Austrians medaled every year less one through 1938. Successes occurred also at the Olympic Games in 1924, 1928, and 1932. In addition to Szabo, they included Gisela Reichmann, Fritzi Burger, Hilde Holovsky, Liselotte Landbeck, Ilse Hornung, and Emmy Putzinger.[22] Beginning in 1927, three of them, Szabo, Burger, and Holovsky, along with five others from Sweden, Britain, the United States, and Canada placed second to Sonja Henie during that skater's ten-year reign as World and Olympic champion.

Fritzi Burger (1910–99), a four-time Austrian national champion, claimed the silver medal at the Olympic Games and the bronze medal at the World Championships in 1928, her first year on the international scene. She was the silver medalist in 1929, did not compete in 1930, and was the bronze medalist in 1931. For her final year of competitive skating, 1932, Burger claimed silver medals at the Olympic Games and the World Championships.

Hilde Holovsky (1918–33) followed Burger as a two-time Austrian national champion. A year earlier, at thirteen, she was the bronze medalist at the European Championships and the silver medalist at the World Championships. Holovsky was thought by many to have the potential to dethrone or at least succeed Henie as World champion, but, tragically, the talented young skater died following the 1933 season at just fifteen years of age.

Following Holovsky as the Austrian national champion was Liselotte Landbeck (b. 1916). She won three international medals, two silver at the European Championships and one bronze at the World Championships. In 1936, her final year of competitive skating now representing Belgium, she placed fourth at the European Championships and the Olympic Games.[23]

Holovsky's early death and Landbeck's retirement ended Austria's talented line of competitors. Henie, who had reigned supreme since 1927, retired in 1936, the same year as Landbeck, clearing the way for two talented British skaters, Cecilia Colledge and Megan Taylor. They, too, had skated in Henie's shadow, but unlike the Austrians they continued competing after Henie's retirement. The three prewar years belonged to them as they stood atop the medal stand at the World Championships, Colledge in 1937 and Taylor in 1938 and 1939.

Cecilia Colledge (b. 1920) was in the audience in 1928 when Henie defended her World title in London. Captivated by Henie's spins and jumps, the young and impressionable Colledge turned to her mother and said, "I should like to skate like her."[24] She did, and in one way surpassed her idol. Training with the legendary coach Jacques Gerschwiler, it was just four years later at the age of eleven years and four months that she became the youngest figure skater ever to compete in Olympic competition. Henie, who competed at age eleven years and ten months, placed last in a field of eight; Colledge, six months younger, placed eighth in a field of fifteen. Four years later she won the silver

Fritzi Burger, one of several outstanding skaters who placed second behind the unbeatable Sonja Henie. (World Figure Skating Museum and Hall of Fame)

medal.

Colledge was a fine free skater credited with several firsts, including the first camel spin, then called a parallel spin; the first layback spin; and the first one-foot Axel
Paulsen jump. She was also the first lady to execute a double jump in international competition, a Salchow at the European Championships in 1936. During the war, Colledge
served her country as a driver in the Mechanized Transport Corps. After the war, she
skated again in the British Championships and won a sixth title. Colledge's international
medal count included three gold, two silver, and one bronze at the European Championships; one gold and two silver at the World Championships; and one silver at the Olympic Games. Her professional career included skating in ice shows. She emigrated to the
United States in 1951, where she became a highly respected and long-time coach in the
Boston area. She was elected to the World Figure Skating Hall of Fame in 1980.

Megan Taylor (1921–94), a year younger than Colledge, is one of several major skaters taught by a parent. Her father, Phil Taylor (1895–1959), also coached Graham Sharp
and in 1939 led both skaters to World titles, a rare occurrence in the coaching world. Taylor began her remarkable career in 1932 at age eleven as Great Britain's national champion and ended it seven years later as the only British skater other than Madge Syers
to twice become a World champion. Taylor's international medal count included three
silver and one bronze at the European Championships and two gold and three silver at
the World Championships. As a professional, Taylor remained active in skating circles,
primarily as a coach, until retirement in 1982.

In line to continue the tradition started by Colledge and Taylor was the young Daphne
Walker (b. 1925), bronze medalist at the last World Championships before the war. She
first appeared in 1936 at the British National Championships as yet another talented
eleven-year-old. An amusing story comes from that first outing. Under the British Children and Young Persons Act, which had apparently not been enforced in the past, children under age twelve could not participate in events for which admission was charged.
The only solution was to have her skate in front of very tired judges late at night after the
paying audience had left. She placed seventh.[25] The following year Walker advanced to
third behind Colledge and Taylor. At her first World Championships in 1938 she placed
seventh, and a year later at the last championships before the war she won the bronze
medal. Walker reappeared in 1947 and had her career-best finish, a silver medal, after
which she turned professional.

Colledge could not skate at the 1939 World Championships owing to a strained Achil-
les tendon, which allowed the advancement of Hedy Stenuf (b. 1922) to a silver medal
behind Taylor. Stenuf, the reigning bronze medalist, was a strong free skater who in a
relatively short career skated for three countries: Austria, France, and the United States.
She represented Austria at the European and World Championships in 1935, France at

World Champion Cecilia Colledge with her teacher Jacques Gerschwiler. They invented the parallel spin, today called the camel spin. (World Figure Skating Museum and Hall of Fame)

the European and World Championships and the Olympic Games in 1936 and 1937, and the United States at the World Championships in 1938 and 1939. Her only medals were bronze and silver at the World Championships in 1938 and 1939.

SONJA HENIE

Sonja Henie (1912–69) dominated ladies' skating in the 1930s and changed the direction of skating more than any person since Jackson Haines. She was a gifted skater whose wealthy parents had the financial means to support and foster her infinite talent and dogged determination. Born in Oslo, Norway, Henie skied, skated, and studied ballet from childhood. Her athletic father, a highly successful furrier, had twice been a bicycling champion in the 1890s. He and his wife devoted themselves completely to their daughter's career from the time her talent first appeared. Henie began skating at age five and won a children's competition at age eight. She became Norway's junior champion at age nine and senior champion a year later. The last ten years of her amateur career resulted in ten consecutive World titles and three Olympic gold medals. Beginning in 1927, she won every competition entered, a record matched by only one other, the Russian pair skater Irina Rodnina. After her long career as an unbeatable competitive skater Henie continued her quest for fame in the professional world of ice shows and the cinema.

As an eleven-year-old national champion, Henie entered the Olympic Winter Games at Chamonix in 1924. Although she placed last in the field of eight, she was sixth in free skating. Her next international competition, two years later, was the 1926 World Championships in Stockholm, where just two months short of her fourteenth birthday she placed second to five-time champion Herma Szabo. A year later Henie upset Szabo, resulting in one of figure skating's most famous judging controversies. The World Championships that year were held in Oslo, with three of the five judges from Norway and the other two from Austria and Germany. The Norwegian judges all placed Henie first, whereas the Austrian and German judges placed Szabo first. The upshot was an ISU rule still employed today that limits the number of judges in international competition to one from a country, but the 1927 rankings stood. Henie had won her first World title.

A strong interest in dance affected Henie's approach to skating. She was enthralled when, as a child, her mother took her to see the famous Russian ballerina Anna Pavlova (1885–1931). She vowed then to incorporate balletic movement and interpretation into her skating routines. It is significant that like Jackson Haines before her and John Curry much later, a love of ballet guided strongly her skating artistry. At a time when free skating still tended to be a series of figures loosely strung together with dance steps, Henie devised meticulous choreography and created continuous, flowing programs. She became known as the "Pavlova of the Ice," and it was that ballerina's famed dance that inspired Henie's interpretation of Saint Saëns's Dying Swan, first performed at an exhibition in 1932. Wearing a white costume adorned with downy feathers, she electrified audiences, first in Milan and later in Paris, New York, and elsewhere. It became one of the most famous routines in the history of figure skating, one she presented throughout her amateur and professional careers.

Henie's moves were connected and balletic, but her programs were not devoid of athleticism. It has been reported that she had nineteen different spins in her repertoire and could manage up to ninety revolutions. Jumping was still limited largely to single jumps, but Henie employed them all, including the Axel Paulsen jump. Her later films show her phenomenal spinning ability, but by then she seemed to prefer simple waltz jumps. Henie was honored as one of the original inductees into the World Figure Skating Hall of Fame.

NORTH AMERICAN SKATERS

Louis Rubenstein competed abroad in 1890, and Irving Brokaw represented the United States at the 1908 Olympic Games. But not until the period between the wars did figure skaters from Canada and the United States compete internationally on a regular basis. North American skaters appeared at every postwar Olympic Games and returned home with medals from all but one, a total of four bronze and two silver. Less participation occurred at the World Championships. Canadians competed four times, two of them being the ones held in North America, and won three medals, two silver and one bronze. Americans competed at ten World Championships and won nine medals, four silver and five bronze. Canada owes its success to two skaters, Cecil Smith (1908–97) and Montgomery Wilson (1909–64). Smith, twice the national ladies' champion, won Canada's first World medal, silver, at New York in 1930, and Wilson, nine times the national champion, won Canada's first Olympic medal, bronze, at Lake Placid in 1932. He followed that with a silver medal at the World Championships in Montreal two weeks later.

Wilson competed at the St. Moritz Games in 1928, placing thirteenth, and remained in Europe for the World Championships, placing seventh. He returned to Europe in 1936 and placed fourth at the games and fifth at the World Championships. Wilson was an all-round skater who competed also in pairs with his sister, Constance. They claimed five national titles and competed twice at the World Championships, placing fourth in 1930 and sixth in 1932. Constance Wilson Samuel (1908–53), like her brother, was a talented singles skater. She won the Canadian title nine times and a bronze medal at the World Championships in 1932. The Wilson siblings dominated the biennial North American Championships beginning in 1929. Montgomery won five consecutive titles, Constance won four, and together they won three pair titles. After retirement Montgomery Wilson became a highly respected coach, first in St. Paul, Minnesota, and later in Boston. In 1976 he was elected to the World Figure Skating Hall of Fame.

American skaters collected fourteen World and Olympic medals between the wars.

Roger Turner (1901–93), holder of seven national titles between 1928 and 1934, was less consistent in the international arena. Two successive silver medals at the World Championships in 1930 and 1931 were sandwiched between fifth-place finishes in 1929 and 1932. In two Olympic efforts he was held to tenth- and sixth-place finishes.

The women had greater success, carrying home four Olympic and six World medals. Theresa Weld (1896–1978) won the national title in 1914. When competition resumed in 1918 she placed second. The competition was not held in 1919, but a year later the now-married Theresa Weld Blanchard reclaimed the title and held it for five years. Representing the United States at the Antwerp Olympic Games in 1920, she won the bronze medal, the first of any color for a North American skater.

Blanchard had an almost equally distinguished career in pairs over a period of eighteen years with Nathaniel Niles (1886–1932). At the national level they won the silver medal in 1914 and after the war amassed nine gold and two silver medals. They competed in three World Championships and three Olympic Games with a career-best finish of fourth at the Antwerp Games. Niles skated singles events as well, winning gold or silver medals at the national level every year less one from 1920 through 1927. His efforts on the international stage were less successful.

Beatrix Loughran (1900–1975), three times the national champion from 1925 through 1927, was four years younger than Blanchard. She twice won silver medals behind Blanchard before their roles were reversed. Loughran represented the United States at the Chamonix Olympic Games and the World Championships in 1924, where she won silver and bronze medals. It was the first World medal won by a North American. Four years later she competed at the St. Moritz Games and claimed the bronze medal. Like Blanchard, Loughran distinguished herself in pairs as well, skating with Sherwin Badger (1901–72). They were national champions for three years, beginning in 1930, and bronze medalists twice at the World Championships. Although Badger was the national champion from 1920 through 1924, he did not compete as a singles skater in World competition.

Blanchard and Loughran represent the high quality of American lady skaters in the 1920s. The next champion was even more remarkable. Maribel Vinson (1911–61) was the national champion for nine years, a record still not surpassed by any skater, man or woman.[26] Along the way she collected a bronze and a silver medal at the World Championships and a bronze medal at the 1932 Olympic Games. Sonja Henie's brother, Leif, reported that his sister was always more concerned about Vinson as an opponent than she was about either Colledge or Taylor.[27]

Opposite: Maribel Vinson, America's most successful skater before World War II. (World Figure Skating Museum and Hall of Fame)

After retiring from amateur competition, Vinson married the 1929 Canadian junior champion, Guy Owen (d. 1952). Their two daughters, Maribel V. Owen (1941–61) and Laurence Owen (1945–61), coached by their mother, became fine skaters in the late 1950s, but they were just two of many who benefited from Vinson's coaching. The most notable was Tenley Albright, who in 1956 became the first American woman to win an Olympic gold medal. Like so many of the people mentioned in this book, Vinson was multifaceted. Champion and coach, she also wrote for the *Boston Globe* and *New York Times*. Three books on the sport were published, two before the war dealing with elementary and advanced figure skating and one twenty years later, *The Fun of Figure Skating,* the title of which expressed her deep love for the sport. It was in a airplane crash en route to the 1961 World Championships that Maribel Vinson Owen and her two daughters as well as the entire U.S. World team lost their lives. America lost a generation of skaters, including the talented Owen family.

SEVEN

Skating with a Partner

SKATING with a partner of the opposite sex in which there is physical contact, the disciplines of ice dancing and pair skating, had its real beginning in England, bastion of combined skating, and yet they were the antithesis of combined skating. There in the 1890s hand-in-hand skating surfaced strongly, became popular, and then died away, all in a short period of time. As far back as 1836 the Oxford Skating Society had a simple program of "club figures" suitable for hand-in-hand skating, but it was in the 1890s that hand-in-hand skating became fashionable and moved from the static confines of basic figures to continuous movement around a rink. The rigid English style still ruled supreme, but in that same decade the introduction of the first true skating waltz, which capitalized on speed and flow across the ice with partners in a true dance position, not just holding hands, dealt a death knell to hand-in-hand skating.

The direction of couple skating changed rapidly and permanently when in 1895 the three-step waltz ushered in the era of ice dancing. As a competitive discipline at the international level ice dancing was many years in the future, but dances and steps from them provided from the beginning basic material employed in competitive programs for singles and pair skating. Before discussing ice dancing as it evolved between the wars, we must retreat and describe briefly the discipline's genesis, its early popularity, and the first ice dances.

DANCING ON ICE

Jackson Haines danced on ice in Vienna at his first exhibition there in 1865, but it was not ice dancing as we know it today. The Viennese love of music and dance whetted their appetite for dancing on skates, and Haines affected their approach to it. Those skaters who first experimented with dancing on ice quite logically attempted steps similar to those employed on the ballroom floor, which is inconsistent with the inherent characteristics of modern ice dancing. In transferring ballroom dancing to the ice, early ice dancers naturally kept both feet on the ice much of the time. Thus the earliest ice dances displayed a basic characteristic of grapevines. What was lacking was the long and flowing edges associated with graceful figure skating.

The American waltz and Jackson Haines waltz were among the most popular ice dances by the 1880s. The American waltz was a simple four-step sequence repeated as one skater or a couple moved in a circular pattern. Its steps were a right inside forward edge, a left outside forward edge, and a Mohawk to a right outside backward edge followed by a left inside backward edge. Another Mohawk put the skater on the original edge, and the pattern repeated. Each step received one measure of music.

The Jackson Haines waltz evolved into variants during the 1880s. Originally it was a four-step repeating pattern in which the skater kept both feet on the ice throughout. Like the American waltz, the Jackson Haines waltz included two steps forward and two steps backward. Describing it as the "most popular of all dance steps," the authors of *Spuren auf dem Eise* called it "an interesting example of the emergence of the dance step out of the grapevine."[1] In variant forms, feet were lifted during the turns.

Dances in triple meter, waltzes and mazurkas, were most popular. The 1892 edition of *Spuren auf dem Eise* includes nine waltzes and four mazurkas, most of which had been forgotten by the end of the century. In the popular Swedish mazurka, an expanded version of the Jackson Haines waltz, additional steps and turns were added before the pattern was repeated. Its unique feature was a spring off the ice from the toe of the skate, a characteristic of the original Polish peasant dance. This "mazurka step," it was said, "creates a charming effect and makes a brilliant finish to a free-skating program."[2]

The direct predecessor of ice dancing in the modern sense, featuring speed and flow across the ice, was not from Vienna. It was a waltz reportedly first skated in 1894 by Monsieur Richard, the skating instructor at the Palais de Glace in Paris, although there is evidence of a similar dance being skated earlier in Canada.[3] Within a year the three-step waltz became a craze throughout Europe as well as across the channel in England. Soon it was being skated in Berlin, Brussels, Davos, London, St. Moritz, St. Petersburg, Stockholm, Vienna, and elsewhere. In England some diehard Victorian-minded combined skaters made their disgust known by purposely interfering with dancers who moved around the rinks. For them, the waltz was "derogatory to the austere dignity of the sport and a frivolous lowering of the lofty ideal of continuous going in combined forms round and round an orange."[4] But the explosive popularity of waltzing could not be quelled. This first true ice dance, a waltz containing only three steps, was natural, easy, and idiomatic. More important, it was fun. One enthusiastic skater writing in *Vanity Fair* magazine philosophized, "Is there anything in the whole world to come up to valsing on ice? The only drawback is that it quite spoils you for valsing in a ballroom." She continued, "Who that has once known the glorious intoxication of a mad whirl round on flying skates, can ever care again to dance in satin slippers on an ordinary parquet floor? Why the two are as far apart as water from champagne."[5]

As waltzing became "all the rage," reports abound of beginning skaters with but one desire, to waltz on ice. From France, we hear that "Knowing how to waltz, this is the ideal, this is what the young girls dream about, even before knowing how to do an outside edge."[6] It was the same in England. "The first thing beginners want to do, as soon as they come on the ice, before they can scarcely stand upright on their skates, and long before they can trace an outside edge, or even attempt to cut a three turn, is to ask: how soon they will be able to valse?"[7]

THE THREE-STEP WALTZ

The three-step waltz, known on the Continent as the English waltz, became the standard for waltzing competitions by century's end. The *Rules and Regulations for Competitions in Valsing on Ice,* as adopted by the Prince's Skating Club in London, dealt specifically with the three-step waltz and were based on ice dancing regulations already adopted by the ISU.[8] Relatively inexperienced skaters could manage the simple dance; those more skilled could introduce variations such as the substitution of more difficult one-foot turns for the prescribed three turns. Two-footed movements such as spread eagles or grapevines, like those used in the Jackson Haines waltz, were specifically prohibited. Waltzing competitions became extremely popular. They usually included a qualifying round, called the preliminary test, and a final round of the top four or five couples. Judging categories included carriage, grace, unity, and time, but the major concern was always with artistry. Judges looked for long and sweeping edges and great speed.

As the name implies, this early form of the waltz required only three steps: a forward outside edge, a three turn to a backward inside edge, a backward outside edge on the opposite foot, and a step to the original forward outside edge. The pattern was repeated as skaters moved around the rink in circular motion and could be elongated by adding additional outside edges at the end of the three steps. Skaters could then move down the rink in a basic serpentine pattern, allowing full use of any rink, regardless of size.

Partners faced each other so that when one was on a forward edge the other was on a backward edge, when one was doing a three turn the other was doing a Mohawk. The position was similar to the face-to-face position previously employed in hand-in-hand skating, but partners were now in a true waltz position rather than just holding hands. The man's right hand was lightly but firmly placed on his partner's waist; his left hand was carried freely, just below shoulder height and supporting, not clutching, his partner's right hand. Her left hand was usually placed on his shoulder, although sometimes it rested on his right arm. Tempos for waltzes were to be slow, allowing long and graceful edges. One writer spoke for many when he described his ideal as a "beautiful ska-tress . . . gliding with liquid smoothness over the surface of the ice, in even, measured sweeps and harmonious, rhythmic circles."[9]

THE TEN-STEP

The ten-step is the basis of the oldest dance still done. With the first sequence of steps repeated, it became the fourteen-step. There has been confusion regarding the history of this dance. It began as the ten-step or Schöller march, reportedly first skated in Vienna by Franz Schöller in 1889, and it is included in the 1892 edition of *Spuren auf dem Eise.* Brokaw, writing in 1910, describes a slightly simplified version of the dance, which he calls the Bohatsch march or two-step, possibly crediting it to Max Bohatsch, the Austrian skater who placed second to Salchow in 1905 and 1907.[10] Brokaw meant "ten-step" not "two-step." The term *two-step* is not used in the body of his text, there is no further reference to a two-step march in skating literature, and the American social dance known as the two-step was still ten years in the future. Brokaw provides no history of the dance, and there is no mention of the additional four steps until 1915, when he describes the fourteen-step as a "recent and beautiful variation of the ten-step" which, he says, originated in Berlin.[11]

The fourteen-step is derived from the Bohatsch version of the ten-step, and its history is clarified by Herbert Yglesias, who called the ten-step "a simplified version of the old Schöller march."[12] The fourteen-step is now skated to music in duple meter, but in its early history waltz music, that is music in triple meter, could be used as well by strok-ing on the accented beat of each measure. The position of the partners is the same as for the three-step waltz, with the lady starting backward. Mohawk turns are employed at changes of direction.

Vienna in the nineteenth century was the dancing capital of Europe, both on and off skates. Seventeen ice dances are described in the 1892 edition of *Spuren auf dem Eise,* but by the end of the century in Vienna and elsewhere ice dancing included primarily the two dances described, the three-step waltz and the ten-step. The European waltz, included in the USFSA pre-silver test, is credited with having been skated before the turn of the century, but its inventor is unknown, and writers of the period fail to mention it.

The kilian, the last of the prewar dances still done today, was apparently first skated in 1909 by Karl Schreiter at the Engelmann Rink in Vienna. It employs a side-by-side position that bears the name of the dance. The couple skates hip to hip with the man's right shoulder just at the rear of his partner's left shoulder. The lady's left arm is stretched across her partner's body, and their left hands are joined at about waist height. The man's right arm goes around his partner's back, and their right hands are clasped on or just above her right hip. The kilian is a fast dance with progressive steps and cross steps, all but two of which are of one-beat duration. It takes just four measures of music—sixteen beats—to complete the entire pattern.

Skaters throughout the skating world were dancing on ice in the years preceding World War I. It was primarily recreational, but at the local level it was sometimes competitive. Years before becoming an official discipline under national and international control, dancing contests were commonplace at individual clubs and were occasionally added attractions at major skating events.[13] Between the wars, national organizations began overseeing dance competitions: England in 1934, Canada in 1935, the United States in 1936, and Austria in 1937.

International competitions had to wait much longer. Ice dancing was not contested at the World Championships until 1952, at the European Championships until 1954, or at the Olympic Games until 1976. Between the wars ice dancing evolved into a competitive discipline at the national level, and skating's first notable ice dancers made major contributions to the discipline.

ICE DANCING BETWEEN THE WARS

Singles skaters as well as pair skaters and nominally proficient skaters as well as elite skaters all enjoyed dancing on ice. It became a part of open sessions in many rinks as well as an added event at competitions. Several skaters, not necessarily major contenders at the elite level of singles or pair skating, made significant contributions to the discipline during the 1930s. Erik van der Weyden, the author of *Dancing on Ice*, with his partner and wife Eva Keats, invented the foxtrot, rocker foxtrot, Viennese waltz, and Westminster waltz. Reginald J. Wilkie and Daphne B. Wallis invented the Argentine tango, paso doble, and quickstep. They won competitions under the auspices of the NSA in 1937 and 1938 and became the first British champions in ice dancing when the discipline was elevated to that level in 1939. Authors Robert Dench and Rosemarie Stewart, whose *Pair Skating and Dancing on Ice* remains valuable, are remembered primarily as show skaters and choreographers, but Dench, with an earlier partner, Leslie Turner, invented an ice dance entitled "the blues." Thus three British couples are collectively responsible for one-fourth of the compulsory dances still on the ISU's list, and they invented them in a period of just six years, 1933 through 1938.

The invention of new dances was not happenstance; it was necessary. As the decade of the 1930s began, available set-pattern dances were still primarily those already mentioned: the ten-step, the kilian, and the European waltz. Ice dancers either had to be ingenious in devising variations to the established dances or create new ones. Competitions specifically to encourage new designs were sponsored by the Westminster Skating Club and the *Skating Times* in 1933, the same year the NSA established its ice dance committee. The following year, at an NSA competition held to evaluate new dances, van der Weyden and Keats won first and third places with the Viennese waltz and rocker foxtrot. Dench and Turner were the runners-up with the blues.

The growing popularity of ice dancing served as a catalyst drawing ever-increasing numbers of recreational skaters to local rinks and fed their enthusiasm for the sport. New skaters practiced diligently so they could participate in dancing intervals, which had become part of open skating sessions at many rinks. As they gained proficiency they entered dance competitions. The new ice dancers swelled membership, indeed became the backbone of skating clubs. One did not have to be an advanced skater to enjoy ice dancing at a reasonable level of competence and have fun doing so. Thomas Dow (T.D.) Richardson expressed it well: "Skating rinks, like golf clubs, are full of the eighteen handicappers."[14]

THE BEGINNINGS OF PAIR SKATING

Pair skating today is arguably the most difficult discipline technically. Pair skaters do the same jumps and spins as singles skaters, sometimes with fewer revolutions, but timing is far more critical because they must execute moves in perfect unison. In addition to jumps and spins, pair skaters perform lifts unique to their discipline. More intangible but no less important is the necessity for expressive and convincing interaction between partners as they interpret the music. To understand pair skating at the beginning of its history, however, one must first dismiss today's concept of it. It was not originally the athletic and acrobatic discipline it has become. There were no lifts, throw jumps, or death spirals. Side-by-side jumps and spins, which were not a requirement, were employed but only conservatively and by the best pairs. Pair skating was closely allied to ice dancing, with skaters relating to each other as in dance.

Pair skating was first contested internationally at the World Championships in 1908 and later that same year at the Olympic Games in London. A German pair, Anna Hübler and Heinrich Burger, offered programs of speed with gracefully executed dance steps, while a British husband and wife, Phyllis and James Johnson, showed their English background with programs of carefully placed choreography presented with absolute technical precision. Although lingering signs of the international versus English styles appear evident in the two pairs, basic figures with alterations necessary to accommodate two skaters were fundamental to both with dance steps and simple free-skating moves melded into a homogeneous program. The Johnsons, in their article "Pair-Skating," written a year after their first World title, provide an illuminating discussion of the discipline in its infancy.[15]

The Johnsons stressed the importance of proficiency in basic figures that could be done by a pair. Elements employed in pair skating included spirals, dance steps, jumps, and pirouettes. Spirals were considered especially beautiful because they could be skated in an "endless variety" of ways. Importance was placed on giving the impression of ease and grace. Long flowing edges were emphasized for the beauty they provided, and dance steps were basic to all programs. Jumps and pirouettes were not a requirement and were reserved for advanced skaters because "after all, [they are] only what one might describe as the varnish to the picture." Joining elements into a "concrete whole" was viewed as essential in providing continuity while avoiding monotony. Connecting steps were critical to a successful program and were to be employed so showier elements would flow smoothly from one to another. Success in these connections was the ultimate test of pair skaters, and the Johnsons noted that "clumsy joining is a fault very frequently observed in the novice pair's programme," which, they said, could also be "seen in the skating of pairs long past their motivate." Choreography was to be designed, if possible, so the entire skating surface would be used. When the entire surface was not used, the program was to be done on the central portion of the ice. For reasons not explained, programs were never to end at center ice but rather at the extremity of the surface employed.

National differences are described. The Viennese used primarily dance steps, which were done quickly and gracefully with intricate passes. The Germans showed "more devotion to action of the limbs," which the British viewed negatively as "theatrical effect." British skaters were, not surprisingly, "more rigid and cramped." The Johnsons had not at that time had the opportunity of observing North American pairs.

Pair skating had been contested in Canada as early as 1905, when Katherine and Ormond Haycock won two years in succession. The first U.S. champions were Jeanne Chevalier and Norman Scott in 1914. While pair skating was a part of the prewar scene in North America, few contemporary descriptions of it have survived. Writing just after the war, George Meagher, a Canadian, defined pair skating as "the execution of single movements by two persons," stating that nearly all movements that can be performed singly can be performed by pairs as well. After describing the figures most frequently done, including waltz steps, threes, brackets, rocking turns, and eights, he goes on to say that "it is possible to add not a few but hundreds of other beautiful creations to these somewhat simple and 'skated to death' movements." Meagher called pair skating "unquestionably the most fascinating of all styles" and reported that in North America, as in Europe, it was increasing in popularity.[16]

The Johnsons credited pair skating's growing popularity in England to "the fact that ladies have become so proficient in the art [of skating], and also [owing] to the encouragement given to pairs [as a discipline] by the International Skating Union."[17] Thus the stage was set in Europe and North America for expansion of the discipline in the years between the wars. Interest existed and international competitions were in place.

In the 1930s pair skating became more athletic as skaters such as Andrée Joly and Pierre Brunet, and later Maxi Herber and Ernst Baier, pushed the envelope with greater speed and the addition of spectacular lifts, but in the early 1920s side-by-side skating, with partners executing the same movements in unison, received greater emphasis. When T. D. and Mildred Richardson presented almost an entire program in this style in 1923, a journalist called it "shadow skating," a label that stuck. Controversy soon developed within the skating community, which debated passionately the question of what pair skating was or should be. Some considered shadow skating the highest and most difficult form of the discipline, a view obviously espoused by Richardson.[18] Others, including Yglesias, argued that it was not pair skating at all.[19]

By the mid-1930s pair skating had evolved into a balanced blend of shadow skating coupled with increasingly spectacular pair moves, including spins, death spirals, and lifts. Richardson, writing shortly before World War II, acquiesced by saying, "There is much to be said for both schools," but "for the moment shadow skating is definitely on top, owing to the . . . success of the German pair, Maxi Herber and Ernst Baier . . . who perform the most difficult movements side by side, often not even hand in hand but in the most perfect unison and with impeccable timing."[20] He could have included the Brunets as well. They, too, had incorporated effective side-by-side moves in classically oriented programs, but the same pairs included exciting athletic elements and can be credited with directing pair skating toward the balanced programs of today that require pair spins as well as side-by-side spins, throw jumps as well as a side-by-side jumps, and lifts as well as footwork sequences done side by side.

Descriptions of pair skating by two major writers, one at the beginning the other at the end of the period, are enlightening. Bror Meyer, writing in 1921, described the discipline as it had evolved in the years before World War I. "Pair skating to a certain extent is merely a free skating performance executed by two persons."[21] Prerequisite for success, he wrote, is "absolute unity of movement." He makes no mention of jumping or spinning either side by side or together, which supports the Johnsons' statement of a decade earlier that those acrobatic moves were unnecessary. Seventeen diagrams show characteristic pair figures of the time. Hand-in-hand, kilian, and waltz positions were all employed; six include separation of the pair for a portion of the figure, with symmetry being especially important, even to the extent that skaters were often on opposite edges and opposite feet at points of separation, that is, mirror skating. There is straight-line skating, and there are long sweeping curves. The closeness or relationship to dance is evidenced by the titles of the basic figures, including the waltz, the Mohawk dance, and the ten-step and also by the fact that waltzing on ice is included in the chapter on pair skating.

Writing sixteen years later, Willy Böckl began his section on pair skating by observing that "a modern pair should be naturally developed by a couple who have danced together on the ice with a degree of success."[22] In constructing a program, Böckl says, skaters must "start with a repertoire of spirals and a few good dances," but, he continues, they should include "lifts, spins, and specialties adapted from the theater." His use of the word *theater* is telling. These moves, although now a part of pair skating, were still viewed as tricks employed specifically as showy elements, but they were growing in popularity. Böckl provided guidelines for them. Lifts were to be graceful and adapted from true one-foot figures. Spins could be done singly or together, but single spins were effective only if skaters were very close together. Shadow skating was effective when coupled with well-timed, non-separated moves, but in the final analysis, Böckl emphasized, dances were still "the life and substance of pair skating."[23]

Thus, pair skating advanced tremendously during the 1930s. It was not yet viewed equally with singles skating, at least from a technical standpoint, but it had grown to be a much-appreciated discipline. Böckl called it "the most popular form of skating."[24] He lauded it for the pleasure it provided both skaters and audiences and appreciated it for the variety and originality possible. He noted also that it was less of a strain on the skaters. Many singles skaters of that era entered pair events. One prewar American champion told me that she had paired up with her partner for that particular competition because they were there anyway.[25] But we should not deduce from such statements that highly trained pair skaters were not competing internationally. The Brunets and others directed pair skating toward the important and highly competitive discipline it was to become after World War II, a time when it would equal singles skating in importance and no longer be "less of a strain on the skaters."

PAIR CHAMPIONS

Ludowika and Walter Jakobsson capped their highly successful prewar career with Olympic gold in 1920 and a third World title in 1923. Helene Engelmann, who, with Karl Majstrik, won the 1913 World title partnered after the war with Alfred Berger (b. 1894). They won three national titles, in 1921, 1922, and 1923; two World titles, in 1922 and 1924; and an Olympic gold medal in 1924. The dynamic singles champion Herma Szabo, also a member of the Engelmann family, skated both pair and singles events during the last three years of her competitive career. She and Ludwig Wrede (1894–1965) were World champions in 1925 and 1927. After Szabo's retirement, Wrede partnered with Melitta Brunner (b. 1907). They won bronze medals once and silver medals twice at the World Championships and bronze medals at the 1928 Olympic Games.

The nemesis for Brunner and Wrede was a young French pair destined to leave their special mark on the history of figure skating. Andrée Joly (1901–93) and Pierre Brunet (1902–91) were the first skaters from France to medal in European, World, or Olympic competitions.[26] Their first outing, the 1924 Olympic Games, resulted in a bronze medal behind the more experienced teams of Engelmann and Berger and the Jakobssons. The following year at the World Championships they placed second behind Szabo and Wrede in one of the closest contests in pair-skating history. Thereafter, the Brunets won every competition entered. They were European champions once, World champions four times, and Olympic champions twice. Beginning in 1926 they competed only in even-numbered years. They were married in 1927, and their son Jean Pierre Brunet was born in the fall of 1930.[27] Retiring from amateur skating after the 1932 season, they moved to New York, where they became highly respected and successful coaches. Among their many students was the 1960 Olympic gold medalist Carol Heiss. The Brunets are remembered for expanding the scope of pair skating by making it more athletic and moving it farther away from dance. Magnificent lifts and spectacular side-by-side jumps created excitement and variety in their programs. They were honored with election to the World Figure Skating Hall of Fame with the initial group in 1976.

In the shadow of the Brunets were Lily Scholz (b. 1903) and Otto Kaiser (b. 1901), three times the Austrian national champions. Following bronze medals at the World Championships in 1925, they won silver medals, once behind Szabo and Wrede and twice behind the Brunets, before realizing a long-sought-after World title in 1929. Their one Olympic effort in 1928 resulted in a silver medal.

The Brunets' retirement allowed a talented Hungarian pair to claim World titles for the next three years. Emilia Rotter (1906–2003) and László Szollás (1907–80) had won their first World title in 1931, the season Andrée Brunet had her son, but settled for silver medals when the Brunets returned for their final World Championship in 1932. Afterward, Rotter and Szollás proved unbeatable in World competition. They won bronze medals at the 1932 and 1936 Olympic Games.

The second half of the 1930s belonged to a dynamic German pair, Maxi Herber (b. 1920) and Ernst Baier (1905–2001). Baier, fifteen years Herber's senior, skated singles for six years, beginning in 1931, winning two bronze and two silver medals each at the European and World Championships and a silver medal at the 1936 Olympic Games. Herber skated singles twice at the European Championships, 1935 and 1936, placing fourth and seventh. In their first outing as a pair, the World Championships of 1934, they

Andrée Joly and Pierre Brunet, four-time World pair champions and two-time Olympic gold medalists, the first champions from France in any discipline. (World Figure Skating Museum and Hall of Fame)

won bronze medals. Owing to an injury they did not compete in 1935 but returned in 1936 and were unbeatable for the remainder of the prewar period, winning four consecutive World titles plus Olympic gold in 1936. Like the Brunets, they pushed the envelope of pair skating both athletically and artistically. Herber and Baier were honored with election to the World Figure Skating Hall of Fame in 1979.

Throughout the history of competitive figure skating there have been outstanding

Maxi Herber and Ernst Baier, four-time World pair champions and Olympic gold medalists in 1936. (World Figure Skating Museum and Hall of Fame)

Ilse and Erich Pausin, a talented young brother-and-sister pair, consistently placed second behind Herber and Baier. (World Figure Skating Museum and Hall of Fame)

skaters who in normal situations would probably have been World champions had they not had the misfortune of competing against unusually gifted skaters. One example is a brother and sister, Ilse (b. 1919) and Erich (b. 1920) Pausin, who were six times the Austrian national champions. For five years beginning in 1935 and missing only one event, they skated at every European, World, and Olympic competition and always placed second, once behind Rotter and Szollás and ten times behind Herber and Baier.

FOURS

No history of figure skating would be complete without mention of a discipline that although still contested occasionally lasted in its heyday just over a generation and was uniquely North American. Fours skating was immensely popular in Canada and the United States both competitively and in exhibition. Dating from the first decade of the new century, it began as an innovation of Canadian skating clubs, first at the Rideau and Minto clubs in Ottawa, but the United States was not far behind. Fours is a discipline specifically for two mixed couples. Böckl lauded the discipline, saying "there is no branch of skating which gives more exercise and fun than a four," and, he continued, "all four—indeed none of the four—need be expert."[28]

The team of Elaine Asanakis, Calla Urbanski, Rocky Marval, and Joe McKeever performing a fours death spiral at the 1991 U. S. Nationals, the last time a fours competition was held. (World Figure Skating Museum and Hall of Fame)

The discipline evolved and gained popularity contemporaneously with pair skating and like it became continually more demanding technically. Fours skating incorporates most of the moves of pair skating as well as others unique to the discipline, such as lifts involving partner exchanges and, more recently, "quad" death spirals in which the ladies skate close together, almost on top of each other, around the men's closely placed pivots. Emphasis is placed on unison, which becomes far more difficult with four skaters.

Canadian fours have dominated throughout most of the competitive history of the discipline. It was a strongly contested event at the Canadian National Championships beginning in 1914 and continuing every year between the wars. Fours appeared competitively in Ottawa as early as 1908, following the donation of the Earl Grey Trophy by the then-governor-general of Canada. The trophy was awarded for team competitions in singles, pairs, and fours. More important was a special competition specifically for fours created in 1913 with the coveted prize being a cup donated by the Duke of Connaught, the new governor-general of Canada and a son of Queen Victoria. The Connaught Cup was first contested at Ottawa in a match between the Minto Skating Club and the Skating Club of Boston. The Canadian team won. Contested only in odd-numbered years, the competition was not held again until after the war. Reinstated in 1921, it continued through 1931, always with the same results. The cup never left Canada.

The North American Championships, established in 1923, were also biennial events held in odd-numbered years. Beginning in 1933, the Connaught Cup was contested at the North American Championships rather than at a special competition. Canadian teams won it four more times. Most successful was the "Minto Four": Margaret Davis, Prudence Holbrook, Guy Owen, and Melville Rogers. They won the cup three times, in 1933, 1935, and 1937, and are the only team in the history of the event to repeat as champions. Not until 1941 did an American team prevail. The "St. Paul Four" of Janette Ahrens, Mary Louise Premer, Robert Uppgren, and Lyman Wakefield Jr. won that year.

World War II interfered with continuation of the North American Championships. They were not held in 1943, and only a ladies' event was held in 1945. Full revival came in 1947 but without a fours event. At one final offering in 1949 another St. Paul team, Janet Gerhauser, Marilyn Thomsen, John Nightingale, and Marlyn Thomsen, called the "Little St. Paul Four," possibly because all were teenagers, won the event. They were national champions in the discipline for three years, 1947, 1948, and 1950. Only once since has fours been contested at the U.S. Nationals, and that was forty-one years later, 1991, with just two teams competing.[29]

In Canada, fours has remained on the books. For many years the event was skated only occasionally. Some years there were no entrants, and in others the event was not offered. Only six times was it held, with winners between World War II and 1983, but then a significant revival of interest occurred. Successful competitions were held annually for fourteen years, 1984 through 1997. None have been held since. This formerly popular North American discipline has become primarily a national discipline of Canada, where current policy is to offer the event when there are "two pair teams that train at the same rink and are interested in competing."[30] Fours became international when the event was offered at Skate Canada in 1989 and 1990, but it has not been offered since.[31] Reporting on Skate Canada in 1989, one commentator noted, "The [fours] event may have been the most popular of the entire competition."[32] With many skaters flocking to the sport today, might fours not again become a viable competitive event in Canada and perhaps elsewhere?

EIGHT

Skating for an Audience

TELEVISION ratings confirm that in the mid-1990s no sport was more popular with audiences than Olympic figure skating. The ladies' short programs at the Lillehammer Games in 1994 were viewed by forty-five million households in the United States. The media attention surrounding the Harding-Kerrigan incident one month earlier at the U.S. Nationals fueled enthusiasm for an audience that wanted to witness the evolving drama played out on the ice, but the popularity of competitive figure skating, televised and otherwise, had been on the rise for a long time. The public had grown to appreciate the sport as it followed the careers of talented skaters who advanced through the ranks and became elite competitors at the international level. One thinks immediately of favorites such as Peggy Fleming in the 1960s, Dorothy Hamill in the 1970s, and Katarina Witt in the 1980s.

A history of figure skating in the twentieth century must be centered on those skaters who became champions in World and Olympic competition. Since the late 1930s they have had ever-increasing opportunities to enter the professional world and continue pleasing audiences in shows, cinema, and competitions. The generation of skaters preceding World War II was the first to reap substantial benefits from the world of professional skating, and the sport benefited as they elevated and glamorized it.

SKATING CARNIVALS

Show skating is neither new nor unique. Its roots can be traced back farther than competitive skating. Gentlemen amateurs in Victorian England tell of interested observers who watched in amazement as they traced their figures, and they admit that their egos swelled with pride when spectators watched them go through their paces. That was amateur skating at its best, albeit with an element of showing off to those less skilled. Jackson Haines, however, skated professionally in the United States and Canada before moving permanently to Europe to continue his career. Thus, exhibition types of skating, from individuals showing off on local ponds to itinerant professionals were a part of the skating scene in the mid-nineteenth century.

The success of Haines's performances in Europe is legion, but skating shows were popular in America as well. A "Grand Carnival" held at New York's Madison Square Garden in 1879 was described as a lavish event, but carnivals already had a well-established history in Canada, the United States, and elsewhere. At first they were simple club programs in which skaters from beginners to those more skilled presented shows for parents, relatives, and the community at large. By the last quarter of the century, carnivals included large chorus numbers as well as exciting solo routines by the clubs' most advanced skaters. They provided much-appreciated entertainment for audiences, performing experience for skaters, and, not incidentally, revenue for the sponsoring clubs. As the days of intimate club carnivals passed, expanded and more lavish shows, still sponsored by local clubs, frequently included guest performers, and that further increased their popularity. Proceeds sometimes supported local charities.[1]

Shortly after its founding, the USFSA adopted the innovative idea of holding annual associationwide carnivals. Beginning in 1924 and continuing for three years, carnivals were held successively at three major skating centers: Boston, Philadelphia, and New York. These gala events featured professional stars, including Charlotte Oelschlagel, as well as elite amateurs. Carnivals thereafter were again relegated to the domain of individual clubs, but they remained as popular as before. Sonja Henie appeared as a guest of the New York Skating Club during her first trip to the United States for the World Championships in 1930. Other World and Olympic champions, including Gillis Grafström, Karl Schäfer, and pair skaters Andrée and Pierre Brunet and Maxi Herber and Ernst Baier, graced the ice at American club carnivals during the 1930s. Carnivals increased public interest in show skating and provided a strong impetus for establishing professional touring ice shows then on the horizon.

The importance of carnivals to the advancement of the sport cannot be overemphasized because they provided performance experience to skaters at all levels. Large chorus numbers were always featured so many could participate. Up-and-coming competitive skaters had the opportunity of performing before large audiences, and talented guests received top billing and valuable exposure as they neared completion of their amateur careers and sought the limited professional opportunities then available. There was a less tangible but equally important benefit provided by the carnivals. A contemporary writer observed, "One of the functions of carnivals to figure skating is as a stimulant, to arouse, to re-create, and to vivify extensively and intensively in the art."[2] Before television, before cinema, and before established touring ice shows, carnivals took figure skating to the public.

CHARLOTTE AND THE ICE BALLET

Jackson Haines was skating's first matinee idol. Charlotte Oelschlagel (1898–1984) a half century later was skating's first theatrical star. Musically gifted, she reportedly appeared as a guest with the Berlin Philharmonic at age seven. At about that time she began skating and demonstrated almost immediately a special flair for grace and artistry. She participated in an ice show at age ten and just two years later began appearing in "ice ballets" produced at the Admirals Platz in Berlin. Entitled *Montreal the Town on Skates, The Magic of the Alps, Yvonne,* and *Flirting at St. Moritz,* the popular productions were described as a kind of pantomime and musical comedy on ice.

Soon after the outbreak of war in 1914 and armed with an attractive offer from the American entrepreneur Charles Dillingham, Oelschlagel and twenty members of the company traveled to America for the reopening of New York's Hippodrome.[3] Their ice ballet, which served as the climatic act to a musical revue entitled *Hip-Hip-Hurray!,* enthralled audiences for a run of 425 performances in three hundred days, a record at that time. Like the *Ziegfeld Follies* of the same era, a chorus of beautiful women thrilled New York audiences.

Oelschlagel's hard-to-pronounce surname was dropped. New York's newfound theatrical star was billed simply as Charlotte. Her costumes, manner, and brilliant skating electrified audiences. She wore white boots, and her skirts were daringly short for their day, barely covering her knees. It was art, it was theater, but it was much more. Charlotte was an athletic skater, the first woman to include an Axel Paulsen jump in her programs.[4] But a move she invented is most associated with her today. A spectacular spiral in which the body is brought forward until the head is near the ice with the free leg extended very high is called the Charlotte stop. Henie incorporated it in some of her performances, including her Garmisch-Partenkirchen Olympic program and some of her films, and it has appeared periodically since the war.[5] Michelle Kwan included it in her long program during the 1999 season, and others soon followed, including her younger challengers Sasha Cohen and Sarah Hughes.

After its New York run, the ice ballet was taken to other cities. Charlotte then returned to Berlin but was soon back in New York for another Dillingham production.

Charlotte Oelschlagel, skating's first theatrical star. (World Figure Skating Museum and Hall of Fame)

Get Together was almost as successful as *Hip-Hip-Hurray!* and had a run of nearly four hundred performances.[6] During the 1920s and 1930s, Charlotte appeared throughout Europe and North America, including performances in Mexico and Cuba. In 1925 she married her skating partner, Curt Neumann (d. 1971). They are credited with inventing the backward outside death spiral, reportedly first done in Hungary in 1928. Tragically, the couple returned to Berlin in 1939 for the funeral of Charlotte's mother and were trapped, unable to leave, for the duration of the war. After the war they made their way to the western sector of the city, leaving their possessions in what became East Berlin. Then forty-seven years of age, Charlotte taught skating for many years before retiring and living out her life in West Berlin. She was elected to the World Figure Skating Hall of Fame in 1985.

Charlotte, the first skater to appear in cinema, was the heroine in *The Frozen Warning,* a 1916 six-part serial. Learning of a sinister plot by enemy agents to steal government secrets, a college student from Vassar, played by Charlotte, warns of impending danger by tracing the word *spies* on the ice during a skating party.[7] Still the era of special figures, fascination with tracing letters and numbers on the ice remained.

Often forgotten is another important but short-lived aspect of Charlotte's professional work in New York. For a short time she taught at the Hippodrome Skating Club. There in 1916 *The Hippodrome Skating Book* was published. It is subtitled *Practical Illustrated Lessons in the Art of Figure Skating as Exemplified by Charlotte.* She was not complimentary about American skating, saying that "the serious study of the fundamental theories of skating strokes is almost unknown in this country. Most American skaters have not the slightest idea of what they are doing, how they do it, or how they would do it ever again."[8] On a more conciliatory note she admitted that "the energy and the enthusiasm of the [American] skaters was wonderful."[9] *The Hippodrome Skating Book* deals primarily with fundamentals and compulsory figures but includes short sections on free skating and pair skating.

When a young skater, Charlotte saw Anna Pavlova dance, an event that nurtured her fertile musical and artistic mind and influenced her approach to skating. Years later Pavlova appeared with Charlotte at the Hippodrome in one of Dillingham's productions and autographed a picture, which she inscribed to "the greatest ballet dancer on ice."[10] One of Charlotte's most famous show numbers, the "Dying Swan," was a dance made famous by Pavlova. It is not surprising that she was called the "Pavlova on ice." That same dance and title were soon to be linked to another great skater, Sonja Henie.

SONJA HENIE: QUEEN OF THE ICE

In 1936, twenty-two years after Charlotte left her native Germany, moved to the United States, and became skating's first theatrical star, Sonja Henie retired from amateur skating and departed for the United States. She, too, wanted to star in major skating shows, but foremost in her plans was a Hollywood career, not just as a skater but as a leading actress. Her American career, like Charlotte's, began in New York but not as the star of an established ice ballet. In a less auspicious beginning, Henie first appeared in a club carnival, but she had arrived in America with unequaled credentials as a talented, unbeatable, and well-known World and Olympic champion, one who possessed an all-encompassing passion for professional success.

Henie's first trip to the United States six years earlier, 1930, had been to compete at the World Championships in New York City. Already a three-time World champion, she was invited that year to appear in a New York Skating Club carnival entitled *The Land of the Midnight Sun,* which was held at Madison Square Garden and dedicated to her homeland. There, Americans saw for the first time the Norwegian skater who would later elevate show skating to new heights.

Henie's second trip across the Atlantic, just two years later, was to compete at the 1932 Winter Games at Lake Placid and the World Championships at Montreal. Her popularity now preceded her. She was such a draw that standing-room-only tickets at Lake Placid sold for $5 each, this at the height of the depression.[11] Her fame continued to grow. Four years later she capped her amateur career at the 1936 Olympic Games and World Championships, having compiled a competitive record surpassing that of any skater, male or female, in the history of the sport other than the Russian pair skater Irina Rodnina, who with two partners equaled it in the 1970s.[12]

In March of 1936, accompanied by her mother, father, and a skating friend, Jack Dunn of England, Henie crossed the Atlantic for the third time, prepared to begin her path to professional stardom and fortune.[13] Again, she appeared in a carnival sponsored by the New York Skating Club, but it was a short tour afterward arranged by Chicago businessman Arthur Wirtz, an associate for many years, that began her professional career and journey to Hollywood. In twenty-three days seventeen shows were presented from the East Coast as far west as Minneapolis, but Henie had not yet reached Hollywood. To accomplish that, a plan was devised by Wirtz and her father. They rented the Polar Palace, Hollywood's only ice rink, and put on a spectacular show to which many film executives and stars were invited. Hollywood's elite filled the small rink, including Gary Cooper, Bette Davis, Carol Lombard, Jeanette MacDonald, Ginger Rogers, and James Stewart as well as executives from most of the film studios.

Henie's talent and her father's business acumen produced the desired results. She was able to negotiate a favorable contract with Twentieth Century Fox, the result of which was a series of nine motion pictures over a period of seven years. Two additional films were released later, one each by RKO and Universal International.

Henie also directed and performed in her own ice shows as she settled into a routine of filming during the summer, stipulated by a clause in her contract, and touring during the winter. Her father's premature death in 1937, a year into her professional career, was a tremendous blow, but she had learned well. He had successfully guided her through her amateur career and set her on her way to professional stardom. "My luck was my father," she said. "His shrewdness took me safely through the writing of my contract, the making of my first picture, and the first gleams of its financial aftermath."[14] He was gone, but Sonja possessed his astute business sense. At age twenty-five she was capable of fending for herself: "I had cut through the haze and learned to make no decision hastily, to judge no man by his front, and to remember that the world never puts a price on you higher than the one you put on yourself."[15]

She trusted only one other person in business matters. Arthur Wirtz had arranged her first tour and helped her get to Hollywood. In late 1937 Wirtz proposed an extravaganza to be presented at his Chicago Stadium, featuring Henie as the star of a two-hour ice show with a fully professional supporting cast. She had moved to the United States to fulfill the dual dreams of becoming a movie star and combining skating, dance, and drama into one unified and artistic whole. Both goals were accomplished within a year.

The extravaganza was an unqualified artistic and financial success. The arena was filled to capacity, ten thousand for each of five nights. A major tour was arranged for the following season that included performances in Los Angeles, Houston, St. Louis, Minneapolis, Toronto, Montreal, Boston, Chicago, Detroit, Cleveland, and New York City. The show was rehearsed at the Polar Palace during the filming of *Happy Landing*. Billed as "Miss Sonja Henie with Her Hollywood Ice Review," it included a cast of sixty skaters who played consistently to sold-out houses, a scenario that continued for many seasons.

Henie's popularity never diminished. As late as 1953 no less an impresario than Claude Langdon reported on a performance at Empress Hall. Not only was it a box-office success but it was also "one of the most outstanding spectacles of London entertainment during the coronation season." Langdon noted that "a new postwar generation who knew Sonja only as a legend and had never seen her were captivated by her skating skill and personality."[16]

Henie was then in her forties. Her skating skills were beginning to wane but not her persona. There were no more movies and only occasional ice shows, but she remained dominant and forceful. Fifteen years later, and just a year before her death from leukemia, she said, "I brought the ice review to America and motion pictures. Now I am going to introduce the full-scale ice extravaganza to television."[17] But the grande dame of skating was living in the past. That would be left to future skaters.

Opposite: Ten times a World champion and three times an Olympic gold medalist, Sonja Henie moved to the United States for her professional career. She starred in a series of Hollywood films and head-lined her own touring company, the Hollywood Ice Review. (World Figure Skating Museum and Hall of Fame)

THE ICE FOLLIES AND ICE CAPADES

Henie's Hollywood Ice Review was not the first major American traveling ice show. That credit goes to the Shipstads, Roy (1911–75) and Eddy (1907–98), and to Oscar Johnson (d. 1970) of St. Paul, Minnesota, who took their Ice Follies on the road in 1936. Unlike Henie's troupe a year later, the Ice Follies began on a shoestring budget. Eddy Shipstad and Oscar Johnson, who performed frequently during intermissions at hockey games and as guests at carnivals, shared since their youth a dream of creating a professional touring ice show. Heading a troupe of twenty-four skaters, including Eddy's brother, Roy, they departed from St. Paul in November and headed for Tulsa, Oklahoma, their first performance outside the Twin Cities.

The company experienced a precarious and problem-ridden beginning. An infantile paralysis outbreak in Tulsa kept the audience away. Their second stop was Kansas City, where a blizzard kept the audience away. Not to be dissuaded, and armed with youthful optimism, they pressed on to St. Louis, but there, too, and for unexplained reasons, the audience was small. It was not until they reached Philadelphia, a longtime skating capital, that the young company had its first break and performed for two large and appreciative audiences. Similar receptions followed in New York and Boston. Perseverance triumphed, and by the end of the tour the Ice Follies was booked completely for a second season.

Continued success resulted from imaginative shows that featured much variety. Especially popular were cast members Frick and Frack, who joined the company in 1942. Hailing from Switzerland, Werner Groebli (b. 1915), Frick, and Hans-Rudi Mauch (d. 1979), Frack, performed professionally in ice shows on the Continent and in England before crossing the Atlantic and performing in carnivals and ice shows throughout North America. They are remembered for their unusual cantilever spread eagles that gave the illusion of defying gravity. With much speed, they bent backward from their knees until their bodies were parallel to the ice. A crippling illness forced Frack to retire in 1953, but the indefatigable Frick remained with the company, skating solo as Mr. Frick until 1980. He was inducted into the World Figure Skating Hall of Fame in 1984.

Another major and long-lived traveling ice show began four years later. Germany had already invaded Poland, but the United States was nearly two years away from suffering the Japanese attack on Pearl Harbor when in February 1940 a group of arena owners met in Hershey, Pennsylvania, to plan an ice show that would play at their arenas during the coming season. They selected the name Ice Capades. The company debuted in New Orleans and performed also in Atlantic City and Philadelphia while rehearsing for its premier season. Ice Capades of 1941 began a tour of twenty-five cities in Philadelphia on November 5, 1940.

Boasting a cast of seventy-five, the company's first headliner was billed as Belita,

Mr. Frick, a star of the Ice Follies, performing his famous cantilever move. (World Figure Skating Museum and Hall of Fame)

the "world's greatest skating star." Gladys Lynne Jepson-Turner (b. 1923), a young British skater, had placed sixteenth at the 1936 Olympic Games before turning professional a year later at age fourteen.[18] Under the stage name Belita, her popularity soared in 1937 when she skated in two special ice ballets at the Royal Opera House at Covent Garden. *The Brahmin's Daughter* and *Enchanted Night* were extravagant productions, each with a cast of 120 skaters supported by a fifty-piece orchestra. Although conceived in a grand manner, the productions were not successful artistically or financially. Historian Nigel Brown explained why. "These performers needed space, they were cramped on a stage fifty five by seventy feet and [were] obliged to execute too many movements 'on the spot.' The essential of skating art, 'gliding or sliding,' was lost. The *corps de ballet,* too numerous for such a stage, crowded and collided, showing to a disastrous degree the failure on the part of the director to grasp the artistic aim of skating."[19]

The popular Belita was also a talented actress, pianist, ballerina, and swimmer. After the war she left Ice Capades and returned to England, where she continued her career as a show skater. She appeared in several films as well, the most important of which was a 1953 MGM release *Never Let Me Go* with Clark Gable.

Another long-time member of the company deserves special mention. Donna Atwood, the U.S. pairs champion with Eugene Turner in 1941, turned professional following the cancellation of the World Championships that year. She joined Ice Capades and enjoyed a distinguished career as a pairs skater, first with Jimmie Lawrence but then for nearly two decades with Bobby Specht, the 1942 U.S. men's champion. Atwood and Specht characteristically anchored musical numbers, including "Anthony and Cleopatra," "Snow White," "The Student Prince," "Cinderella," and "An American in Paris." Atwood remained with the company until it was sold in 1963.

Turner, Atwood's pair partner at the 1941 National Championships, also toured with Ice Capades for a short time. In spite of a remarkable beginning, the war had precluded his continuation as a competitive skater. As a professional, he enjoyed a year-long tenure as Henie's skating partner in the Hollywood Ice Review before joining the Army Air Corps and completing sixty-nine missions over Germany. After the war he devoted his efforts to teaching skating and for many years wrote articles for *Skating* magazine under the heading "Turner's Turn."

The Ice Follies and Ice Capades both survived the war and, along with Holiday on Ice, dominated the market for skating shows, but they were products of skating before the war. Professional skaters in the United States and elsewhere had begun blazing the trail in the 1920s. England was especially rich in its offerings, possibly owing to a strong national interest in ice dancing. Chorus numbers in show skating were often dance-oriented. Entrepreneurs there viewed skating as entertainment for which the public would pay and anticipated the potential for profit. Shows were held at the Manchester Ice Palace as early as 1921, but the first major professional ice show in England is said to have been staged at London's Hammersmith Rink in 1927. Soon thereafter shows appeared in other cities, including Blackpool, Bournemouth, and Brighton. Among the most remembered was an ice extravaganza entitled *Marina* that was first produced at Brighton and then taken to other venues. Special music was composed for it, comedy was employed as an important element, and talented professional skaters assured its success.

Brief mention must be made of "tank" shows. They date from the early years of the century but continued between the wars and beyond. Extremely small portable ice surfaces, called tanks, could be set up in hotel dining rooms, on roof gardens, or at almost any facility. Isabel Butler and Eddie Basset are said to have performed in 1908 on a tank of just sixty square feet. These cabarets on ice had a significant effect on popularizing figure skating because they reached audiences that often had no other opportunity to see figure skating. Skating as live theatrical entertainment by professional skaters at large and small venues contributed greatly to the sport's development as an art form between the wars, undoubtedly leading many people to don skates wherever rinks were available.

SKATING AND THE CINEMA

The popularity of skating shows sent a signal to Hollywood. Skating could have a place in cinema, and the persistence of Sonja Henie made that happen. She was not the first skater to grace the movie screen. That honor had gone to Charlotte two decades earlier in *The Frozen Warning,* but a serial that included a skating star only incidentally was not Henie's goal. She believed skating had a place in cinema, but more important, she wanted to be a legitimate actress. Her skating skills provided the means to that end. Twentieth-Century Fox released nine successful motion pictures starring Henie over a period of seven years.

One in a Million, the first of her two films produced in 1937, was based on an original script by the Fox writers Lenore Praskins and Mark Kelly. Henie plays Greta Muller, a talented young Swiss skater who wants to win an Olympic gold medal for her father, who years earlier had unfairly lost his own Olympic bid. She becomes entangled in a web of potential ineligibility caused by a small-time hustler who schedules her into a skating show. Her leading man, the popular Don Ameche, saves the day, and her Olympic medal becomes reality. The script provided five skating scenes, including ones representing the ice at St. Moritz, the Olympics, and Madison Square Garden.

Her second film, *Thin Ice,* is based on *Der Komet* (The Comet), a novel by Attilla Orbok. Henie plays Lili, an innocent peasant employed as a skating instructor at a Swiss resort. Skiing daily with a guest who unbeknown to her is actually a prince results in attention that becomes top media fare around the world. In her naïvete, Lili remains oblivious to it all. Tyrone Power played the Prince Charming. Magnificent skating scenes with a large chorus of skaters were set to classical music, including Alexander Borodin's popular "Polovtzian Dances" from the opera *Prince Igor,* still a standard for skating routines. *Thin Ice,* like *One in a Million,* was a great success, enough so that Henie was able to renegotiate her already highly favorable contract.

Fox released seven more films over the next several years, including *Happy Landing* (1938), *My Lucky Star* (1938), *Second Fiddle* (1939), *Everything Happens at Night* (1939), *Sun Valley Serenade* (1941), *Iceland* (1942, and *Wintertime* (1943). In addition to Don Ameche and Tyrone Power, both of whom appeared in later films as well, Henie's other leading men included Richard Greene, Ray Milland, John Payne, and Jack Oakie. Music served always as an important element in the productions, and not just for skating scenes. In the last three Fox releases, major big bands participated as key elements of the story line. They included those of Glenn Miller in *Sun Valley Serenade,* Sammy Kaye in *Iceland,* and Woody Herman in *Wintertime.*

After leaving Fox, Henie made two additional films. *It's a Pleasure* was released by RKO in 1945, and *The Countess of Monte Cristo* by Universal Studios in 1948. Her success in cinema is unique. Only a few motion pictures have since included figure skating as an integral part of a story line, and no other skater has been able to become an actor or actress who starred in a series of successful films.

Henie's films boosted attendance at her skating shows, and her skating shows made people want to see her movies. This success occurred in the United States, although the films were shown in other countries. It is significant that no American skater had at that time won an Olympic gold medal or been a World champion, and no American skater had the financial wherewithal or the business acumen of a Wilhelm Henie to foster their cause. Sonja Henie was a celebrity recognized as the best skater in the world. Hollywood capitalized on her talent, sense of theater, winning smile, and reputation and by doing so provided the opportunity for many people to view the beauty of figure skating.

WAR AND ANOTHER ERA

Figure skating evolved rapidly in the years between the wars. Talented skaters molded it into a highly competitive sport at the amateur level and lavish entertainment at the professional level. Compulsory figures remained the most practiced and appreciated part of the sport. Special figures receded into skating's past. Spins and jumps connected by dance steps molded into flowing free-skating programs became skating's future. The number of competitors nationally and internationally grew steadily as the sport's popularity increased. North Americans as well as Europeans competed in World and Olympic competitions now held on both sides of the Atlantic.

Carnivals, ice ballets, and other shows were enjoyed throughout the skating world early in the century, but no one would have thought that a quarter century later, on the eve of World War II, professional touring ice shows would be presenting lavish entertainment to huge audiences in America, Europe, and elsewhere. The cinema took skating to an even broader public, much of which lacked the opportunity to see live ice shows. Ice skating was contagious. Shows and cinema led many to take up the sport as an increasing number of ice rinks provided the opportunity for them to experience the thrill of gliding across the ice.

As war again engulfed Europe, skating, as it had a quarter century earlier, suffered a temporary setback. Talented skaters had their competitive aspirations destroyed not by other skaters but by canceled competitions. Seven World Championships and two Olympic Winter Games were not held. Many skaters were called to serve the war efforts of their respective countries; a few were able to undertake professional careers. The generation of skaters between the wars advanced the sport tremendously. A new generation would appear after the war to continue where the others left off.

PART THREE

Skating since World War II

NINE

The Golden Age
of American Skating

WORLD War II was more devastating to the skating community than was World War I, primarily because figure skating between the wars had become more widespread. Before World War I, skaters from just nine countries participated in forty-two European, World, and Olympic competitions; between the wars, skaters from twenty-one countries competed in forty-one European, World, and Olympic competitions.[1] North American skaters competed most years, and Japanese skaters became the first Asians to compete.

Many countries joined the ISU, including Czechoslovakia and the United States in 1923, Poland in 1925, Japan and Latvia in 1926, Italy in 1927, Estonia and Yugoslavia in 1928, Australia in 1932, Romania in 1933, and South Africa in 1938 as membership expanded from one continent to four. Then for a second time the most developed skating nations became belligerents. Skaters who had competed against each other as sportsmen found themselves fighting for their countries against those of their former competitors. A second seven-year lapse in international competition retested figure skating's resilience. Again, it not only survived but it also developed into a greater sport than it was before.

A few European countries, including Austria, Belgium, and Germany, managed to hold national championships sporadically during the war years. North American countries were able to continue their national championships almost unabated. Not surprisingly, skaters from Canada and the United States led the way as international competition resumed in 1947.[2] North Americans won no European, World, or Olympic titles before the war, although they claimed one bronze medal at the European Championships, six silver and six bronze medals at the World Championships, and two silver and three bronze medals at the Olympic Games.

When the European and World Championships were reestablished in 1947, Barbara Ann Scott of Canada won gold medals. The following year Scott and Dick Button of the United States won gold medals at those competitions and at the Olympic Games as well. From 1947 through 1960 North American skaters were gold medalists in at least one discipline every year, and they dominated the sport in singles skating, changing it dramatically through expanded athleticism. The leader in what has been called the golden age of American skating was Dick Button.

RICHARD BUTTON AND THE NEW ATHLETICISM

Perhaps no name is better known in the sport of figure skating than that of Richard T. (Dick) Button (b. 1929), a result of his visibility for forty years as a commentator on ABC's *Wide World of Sports*. Through that forum he has had opportunity to champion the sport more than any other person. His tenure with ABC, which began in 1962, exactly ten years after his remarkable career as a competitive skater ended, has provided him with a historical perspective possible only from watching the sport evolve for more than a half century. From his double Axel Paulsen jump at the 1948 Olympics to the quadruple jumps of today, Button has witnessed firsthand figure skating's unprecedented expansion and development in the post–World War II era.

Button's athleticism reflected North American developments during the war years. Guided by the legendary coach Gustave Lussi, Button's determination, intelligence, and athletic ability led to five World and two Olympic titles. Those were crowning achievements because just six years after beginning lessons at age twelve he returned home as America's first Olympic gold medalist in figure skating. Four years later he won a second Olympic gold medal, the only man since World War II to do so. Button's competitive years required difficult juggling of skating and a demanding undergraduate curriculum at Harvard University.

After retiring from amateur skating, Button enjoyed a short career as a show skater, but it is in other roles that he has had the greatest influence. In addition to television work, he has been a tireless leader in the promotion of skating through the establishment and management of ice shows and professional competitions. For his numerous accomplishments in the sport as a competitor and commentator he was honored as one of the original inductees into the World Figure Skating Hall of Fame.

Dick Button, America's first World and Olympic champion. (World Figure Skating Museum and Hall of Fame)

Button's competitive career as a senior skater began at the 1946 National Championships. It was the first time the senior men's event had been held since 1943, although the other disciplines had continued unabated through the war years. Having won the novice title in 1944 and the junior title in 1945, Button completed an unprecedented three-year sweep through the ranks of men's skating by winning the senior title in 1946. It was his first of seven consecutive National titles, a record not since duplicated by skaters in any discipline.[3] More important, 1946 marked the beginning of a new generation of American skaters who would lead the United States to World domination for the next fifteen years.

Button traveled to Stockholm in 1947 for the World Championships. There, Europeans witnessed for the first time a more athletic style of skating soon to be labeled the "American school." The European skating community was not prepared for the athletic free skating it witnessed. Rumors of a young, athletic jumper preceded Button's appearance but had not been taken seriously. One British writer reported that "the strength and virility of his performance simply crashed into the sober circles of the ice world and staggered for a moment their conventional ideas," but that same writer evaluated incorrectly its impact. Sounding like British writers fifty years earlier in discussing the continental style, he continued, "Button was not an artist but an athlete on ice."[4] Speed and high jumps set Button apart, but his athleticism was well balanced with artistry that created convincing harmonious programs, albeit ones ahead of their time. Button was on the cutting edge of a new kind of skating, and historical perspective shows that in 1947 the world witnessed a new direction for figure skating.

Just five men from as many countries competed in Stockholm that year. Hans Gerschwiler (b. 1920) of Switzerland defeated Button in a close competition with the judges split three to two, but a year later the placement changed dramatically when seven of an enlarged panel of nine judges placed Button first. Perusal of the scores shows Button's strength. All nine judges placed him first in the free skating, but he was clearly competitive in compulsory figures as well. Five judges marked him higher than Gerschwiler. Button and Gerschwiler had met twice in the previous thirty days. Button won the European Championships, winning first place in free skating from six of seven judges, whereas Gerschwiler bettered him in compulsory figures by placement from four judges.[5] At the Olympic Games, Button prevailed decisively, winning the free skating from every judge and compulsory figures from all but one. For the remainder of his career, four more years, Button won unanimously every competition he entered, and on just two occasions did an individual judge not place him first in both compulsory figures and free skating.

Gerschwiler represented the older, prewar style of skating. Although he skated for Switzerland, most of his training had been in England under the guidance of his famous uncles, Jacques and Arnold Gerschwiler. He first appeared internationally at the European Championships in 1939, where he placed fifth behind a talented roster of skaters, including Graham Sharp and Freddie Tomlins of Great Britain, Horst Faber of Germany, and Edi Rada of Austria. None of those top finishers from 1939 competed in 1947, the year Gerschwiler won the World title, although Sharp and Rada did reappear in ensuing years. Following his competitive career, Gerschwiler moved first to Canada and then to the United States, where he became, like his uncles, a respected coach.

Button was the first exponent of the new American school of skating. He amazed the Olympic audience at St. Moritz with the first double Axel Paulsen jump and at Oslo four years later with the first triple jump, a loop, but the new American school of skating was more than explosive athleticism.[6] The new jumps obviously stood out in those performances, as do the quadruple jumps of today, but Button's programs were skated with meaningful musicality. He had studied piano, and that musical training was carried onto the ice. As a commentator he has promoted tirelessly and praised constantly musicality in skating. The new American style in the hands of great skaters increased the envelope of athleticism, but it was successful because it was done within the artistic boundaries of musical interpretation.

Button was the instrument through which Gustave Lussi (1898–1993) of Switzerland put his ideas into practice. A former skier who had suffered an accident, Lussi turned to skating not as a competitor but as a coach. He once said, "Not able to become an amateur champion myself because I had turned professional to earn a living, I made one vow. If I cannot be World's champion myself, I will make one through my teaching."[7] Lussi was a taskmaster who approached skating through analysis of the physics of the sport, specifically jumps and spins, but he also understood the importance of compulsory figures and emphasized the necessity of performing them well. His concepts of skating and coaching evolved after 1927, the year he arrived in the United States, a fact Button viewed as a strength: "He was not, therefore, a competitor trained in the European style and limited to its teaching."[8] Lussi taught many skaters during a long career and along with his most famous student was among the original inductees into the World Figure Skating Hall of Fame.

THE JENKINS BROTHERS

Following Button's retirement in 1952, two brothers dominated American skating for the next eight years. In turn, Hayes Alan Jenkins (b. 1933) and David Jenkins (b. 1936) claimed successively seven World and two Olympic titles. Guided early in their careers by Button's coach, Gustave Lussi, the Jenkins brothers' technique had been well established when in 1954 they moved to Colorado Springs to train with another highly respected coach, Edi Scholdan (d. 1961). Hayes was the reigning World champion; David had placed second behind his brother at the National Championships and fourth at the World Championships that year.

Hayes Jenkins first appeared on the national scene in 1946 as a novice, placing fourth. Two years later he won the junior title. Progressing to the senior level, he consistently placed third or fourth for four years before becoming the national champion in 1953 and repeating three times. David Jenkins, three years younger, placed fifth in 1949, his first year as a novice. He won the junior title in 1953. Four years later, following his brother's retirement, he became the national champion and repeated twice.

Collectively, Button and the Jenkins brothers were national champions from 1946 through 1960, but their successes surpassed national boundaries. The biennial North American Championships were fully revived in 1947. Button won from 1947 through 1951, Hayes Jenkins won in 1953 and 1955, and David Jenkins won in 1957 but did not compete in 1959. Button was the World champion from 1948 through 1952. Hayes Jenkins, who had collected two bronze medals, followed Button as the World champion and repeated three times. David Jenkins, who like his brother had collected two bronze medals, became the World champion in 1957 and repeated twice. From the reinstatement of the World Championships in 1947 through 1960 this trio of skaters, representing the new American style, won all but two of them, the first in which Button placed second to Gerschwiler and the last after they had all retired.

The Jenkins brothers, like Button, balanced skating careers with college educations. As David followed his brother in competitive skating he also followed him to Colorado College, where, like his brother, he graduated with honors. Hayes continued his education at Harvard University, earning a law degree. David proceeded to medical school at Case Western Reserve University. Both skated professionally for short periods of time, Hayes for two summers with Holiday on Ice and David for one season with Ice Capades, before retiring to pursue educational goals and professional careers in their chosen fields. The Jenkins brothers were among the original inductees into the World Figure Skating Hall of Fame.

Another trio of American skaters deserves brief mention. None of them received gold medals in World or Olympic competition, but collectively they demonstrate the strength of American skating during the 1950s. For eight years, from 1951 through 1958, James Grogan (b. 1931), Ronald Robertson (1937–2000), and Tim Brown (b. 1938) in succession won silver medals behind Button and the Jenkins brothers at the World Championships.

The four postwar Olympic gold medals were won by the impressive trio of Button and the Jenkins brothers. North American men, all but one from the United States, also claimed one of the silver medals and three of the bronze medals. The silver medal was won by Ronald Robertson in 1956, and the bronze medals by James Grogan in 1952, David Jenkins in 1956, and Donald Jackson of Canada in 1960. European skaters claimed the remaining four medals, three silver and one bronze. The silver medals were won by Hans Gerschwiler of Switzerland in 1948, Helmut Seibt of Austria in 1952, and Karol Divin of Czechoslovakia in 1960, and the bronze medal by Edi Rada of Austria in 1948.

For figure skating in the United States 1956 was a banner year as American men—Hayes Jenkins, Ronald Robertson, and David Jenkins—swept the medals for just the second time in Olympic history. The only other sweep of the medals in any discipline was by Swedish men led by Ulrich Salchow in 1908. American domination of men's figure skating ended in 1960; not until 1984 would another American win an Olympic gold medal.

BARBARA ANN SCOTT

Dick Button was not the first North American to win a gold medal at the European Championships. That honor went to his exact contemporary, Barbara Ann Scott (b. 1929), a popular, blue-eyed dynamo from Canada who surprised the World in 1947 when five of seven judges placed her first at the European Championships. Just two weeks later eight of nine judges placed her first at the World Championships. Competing at those first postwar competitions was a large and almost entirely new slate of women skaters. Great Britain's popular Daphne Walker, who had competed in 1939, returned and was favored to win, but Scott managed the upsets and claimed everyone's attention.[9] The petite

Barbara Ann Scott, Canada's
first World and Olympic champion. (World Figure Skating
Museum and Hall of Fame)

eighteen-year-old traced outstanding figures and was a strong free skater. Her success
in Europe was the continuation of a pattern already well established at home. From 1944
until retirement in 1948 she was never defeated. In addition to four national titles she
was twice the North American champion, and the Canadian in Europe claimed two European and two World titles as well as Olympic gold.

Scott was Canada's junior champion in 1940. As a senior, she twice placed second
behind Mary Rose Thacker. Senior events were not held in 1943, but when they resumed
Scott became the national champion and repeated three times. As early as 1941 she
competed at the North American Championships and placed fifth. It was a remarkable
feat given that just an hour after skating she was diagnosed with German measles.
When competition resumed in 1945 she won twice.

Scott included double jumps in her programs, an athleticism not necessarily expected of women although her British predecessors had included the same jumps before
the war. Scott's success was the result of a near-perfect balance of athleticism and art-

istry. Like Button, she had studied piano, and that undoubtedly influenced the musicality always associated with her free skating.

Upon retirement from amateur competition Scott skated professionally for five years with Ice Capades and the Hollywood Ice Review, but show skating did not provide the satisfaction of amateur skating. She found living out of a suitcase, skating on small surfaces, and performing for audiences who failed to appreciate the finer aspects of the sport to be unrewarding. Her decision to retire was total. "I still love to see other people do it," she said, but "I can't go out and skate as well as I used to, and since you can't live in the past, I won't skate at all."[10] Scott's desire to lead a domestic life was realized in 1955 when she married Tom King, then the Hollywood Ice Review's publicity director, and moved to Chicago, where she lived for many years before retiring to Florida. She was inducted into the World Figure Skating Hall of Fame in 1979.

Scott and Button were the last North American skaters to compete at the European Championships because after 1948 the competition was closed to non-Europeans. Three other North Americans, all from the United States, competed in the postwar championships. Gretchen Miller won the silver medal behind Scott in 1947, Roberta Scholdan placed thirteenth in 1947 and eighteenth in 1948, and John Lettengarver placed fifth in 1948. Two Americans had competed before the war. Maribel Vinson won the bronze medal in 1934, and Audrey Peppe placed eleventh in 1937. Thus, a total of just seven North American skaters competed at four European Championships, two before and two after the war, but they carried home four medals, three of them gold.

The Olympic cycle following Scott's retirement, 1949 through 1952, was a period of rejuvenation for European women as Aja Vrzáňová of Czechoslovakia, Jeannette Altwegg of Great Britain, and Jacqueline du Bief of France in turn became World champions, but before describing their successes I will continue with two Americans who in 1953 were poised to become the next dominant force in ladies' figure skating. It is the story of two teenagers, one eighteen, the other thirteen, who first competed against each other at the National Championships that year.

TENLEY ALBRIGHT AND CAROL HEISS

The years 1953 through 1960 belonged to Tenley Albright (b. 1935) and Carol Heiss (b. 1940). Albright won five consecutive national titles, 1952–55, and Heiss followed with four more, 1956–60. Albright won two World titles, 1953 and 1955, and Heiss followed with five more, 1956–60. Albright won Olympic gold in 1956, and Heiss followed in 1960.

Albright, already a budding skater, was stricken at age eleven with a mild case of nonparalytic poliomyelitis. Although it left her back, legs, and neck weak, she defeated the disease and with tenacity returned quickly to the ice, where skating provided much needed physical therapy. At age thirteen she became the novice champion and at four-

Tenley Albright, America's first lady World and Olympic champion. (World Figure Skating Museum and Hall of Fame)

teen the junior champion. Then, in 1952, a month before becoming the senior national champion, she surprised the skating world by winning the silver medal at the Olympic Games behind Jeannette Altwegg, actually placing ahead of Altwegg in the free skating.[11] At the World Championships later that month, Albright withdrew after placing second in the compulsory figures owing to a bout with the flu. Over the next four years she collected two silver and two gold medals at the World Championships, a gold medal at the Olympic Games, and gold medals at two biennial North American Championships.

Like Button and the Jenkins brothers, Albright pursued a college education during her competitive years. First there was a strenuous premedical program at Radcliffe College while defending her national and World titles. Then, at Harvard Medical School she pursued a specialty in general surgery. Throughout her medical career she has supported her sport in many ways, especially in the area of sports medicine. She served also as secretary of the U.S. Olympic Committee.

In spite of a five-year age difference, Albright and Heiss provided the first of several postwar rivalries in figure skating. Albright was nearing the end of her competitive career as Heiss was beginning hers at the senior level. Their styles and personalities were different, but their innate talent was equal. Albright, an inwardly serious competitor, was known for balancing artistry and athleticism to perfection. Heiss was an outwardly charismatic skater who in 1956 won the hearts of television audiences at the first televised Olympic Games. Americans watched as their two stars competed head to head in World and Olympic competition.

Albright's Olympic gold medal in 1956 came in the same year that Hayes Jenkins won his. It was the second of only three times that gold medals have been won by a man and woman from the same country. Gillis Grafström and Magda Mauroy-Julin of Sweden won gold at Antwerp thirty-six years earlier, and Heiss and David Jenkins would accomplish the feat again at Squaw Valley four years later. Albright was another of the original inductees into the World Figure Skating Hall of Fame.

The rivalry between Albright and Heiss spanned just four years. With one exception, the younger Heiss placed second behind the older, more experienced Albright. In 1956 Albright seriously cut her leg in a fall during an Olympic practice session but recuperated sufficiently to win soundly both the compulsory figures and the free skating. She was placed first overall by ten of the eleven judges. Heiss won the silver medal. At the World Championships two weeks later Heiss managed to upset the champion in an exciting and close finish, winning by the margin of five judges to four. The U.S. Nationals followed the World Championships in those years, and there, in her final competition, Albright once again prevailed. As David Jenkins was positioned to continue the American domination in men's skating following his brother's retirement that year, Heiss was likewise positioned to continue the American domination in ladies' skating following Albright's retirement.

Heiss's talent showed early. A native of New York City, she had the opportunity of studying from childhood with the legendary coaches Pierre and Andrée Brunet, twice the Olympic pair champions from France. In just five years Heiss began her steady climb through the national ranks as novice champion, junior champion, and senior contender. Years of nipping at Albright's heels prepared her for a four-year undefeated reign as another "queen of the ice." In addition to her Olympic gold medal she won four national, two North American, and five World titles. Coupled with outstanding athleticism, Heiss's charm and beauty made her one of the most appealing skaters in the history of the sport.

Retiring from competitive skating, Heiss pursued a short career as a professional skater, including appearances in ice shows and a role in a Hollywood film, *Snow White and the Three Stooges*. Just three months after receiving her Olympic gold medal she married Hayes Jenkins and curtailed her professional career to become a wife and mother, but skating had been such an important part of her life that she later returned to

Carol Heiss, a five-time World champion and the 1960 Olympic champion. (World Figure Skating Museum and Hall of Fame)

the sport as a coach. Like her teachers the Brunets, she has guided and influenced the careers of several international competitors, including Tonia Kwiatowski, Lisa Ervin, and Timothy Goebel. Heiss like Albright was elected to the World Figure Skating Hall of Fame with the original class in 1976.

EUROPEAN CHAMPIONS AND CHALLENGERS

Although the postwar period was one of North American domination, European skaters excelled as well. Most important among the men were Ede Király of Hungary, Carlo Fassi of Italy, and Alain Giletti of France. Király (b. 1926) is best remembered for a remarkable although brief career as a pair skater with Andrea Kekéssy, but he was also a strong singles skater. He medaled in both disciplines simultaneously at the World Championships in 1948 and 1949. His record as a singles skater in just three years of competition includes a fourth-place finish followed by silver and gold medals at the European Championships, a bronze and two silver medals at the World Championships, and a fifth-place finish at the Olympic Games.

Fassi (1930–97), a bronze medalist at the World Championships in 1953, is one of only two Italian singles skaters to medal in World or Olympic competition, the other being the American-born Suzanne Driano, bronze medalist in 1978. Fassi competed at the European Championships for six years, beginning in 1949, and advanced consistently in the rankings from fourth place that year through two bronze, one silver, and two gold medals, but four appearances at the World Championships netted only a single bronze medal. Although Fassi remains Italy's most successful skater, his importance is not found in his competitive record but rather in his role as one of the most respected and successful coaches in the history of the sport. Emigrating to the United States in 1961 to replace Edi Scholdan at the Broadmoor Skating Club in Colorado Springs, he devoted his professional career, assisted by his wife, Christa, to teaching and coaching. World and Olympic champions Peggy Fleming, John Curry, Dorothy Hamill, Robin Cousins, and Jill Trenary were his students. At the time of his death from a heart attack during the World Championships in 1997 he was coaching Nicole Bobek of the United States. In describing Fassi's competitive skating, Dick Button, who competed against him on two occasions, said it had "flare, talent, excitement, and fun."[12] Those are exactly the characteristics that his former students describe when discussing his teaching, and it is those students who represent his greatest legacy. Of importance to the history of figure skating, Fassi is the most recent of the elite coaches who have left their ideas and methodology in written form. *Figure Skating with Carlo Fassi* is a valuable resource for students of skating at all levels. Recognizing his contributions to the sport, he was elected to the World Figure Skating Hall of Fame in 1997.

Giletti (b. 1939) was the first man from France to medal in World or Olympic competition. A national champion from age twelve, his international career spanned a decade. Beginning with a fourth-place finish in 1952, he went on to garner four silver and five gold medals at the European Championships, but eight appearances at the World Championships resulted in just two bronze medals before 1960. His success at the European Championships demonstrates that he was probably the best skater in Europe. At the World Championships with the Americans present, specifically the Jenkins brothers, Ronald Robertson, and Tim Brown, top placements could not be achieved, but the indefatigable Giletti outlasted them all. In 1960, after the Americans retired, he became the World champion.

Not all skaters who have significantly influenced the sport have had strong competitive careers. Several writers and coaches have already been mentioned. Josef Dědič (1924–93) of Czechoslovakia, whose only international appearance was at the 1948 European Championships, is another. His contribution to the sport came later through service to the ISU as a member and chair of the figure skating technical committee, as a council member, and as a vice president. A respected international judge and referee, he wrote one of the most definitive books on skating technique, *Single Figure Skating for Beginners and Champions,* and was coauthor of two of the ISU's Judges' Handbooks. For his dedication to the sport, Dědič was elected to the World Figure Skating Hall of Fame in 1998.

Four European women deserve special mention. All were World champions who came to the fore after Scott's retirement in 1948, three of them before the rise of Albright five years later. Alena (Aja) Vrzáňová (b. 1931), one of several Czech skaters who distinguished themselves in the postwar years, was coached in England by Arnold Gerschwiler. She arrived on the scene immediately following the war and competed in every European, World, and Olympic competition for four years. From sixth place at the European Championships in 1947, she progressed in the next three years through medals of every color. Placing seventh at the World Championships that first year, she advanced to fifth a year later before becoming the World champion twice. Her one Olympic appearance in 1948 at age sixteen resulted in a fifth-place finish. After retiring from competitive skating, Vrzáňová moved to the United States and toured with Ice Capades. She has resided in New York City since retirement. For several years she promoted *Super Skates,* a series of fund-raising shows held at Madison Square Garden.

Jeannette Altwegg (b. 1930) was the only singles skater not from North America to win a gold medal in the four postwar Olympic Winter Games and only the second British woman to ever win one, the other being Madge Syers in 1908. Altwegg was an all-around athlete who could have had a successful career as a tennis player. She placed second in the junior finals at Wimbledon in 1946, the same year she became the British junior champion in figure skating. Recognizing that she could not compete successfully at the senior level in two sports, Altwegg gave up tennis and directed her efforts to skating. She was one of the sport's best practitioners of compulsory figures and might not have won gold medals had free skating held the value it does today. Her competitive record includes four years as the British national champion. Placements of fourth at the European Championships and fifth at the World Championships in 1947 and 1948 were preludes to successive bronze, silver, and gold medals at those competitions.[13] Her two Olympic bids resulted in as many medals—bronze in 1948 and gold in 1952.

Altwegg's joy in skating was compulsory figures. She retired with no desire to enter the professional world of show skating, although she received lucrative offers. Her response was "I'm sorry . . . but I'm quitting the ice world. I'm going out to Pestalozzi."[14] She loved children and chose to devote herself to humanitarian work with the Pestalozzi village located at Trogen, a small town in eastern Switzerland, where hundreds of orphaned children had been taken from Europe's refugee nations. Altwegg is one of the few skaters who have had the opportunity and ability to experience the thrill of achieving at such a high level in sport and the satisfaction of giving so completely to a humanitarian cause. In 1953 her country, on the recommendation of Winston Churchill, awarded her the highest honor given to a figure skater, Commander of the Order of the British Empire (CBE). In 1993 she was inducted into the World Figure Skating Hall of Fame.

Following Altwegg as World champion was a popular French skater, Jacqueline du Bief (b. 1930). Although she appeared internationally a year after Altwegg, she retired the same year, never having defeated her. Competing at four European Championships, du Bief won one bronze and two silver medals. At four World Championships she won one silver and one gold medal. Becoming the World champion in 1952 was a significant accomplishment, and she remains the only French lady World champion.

Unlike the reserved Altwegg, the outgoing du Bief was always a crowd-pleaser and played to the audience; she readily answered the call of show skating. Turning professional after winning the World Championship, she moved to the United States and joined Ice Capades. The confidence and zeal she displayed whether skating as an amateur or a professional is evident also in her book *Thin Ice,* published just four years into her professional career.

It was five years after the war before German skaters participated in the European and World Championships. They returned in 1951, two men, four women, and three pairs. Ria Baran and Paul Falk won the pairs event at both competitions. Horst Faber placed second at the European Championships, but no singles skater placed higher than tenth at the World Championships. Three years later, 1954, Gundi Busch (b. 1935) became the World champion. As the German national champion she had placed sixth at the European Championships and tenth at the World Championships in 1952. Silver medals followed in 1953 and gold medals in 1954. Turning professional, she moved to the United States and toured with the Hollywood Ice Review. Busch is remembered as a skater who paid meticulous attention to detail and possessed a strong sense of musicality.

One other German skater must be mentioned, not for her competitive success but rather for the dramatic free-skating move she invented and that today bears her name. Ina Bauer competed from 1956 through 1959, achieving career bests of fourth-place finishes at the European and World Championships in 1959. The move she made famous is a variation of the spread eagle figure in which the two feet trace parallel lines. The front

Ina Bauer in a variation of the spread eagle figure, a move she invented and that now bears her name. Ina Bauers are included in many free-skating programs. (The Broadmoor)

leg is deeply bent at the knee while tracing a flat or a shallow forward outside edge. The body is bent backward so the other leg is on a parallel line, tracing a backward inside edge. Known today as the Ina Bauer, it is employed in many free-skating programs.

Although Americans dominated singles skating throughout the period, strong European skaters were always in contention and represented a majority of the contestants at international competitions. It is true that rinks had been destroyed and remained closed in many parts of war-ravaged Europe, making it difficult for skaters to practice, but it is equally true that North America, primarily the United States, produced at that time a generation of unusually gifted skaters. It was the golden age of American skating.

TEN

Recovery in Europe, Pair Skating, and Ice Dancing

WORLD War II devastated Europe. As the war clouds passed, skaters in most countries found few facilities where they could practice. By the early 1950s the situation had improved, but only slightly. Sweden had rinks in Gothenburg and Stockholm. Belgium, Holland, and Norway had one rink each. Several existed in Russia and Switzerland. Czechoslovakia had fourteen rinks, possibly a factor in the successful amassing of fifteen World and Olympic medals between 1948 and 1973. There were two rinks in Hungary, several in Austria and France. Poland opened its first in 1955. Germany, in spite of massive Allied bombings, soon rebuilt year-around facilities.[1]

Germany held national championships during the first two years of the war, and Austria held championships through 1943. Even more remarkable was Belgium's ability to hold championships through 1944 in spite of its capitulation to German forces in May 1940. Undoubtedly, that tenacity contributed to Belgium's success in claiming gold and bronze medals at the European and World Championships in 1947.

The war in Europe ended in May 1945, but not until atomic bombs were dropped on Hiroshima and Nagasaki in August did Japan capitulate. Formal terms of surrender were signed a month later. The ISU Council met in July 1946 and set dates for the resumption of competition. European Championships commenced at Davos on January 31, 1947, sixteen months after the surrender in the Pacific. World Championships followed two weeks later at Stockholm.[2] Switzerland and Sweden, host countries for the competitions, were two of only four European nations that had managed to remain neutral during the war.

Participation at the championships demonstrated the sport's durability and stature. The ladies' and pairs' events boasted more entries than in 1939. Not surprisingly, men's events had fewer entries. Ten countries were represented at the European Championships and twelve at the World Championships, all of which had been allied against Germany, been annexed or captured by Germany, or remained neutral. They included Australia, Belgium, Canada, Czechoslovakia, Denmark, Finland, France, Great Britain, Norway, Sweden, Switzerland, and the United States. Absent were Austria, Germany, and Italy. Invitations to participate had been extended only to those countries "not under control of foreign forces," a practical, not punitive, decision because national organizations, which were needed to enter skaters, no longer existed in those countries.[3]

Participation increased in the men's event in 1948 but not to the prewar level. Fewer countries sent competitors to the championships that year, but skaters from former strongholds, specifically Austria and Hungary, returned and won medals.[4] Italy and Germany did not compete until 1949 and 1951 respectively.

	Men	Ladies	Pairs
European Championships			
1939	12	12	9
1947	6	20	11
1948	9	19	11
World Championships			
1939	11	15	10
1947	5	19	11
1948	14	20	15

THE REBIRTH, REVITALIZATION, AND GROWTH OF THE ISU

Stockholm hosted the July 1946 meeting of the ISU Council. In addition to setting dates for competitions, other items of business included an evaluation of the state of the union, primarily to determine its financial condition and which countries maintained viable associations or could readily reestablish them. Financially, the union was solvent, and sixteen countries had associations in good standing. Those countries were deemed eligible to send skaters to the 1947 Championships.

The championships were skated under prewar rules, but already at the first postwar congress held the following June the process of debating and evaluating those rules began. The first in a long series of changes that diluted and eventually eliminated compulsory figures was the reduction from twelve to six in the number to be prepared for competition. Those prepared were then skated on one foot rather than both feet. Technical changes in judging figures placed greater emphasis on tracing and carriage and less on the accuracy of triple repetition, but the importance of figures was not diminished. Scoring values remained the same, 60 percent for compulsory figures and 40 percent for free skating.

Ice dancing received strong impetus by the appointment of an ad hoc committee charged with proposing rules for international competition. Included on the committee was Reginald Wilkie, who with his partner, Daphne Wallis, invented the Argentine tango, quickstep, and paso doble in the 1930s.[5] He later served as chair of the ice dancing technical committee.

Some administrative changes were made, including establishing a permanent headquarters at Davos, Switzerland.[6] English replaced German as the official language for the union, although some publications as late as 1962 still appeared in German. It was decided that after 1948 eligibility to compete at the European Championships would be limited to members of European associations. Barbara Ann Scott of Canada, the reigning ladies' champion, won again in 1948, as did Dick Button of the United States. They are the only non-European champions of figure skating's oldest competition.

By 1960 the ISU's membership had expanded to twenty-nine countries. Austria, Hungary, and Italy rejoined in 1947. Russia, soon to become a dominate force in pair skating and ice dancing, joined in 1948. The defeated nations of Germany and Japan were readmitted in 1951, as was Romania. The German Democratic Republic (East Germany), created as an independent nation in 1949, joined in 1953 but not without significant opposition. The ISU refused initially to differentiate between the two Germanies in competition. Thus, Gundi Busch, the ladies' gold medalist at the European and World Championships in 1954, is listed officially as being from Germany although she actually represented the Federal Republic of Germany (West Germany). That practice lasted only a year at the European and World Championships but continued through 1964 at the Olympic Games. Other new countries included the Republic of Korea (South Korea) in 1948, China and Spain in 1956, the Democratic People's Republic of Korea (North Korea) in 1957, and Mongolia in 1960.

WORLD PAIR CHAMPIONS, 1947–53

Americans, especially the men, dominated singles skating throughout the postwar years. Beginning in 1954, Canadians dominated pair skating, collecting ten of the twenty-one World Championship medals awarded, six of them gold. But before 1954 five other countries, Belgium, Germany, Great Britain, Hungary, and the United States, won nineteen of the twenty-one medals awarded, including all of the gold.

No pair from the prewar era returned to the European and World Championships in 1947, where Micheline Lannoy (b. 1925) and Pierre Baugniet (b. 1925) of Belgium won gold medals. They did not compete at the European Championships in 1948 but successfully defended their World title and won Olympic gold as well.

Andrea Kekéssy (b. 1929) and Ede Király of Hungary followed Lannoy and Baugniet as World champions. Király, a highly successful singles skater as well, is the last skater in the history of the World Championships to medal in two disciplines in the same year. Kekéssy and Király amassed two silver and three gold medals at the European and World Championships.

Next was the first of just two American pairs that have prevailed in World competition.[7] Sister and brother Karol (1932–2004) and Peter Kennedy (b. 1927), silver medalists at the U.S. Championships, proceeded to the World Championships in 1947, where they won silver medals behind Lannoy and Baugniet. They slipped to fourth place in 1948. Questions were raised about that placement, but all medal winners, representing three countries, had consistent marks from a majority of the judges. Still, some judging was open to question. The French and Hungarian judges placed the Americans second, and the Swiss judge placed them ninth. The Kennedys won silver medals behind Kekéssy and Király in 1949, but in 1950, with all former medal winners retired, they stood atop the medal stand as America's first World pair champions. Unable to successfully defend their title, they twice collected silver medals behind Ria Baran and Paul Falk of Germany. Their Olympic bids resulted in a sixth-place finish in 1948 and silver medals in 1952.

An unfortunate incident occurred at the 1952 World Championships, where Peter Kennedy allegedly assaulted a press photographer.[8] There was provocation, but the altercation resulted in his permanent suspension by both the ISU and the USFSA. Neither sibling had further involvement with the sport. The Kennedys' place in the history of figure skating is in representing the new American style in pair skating. Other pairs watched and imitated their speed and flair.

German skaters reappeared internationally in 1951. Ria Baran (1922–86) and Paul Falk (b. 1921), national champions since 1947, were one of three pairs entered in the European Championships that year. They won decisively, receiving first-place marks from all seven judges. Three weeks later they wrested the World title away from the Kennedys by a four-to-three decision. Marriage followed that spring. In 1952 the Falks successfully defended their European and World titles and added Olympic gold to their record. They demonstrated that German skaters were again a major force in competitive figure skating and that they were worthy successors to the prewar German champions Maxi Herber and Ernst Baier. Turning professional, the Falks skated in shows on both sides of the Atlantic, after which Paul continued his involvement as a prominent coach in Germany.

The Falks' amateur career was curtailed by the war. In 1940, as teenagers, they placed fourth at the German Nationals, but their international career had to wait more than a decade, when they were nearly thirty years of age. Remarkably, they were also the World pair champions in roller skating. The Falks, who are remembered for exciting lifts and spectacular side-by-side moves always done with elegance and grace, were elected to the World Figure Skating Hall of Fame in 1993.

When pair skating was first contested at the World Championships and Olympic Games in 1908, two British husband-and-wife pairs, Phyllis and James Johnson and Madge and Edgar Syers, demonstrated medal-winning talent. The Johnsons became World champions twice. The years between the wars provided three additional medals but no World or Olympic titles for British pairs.[9] A brief but strong rejuvenation occurred after World War II, when a sister and brother, Jennifer (1932–80) and John Nicks (b. 1929), began a distinguished career as Britain's most successful pair skaters since the Johnsons forty years earlier. There have been no British medals in pairs since.

The siblings first appeared internationally in 1947 and competed at every European, World, and Olympic competition through 1953. Medals at the European Championships included bronze in 1950 and 1951, silver in 1952, and gold in 1953, and, at the World Championships, silver in 1950, bronze in 1951 and 1952, and gold in 1953. Medals eluded them in two Olympic bids. Following a professional career with touring shows, including their own, the siblings emigrated to North America, where John Nicks has enjoyed a long and distinguished career as a coach, first in Canada and then in the United States. Most notable of his students are the 1979 World pair champions Tai Babilonia and Randy Gardner. Others include the popular pair Alicia Jo (JoJo) Starbuck and Kenneth Shelley, World bronze medalists in 1971 and 1972, and Jenni Meno and Todd Sand, World bronze medalists in 1995 and 1996 and silver medalists in 1998. Nicks was elected to the World Figure Skating Hall of Fame in 2000 for his positive influence on many skaters.

Before turning to the Canadians who dominated pair skating for the remainder of the decade, one other pair deserves special mention. Elisabeth (Sissy) Schwarz (b. 1936) and Kurt Oppelt (b. 1932) of Austria were the only pair able to defeat the Canadians during their years of domination (1954–62). As national champions from 1952 to 1956 they appeared at every European, World, and Olympic competition except the 1955 European Championships. Their medals included silver and gold at the European Championships in 1954 and 1956; bronze, silver, and gold successively at the World Championships from 1954 through 1956; and gold at the Olympic Games in 1956. Their post-amateur career included show skating in both Europe and America.

THE ERA OF CANADIAN SUPREMACY

Canada tended to be selective during the early 1950s, not sending its full quota of skaters to the World Championships. No woman won a medal after Barbara Ann Scott until Petra Burka in 1964, and no man won a medal after the war until Charles Snelling did so in 1957. Canada's forte was pair skating. Four pairs medaled at the World Championships, and the last three won collectively every World title less one from 1954 through 1962. The first pair had a relatively short career. Suzanne Morrow (b. 1930) and Wallace Diestelmeyer (1926–99), national champions twice and North American champions once, collected bronze medals at the European and World Championships and the Olympic Games in 1948 after which they retired.[10] Morrow followed her pair skating career with a second career in singles, competing at the World Championships for four years, beginning in 1950. She placed fourth three times and fifth once. Morrow, later Dr. Suzanne Francis, a veterinarian, remained active in the sport for many years and held leadership roles in the CFSA. Diestelmeyer became a successful coach.

Canadian skaters did not compete at the 1949 World Championships, and Morrow was the only experienced member on the World teams in 1950 and 1951. Canadian skaters became a competitive factor in 1952, when in addition to Morrow, the dynamic pair of Dafoe and Bowden placed fourth at their first World Championships.

Frances Dafoe (b. 1929) and Norris Bowden (1926–91) placed a close second when Jennifer and John Nicks won their World title in 1953. Three of the seven judges placed them first. Two had the Canadians on top.[11] Dafoe and Bowden easily became World Champions in 1954 and repeated for a second year, but in 1956 they slipped to second place behind the Austrians Elisabeth Schwartz and Kurt Oppelt at both the Olympic Games and the World Championships.

The Olympic results were hotly debated, partly because Dafoe and Bowden had defeated Schwartz and Oppelt consistently for four years, but the controversy related primarily to the Canadians' overhead lifts, which, some critics claimed, violated ISU rules. Questions were raised regarding the number of revolutions done at full extension, and charges contended that Dafoe was being carried. Although athletic movements not yet covered in the rulebook were incorporated in their routines, increased athleticism was not new. It was the wave of the future and in the spirit of the postwar style.

The controversy caused the ISU to debate, review, and amend pair skating rules over the next several years, especially with regard to the number of revolutions of the lifting partner allowed at full extension. The number, set at three, was later increased to three and a half. An indirect result of the controversy was movement toward a short or technical program.[12] Pair skating at that time was decided on the basis of a single free skate.

The Canadians finished ahead of the Austrians by a tenth of a point, 101.9 to 101.8, at the Olympic Games, but points decided a winner only if the total ordinals and ma-

Frances Dafoe and Norris Bowden, Canada's first World pair champions. (World Figure Skating Museum and Hall of Fame)

jorities were tied. Both pairs received four first-place ordinals, but the Austrians received more second-place ordinals than the Canadians. At the World Championships two weeks later the Austrians received five first-place ordinals and the Canadians four. Dafoe and Bowden retired following the World Championships but continued to serve their sport as international judges. They were honored in 1984 with election to the World Figure Skating Hall of Fame.

With the retirement of Dafoe and Bowden and their competitors Schwarz and Oppelt, Barbara Wagner (b. 1938) and Robert Paul (b. 1937) became four-time World champions. In 1952 their coach Sheldon Galbraith had paired them for pedagogical reasons having nothing to do with developing a champion pair. Galbraith viewed Wagner's free skating as strong and her stroking as weak, while he viewed Paul's compulsory figures as strong and his free skating as weak. Galbraith believed they would improve by skating together. Their ages were twelve and thirteen, and they were the same height. Paul grew but Wagner did not. Soon he was twelve inches taller than she. Such height differences were to become characteristic of pairs a decade later, but such a differential was unusual in the 1950s.

Wagner and Paul were Canada's junior champions in 1954, runners-up as seniors in 1955, and national champions from 1956 through 1960. At the World Championships

Barbara Wagner and Robert Paul, four-time World pair champions and Olympic champions in 1960. (World Figure Skating Museum and Hall of Fame)

they twice placed fifth before winning four consecutive titles. North American titles were added to their record in 1957 and 1959. Olympic gold came in 1960. Their cumulative record of twelve national and international titles is the best among Canadian skaters in any discipline. Only Kurt Browning has won four World titles, and only Barbara Ann Scott has won Olympic gold.[13]

Retiring after the 1960 World Championships, Wagner and Paul starred in Ice Capades for four years. Wagner has continued her involvement in the sport as a coach, and Paul became a highly respected choreographer, creating routines for Peggy Fleming, Dorothy Hamill, and Linda Fratianne among others. Wagner and Paul were elected to the World Figure Skating Hall of Fame in 1980.

ICE DANCING COMES OF AGE

Ice dancing in the early years of the century was closely related to pair skating, which included simple side-by-side free-skating elements connected artistically by dance steps and variations of them. By the 1930s pair skating had become more athletic. Men were lifting their partners high above the ice and spinning them in death spirals low to the ice. As pair skating became more athletic it moved further away from its companion discipline. At the same time, ice dancing grew in popularity as a separate discipline, especially in England, one in which less-proficient skaters could participate both at open skating sessions and in competition at local and national levels. New and more difficult dances were invented, providing greater challenges for more advanced skaters. Not surprisingly, as talented ice dancers became national champions, their desire to compete internationally led the discipline toward World and Olympic competition.

As a result of seeds sewn during the 1930s, establishing ice dancing as an international sport was a high priority for the ISU after the war. An ad hoc committee appointed in 1947 was charged with proposing rules for competition in ice dancing, and its recommendations were adopted at the 1949 Congress. In anticipation of World Championships commencing as early as 1950, judges were appointed, a move that proved overly ambitious.

The regulations called for skating four pre-selected dances, one from each of four groups entitled easy dances, waltzes, quick dances, and slow dances in addition to a free dance of three minutes' duration.[14] The compulsory dances, like compulsory figures in singles skating, counted for 60 percent of the score. They were skated in the numerical order of the groups from which they were selected, and all couples performed them to the same music. The free dance, which counted 40 percent, was skated to music selected and furnished by the couple. It consisted of "a non-repetitive performance of novel movements and variants of known dances or parts thereof, combined into a program with originality of design and arrangement."[15] There were strict limitations on moves associated with pair skating, specifically jumps, spins, and lifts. Jumps were limited to a half-revolution when done side by side, lifts were strictly limited to one measure of music, and spins were limited to a maximum of one and a half revolutions when done by one partner and two and a half revolutions when partners revolved around each other. Separation of partners was limited to "the time necessary to change positions." The rules, which dealt extensively with what couples could not do, assured that the discipline was clearly distinctive from pair skating.

Although not yet contested as a World Championship sport, ice dancing under the newly adopted rules and called an "international dance competition" received its first showing at Wembley Stadium in London as a special event at the 1950 World Championships. Three members of the newly elected technical committee were among the five judges as three couples from the United States challenged three from England. Much to the chagrin of the British, Lois Waring and Michael McGean of the United States won the event. Although the newly adopted rules for free dancing were followed, an established style was far from evident. Significantly different approaches were offered. One British writer described the American style as "somewhat dull stepping and turns very neatly executed." English couples, by contrast, "entered with a timid imitation of pairs skating performed rhythmically to music."[16]

The British, who viewed themselves as the masters of ice dancing, were embarrassed that an American couple not only defeated them in their discipline but also in their stadium. It became a matter of national pride to avenge the loss. A second "international dance competition" was held at the World Championships in Milan the following year, where a growing interest in ice dancing was evident. In addition to couples from Great Britain and the United States, others from Austria, Belgium, the Netherlands, and Switzerland competed. The British had their revenge as Jean Westwood and Lawrence Demmy, who had not competed the previous year, began a five-year domination of ice dancing, including four years as the discipline's first World champions. Teammates Joan Dewhirst and John Slater placed second, a position they would hold for three years. The Americans trailed the British, and couples from the Continent trailed the Americans.

LEGITIMATIZED AT LAST AND BRITISH DOMINATION

Ice dancing became an official discipline at the Paris World Championships in 1952. It was an appropriate location because in that same city, fifty-eight years earlier, Monsieur Richard demonstrated the three-step waltz. From there the widespread craze for ice dancing had spread. Nine couples competed for those first medals. Westwood and Demmy of Great Britain, Dewhirst and Slater of Great Britain, and Carol Peters and Daniel Ryan of the United States won them. Other couples from the United States, Austria, the Netherlands, and Switzerland competed. Among them was Nigel Brown and his wife, Albertine, representing Switzerland. Brown later wrote the first historical survey of figure skating, *Ice Skating: A History.*

English dominance continued in 1953 as twelve couples competed with identical medal results. All but two couples from the previous year returned, and one man had a new partner. A significant decrease in participation occurred in 1954, when just seven couples competed, three each from Great Britain and the United States and one from Austria. Westwood and Demmy continued their reign, but the former silver and bronze medalists had retired, allowing Nesta Davies and Paul Thomas of Great Britain and Carmel and Edward Bodel, a husband-and-wife couple from the United States, to move into those positions. Two weeks earlier all except the Americans were among twelve couples that competed in the first offering of ice dancing at the European Championships, possibly the reason for lesser participation at the World Championships. Without the Americans present, three British couples—Westwood and Demmy, Davies and Thomas, and Barbara Radford and Raymond Lockwood—swept the medals. Others from Austria, France, Italy, the Netherlands, and Switzerland completed the roster.

Jean Westwood (b. 1931) and Lawrence Demmy (b. 1931) won every European and World title in ice dancing through 1955 and continued to leave their mark on figure skating following retirement. Westwood crossed the Atlantic, where she taught at major skating centers and coached several national champions and World medalists. Demmy remained in England and managed a company that manufactured electronic components, but he continued to serve his sport as a member and chair of the ISU's ice dancing technical committee. Westwood and Demmy did not have the opportunity to win an Olympic medal because ice dancing was not yet contested as an Olympic sport. Demmy was, however, selected to serve as the referee for the first Olympic ice dancing competition at Innsbruck in 1976. The couple was honored in 1977 as the first ice dancers elected to the World Figure Skating Hall of Fame.

Runners-up at the European and World Championships in 1954 were Paul Thomas and his first partner, Nesta Davies, then in their second year of international competition. Thomas reappeared in 1955 with a new partner, Pamela Weight, and they, too, were runners-up to Westwood and Demmy. It was a banner year for British ice dancers, who accomplished the first of three medal sweeps in World competition. Bronze that year went to Radford and Lockwood. In 1956, following Westwood and Demmy's retirement, Weight and Thomas became World champions, after which they retired but not before leading a second British medal sweep. Courtney Jones and his first partner, June Markham, were the silver medalists, Barbara Thompson and Gerald Rigby the bronze medalists. Twelve years later, in 1968, British ice dancers swept the medals for a third time.

Courtney Jones (b. 1933) holds a unique position in the history of ice dancing. He was a World champion for four consecutive years, twice with each of two partners. June Markham (b. 1939), his first partner, retired following gold medal performances in 1957 and 1958. Jones quickly selected Doreen Denny (b. 1941) as his next partner. Two additional gold medals followed. Today, one does not expect ice dancers to mesh and become serious competitors in such a short time; a long period of development is viewed as being necessary for partners to relate naturally one to the other, but Jones, throughout a long and distinguished career that crossed disciplines, demonstrated uncanny skating ability. His career began in 1947, fifteen years before ice dancing was contested at the World Championships. As an ice dancer he competed in local and national competitions with several partners; as a pair skater he competed successfully at the national level; and as a singles skater he won several national competitions.

Partnering with Markham in late 1955, second-place finishes came within months at the European and World Championships, accomplished amazingly while he was on active duty with the Royal Air Force. Decisive wins followed for two years, with all judges placing them first. Jones and Denny in their three years together proved equally remarkable. With one exception, all judges placed them first. Jones and his two partners dominated ice dancing completely for five years. It was a strong continuation of the British dynasty, but one that came to an end with Jones's retirement. Only two British couples have since become World champions, Diane Towler and Bernard Ford in the late 1960s and Jayne Torvill and Christopher Dean In the early 1980s.

Doreen Denny continued to be involved with the sport in the United States as a coach at Colorado Springs. Jones served the ISU as a judge and referee for ice dancing and the NSA in several positions, including its presidency in 1985. As a fashion designer, he constructed costumes for Torvill and Dean. Still skating, he and a later partner, Peri Horne, invented two new dances, the silver samba and the starlight waltz, both of which were subsequently adopted by the ISU as compulsory dances. Jones was elected to the World Figure Skating Hall of Fame in 1986. His country honored him for his skating achievements when Queen Elizabeth II named him Member of the Order of the British Empire (MBE) in a ceremony held at Buckingham Palace in 1989. He was elevated to OBE in 1995.

The British ice dancing dynasty ended with the retirement of Denny and Jones in 1961, and American domination of singles skating ended with the retirement of Carol Heiss and David Jenkins in 1960. But the Canadians retained control of pair skating through 1962, when Maria and Otto Jelinek won the World Championship in Prague and then retired.

The 1950s was an exciting decade in the history of figure skating, a time of rebuilding and expansion for the ISU. With the acceptance of Mongolia in 1960, the union counted twenty-eight countries among its members, a growth of 75 percent in just fifteen years. The newest members had yet to enter skaters in international competitions, but expanding interest in the sport was evident. Overall participation at the European and World Championships increased by 40 percent during the period as many talented skaters advanced the sport athletically and left it the better because they were in it.

JUDGES, JUDGING, AND CONTROVERSY

The challenge of providing competent and fair judging has plagued the ISU throughout its history. The difficulty of obtaining objectivity in a subjectively judged sport has persisted since the earliest skating competitions and continues to the present. Coupled with the inherent problems of subjective judging have been efforts to prearrange results. Questions were raised regarding the ice dancing results at the Nagano Olympics in 1998 and the pair skating results at the Salt Lake City Olympics in 2002, but such questions have been raised over discrepancies, some real and some imagined, throughout figure skating's history. Among those mentioned is Sonja Henie's 1927 defeat of Herma Szabo at the World Championships in Oslo, where three of five judges, all from Norway, placed Henie first in both compulsory figures and free skating while the others from Austria and Germany placed Szabo first. The war was scarcely over when Dick Button was narrowly defeated by Hans Gerschwiler at the World Championships in 1947. In the annals of figure skating history, that result too was considered controversial, fueled perhaps by the generosity of Ulrich Salchow, who, in awe of Button's outstanding free skating, gave him one of his own World trophies, but the judges there had showed no inconsistency. All five placed Button first in the free skating, and four of them, all except the American, placed Gerschwiler first in compulsory figures. The weighting factor that favored compulsory figures over free skating, not the judging, defeated Button.

Those examples demonstrate fundamental but very different kinds of challenges with which the ISU has had to deal, ones of honesty, competency, perception, and what should be emphasized in figure skating. The ISU has historically taken its obligations seriously, and in the 1950s it acted positively and decisively. As early as 1949 a rule was adopted requiring that referees request an immediate explanation if an individual judge's marks were significantly different from those of others on the panel. The discrepancy in the Kennedys' marks by the Swiss judge at the World Championships in 1948 provides an excellent example of the problem that rule addressed. It was an important first step toward the eventual establishment of formal procedures for evaluating judges. Over the next several years a system for instituting sanctions against judges who displayed incompetency or dishonesty evolved and it was placed under the jurisdiction of elected technical committees. Another major problem stemmed from attempts to influence the outcome of events by external means, and here too the ISU Council has acted firmly to curb the practice. Among the rules adopted was one requiring referees to submit reports on the judging to the technical committees following every event. As a result, and acting on recommendations made by technical committees, twenty-one judges were suspended during the 1950s.

Training for judges was needed because in some cases their qualifications were rightly called into question. Schools and seminars where judging criteria could be clarified were proposed, and a major step was taken in 1957 with a constitutional amendment requiring instructional courses for judges of figure skating and ice dancing. Thus, long-existing judging problems that had demonstrated the need for change were addressed. Actions taken during the 1950s pursuant to those problems demonstrated that the ISU was prepared to take all steps necessary to assure fairness and promote good sportsmanship.

Rules adopted by the ISU contributed ultimately to the demise of one well-established and successful international competition. The North American Championships provided friendly biennial competition between Canada and the United States for nearly fifty years, from 1923 to 1971.[17] Since 1945 an equal number of judges from each country had been employed with the scoring based on a ten-point scale. In 1954 the ISU declared that its regulations, which require an odd number of judges and a six-point scale, must be followed if the North American Championships were to continue. Reverting to a six-point scale created no problem, but requiring an odd number of judges resulted in an alleged bias, one that cannot be substantiated by actual results but one that led to the refusal of some skaters to participate. Held alternately in Canada and the United States, the required extra judge came from the host country. Perceived as an advantage to that country's skaters, the issue became a catalyst for discontinuance of the once-popular competition.[18] Out of its ashes came Skate Canada in 1973 and Skate America in 1979, events on the Grand Prix Series today.

ICE RESURFACING MACHINES

The most significant technical advancement between the wars was increased efficiency in producing artificially frozen ice. That allowed the sport to develop in countries where it had not previously been possible and provided year-around practice in all countries. Throughout skating's history, ice quality had been a limiting factor affecting what skaters could accomplish. Perhaps no technical advancement other than artificial ice has had a greater impact on the sport than the invention of the ice resurfacing machine by Frank J. Zamboni (1901–88), who opened an ice rink in southern California in 1940.[19] Concerned about the time it took to resurface the ice manually, Zamboni sought a mechanical method for doing so. Experimentation began in 1942, but it was not until 1949 that the first resurfacing machine actually replaced a crew of men at his Paramount Ice Rink. Sonja Henie was so impressed by the machine's efficiency that in 1950 she bought two for her traveling ice show. Not to be outdone, Ice Capades also purchased one.[20] Rinks throughout the United States and beyond soon found the machines to be indis-

Frank Zamboni's first ice-resurfacing machine, the Model A. (© Zamboni Co.)

pensable. Six were used at the Squaw Valley Winter Olympic Games in 1960, and by 1998 more than five thousand had been sold worldwide.[21]

Before Zamboni's invention, resurfacing was done by pulling a metal plane across the ice to collect trash, dirt, and excess snow. Water was then sprayed on the surface, and squeegees were employed to complete the process. Owing to the time required, sometimes as much as an hour, it was usually not practical to resurface ice more than once or twice each day, and the quality was characteristically inconsistent. With a resurfacing machine, ice can be resurfaced in fewer than fifteen minutes, and skaters are assured of an ice surface of uniform quality. The process, technically simple, accomplishes mechanically what was formerly done by hand. A blade shaves a thin layer of ice from the surface. Behind the blade, a cloth evenly distributes a thin layer of water that freezes quickly. The machines are well known to all skating fans, who enjoy watching the process during intermissions. Sometimes at major events one sees the drivers dressed formally.

SKATING'S GREATEST TRAGEDY

The 1950s was the golden age of American skating and also a decade of unprecedented growth for the sport internationally, the 1960s began with skating's greatest tragedy. On February 15, 1961, at 10:15 A.M., Sabena Airlines flight 548 crashed near the Brussels, Belgium, airport while attempting a landing. Among the seventy-two passengers and crew on board the Boeing B-707–320 airliner, all of whom perished, was the entire U.S. World Figure Skating Team, including referees, coaches, and parents en route to Prague, Czechoslovakia, for the World Championships. The cause of the crash has never been adequately explained. One possible scenario is that control of the aircraft was lost owing either to jamming of the outboard ailerons or unwanted extension of the spoilers. Eyewitnesses reported that a landing in clear weather had been aborted, probably the result of another aircraft on the runway, after which the airplane climbed to perhaps as much as 1,500 feet before control was lost. It stalled, nosed down, and crashed about four miles from the airport.

Those lost included Bradley R. Lord, men's champion; Gregory E. Kelley, men's silver medalist; Nathalie Kelley, his sister; Douglas Ramsey, men's alternate; Laurence R. Owen, ladies' champion; Stephanie Westerfeld, ladies' silver medalist; Sharon Westerfeld, her sister; Rhode Lee Michelson, ladies bronze medalist; Maribel V. Owen and Dudley S. Richards, pair's champions; brother and sister Ila and Ray Hadley, pair's silver medalists; Alvah Hadley, their mother; brother and sister Laurie and William Hickox, pair's bronze medalists; Diane Sherbloom and Larry Pierce, dance champions; Dona Lee Carrier and Roger Campbell, dance silver medalists; Ann Campbell, mother of Roger; husband and wife Patricia Major and Robert Dineen, dance bronze medalists; Maribel

Vinson Owen, mother and coach of Laurence and Maribel, herself a former World and Olympic medalist; Walter S. Powell, a World referee and ISU Council member; Harold Hartshorne, a World dance judge and member of the ISU ice dancing technical committee; Louise Heyer Hartshorne, his wife; Edward LeMaire, a national judge; Richard LeMaire, his son; Edi Scholdan, a coach; James Scholden, his son; William Kipp, Daniel C. Ryan, and C. William Swallender, coaches; and Deane E. McMinn, the World team manager.

There were calls for cancellation of the World Championships in respect for the U.S. team, but F. Ritter Shunway, acting president of the USFSA, requested that the competition continue as scheduled, stating that he was sure that was what the U.S. team would have wanted. Georg Häsler, honorary secretary of the ISU, announced the following day, however, that the ISU Council had voted for cancellation "as a sign of mourning over the deaths of our United States comrades."[22] With that the 1961 skating season came to an end. In memory of and as a lasting tribute to those lost, a memorial fund was established by the USFSA that continues to provide financial assistance for the training of American figure skaters.

ELEVEN

The Artistic Sixties

THE entire U.S. World team died in the crash on the way to Prague in 1961. One year later, two skaters from former teams, Barbara Ann Roles and Yvonne Littlefield, traveled to Prague as part of an otherwise inexperienced team of American skaters. Roles had been the World and Olympic bronze medalist in 1960, and Littlefield, an ice dancer, had partnered with Roger Campbell in 1960. He was on the ill-fated airplane with a new partner, Dona Lee Carrier. As members of the 1962 team, Roles placed fifth, and Littlefield with her new partner, Peter Betts, placed eighth. Other members of the team included two men, Monty Hoyt and Scott Allen; two women, Lorraine Hanlon and Victoria Fisher; and two pairs, Dorothyann Nelson and Pieter Kollen and sister and brother Judianne and Jerry Fotheringill. Nelson and Kollen also competed in ice dancing. Only one new member of the 1962 team, Scott Allen, would ever win a World or Olympic medal, but collectively the team provided the foundation on which the United States built its next generation of international champions.[1]

MEN OF THE SIXTIES

While the United States lost its current best skaters in the airplane crash and was thrust into the necessity of developing new ones, across the skating world, a largely new slate of skaters appeared at the 1962 World Championships. Combining all disciplines, only a third of those who competed in 1960 reappeared in 1962. Three of the men, Donald Jackson, Manfred Schnelldorfer, and Alain Calmat, were destined to become World champions.

Donald Jackson (b. 1940) became in 1962 the first Canadian man to win a gold medal in World competition, and it was a historic event. In an amazing, come-from-behind victory, all judges placed him first in the free skating, rewarding him for his history-making triple Lutz jump. Karol Divin of Czechoslovakia, the hometown favorite and expected winner, held a substantial lead after the compulsory figures, but Jackson won the free skating decisively, receiving seven 6.0s. Dick Button, commentating on ABC's *Wide World of Sports,* called the event "thrilling, a moment that shall stand as one of the greatest in skating history."[2] Ironically, it was exactly a decade after Button himself had completed the first triple jump of any kind in international competition.

Jackson was the Canadian national champion four times and the North American champion twice. Five World appearances produced two silver medals before he won gold in Prague. His one Olympic bid in 1960 resulted in a bronze medal. Upon retiring from competitive skating, Jackson skated professionally as a headliner with the Ice Follies for six years, after which he devoted his efforts to coaching. He was elected to the World Figure Skating Hall of Fame in 1977.

Among a younger generation of skaters who first appeared on the international scene in the early 1960s was Donald McPherson (b. 1945), the Canadian junior champion in 1959. As a senior competitor he skated in the shadow of Donald Jackson, but following Jackson's retirement McPherson became the Canadian, North American, and World champion. He had just turned eighteen. Retiring immediately, he enjoyed a long and distinguished career with Holiday on Ice in Europe. One Canadian writer lamented that because McPherson's amateur career had been so short and was followed by a professional career pursued abroad, he remained largely unappreciated in his homeland.[3]

Manfred Schnelldorfer (b. 1944), ten times the Federal Republic of Germany champion, competed at as many European Championships and collected three bronze and two silver medals.[4] He had garnered only a single bronze medal from six World Championships when in 1964 he managed a surprising upset at the Olympic Games, winning both the compulsory figures and the free skating. Just three weeks later he defeated the same skaters almost as decisively at the World Championships. Schnelldorfer skated professionally for only a short time because during his competitive years he pursued university studies in preparation for a career as an architect.

One of the longest amateur careers in postwar skating was that of France's Alain Calmat (b. 1940), who skated internationally for twelve consecutive years and never missed a European, World, or Olympic competition. His slow but consistent development is demonstrated by three Olympic placements: ninth in 1956, sixth in 1960, and second in 1964. During his last five competitive years Calmat won nine medals in international competition, including European titles from 1962 through 1964 and the World title in 1965. Calmat is yet another skater who successfully juggled higher education with skating. As a medical student, he did his internship at a Paris hospital during his final competitive year. Calmat remained active in figure skating for many years as a World judge and referee and was honored as the person selected to light the Olympic flame at Grenoble in 1968. He served in the French government as minister of youth and minister of sports.

Emmerich Danzer (b. 1944) of Austria followed Calmat as the World champion. He first competed internationally in 1961. Competing every year for eight years, he developed into a strong and consistent competitor, winning the European title four times (1965–68) and the World title three times (1966–68). Following retirement from competitive skating, he, too, joined Holiday on Ice.

Wolfgang Schwarz (b. 1947) of Austria was the 1968 Olympic gold medalist. Danzer, his nemesis through most of a relatively short competitive career, defeated Schwarz in twelve national and international meetings before Schwarz managed the unexpected Olympic upset to claim his only national or international title.

Tim Wood (b. 1948) was America's most successful men's skater for two decades after the airplane crash. He was the novice champion in 1962, the junior champion in 1964, and the senior champion from 1968 through 1970. His international career began

Tim Wood, the first American man to become a World champion after the airplane crash. (World Figure Skating Museum and Hall of Fame)

with a thirteenth-place finish at the World Championships in 1965. Skipping a year, he placed ninth in 1967. In a major leap forward he collected silver medals at the Olympic Games and World Championships in 1968. Competing for two additional years, he won consecutive World titles. A short professional career followed.

A BRILLIANT TRIO: DIJKSTRA, FLEMING, AND SEYFERT

As Tenley Albright and Carol Heiss dominated ladies' figure skating in the 1950s, three great athlete-artists from as many countries dominated in the 1960s. Sjoujke Dijkstra, Peggy Fleming, and Gabriele Seyfert claimed every World championship less one and both Olympic gold medals after Heiss retired in 1960.

Had Sjoukje Dijkstra (b. 1942) of the Netherlands retired in 1958 after five years of international competition she would now be forgotten. At that point her best showing was a sixth-place finish at the European Championships. Judges and the audience must have been stunned in 1959 when she won the silver medal at the European Championships and the bronze medal at the World Championships, upsetting several skaters who had previously defeated her. The following year, 1960, she became the European champion and carried home silver medals from the Olympic Games and World Championships. Competing for another four years, from 1961 to 1964, she was unbeatable. Dijkstra was a national heroine, the first of only two figure skaters in any discipline from the Netherlands to medal in World or Olympic competition.[5] Queen Juliana sat proudly in the audience at Innsbruck in 1964 as Dijkstra won her Olympic gold medal, performing what is reported to have been her finest free skate. Following retirement from competition she toured with Holiday on Ice.

The bronze medalist at the Olympic Games and the World Championships in 1964, Dijkstra's final year of competition, was Petra Burka (b. 1946) of Canada. She became the World champion a year later, regressed to bronze in 1966, and then retired. Burka's World title resulted from defeating decisively the usually consistent Regine Heitzer (b. 1944) of Austria, the only time she did so in five World and Olympic meetings. Heitzer was twice the European champion but never the World champion. Dijkstra's retirement provided her with a window of opportunity but one not realized.

Placing sixth at the Olympic Games and seventh at the World Championships in 1964 was a vivacious young American, one of the most respected skaters of all time, whose subsequent climb to World and Olympic titles was meteoric. Peggy Fleming (b. 1948) was a surprise winner at the National Championships in 1964, her first year as a senior, not having won the junior title. She remained the U.S. champion for five years. Her first World medal a year later was bronze. For the next three years (1966–68) all of Fleming's medals at every competition, national, North American, World, and Olympic, were gold. Like Dijkstra before her, Fleming's gold medals were won decisively. Her

Sjoukje Djikstra, three-time World champion and Olympic gold medalist in 1964, the Netherlands' most decorated skater. (World Figure Skating Museum and Hall of Fame)

senior career was under the tutelage of Carlo Fassi in Colorado Springs, but her success resulted from natural talent, an innate musical sense, and a driving work ethic.

The 1968 Olympics, televised for the first time in color, showed the always feminine Fleming wearing a chartreuse dress while skating a beautifully choreographed program. It was not her all-time best performance, but it made an indelible mark on the history of the sport and endeared her permanently in the hearts of skating fans. The free skate included an artistic jump frequently associated with her, a double Axel Paulsen approached and finished in a spread eagle position. Just seven years after the airplane crash that took her coach, Bill Kipp, the United States produced one of its finest skaters. After winning a third World title in 1968, Fleming retired from competition but not from

Peggy Fleming's artistry is seen here in an inside spread eagle. She is remembered also for her double Axel Paulsen jump done from and landed in an outside spread eagle. (World Figure Skating Museum and Hall of Fame)

skating. She toured with the Ice Follies, skated in television specials, and continued to perform in exhibitions well into the 1990s. Among her most moving performances was a tribute to Fassi following his death in 1997. She continued to serve her sport as a commentator on ABC's *Wide World of Sports* alongside Dick Button, Peter Carruthers, and Terry Gannon. Fleming was honored in 1976 as the youngest of twenty persons in the initial class elected to the World Figure Skating Hall of Fame.

Following Fleming was the first skater from the German Democratic Republic to medal at the World Championships. Gabriele Seyfert (b. 1948) placed second behind Fleming three times, but when Fleming retired the title was open. For the next two years Seyfert proved to be a worthy successor. Hers was a long career that showed steady improvement through the early 1960s. Seyfert was reportedly just three when her mother, Jutta Müller, a coach and former competitor, first put skates on her feet.[6] Progress was not particularly rapid. At age thirteen she skated in her first World competition and placed last. Three years later, the year Fleming won her first World medal, Seyfert was fifth. She never again failed to medal, and none were ever bronze. There were three silver medals behind Fleming at the World Championships and another at the Grenoble Olympics, but only gold medals followed. During her ten-year career Seyfert was seven times the German Democratic Republic champion, three times the European champion, and two times the World champion. She was a well-balanced skater, strong at compulsory figures, but is remembered especially for her athletic style of free skating always presented with crowd-pleasing personality.

PAIR SKATING

The World Championships at Prague in 1962 were a high point for Canadian figure skating. Gold medals were won in two disciplines, men and pairs, a scenario that had not occurred before and would not occur again for more than thirty years, when Kurt Browning and the pair of Isabelle Brasseur and Lloyd Eisler would do so in the same city. Donald Jackson upset his competition and brought the audience to its feet as he landed a perfect triple Lutz jump, the first in international competition, but more anticipation and greater excitement that week stemmed from the pairs event in which brother and sister Maria (b. 1943) and Otto Jelinek (b. 1941) returned to Prague, the city from which they had escaped as children in the middle of the night fourteen years earlier.

Henry Jelinek, their father and an astute businessman, owned a large cork-manufacturing company. Following the communist takeover, he made arrangements for his wife and children to escape to Austria in a foreign diplomat's automobile. The year was 1948, and the escape was a daring gamble. In 1962 Henry and Jarmilla Jelinek could not be in the audience for their talented children's historic performance in the city of their birth. The Czechoslovak government, in order to gain the privilege of hosting the championships, had guaranteed safety for the siblings but not for their parents, who watched on television from nearby Switzerland. The audience that evening was not concerned with the Jelineks' earlier defection. On the contrary, they cheered proudly for their compatriots, who offered them an outstanding program of pair skating. Otto reported that "we got showered with thousands of gifts not only because we were top figure skaters but because we were a symbol of freedom."[7]

The Jelineks had won the Canadian junior title in 1955, but six years passed before they won the senior title. Those years coincided with the reign of the indomitable Wagner and Paul. In 1961, following Wagner and Paul's retirement, the Jelineks won the Canadian and the North American Championships, but cancellation of the World Championships brought the season to a close. A year later they stood atop the World podium.

Retiring from competitive skating, the Jelineks toured for several years with Ice Capades. Otto later managed the family business and had a distinguished career in politics as well, including terms in the Canadian Parliament and appointments to head two ministries, sports and finance. He also served as a figure skating analyst for Canadian television. More recently, he returned to his native Prague, where he resides today. Maria attended the University of Michigan, married, raised three sons, and works in the travel business.

Maria and Otto Jelinek, World pair champions in 1962. (World Figure Skating Museum and Hall of Fame)

No Russian skater in any discipline had competed in international competition since the days of the czarist state, when in 1956 three men and two pairs from the Soviet Union appeared in Paris for the European Championships. It was a humble rebirth that included a last-place finish in the men's competition but a hopeful one, with an eighth-place finish by the pair of Lidia Guerassimova and Turii Kissele.[8] Soviet skaters have since competed at every European Championships other than one held in Berlin and skipped for political reasons. In 1958 Nina and Stanislav Zhuk carried home their country's first medals, silver. That same year the Soviets competed at the World Championships for the first time.

Soviet men did not medal until Sergei Chetverukhin won bronze at the European Championships in 1969. Soviet women did not medal until Elena Vodorezova won bronze at the European Championships in 1978. Soviet skaters found their first niche in pair skating and since 1965 have dominated the discipline. Silver medalists behind the Jelineks at the World Championships in 1962 were Liudmila Belousova and Oleg Protopopov. Although the Jelineks retired, Belousova and Protopopov's time as World champions had not arrived. Marika Kilius and Hans Jürgen Bäumler of the Federal Republic of Germany held them at bay for two years.

Marika Kilius (b. 1943) enjoyed an international career that spanned ten years and included two partners. From 1955 through 1957 she paired with Franz Ningel (b. 1936), and they won bronze medals at the European Championships. Those same years included bronze and silver medals at two World Championships and a fourth-place finish at the Olympic Games. Changing partners, both continued to compete. With placements ranging from second to fifth, Ningel and his new partner Margret Göbl (b. 1941) consistently placed behind Kilius and her new partner Hans Jürgen Bäumler (b. 1942) as they captured six European titles, two World titles, and two Olympic silver medals. The pairs event at Innsbruck has been called "the story" of the 1964 Olympics. As reigning European and World champions and silver medalists from the previous Olmpics, Kilius and Bäumler were strongly favored to win, but by a decision of five judges to four Belousova and Protopopov upset them to claim the Soviet Union's first Olympic gold medal. Enterprising merchants had been so sure of the outcome that souvenirs proclaiming the Germans as champions had gone on sale before the event was skated.[9]

Kilius and Bäumler offered an exciting, theatrical style of skating and are sometimes remembered for a showy but not difficult death spiral in which her hair, worn on top of her head, would collect shavings from the ice. A decision to turn professional and join Ice Capades at the conclusion of the 1964 season had been made before the games, and that resulted in controversy. Although they had signed a contract they had received no compensation and had never skated outside of approved amateur competitions. Because the signing was viewed by some as turning professional, Kilius and Bäumler returned their Olympic medals, but the records of the Olympic Games published by the

ISU list them as being the silver medalists. No official action was taken by either the ISU or the IOC. Kilius and Baumler competed four weeks later at the World Championships and won the gold medals, defeating Belousova and Protopopov by a five-to-four decision. The Olympic medals were returned to them more than twenty years later.

A NEW STYLE OF PAIR SKATING

The close decisions between Kilius and Bäumler and Belousova and Protopopov in 1964 had less to do with which was the better pair than it did with a new style of pair skating. A more flowing style presented by the Russians was replacing an older, more disconnected style. Pair skating had become more athletic and theatrical since the war, but tricks such as Kilius collecting ice shavings in her hair had little to do with the style of skating the Soviets introduced. Kilius and Bäumler skated in what can be called the old style. Belousova and Protopopov created a new, more romantic style, one that clearly reflected its roots in classical ballet. Difficult technical elements remained, but they were integrally woven into more continuous and balletic programs.

Liudmila Belousova (b. 1935) and Oleg Protopopov (b. 1932) began skating together in 1955 when she was twenty and he was twenty-three. Oleg, from Leningrad, studied piano and had musical ambitions but failed his entrance audition at the conservatory. At fifteen he began skating and was coached by Nina Lepninskaya, a former a student of Nikolai Panin. Liudmila, born in Ulyanovsk on the Volga River, moved with her family to Moscow following the war. Her interest in figure skating developed after seeing Sonja Henie's *Sun Valley Serenade.* Undissuaded when told that she was too old to begin, she joined an adult class taught by Larisa Novozhilova, a former Russian ice dancing champion. She met Oleg at a Moscow rink when he was on leave from service in the Russian navy. Later, in Leningrad, they met for a second time. He was again on leave, and she was preparing to take the tests prerequisite to acceptance into an engineering curriculum at the university. Like Oleg, who failed his audition at the conservatory, Liudmila failed portions of the test required to study engineering. Recognizing their affinity for skating and the fate that had brought them together twice, they devoted themselves to a partnership in skating and ultimately in marriage.[10]

Belousova and Protopopov, in their first year of international competition, 1958, placed tenth at the European and thirteenth at the World Championships. In 1959 they advanced to ninth at the European Championships but were not sent to the World Championships. The year 1960 saw jumps in their placements to fourth and eighth at those competitions and ninth in their first Olympic effort. The next year, 1961, was a lost one because the European Championships were held in West Berlin without Soviet participation, and the World Championships were canceled. The years between 1962 and

Liudmila Belousova and Oleg Protopopov, four-time World pair champions and two-time Olympic gold medalists, were the Soviet Union's first winners in any discipline. (World Figure Skating Museum and Hall of Fame)

1964 were ones of anticipation because, except for the Olympic upset, they continually placed second behind the Jelineks and Kilius and Bäumler.

After the former champions retired, Belousova and Protopopov won every competition through the next Olympic cycle. They competed for one additional season, 1969, but slipped to silver and bronze at the European and World Championships. At ages thirty-four and thirty-seven they retired from competitive skating, among the oldest Olympic champions in the history of the sport. They had amassed four European, four World, and two Olympic titles. As professionals, they skated in Russia and abroad. While on tour in 1979 they defected and were granted political asylum in Switzerland. Three years with Ice Capades followed, after which they curtailed touring but continued skating, making appearances into the twenty-first century. In recognition of their contributions they were recipients of the Jacques Favart Trophy in 1997 and were elected into the World Figure Skating Hall of Fame in 1978.

The Protopopovs were an anomaly in several respects. They were older than usual when they began skating, much of their amateur career was done without the benefit of coaching, and their success was not a meteoric rise to the top but rather a long period of development. They created a new and personal style of pair skating with emphasis placed on musical interpretation, and they selected the most romantic of nineteenth century music. Among their most-remembered programs are ones to Liszt's *Liebesträum,* Massenet's "Meditation" from the opera *Thaïs,* and Beethoven's *Moonlight Sonata.* Once selected, music was interpreted as in ballet. Oleg explained, "We don't agree with those coaches who regard a duet of a man and a woman as a union of two single skaters." As an example, he added, "If Tchaikovsky's First Concerto is performed in concert, the pianist plays his part, the orchestra members play theirs. They hardly ever duplicate one another and still create a concord of sounds."[11] The analogy is an excellent one because it describes completely the philosophy behind their skating. The Protopopovs' representation of a romantic relationship between a man and a woman was the complete antithesis of either shadow skating, which although still done at the end of the war had gradually declined in importance, or of a program that included technically difficult but often disconnected tricks.

Like Sonja Henie in the 1930s and Dick Button in the 1940s, the Protopopovs in the 1960s altered dramatically the direction of figure skating, and like their predecessors they won multiple Olympic gold medals. Their career marks the beginning of the Soviet dynasty in pair skating, one that continued almost unabated throughout the remainder of the century.

In the year of the Protopopovs' last gold medals, 1968, one of the greatest skaters in the history of the sport literally popped onto the scene. At the European Championships Irina Rodnina appeared with her first partner, Alexei Ulanov, and placed fifth. They did not compete at the World Championships or the Olympic Games that year, but a year later, the beginning of a new Olympic cycle and the last year of the Protopopovs' amateur career, they won European and World titles.

The coach of many Russian skaters, including Rodnina and Ulanov, was Stanislav Zhuk (b. 1935), one of that country's early pair skaters who, with Nina Bakuscheva, placed sixth at the European Championships in 1957. Married afterward, they continued competing through 1960 and won silver medals twice at the European Championships.

Among Zhuk's many students was his sister Tatiana (b. 1946), whose career with two partners, Alexandr Gavrilov (b. 1943) and Alexandr Gorelik (b. 1945), spanned nearly a decade. Zhuk and Gavrilov won bronze medals at the European and World Championships in 1963. Gavrilov retired a year later, but Zhuk returned with Gorelik in 1965 and again captured bronze medals at both championships. Zhuk and Gorelik never won gold medals, always skating in the shadow of the Protopopovs, but in their final competitive years, 1966 and 1968, all of their medals were silver.[12]

One cannot discuss pair skating of the 1960s without mentioning a Russian couple remembered less for their competitive success than for their years of positive influence on the sport as coaches. Tamara Moskvina (b. 1941) and Alexei Mishin (b. 1941) had a relatively short international career of three years, beginning in 1967.[13] Upon retirement from competitive skating they completed university studies in pedagogical sciences, were honored by their country with the title "Honored Master of Sport," and became coaches for many of the next generation of Russian skaters.[14] Moskvina emigrated to the United States, where she continues to be a sought-after coach. In 1987 she coauthored with Igor Moskvin *Pair Skating as Sport and Art*. Published by the ISU, it serves as a companion volume to Dědič's *Single Figure Skating for Beginners and Champions*.

ICE DANCING IN THE SIXTIES

Ice dancing in the 1960s is the story of two couples, one Czechoslovakian and the other British, both of which were World champions for four years. Because ice dancing was not yet an Olympic sport, becoming World champions denoted the pinnacle of success. Doreen Denny and Courtney Jones won their last international title at the European Championships in 1961, ending temporarily the British dynasty that had dominated the discipline since its elevation to a World Championship sport in 1952. With resumption of the World Championships at Prague in 1962, a young sister and brother, Eva Romanová (b. 1949) and Pavel Roman (1946–71), skating in their hometown and at their first World competition, took the gold medals.[15] It was another upset at that most unusual World Championships. Placing second was a more experienced sister and brother, Christiane and Jean Paul Guhel of France, who just two weeks earlier had decisively defeated Romanová and Roman at the European Championships.

Romanová and Roman first competed at the European Championships in 1959, entering two events, pairs and dance. They placed last in what was their only international pairs' competition, but a relatively strong seventh-place finish in ice dancing marked their future. A majority of the judges placed them third or fourth in the free dance. Their first international medal was bronze at the European Championships in 1962, just two weeks before they upset the more experienced field of competitors in Prague.[16] Throughout the remainder of their amateur career they were unbeatable at the World Championships.

The preeminence of British ice dancers at the World Championships through 1961 made the four-year reign of Romanová and Roman seem an anomaly because another talented British couple, Diane Towler (b. 1946) and Bernard Ford (b. 1947), rose to stardom even more quickly than Romanová and Roman. Their first effort, at the World Championships in 1964, resulted in a thirteenth-place finish. A year later they placed fourth. In 1966, not having won an international medal of any color, Towler and Ford won both the European and World Championships, a pattern that continued for the remainder of their career. They retired in 1969 as four-time European and World champions.

Towler and Ford carried ice dancing to a more dynamic level, creating what one commentator called a "new note of excitement."[17] They selected music from the 1964 film *Zorba the Greek* for their free dance in 1966, a choice said by their coach, Gladys Hogg, to be "much too fast." But their speed, intricate footwork, and exceptionally deep edges created excitement without losing the grace and smoothness expected in ice dancing. Following retirement from competitive skating, Towler and Ford became coaches in England, and in 1993 they were elected to the World Figure Skating Hall of Fame. Their retirement brought the era of British ice dancers to a brilliant close as British couples capped the season by sweeping the medals for a third time at the World Championships. Silver medalists were Yvonne Suddick and Malcolm Cannon; bronze medalists were Janet Sawbridge and Jon Lane.

SKATING AND THE COLD WAR

Skaters from the Soviet Union did not compete at the 1961 European Championships in West Berlin, an early example of the cold war invading sports and a reality that persisted through the 1960s and beyond. There were occasions when member nations of the North Atlantic Treaty Organization refused entry visas to athletes from Warsaw Pact nations, the most notable being a blanket refusal to skaters from the German Democratic Republic for the 1963 World Championships at Cortina, Italy. Although no skater from the German Democratic Republic would have been in medal contention that year, young and developing competitors, including Gabriele Seyfert, were unfairly denied the opportunity of gaining valuable experience.

Cold war politics all too often invaded nongovernment entities, but national differences had been allowed to invade sports long before the cold war. As indicated, the defeated nations were not allowed to participate at the 1920 Olympic Games, and similar but less severe problems existed following World War II.

The establishment of the German Democratic Republic (East Germany) in 1954 created a particularly complex problem. The ISU recognized separate associations for the two Germanys by granting membership to the German Democratic Republic in 1956. Their first competitors, pair skaters Vera and Horst Kuhruber, appeared at the European Championships that year. The IOC, however, refused to recognize two Germanys and through 1964 allowed only combined teams to participate at the Olympic Games. No skater from the German Democratic Republic was on the 1956 team, and only one, Bodo Bockenauer, was on the 1960 team. The problem became more acute in 1964 when the team included six entrants from the Federal Republic of Germany and three from the German Democratic Republic. Gold medalist Manfred Schnelldorfer and pairs silver medalists Kilius and Bäumler represented the Federal Republic of Germany. Future medalist Gabriele Seyfert represented the German Democratic Republic. Bowing to pressure from several international federations, the IOC reversed its policy for the Grenoble Games in 1968.

The ISU, which has successfully avoided most influences of national politics, has consistently strived to maintain an environment for skating that would transcend national differences and offer fairness to all competitors. That was a major reason for its creation in 1892, and there have been numerous examples of efforts to maintain that integrity. Distancing itself from the 1920 Olympics is but one. In spite of that record the ISU could not muster enough votes at its 1963 Congress to approve a rule change that would have prohibited awarding sites for competitions or congresses to nations that would not guarantee free entry to all contestants or participants.[18] Unforeseen problems occasionally frustrated the ISU leadership. One such example occurred at the 1964 World Championships at Dortmond in the Federal Republic of Germany. Skaters from the German Democratic Republic withdrew when the local organizing committee refused to introduce skaters by the name of their country, choosing instead to do so by the name of their federation.

The need for decisive action was evident, and at the 1965 Congress, discrimination, especially the right of free entry for athletes, was on the agenda. An ad hoc committee proposed legislation that was subsequently adopted. Although of necessity general in nature, it was significant cold war legislation that remains in the regulations today. The most important statement says, "The ISU does not approve of interference in sports based on political or any other grounds and will make every effort to avoid such interference."[19] The Union has consistently upheld the integrity of that dictum.

CHANGES IN THE SPORT

Competitive figure skating developed remarkably during the 1960s, both athletically and artistically. Fostering that development was continued and aggressive leadership from the ISU. Significant changes in eligibility and venue requirements were implemented, new regulations for pair skating and ice dancing were adopted, and progress was made in ongoing efforts to provide qualified and honest judges.

Growth of the union continued with the addition of four new countries, Finland, Mongolia, New Zealand, and Bulgaria. The number of competitors at international events increased, bolstered in part by the emergence of talented skaters from the Soviet Union. Russian membership in the ISU dated almost from the beginning, 1893, but ceased after World War I owing to the Bolshevik Revolution and the resulting formation of a communist state. Three decades had passed when in 1948 the USSR joined the ISU, and nearly another decade before Soviet skaters competed in ISU championships. The first efforts were not remarkable, but indications of things to come were evident in pair skating. Not since 1914 had a skater from Russia medaled at the World Championships when in 1962 the Protopopovs won bronze, and not since 1908 had a Russian skater medaled at the Olympic Games when in 1964 the Protopopovs won gold.[20]

The seventy-fifth anniversary of the ISU in 1967 coincided with the hundredth anniversary of the Wiener Eislauf-Verein (Vienna Skating Club). The World Championships, held that year in Vienna, were a gala event made especially notable because celebrations had not been held on the occasions of the ISU's twenty-fifth or fiftieth anniversaries, both of which occurred during war years. The ISU numbered twenty-nine member nations on its anniversary. Sixteen sent competitors to Vienna, and skaters from seven of them returned home with medals.

The World Championships that year marked the end of an era as well as a beginning. For the last time all events except compulsory figures were held outdoors. As had so often happened, skaters found themselves coping with rain and snow, conditions that were soon to become part of skating history because at its congress that year the ISU adopted a rule requiring that the European and World Championships and the Olympic Games be held in covered rinks. Other sanctioned competitions could still be held at outdoor venues, but the number of outdoor competitions diminished rapidly. The rule for a covered facility required only that a roof cover the ice surface. Enclosed indoor venues did not become a requirement until 1980 and for practice sessions not until 1984.

Efforts made throughout the 1950s to improve the quality of judging had clearly been successful. Suspensions of judges in the 1960s numbered only five, a dramatic decline from the previous decade, but concerns about judging remained major topics of discussion at every congress.[21] An important step toward improvement was taken in 1959 when the first *Judges' Handbook* covering compulsory figures was authorized. Written by Josef Dědič and Vladislav Čáp of Czechoslovakia, it was published in 1961. Other handbooks followed, including one for free skating coauthored by Dědič and Miroslav Hasenöhrl of Czechoslovakia in 1965 and one for pair skating by Rudi Marx of Germany in 1966.[22] The handbooks describe skating elements and indicate the criteria judges must employ in making decisions. New rules relating to judges were adopted as well. One required that referees prepare formal reports on the performance of judges following every competition. Another limited the number of events in which a judge could officiate at a competition.

Changes affected the scoring of events. Of great importance for singles skaters was a reduction in the value of compulsory figures, another step along the path toward their eventual elimination. The old ratio of 60 percent for compulsory figures and 40 percent for free skating, in effect since time immemorial, was in 1967 changed to 50 percent for each part.[23]

Changes were desperately needed in the rapidly expanding discipline of pair skating. A major concern resulted from the fact that it was a one-event competition. Compulsory figures were not required for pair skaters, and there was no technical or short program. Success rested totally on the performance of the free skating. Owing to a few controversial decisions in the 1950s and the discipline's increasing technical complexities, support was growing for a second program. As an experiment, at the European Championships, but not the World Championships in 1962 and 1963, programs were skated twice, and scores were combined to obtain the final result. Analysis of those results showed that placements did not change significantly from one performance to the next but that scores were characteristically lower for the second skating. That format was promptly rejected.[24] Adopted instead was a two-and-a-half-minute technical program, later called a short program, which received a third of the total score. Implemented at the European and World Championships in 1964 and at the Olympic Games in 1968, the short program required one element from each of six groups, including lifts, solo jumps, pair spins, solo spins, death spirals, and step sequences. Surprisingly, the value of the short program was reduced to one-fourth at the 1967 Congress, a decision soon undone with a return to one-third, as it is today.

Ice dancing in the 1960s expanded with the addition of three new compulsory dances, the first additions since the war. Three more dances were added in 1975, and three others later.[25] The first in a series of significant changes for ice dancing occurred in 1967. Previously, ice dancers skated four compulsory dances that counted 60 percent and a free dance counting 40 percent. In the initial change, one of the compulsory dances was replaced by an "original set pattern dance," later called the "original dance," with the rhythm and tempo left to the discretion of the couple. Its value equaled that of the compulsory dance it replaced. Amendments adopted at the next two congresses established specified rhythms and tempos for the original dance and increased its value to 20 percent. The three compulsory dances were combined for 30 percent, and the free dance was raised to 50 percent. Another twenty years passed before the number of compulsory dances skated was further reduced to allow a higher value for the original dance. There is now pressure to eliminate compulsory dances completely.

Junior figure skating championships at the international level did not exist in the 1960s, although some national associations have held competitions for junior-level skaters since the 1920s. In 1969 the ISU clarified junior standing by a rule change that established a maximum age of sixteen for singles skaters and eighteen for pair skaters and ice dancers. A former rule defining a junior skater as one who had not won an international senior competition and had not competed in an ISU championship or the Olympic Games was retained with an added restriction that the skater(s) had not medaled in an international senior championship. Another limiting rule dating from 1955 requiring competitors to be at least twelve years of age was also retained.

With the great popularity of winter sports today, especially figure skating, it seems surprising that for a time there was concern over possible discontinuance of Winter Olympic sports. It was an acknowledged fact that Avery Brundage of the United States, president of the IOC from 1952 through 1972, had little interest in the Winter Games.[26] His strongest dislike was Alpine skiing, which he threatened to have discontinued. Following vehement objections, he broadened his threat to cover other winter sports. In reaction, various sports federations formed the Association of the International Winter Sports Federations to be a voice for winter sports. Fortunately, the crisis passed with Brundage's retirement in 1972.

Anniversaries of organizations often provide impetus for histories of those organizations, and two valuable figure skating books were published for the double anniversary in 1967. The first, *100 Jahre Wiener Eislauf-Verein* (A Hundred Years of the Vienna Skating Club), provides a detailed survey covering figure skating, ice hockey, and speed skating. It features many early pictures and excellent appendices, including lists of national medal winners in the various sports and disciplines. The other, *Seventy-five Years of European and World's Championships in Figure Skating,* includes complete, judge-by-judge results of those two ISU championships.

TWELVE

The Dynamic Seventies

NO decade in the history of figure skating includes a longer list of World champions than the 1970s. Fifteen skaters, seven men and eight ladies, took those honors, with only two from each discipline repeating. Pair skating, however, was dominated almost completely by one skater, the incomparable Irina Rodnina, who with two partners won ten World Championships and three Olympic gold medals. In ice dancing, three couples won World titles, and one became the discipline's first Olympic gold medalists as well.

A COLLAGE OF TALENTED MEN

Ondrej Nepela (1951–89) of Czechoslovakia was twice runner-up to Tim Wood before becoming the World champion in 1971. Strong in compulsory figures as well as free skating, he first appeared on the international scene in 1964, just a week past his thirteenth birthday. His ten-year international career displayed consistency. At the European Championships, bronze medals for three years, 1966 through 1968, were followed by gold medals for five years, 1969 through 1973. At the World Championships, silver medals for two years, 1969 and 1970, were followed by gold medals for three years, 1971 through 1973. His second Olympic bid in 1972 resulted in a gold medal.

Men from the German Democratic Republic first competed at the European Championships in 1959 and at the World Championships in 1962, but nearly a decade passed before Günter Zöller (b. 1948) won their first medals, bronze at both competitions, in 1970. His teammate, beginning in 1968, was the much younger Jan Hoffmann (b. 1955), who over a long career won four European and two World titles. Hoffman's record from 1973, the year of his first bronze medals, through 1980, the year of his retirement, includes a combined total of five bronze, three silver, and six gold medals. He was the World champion twice. Since retirement Hoffmann has served the sport as an ISU championship referee.

Soviet men, like those from the German Democratic Republic, first won World medals in the 1970s; collectively, Sergei Chetverukhin (b. 1946), Sergei Volkov (b. 1949), and Vladimir Kovalev (b. 1953) claimed ten of them. Chetverukhin, the first Soviet to medal at the World Championships, won bronze in 1971. He never climbed to the top of the medal stand, but between 1971 and 1973 he collected six silver medals behind the unbeatable Nepela.

Volkov, who followed Chetverukhin, excelled in compulsory figures, which often raised him in the rankings. A silver medal at the European Championships in 1974 came in spite of his placing fifth in the short program and sixth in the free skating. He placed first in compulsory figures. The scenario was similar at his final competition, the 1976 Olympics. But at two previous World Championships he offered more balanced skating; a silver medal in 1974 preceded a gold medal in 1975, when he became the Soviet Union's first World champion.

Kovalev, the third member of the Soviet triumvirate, began and ended his international career in Olympic years. He collected a bronze medal at the World Championships in 1972 but did not compete the following year. His return in 1974 marked the beginning of seven years of strong skating in which he compiled a record of two bronze, seven silver, and three gold medals.

Only one American medaled at the World Championships after Tim Wood's last title in 1970. Charles Tickner (b. 1953) was the national champion for four years (1977–80), but parallel appearances at the World Championships were less consistent. He placed fifth in 1977, became the World champion in 1978, regressed to fourth in 1979, and claimed the bronze medal in 1980. His one Olympic effort resulted in a bronze medal. Turning professional, Tickner skated for several years with Ice Capades.

Robin Cousins (b. 1957), a dashing British skater four years younger than Tickner, was competitively a contemporary. Both ended their careers in 1980. At the national level, Cousins was the novice champion in 1969, junior champion in 1972, and senior champion for four years, beginning in 1976. At the international level, he accumulated four bronze and two silver medals along with one gold at the European and World Championships. Many expected him to win the triple crown in 1980 after winning the European title and the Olympic gold medal, but the World title, as in the past, alluded him. A poor showing in compulsory figures placed him fifth for that part of the competition, a deficit he could not overcome in spite of inspired free skating.

The Lake Placid Olympics provided not an end but rather a brilliant beginning for Cousins. Professional opportunities available to elite skaters in the 1980s allowed Cousins, whose flair and talent is unquestioned, to undertake and enjoy an outstanding career. In addition to touring with Holiday on Ice in Europe, he created his own shows, did guest appearances with Ice Capades, costarred with Peggy Fleming and Dorothy Hamill in made-for-televison films, and competed in professional competitions.

TWO CONSUMMATE ARTISTS: TOLLER CRANSTON AND JOHN CURRY

The Protopopovs created a new artistry in pair skating, one firmly rooted in classical ballet, and it represented a new wave that crossed disciplines. Peggy Fleming, too, endeared herself to the world with her flowing, more balletic style. Two men continued and expanded that movement in the mid-1970s. Toller Cranston and John Curry, although totally opposite in style and temperament, proved to be consummate artists who carried the artistry of their predecessors to new zeniths.

Toller Cranston (b. 1949) was an enigma from the beginning, perhaps the most avant-garde skater in the history of the sport and one whom judges did not always understand or appreciate. Thus, he is remembered not for his competitive record, which would not justify his inclusion in this history, but rather for what he brought to the sport, innovations that influenced the next generation of skaters or at least caused them to contemplate what artistry in skating should be. Cranston was just short of his twenty-first birthday when in 1971 he won the first of six consecutive Canadian titles. He placed second that year at the last holding of the North American Championships and twice won the succeeding Skate Canada. Although he competed at the World Championships from 1970 through 1976, his only medal was bronze in 1974. His one Olympic bid in 1976 also resulted in a bronze medal. Cranston, like Robin Cousins, was weak in compulsory figures. For his bronze medal at the World Championships, he placed first in both the short program and the free skating but eighth in figures. For his Olympic medal, he placed first in the short program, second in the free skating, and seventh in figures.

Cranston's enigma expressed itself in his free skating. He was never a conventional skater but rather a bold modernist who employed angular body movements in a dramatic style while also incorporating a wide variety of music, traditional as well as contemporary. His avant-garde interpretation of *Pagliacci,* which debuted as an exhibition number following the World Championships in Munich, was one of his greatest achievements.

Toller Cranston, a bold modernist, expressed the drama in his programs through innovative choreography. (World Figure Skating Museum and Hall of Fame)

The verismo associated with Leoncavallo's opera suited perfectly Cranston's style as he carried interpretive figure skating to a new level, but as is often the case in artistic endeavors, the avant-garde must wait for wide acceptance.

Cranston is also a successful painter. His study at the Ecole des Beaux Arts in Montreal provided an artistic perspective that carried across to his skating. Like Jackson Haines more than a century earlier, he concerned himself with body position while making new and innovative statements. Cranston's influence on the sport following his competitive career has been primarily through his work as a choreographer. Accolades continue for this skater who expanded the envelope of artistry and left the sport better because he was in it.

John Curry (1949–94) also demonstrated artistry and emotion that could be expressed through body position, not in a modern sense like Cranston but rather in the tradition of classical ballet. From childhood, Curry wanted to study ballet but was denied that opportunity by his father, who viewed skating as a sport and therefore more acceptable for a boy. Although lessons began at age seven, Curry underwent a long period of development. He was twenty-one when he won the British Championship, twenty-five when he won an international medal, and twenty-seven when he won the triple crown, European, World, and Olympic titles.

Curry suffered early in his career from poor jumping technique and weak compulsory figures. Recognizing that he had little chance of progressing without strong jumps and solid figures, and after a poor showing at the World Championships in 1974, he sought out two masters, Gustave Lussi at Lake Placid for jumping and Carlo Fassi at Colorado Springs for figures. Under their tutelage he improved dramatically, medaling at every competition in 1975 and winning every competition in 1976. Coupled with twenty years of artistic development, his then fine-honed technique provided a balance that created one of the greatest artists in the history of the sport. Following Curry's Olympic triumph in Innsbruck, Dick Button called him "the finest classicist I have ever seen."[1]

Turning professional, Curry formed small skating companies where emphasis was placed on carefully choreographed and complex ensemble work skated to classical music and performed to exacting standards. He also established a short-lived school for advanced ice skaters where he fostered his own dance-oriented precepts. Curry was inducted into the World Figure Skating Hall of Fame in 1991.

John Curry, skating's great classicist, was strongly influenced by classical ballet. (World Figure Skating Museum and Hall of Fame)

LADIES' AND COMPULSORY FIGURES

The reign of the remarkable triumvirate of lady champions in the 1960s ended with Gabriele Seyfert's retirement in 1970. Over the next decade seven others claimed World titles. The first became, unwittingly, a major catalyst for the eventual elimination of compulsory figures. Beatrix "Trixi" Schuba (b. 1951) of Austria cannot be given full credit for causing their elimination because other skaters, especially Jeannette Altwegg of Great Britain, benefited from a long-standing scoring system that favored compulsory figures. By the time Schuba was competing, the number of figures skated and their value had been reduced, and there was movement toward further reducing their portion of the total score. But it was Schuba's "unbalanced skating" that caused "a revolution to take place at the 1971 Congress."[2]

Schuba, who is remembered as the last great practitioner of compulsory figures, was not a strong free skater. Competing against her were two unusually popular and outstanding free skaters, a Canadian, Karen Magnussen, and an American, Janet Lynn, neither of whom were particularly strong in compulsory figures. Audiences, especially television audiences, did not see the compulsory figure portion of competitions and did not understand either its importance or skating's scoring system. That resulted in a tendency to view Schuba's skating negatively and unfairly.

Schuba received numerous accolades for her figures from skating afficionados who appreciated and understood their difficulty. Howard Bass called her "the most brilliant exponent of figures the world has seen."[3] Dick Button, a strong proponent for the elimination of figures, praised her skill, noting that "in Trixi's blades there was a drawing-board precision that has never been matched."[4]

Schuba always enjoyed commanding leads following the figure portions of competitions, and even though her free skating was not outstanding it was competent and consistent. She could not be defeated under a scoring system that gave preference to figures. Results from 1969 through her retirement in 1972 always show her first in figures but never higher than fifth in free skating. That sometimes resulted in derision from audiences. A crowd in Toronto reportedly "booed mercilessly" as she skated on tour following her final World title, which she won in Calgary.[5] Janet Lynn, who suffered from skating's scoring system, noted graciously and correctly that "the truth is that some very cruel things have been said about Trixi. She's a very nice, quiet person, and all she's done is play by the rules."[6] Schuba had the good fortune to skate at a time when the rules worked in her favor. Every competition was won fairly.

Schuba's scores at her first international competitions in 1967 fail to suggest results just a year later and for the remainder of her career. At the European Championships, just three of nine judges placed her higher in the compulsory figures than in the free skating, and the results were similar at the World Championships. Dramatic changes occurred a year later as her figures matured but not her free skating. The sixteen-year-old Austrian national champion won the bronze medal at the European Championships. Beginning in 1969, she medaled in every competition, and during her last competitive years, 1971 and 1972, all were gold.

That Schuba was a competent if not an outstanding free skater was a fact sometimes missed in the controversy over the importance of compulsory figures but one demonstrated conclusively by her successful six-year professional career. She skated first in the United States with the Ice Follies and then in Europe with Holiday on Ice.

As a competitor, Schuba had nerves of steel. It has been reported that her pulse rate just prior to one competition was found to be a normal sixty. That same confidence and poise followed her into the business world in Vienna, where she now lives and works.

Schuba ended her competitive career in 1972, winning Olympic gold and a second World title. The other medalists were the two talented North Americans, Karen Magnussen and Janet Lynn. At both competitions Magnussen placed ahead of Lynn in the compulsory figures, and Lynn placed ahead of Magnussen in the free skating, resulting in silver medals for Magnussen and bronze medals for Lynn. In nine head-to-head battles Magnussen defeated Lynn at all except the North American Championships in 1969, and that result remains controversial to Canadians. Audiences could not understand why the results were consistently Schuba, Magnussen, and Lynn when what they saw was actually the reverse, Lynn, Magnussen, and Schuba. Thus, change was not only in the air but also necessary. Public perception was causing questions regarding the validity of judging in figure skating even though irregularities did not exist.

ABC's *Wide World of Sports* had begun covering international figure skating events a decade earlier. The sport's popularity was increasing as television audiences discovered the artistry and athleticism of a sport that could appeal to men and women alike, but they were viewing only the free skating, not the compulsory figures. Thus, a credibility issue existed when the ISU Congress met in 1971. An ad hoc committee recommended reduction in the number of compulsory figures skated, reduction in their value from 50 to 40 percent, addition of a short or technical program of six required elements worth 20 percent, and reduction in the value of free skating from 50 to 40 percent. The recommendations were adopted and took affect in 1973. A further adjustment was made in 1977, specifically a reduction in the number of figures from which those to be skated were selected. The number actually skated remained at three, but the number prepared for competition was reduced to six.

Not all officials, coaches, and skaters supported either the devaluation or the eventual elimination of compulsory figures. Many felt that the technique inherent in their execution and the discipline required to learn them was necessary for the development of quality free skating. Nearly another twenty years passed before their total elimination. Although increasing emphasis on athleticism and diminishing emphasis on compulsory figures would eventually result in some loss of artistry, during the period from the mid-1960s to the mid-1970s some of the greatest artists in the history of the sport—the Protopopovs, Peggy Fleming, and John Curry—competed. They are remembered not for exceptional athleticism but rather for the classic beauty of their performances.

Karen Magnussen (b. 1952), Canada's junior champion in 1965 and senior champion in 1968, competed at the World Championships in 1967 and 1968 but missed most of the next season owing to stress fractures in her legs. Upon returning to competition in 1970 she regained and held the Canadian title for four years. From fourth at the World Championships that year she proceeded through medals of each color on her road to becoming the World champion in 1973. Magnussen's title resulted partially from a disastrous performance by Janet Lynn in the newly required short program. Lynn fell on two required elements, the combination jump and the double Axel Paulsen jump. Having placed second to Magnussen in the compulsory figures, it would have taken a near-perfect free skate coupled with an uncharacteristically poor performance by Magnussen for Lynn to have won. Magnussen presented a beautifully skated program set to music from Rachmaninoff's Second Symphony and Third Piano Concerto that earned all 5.8s and 5.9s for technical merit and artistic impression. Although Lynn's marks were even higher, Magnussen could not be overtaken. Retiring after the World Championships, she skated for several years with Ice Capades. Her unique signature move was a beautiful spiral, called the Magnussen spiral, that featured a sharp change of direction while in the spiral position.

Janet Lynn (b. 1953), one of America's most beloved skaters, was born Janet Nowicki. Her only coach, Slavka Kohout, recognizing the youngster's immense talent and sensing her potential for an international career, suggested for political reasons as well as ease in pronunciation that in skating she use her mother's maiden name, Lynn. She became the U.S. junior champion at age thirteen and senior champion three years later. Unbeatable at the national level, she joined an elite group of skaters, Gretchen Merrill, Tenley Albright and Peggy Fleming, who in the post–World War II era had won five or more consecutive titles.[7] Lynn competed at seven World Championships. For the final three she placed fourth, third, and second, always behind Magnussen. Lynn, a year younger than Magnussen, paralleled her Canadian rival one year later as a junior national champion, senior national champion, and World competitor, but they both turned professional in 1973. One cannot resist speculating about whether Lynn might have become a World champion had she continued for one additional year.

Lynn's weakness was compulsory figures. Her work ethic led to dedicated practice of them, but they provided no joy for her. In 1971, at her coach's suggestion, she worked with Pierre Brunet specifically on figures. There was improvement, but they remained well-learned mechanical exercises not skated at an inspired level. Her effervescent style in free skating, however, was neither learned nor fortuitous. It displayed a natural sincerity that endeared her to skating audiences. Although the scoring system worked against Lynn during most of her competitive career, that was not the case in her final attempt at a World title. The short program was introduced for the first time, Schuba had retired, and only Magnussen stood in the way of her becoming a World champion. Following a career-best showing in compulsory figures, she stood second behind Magnussen at that point in the competition. Many believed she would win with characteristically strong free skating, but disaster struck in the short program. Lynn placed twelfth after

Janet Lynn's natural sincerity and effervescent style endeared her to skating fans everywhere. (World Figure Skating Museum and Hall of Fame)

falls on two required jumps. Showing great inner spirit and the grace that was always as-sociated with her, Lynn reappeared the next day and presented one of her most inspired free skates. It generated two perfect 6.0s but could not overcome the lead held by Mag-nussen.

Lynn ended her amateur career never having won a World championship or an Olympic gold medal, but she established an all-time record for the most perfect scores awarded for artistic impression by a singles' skater in World and Olympic competition.[8] It is a record that shows consistency. During her final three competitive years there were two 6.0s at each of the World Championships and one at the Olympic Games.

Lynn's popularity was confirmed upon turning professional. She was granted a con-tract with the Ice Follies that reportedly made her the highest-paid female athlete in the World. After two seasons of touring she married and began a family, but five years later she returned for three additional seasons. Lynn was inducted into the World Figure Skat-ing Hall of Fame in 2001.

TARGETING THE OLYMPICS

Amateur skating today moves characteristically in four-year cycles ending in Olympic years. It may seem strange that Magnussen and Lynn chose to retire not after an Olym-pic season but a year later, but both were strong candidates for the World title in 1973. During the remainder of the Olympic cycle three talented skaters from as many countries became lady World champions.

Christine Errath (b. 1956) of the German Democratic Republic was one of those vivacious youngsters who has enlivened ladies' figure skating throughout much of its history. Having just turned twelve, she skated at the European Championships in 1970 and placed eighteenth. Three years later she won the European title not yet having won a national title. Sonja Morgenstern, a fine skater and the current national champion, had withdrawn from the European Championships because of an injury. Errath seized the opportunity. In 1974 she added the World title to her credits. Close on her heels was an American, Dorothy Hamill, who won the free skating but placed fifth in the compulsory figures. Errath was a fearless jumper, leading one commentator to call her a "technician rather than an artist" and adding that "she has not the same instinctive grace and musical feelings of the U. S. champion."[9] She was unable to retain the World title, but during four years of European, World, and Olympic competition she amassed four bronze, one silver, and four gold medals.

Dianne de Leeuw (b. 1955), the daughter of Dutch nationals, was born in Orange County, California, and enjoyed the citizenship of two countries.[10] She chose to skate for the Netherlands, which provided the opportunity to compete at the European Champi-onships. Her international career paralleled that of Errath, starting two years later. Both

Dorothy Hamill, one of America's most popular skaters, was a teen idol. Many young women copied the distinctive hairstyle that soon bore her name. (World Figure Skating Museum and Hall of Fame)

skaters showed three years of steady improvement without winning medals, after which they won medals at every competition. De Leeuw collected two bronze, three silver, and two gold medals, winning the World title in 1975 and the European title In 1976. Following retirement from competitive skating she toured with Holiday on Ice and the Ice Follies.

Dorothy Hamill (b. 1956) was just thirteen and still a junior skater when she introduced the layover camel sit spin that bears her name, the "Hamill camel." In 1974 she became the U.S. national champion and repeated twice. Internationally, she engaged in a three-year battle with Errath and de Leeuw to become the World champion. Success was achieved in 1976, two weeks after winning her Olympic gold medal.

Hamill has enjoyed a remarkably long career as a professional. She has retained the attractive, youthful persona that so thrilled audiences throughout her amateur career. Her pixieish, girl-next-door personality that appealed to audiences young and old and caused teen-aged girls around the world to copy her distinctive wedge-cut hairstyle resulted in an extremely lucrative two-year contract with Ice Capades that was extended as her popularity continued to soar. Commercial endorsements surpassed those of other skaters, and there were television specials. Twenty-six years after her Olympic gold medal, Hamill was still exciting audiences, including appearances on Tom Collins's Champions on Ice tours. She was elected to the World Figure Skating Hall of Fame in 2000.

ANETT PÖTZSCH AND LINDA FRATIANNE

The Olympic cycle leading to Lake Placid in 1980 provides the story of yet another rivalry between two competitiors who alternated World titles: Linda Fratianne of the United States in odd-numbered years and Anett Pötzsch of the German Democratic Republic in even-numbered ones. They were almost exactly the same age, born just a month apart, but Pötzsch benefited initially from three years of experience in international competition before Fratianne appeared on the scene, a result of the fact that the American pool of lady competitors was much deeper. At their first meeting, the World Championships in 1976, placements were extremely close, fourth and fifth. Pötzsch scored slightly higher in the compulsory figures. Fratianne edged ahead in the free skating.

Anett Pötzsch (b. 1960) skated in every European, World and Olympic competition for eight years, from 1973 to 1980. At age twelve she placed eighth at the European Championships, a remarkably strong finish in which she was fourth in the free skating. Three weeks later she placed fourteenth at the World Championships. It was the first time a short program was required, and Pötzsch showed her mettle by placing eighth in that part.[11] At fourteen she won the bronze medal at the European Championships. At fifteen she advanced to silver and continued the season with fourth-place finishes at the Olympic Games and the World Championships. During her last four years of competitive skating, from 1977 to 1980, she collected two silver and seven gold medals in as many competitions. The capstone of her career was winning the triple crown: European, World, and Olympic titles. Pötzsch was a master of compulsory figures and also a solid free skater. The placements from 1977 through 1980 in World and Olympic competition are revealing. She consistently placed first in compulsory figures. Her rival, Linda Fratianne, did likewise in the combined free skating (short program and long program).

Linda Fratianne (b. 1960), the World champion following Dorothy Hamill in 1977, alternated titles with Pötzsch. Fratianne, first a roller skater, was nearly ten when she received her first pair of ice skates. In her first year as a senior, 1975, she placed seventh at the U.S. Championships. A year later she was the silver medalist behind Dorothy Hamill, actually winning the free skating. Following Hamill's retirement, Fratianne became the national champion, a title she retained throughout her amateur career. Thus, four of America's most gifted skaters, Fleming, Lynn, Hamill, and Fratianne, collectively held the national title for seventeen years. By comparison, eleven others were to hold it during the next seventeen years, with only four of them repeating.

Fratianne's surprising silver medal performance at the National Championships in 1976 earned her a berth on the World and Olympic teams, where she placed fifth and eighth. During the new Olympic cycle from 1977 to 1980 her World and Olympic efforts resulted in one bronze, two silver, and two gold medals. Fratianne followed three of the most artistic skaters the United States has ever produced. She continued in that tradition but is remembered primarily for energetic and exciting programs featuring triple jumps not included in the programs of her predecessors. Fratianne was coached throughout her amateur career by Frank Carroll and was the first of his students to become a World champion. Her professional career included nearly ten years with Disney on Ice. Marriage and motherhood followed, although she has since made occasional guest appearances and skated in a few short tours.

IRINA RODNINA AND HER PARTNERS

The roster of singles skaters, men and women, presented an abundance of talent and fifteen different World Champions during the 1970s, but the opposite occurred in pair skating. For a decade, from 1969 to 1978, one skater, Irina Rodnina, with two partners won every title. Not competing in 1979, owing to pregnancy, she reappeared for one final season, winning an eleventh European title and a third Olympic gold medal. No skater in the history of the sport, in any discipline, other than Sonja Henie equals her record.

Soviet dominance of pair skating began in 1964 when the Protopopovs upset Marika Kilius and Hans Jürgen Bäumler at the Innsbruck Games. Kilius and Bäumler won their second World title two weeks later, but the wave of the future had arrived. Kilius and Bäumler retired, and for the next fourteen years the Protopopovs and their successors, Rodnina and her two partners, won every European, World, and Olympic title. Continuing to the present, only seven non-Soviet or Russian pairs have become World champi-ons, and none have won Olympic gold.[12]

The incomparable balletic style of the Protopopovs transformed pair skating into an art form of classic beauty but did not advance significantly the athletic aspects of the discipline. In retrospect, it is not surprising that a younger pair with greater speed, more daring lifts, and precisionlike unison would unseat the older champions. The changing of the guard came in 1969, but the previous season provided a stunning climax to the Protopopovs' stellar career as they captured the triple crown, European, Olympic, and World titles. In 1969 Tamara Moskvina and Alexei Mishin succeeded in defeating the six-time champions at the Soviet National Championships. Claiming the bronze medals were Rodnina and Ulanov. Soviet pairs then swept the medals at the European Champi-onships, with Rodnina and Ulanov winning their first title. Moskvina and Mishkin were second, and the Protopopovs third. At the World Championships, Rodnina and Ulanov won again, with the other Soviet pairs trading positions and retiring. The mature sophis-tication of the Protopopovs had given way to the youthful energy of Rodnina and Ulanov. A new era had dawned for pair skating, but it remained the domain of the Soviets.

Irina Rodnina (b. 1949) is another of several Olympic gold medalists, Tenley Albright and Scott Hamilton among them, who benefited medically from skating. At less than two years of age Rodnina contracted tuberculosis. Doctors prescribed fresh air, so her parents took her on brisk walks. A pair of skates was purchased to make the walks more interesting, and soon the youngster was skating at a local amusement park. Lessons followed, and by her early teens she was competing at the junior level. She was sixteen when Stanislav Zhuk took her under his tutelage and paired her with Alexei Ulanov (b. 1947), who was ten inches taller and significantly heavier than Rodnina. With emphasis on difficult lifts, especially one-arm lifts, the weight differential provided a tremendous advantage. To the high-spirited Rodnina, Ulanov's greater size created a challenge that she expressed in words that reflect her credo: "He jumps high, and I try to outjump him; he runs fast and I try to outrun him. I don't like being second to anybody."[13]

Ulanov was more experienced than Rodnina, having skated previously with his sis-ter, but with characteristic lack of concern Rodnina dismissed that, too, in her typically aggressive way: "We joined hands and off we went."[14] Less than two years later, 1968, they appeared at the European Championships in Västerås, Sweden, and placed fifth, but they were not included on the World or Olympic teams. A year later, 1969, at both the European and World Championships they stood atop the medal stand, a position they would retain through the remainder of their career together. Commenting philo-sophically on Rodnina and Ulanov's success, their coach, Stanislav Zhuk, said, "Figure skaters representing a country can win an international title only after someone from their own country earns prestige for their national school. For Irina and Alexei, the way to the top had been paved by the Protopopovs."[15]

The Rodnina and Ulanov partnership continued for three more years with only one minor blemish on an otherwise-perfect record. Liudmila Smirnova and Andrei Suraikin, their compatriots, led after the short program at the World Championships in 1971, but that was the last time in Rodnina's extended career with either partner that she failed to win both parts of a competition. Rodnina and Ulanov ended their career with European and World titles for four consecutive years in addition to Olympic gold medals.

The 1972 World Championships marked the end of their career together because Ulanov had fallen in love with Liudmila Smirnova of the other leading Soviet pair. He left Rodnina to marry and partner with their former rival. Smirnova's partner, Suraikin, retired, but the indomitable Rodnina sought a new partner, and the best years of her career were yet to come. Alexandr Zaitsev (b. 1952) was selected from many partners considered. He was thirty months younger than Rodnina and lacked international experience, but the always perceptive Zhuk, who had paired Rodnina with Ulanov, again guided her wisely. The most successful partnership in the history of pair skating was created. Eventually, the union included marriage. Success was evident in their first season together. Winning the Soviet national title, Rodnina and Zaitsev traveled to Cologne for the 1973 European Championships, where they won by a unanimous decision. Smirnova and Ulanov placed second. At the World Championships in Bratislava, Slovakia, three weeks later, they again won decisively, with Sminova and Ulanov placing second.

One of the most unusual technical problems in the history of competitive figure skating occurred in Bratislava. Less than half way through Rodnina and Zaitsev's free skate, the music stopped owing to an electrical failure. They could have stopped and either continued from the point of interruption or reskated the entire program. Although the referee signaled for them to stop, they completed the program without music. There was no rule at the time requiring competitors to skate to music, so the referee ruled that they could be judged on the entire performance. Ultimately, that led to an ISU rule requiring skaters to stop at a referee's signal, but in 1973 Rodnina and Zaitsev earned seven 5.9s and two 5.8s for artistic impression without music.

Over the next five years, from 1974 to 1978, Rodnina and Zaitsev were never seriously challenged as they amassed gold medals at every European and World competition and at the Innsbruck Olympic Games. Owing to the birth of their son in February, they skipped the 1979 season but returned in the Olympic year for one last competitive season. They won the European Championships with characteristic first-place marks from all judges, and the results were the same at the Olympic Games in a performance that served as their swan song. Undoubtedly, they could have added a seventh World title to their already unmatched record had they competed.[16]

During her amateur career Rodnina and her partners transformed pair skating through expanded and inspired athleticism. They accumulated eleven European, ten World, and three Olympic titles. Perhaps nothing shows consistency more than the

Irina Rodnina and Alexandr Zaitsev, respected for their speed and flare, were unbeatable in seven World Championships and two Olympic Games. (World Figure Skating Museum and Hall of Fame)

range and number of 6.0s awarded. For seven consecutive years, from 1971 to 1977, there was at least one perfect score each year, and they were awarded for technical merit as well as for artistic impression in short programs as well as in free skating. Upon retirement Rodnina turned to coaching and through the 1980s worked with skaters in her homeland. In 1990 she moved to the United States and for more than a decade coached at the Ice Castle International Training Center in Lake Arrowhead, California. She has since returned to her native Russia. Rodnina became in 1981 the first of seven figure skaters to be awarded the Jacques Favart Trophy, and in 1989 she was elected to the World Figure Skating Hall of Fame.

THE OTHER MEDALISTS

During the reign of Rodnina and her partners, 1969 to 1980, six pairs, all from the Soviet Union and the German Democratic Republic, climbed to the second tier of the medal stand in World and Olympic competition. The first was Tamara Moskvina (b. 1941) and Alexei Mishin (b. 1941), who, in a short international career, received their only World medal behind the champions in 1969.

Liudmilla Smirnova (b. 1949), for five years a silver medalist behind Rodnina, is likewise a tale of two partners, one intertwined with Rodnina. Three years of international competition with Andrei Suraikin (b. 1948) produced a total of seven silver medals behind Rodnina and Ulanov. The World Championships in 1972 were traumatic for both Smirnova and Rodnina, being their final competitions with long-time partners. Smirnova married Rodnina's partner, Ulanov, and the couple competed as man and wife for two years, garnering three silver medals behind Rodnina and Zaitsev.

Romy Kermer (b. 1956) and Rolf Österreich (b. 1952), a talented couple from the German Democratic Republic, competed internationally for four years, beginning in 1973. During their final two years they collected five silver medals behind Rodnina and Zaitsev.

Irina Vorobieva (b. 1958) and Alexandr Vlasov (b. 1956), a Soviet pair coached by Tamara Moskvina, first appeared at the World Championships in 1974. Two years later they won bronze medals behind Kermer and Österreich and were fourth at the Olympic Games. Continuing for an additional year, 1977, and benefiting from the retirement of Kermer and Österreich, they climbed to the second tier of the medal stand. Vorobieva with a future partner, Igor Lisovski, would win the World title in 1981.

Manuela Mager (b. 1962) and Uwe Bewersdorff (b. 1958) from the German Democratic Republic first appeared internationally in 1977. She was just fourteen when they placed fourth and fifth at the European and World Championships. A year later they medaled at both competitions. They missed the 1979 season because of injury but returned in the Olympic year for one final season, winning bronze and silver medals at the Olympic Games and the World Championships.

Marina Cherkasova (b. 1964) and Sergei Shakhrai (b. 1958) of the Soviet Union made skating history at the European Championships in 1977 by performing the first quadruple twist lift, a feat made possible by the enormous differences in their height and weight. Criticism of their size differential eventually led to the adoption of an ISU rule requiring that pairs be penalized when there is a "serious imbalance" in physical appearance. But Cherkasova and Shakhrai won the bronze medals that year and continued competing through 1981, collecting a total of eight medals, two bronze, four silver, and two gold. Without Rodnina and Zaitsev present they won the World title in 1980.

For the Americans 1979 was a proud year; they produced their first World pair champions since the Kennedys in 1950. Tai Babilonia (b. 1960) and Randy Gardner (b. 1958) had not reached the second tier of the medal stand behind Rodnina and Zaitzev, but they were the reigning World bronze medalists. With Rodnina and Zaitsev awaiting the birth of their son and Mager and Bewersdorff sidelined because of injury, the stage was set for an American victory. Babilonia and Gardner did not disappoint.

The Olympic year saw the return of Rodnina and Zaitsev as well as Mager and Be-

As reigning World champions, Tai Babilonia and Randy Gardner in 1980 were America's hope for its first Olympic title in pairs but owing to an injury they had to withdraw. (World Figure Skating Museum and Hall of Fame)

wersdorff, setting the stage for an exciting head-to-head battle among three talented pairs. American fans waited with eager anticipation, hoping for their first Olympic gold medal in pairs, but to their disappointment the battle never occurred. Gardner sustained a groin injury two weeks before the competition and reinjured it during an Olympic practice session. It became so painful that medication in the form of a shot of Zylocaine was necessary. Falls on a couple of simple jumps after he entered the ice for the warm-up preceding the short program made it evident that competing was not possible. Rodnina and Zaitsev won gold medals; Cherkasova and Shakhrai, second behind Babilonia and Gardner in 1979, were second again; and Mager and Bewersdorf placed third.

ICE DANCING: AN OLYMPIC SPORT

The Soviets, cautiously but methodically entered World competition. They first sent three men and two pairs to Paris in 1958. No Soviets competed at Colorado Springs in 1959, but two pairs competed at Vancouver in 1960. The championships were canceled in 1961, but the Soviets made history at Prague in 1962, where the Protopopovs ascended to the second tier of the medal stand as the first Soviet World medalists.

Soviet ice dancers first appeared internationally when Nadezda Velle and Alexandr Treschov competed at the European Championships in 1965. A year later another Soviet pair, Liudmila Pakhomova and Victor Rizhkin, competed at both the European and World championships. In 1967 Rizhkin appeared with a new partner, Irina Grishkova, and in 1969 Pakhomova did likewise with Alexandr Gorshkov. Pakhomova and Gorshkov became the first great Soviet ice dancers. In their second year together, 1969, they won World medals, and five consecutive World titles followed. The first, in 1970, was exactly five years after the Protopopovs won the Soviet's first World pairs title and exactly five years before Sergei Volkov won their first World singles' title. Soviet skaters excelled first in pairs, then in dance, and finally in men's singles' skating. By 1975 their cumulative World titles included eleven in pairs, six in ice dancing, and one in men's singles. Their best placement in ladies' competitions at that time was tenth, and nearly another quarter century would pass before Maria Butyrskaya became the first Russian lady World champion.

The 1970s, in ice dancing as in pairs belonged to the Soviets. From 1970 through 1978 they won every World and Olympic title in both disciplines. In pairs it was a continuation of the Protopopovs' successes, but in ice dancing it required overtaking the British in the discipline they had dominated since its inception as a World championship sport.

Liudmilla Pakhomova (1946–86) and Alexandr Gorshkov (b. 1946) ultimately won six World titles, a record not duplicated in ice dancing. In nine years of competitive skating they missed only one competition, the result of a serious bout with pneumonia suffered by Gorshkov just before the 1975 World Championships. From 1970 through 1976 all medals except one were gold, which included the first Olympic ice dancing title.[17]

What the Protopopovs had done in pairs, Pakhomova and Gorshkov did in ice dancing. They excelled through innovative and imaginative programs that changed and improved the discipline. Their choreography reflected Russia's love of classical and national dance. World judges rewarded them with a total of twenty-nine perfect 6.0s, the second-highest number yet in the record books.[18] The tango romantica, their original set-pattern dance introduced in the 1974 season, was later adopted by the ISU as a compulsory dance.

Retiring from competitive skating after the Olympic season, Pakhomova was appointed head of the Department of Sports Choreographers at the Theater Arts Institute in Moscow, a position she held until her untimely death at the age of thirty-nine, a victim of leukemia. Gorshkov became a championship judge and referee and served the ISU for many years as a member, and since 1998 chair, of the ice dancing technical committee. Pakhomova and Gorshkov were honored with election to the World Figure Skating Hall of Fame in 1988.

Pakhomova and Gorshkov were not alone in representing the Soviet Union. From 1976 through 1982 Soviet ice dancers claimed multiple medals at every competition. Irina Moiseeva (b. 1955) and Andrei Minenkov (b. 1954) had previously placed no better than fourth when in 1975, with Pakhomova and Gorshkov sidelined, they came from behind to win the World title, overtaking two couples who had defeated them a month earlier at the European Championships. With the return of Pakhomova and Gorshkov in 1976 they were held to silver medals behind the long-time champions, but after Pakhomova and Gorshkov retired, Moiseeva and Minenkov again stood atop the medal stand as World champions. Ten years of European, World, and Olympic competition resulted in a total of seventeen medals, six bronze, seven silver, and four gold.

Natalia Linichuk (b. 1956) and Gennadi Karponosov (b. 1950) culminated seven years of World and Olympic competition in 1980 by claiming the Soviet Union's second Olympic gold medal in ice dancing. They entered the Olympic season as the reigning European and World champions and were favored to win the triple crown as Pakhomova and Gorshkov had done four years earlier, but after successfully defending their European title and winning Olympic gold they lost the World title to a talented Hungarian couple, Krisztina Regöczy and András Sallay. Linichuk and Karponosov's cumulative record includes six bronze, two silver, and five gold medals.

Regöczy (b. 1955) and Sallay (b. 1953) presented the strongest challenge to the Soviets. She was fourteen and he had just turned sixteen in 1970 when they first competed at the European Championships and placed thirteenth. Following the expected slow development of ice dancers, they improved steadily, winning their first medals, silver at the European Championships in 1977. For the next three years they medaled at every competition, but not until the World Championships in 1980 were they able to dethrone the Soviets. Regöczy and Sallay set the stage for the greatest ice dancers in the history of the discipline, Jayne Torvill and Christopher Dean, to carry ice dancing to new heights in the next Olympic cycle.

ISU CONCERNS OF THE SEVENTIES

The 1970s was a decade of expanded opportunities for the sport and its skaters. Most notable was the inclusion of ice dancing as an Olympic sport twenty-four years after its first offering as the fourth discipline in World competition. Equally significant was the implementation of the World Junior Figure Skating Championships. The union itself experienced limited growth. Luxembourg, the only new member, joined in 1971, and Spain reinstated its membership in 1972 after a sixteen-year absence, bringing to thirty-two the number of countries represented by national organizations or individual clubs.

As we have seen, the quality of judging improved through the 1960s, a result of the ISU's vigorous attack on glaring problems that had occurred in the 1950s, but in an apparent relapse, the suspension of judges reached an alarmingly high twenty-seven between 1970 and 1975, four times the number for the entire previous decade.[19] Renewed and aggressive action resulted. Emphasis was placed on education and the training of judges. Handbooks for singles' and pair skating were updated, and one for ice dancing was written. Seminars and tests for judges and officials were expanded. Reinstatement of inactive judges now required the passing of recertification examinations, and training films were developed. As a result, and for a second time, a significant reduction in the number of suspensions followed. There were only eight during the next decade.

Cold war politics having nothing to do with athletes or their performances continued to plague the sport in the 1970s. The ISU, with membership from both sides of the Iron Curtain, showed remarkable leadership and dealt nonprejudicially with all issues that arose throughout this particularly contentious period. In 1970 the IOC expelled the South African Olympic Association because of the apartheid practiced in that country. A proposal by the Soviet member of the ISU Council to expel the South African Ice Skating Association from the union was denied, however, and the denial was upheld on appeal to the 1971 Congress, but debate on the issue continued for the next eighteen years. Although the Soviet member continued to apply pressure for expulsion, the majority of ISU Council members felt strongly that a constitutional provision calling for noninterference in sport on political grounds prevented such action.[20]

There was also pressure from Eastern Bloc countries for the mandatory playing of national anthems and the raising of flags at all award ceremonies, but the decision to do so remained with local organizing committees. Not until 1984 was a somewhat nebulous constitutional amendment adopted that required the playing of national anthems and flag raising "whenever possible."[21]

WORLD JUNIOR CHAMPIONSHIPS

Junior championships had been held for generations in some countries when the ISU at its 1975 Congress adopted legislation establishing the ISU Junior Figure Skating Championships on a two-year trial basis with the proviso that if successful they would be permanently established as the World Junior Figure Skating Championships. Eligibility required that singles' skaters not be over age sixteen and pair and dance skaters not be over eighteen on July 1 preceding the event. Entrants could not have competed in European, World, or Olympic competitions and could not have won medals in any international senior competition. The age requirement has twice been raised. For singles skating it is now nineteen, and for pair skating and ice dancing it is nineteen for ladies and twenty-one for men.[22] The other prohibitions were removed in 1980, primarily at the instigation of television interests wanting eligible skaters to be able to participate at both the junior and senior levels.

Megève, France, which had previously sponsored an invitational competition for junior-level skaters, hosted the first ISU Junior Figure Skating Championships in 1976. Nineteen men, sixteen ladies, seven pairs, and eight ice dancing couples representing eighteen countries vied for the first medals. Skaters from seven countries returned home with them. There were three each for Great Britain and the United States; two for Canada; and one each for Australia, the Federal Republic of Germany, France, and Japan. Gold medalists in singles were Suzie Brasher and Mark Cockerell of the United States; in pairs, Sherri Baier and Robin Cowan of Canada; and in ice dancing, Kathryn Winter and Nicholas Slater of Great Britain.

Megève hosted the event again in 1977, but controversy arose through no fault of the organizing committee. South Africa entered competitors in the ladies' and pairs' events, leading to the withdrawal by the Warsaw Pact nations of all their skaters and a written protest filed by the Soviet member of the ISU. The result was a 20 percent reduction in participation. In a judicious compromise, the ISU voted once again against expulsion of South Africa from the Union, but recognizing the number of skaters who had been denied the opportunity of participating at Megève it placed against South African skaters a "temporary restriction of not taking part in ISU Championships."[23]

The quality of skating at both competitions was high, exceeding ISU expectations and justifying the elevation of junior-level skating to World status, beginning in 1978. It was appropriate that the first World Junior Figure Skating Championships were held in Megève. South African skaters could not compete, but overall participation increased by more than 50 percent from the previous year. The first World junior champions were Jill Sawyer of the United States, Dennis Coi of Canada, pair skaters Barbara Underhill and Paul Martini of Canada, and ice dancers Tatiana Durasova and Sergei Ponomarenko of the Soviet Union.

THIRTEEN

Skating Redirected:
Lake Placid to Albertville

MEDIA interest in figure skating has grown steadily since 1962, when ABC's *Wide World of Sports* began covering the World Championships, but the Olympic Games have provided the most popular televised skating events. By the Games at Lake Placid in 1980, a well-established pattern of aiming toward the quadrennial Olympics existed as media attention popularized the sport, especially Olympic competition. The sport has benefited from the public's demand for more televised events, amateur and professional. Skaters have benefited from increasingly lucrative ways to continue as professionals in the sport they had devoted many years to developing. And the public has benefited from the opportunity to watch its favorite skaters advance through the amateur ranks and develop as artists in the professional world.

Media attention has resulted in a redirected emphasis in competitive skating toward aspects of the sport that can be easily understood by the casual viewer, especially jumping, but it would be wrong to credit such change to the media alone. Since 1948, when Dick Button performed the first double Axel Paulsen jump, the envelope has continually expanded, but, sadly, when Vern Taylor of Canada, a second-tier skater who never won a World or Olympic medal of any color, performed the first triple Axel Paulsen jump at the

World Championships in 1978, the media demanded that the ISU declare whether the jump had been completed.[1]

The concern was not with whether it represented good skating or how well the jump was executed. It was simply a question of whether a new plateau had been reached. Ten years later, a similar scenario occurred when Kurt Browning, a more talented skater, successfully completed the first quadruple jump at the 1988 World Championships. But artistry in skating achieved through deep edges and perfectly centered, beautifully positioned spins is less easily recognized and appreciated by the casual viewing public and proportionally less important to the media. With multiple quadruple jumps now expected from men, the first quintuple jump may be next, and it will be celebrated by the media.

TWO MATINEE IDOLS: SCOTT HAMILTON AND KURT BROWNING

Increased visibility spurred unprecedented interest in figure skating. Television audiences wanted to see in person those competitors they had watched compete for World and Olympic medals. The result has been phenomenal. An ever-increasing number of ice shows and professional competitions have provided opportunities for former competitors to enjoy lucrative careers while continuing to excite audiences. Some have sustained unusual longevity. Two, Scott Hamilton and Kurt Browning, can be classified as matinee idols.

Hamilton (b. 1958), adopted as an infant by a university professor and his wife, was soon overcome by an unidentified disease that severely stunted his growth.[2] Unlike Tenley Albright and Irina Rodnina, skating was not employed as treatment for Hamilton's medical problem. It began when the small and sickly but always energetic youngster tagged along with his sister on an outing to a local ice rink in Bowling Green, Ohio, an experience that kindled his enthusiasm almost immediately. Soon the nine-year-old began lessons with Rita Lowery. Unexpected physical benefits resulted as his stamina improved and he began to grow. Seven years later he was declared completely cured.

Hamilton's tremendous talent developed slowly but consistently. He placed last in his first novice event at age fourteen and seventh in his first junior event at sixteen. A year later he became the U.S. junior champion. He placed ninth in his first senior event. A year later he won the bronze medal and a place on the World team. Through the Olympic year, 1980, his best results were bronze medals at two National Championships and fifth-place finishes that year at the Olympic Games and the World Championships. Although Robin Cousins, Jan Hoffmann, and Charles Tickner all retired, it is unlikely that anyone would have predicted Hamilton's success over the next four years. He was unbeatable, claiming four national and four World titles in addition to the Olympic gold medal. His greatest strength was free skating, but he also traced excellent compulsory figures. Mature and balanced skating assured the victories.

There is a mystique about Hamilton that is hard to define, one that results from his being an inwardly serious but outwardly fun-loving person. Standing just five feet three inches tall, a result of his childhood illness, he refused to let size be a hindrance. Concerned with the image of figure skating, particularly that of male figure skaters, Hamilton changed costume design from that in vogue in the early 1980s to a more masculine style, eliminating beads and other ornamentation. His athletic prowess and on-ice personality made him extremely popular within the skating community as well as with the public. He has served as a mentor to many young skaters.[3]

A natural showman, he loved audiences and revealed his enthusiasm when performing for them. Hamilton became the most popular professional male skater in the history of the sport. After two years with Ice Capades, he organized the highly successful Scott Hamilton American Tour, which became Stars on Ice, and performed with the company

Scott Hamilton could not be defeated in the early 1980s as he amassed four World titles and an Olympic gold medal. (World Figure Skating Museum and Hall of Fame)

until his retirement after the 2001 season. Off the ice he has become a popular television commentator and since 1992 has covered Olympic figure skating events for CBS. His accolades include receiving the Jacques Favart Trophy in 1987 and election to the World Figure Skating Hall of Fame in 1990.

After Hamilton's retirement from amateur competition in 1984, two North Americans, Brian Boitano and Brian Orser, dominated men's skating through the next Olympic cycle, but before examining that period we move ahead four years to meet the next matinee idol. Kurt Browning (b. 1966) was Canada's novice champion in 1983 and junior champion in 1985. His senior record includes three silver and four gold medals. Internationally, four World titles in the post-Calgary period were interrupted by a silver medal in 1992, a year in which he suffered a severe back injury that kept him out of the Canadian Nationals and had a negative affect on his Olympic bid at Albertville.

The Winter Olympics were moved ahead two years after the 1992 Games, influencing Browning's decision to remain eligible with the hope of winning a medal in 1994, but again a medal proved illusive. Although he placed just fifth overall, his free skate remains one of the most memorable in Olympic history. The program, choreographed by Sandra Bezic, was set to music from the film *Casablanca*. Dressed in a white dinner jacket, Browning portrayed Rick Blaine, as Humphry Bogart had done fifty-two years earlier. With that program Browning stretched the boundaries of interpretive free skating to a new plateau. Since retiring from competitive skating the ever-popular Browning has continued to please audiences with interpretive-type programs, a genre in which he excels. He has appeared in made-for-television films and toured with Stars on Ice. Browning, like Hamilton, was honored by the ISU with the Jacques Favert Trophy.

"THE BATTLE OF THE BRIANS"

Between the competitive eras of Hamilton and Browning one of the great rivalries in modern figure skating developed and climaxed at the Calgary Games. Fanned by the media, the Battle of the Brians actually had begun five years earlier. Canadian Brian Orser and American Brian Boitano first met at the World Championships in 1983, where the more experienced Orser in his third World effort won the bronze medal. Boitano placed seventh. Both skaters advanced one place in 1984. During the next Olympic cycle, 1985 to 1988, they alternately defeated each other at the World Championships, with Boitano winning titles in 1986 and 1988 and Orser in 1987. Media hype for the Calgary Games was augmented by the fact that Orser was not only the reigning World champion but also competing in his own country. The pressure to become the first Canadian man to win an Olympic gold medal was daunting.

Brian Orser (b. 1961) became the Canadian novice champion at age fifteen, junior champion at age seventeen, and senior champion at age nineteen. He held the senior title for eight consecutive years, 1981 through 1988, a record not duplicated in any discipline. He also represented Canada at the World Championships each of those years and accumulated six medals: one bronze, four silver, and one gold.[4] His free skating was always stronger than his compulsory figures. Never having placed above fourth in the compulsories, and at the suggestion of his coach, Doug Leigh, in 1986 he sought out James Grogan, Dick Button's rival in the early 1950s, who was well known for coaching figures. Success followed as Orser won the World title in 1987. His figure placement improved from fifth the year before to third that year, and he won both the short program and the free skating. As the reigning World champion, Orser entered the Olympic year favored to win gold at Calgary.

Brian Boitano (b. 1963), the U.S. junior champion in 1978, won the bronze medal at the World Junior Figure Skating Championships held for the first time that year, but as a senior he competed for five years at the National Championships before placing high enough to be named to a World team. His World and Olympic efforts in 1983 and 1984 produced no medals, but with the changing of the guard following the Olympic season the rivalry leading to Calgary began. Boitano assumed and retained for four years the national title vacated by Hamilton and twice won World titles.

Twenty thousand fans crowded into the Saddledome in Calgary the night of the men's long program, at that time the largest audience ever assembled for an Olympic skating event, and the fans were not disappointed. The Battle of the Brians proved to be one of the greatest head-to-head match-ups in figure skating history. A preview had occurred in the same venue four months earlier at Skate Canada when the two skaters debuted their Olympic long programs, both of which featured military motifs. Orser skated to music from Dmitri Shostakovich's ballet *Bolt,* and Boitano to music from the film *Napoleon.* The results at Skate Canada did not match those of four months later. Orser defeated Boitano decisively, winning all three parts of the competition. At the Olympic Games, Boitano placed second in figures, as he had at Skate Canada, but Orser slipped to third. Orser won the short program, with Boitano second. It was a virtual dead heat. The winner of the free skating would be the Olympic champion. Boitano skated first in the final group and presented one of the finest performances in the history of competitive figure skating. Two skaters later Orser also presented a fine performance, but there were minor flaws, primarily a slight turn-out on the landing of his triple flip jump. Boitano, by a five-to-four vote, won the Olympic title.

In his *Napoleon* program, Boitano introduced a variation of the triple Lutz jump that was to become his trademark and bear his name. The "Tano Lutz" is done with one arm extended vertically above the head during the rotation, significantly increasing the difficulty of the jump. His signature move, however, is a spectacular outside spread eagle. Boitano was honored with election to the World Figure Skating Hall of Fame in 1996.

Joining the professional ranks after Calgary, both Brians embarked on highly successful careers, including the film *Carmen on Ice,* major tours, and competitions. Boitano was one of several skaters who reinstated and competed at the Lillehammer Olympics in 1994. He placed sixth, after which he returned to an active professional career.

Third and fourth behind the Brians at Calgary were a former and a future World Champion. In fourth place was the 1985 champion, Alexandr Fadeev (b. 1964) of the Soviet Union. He first appeared at the World Junior Championships in 1979 and won the bronze medal; then, a year later, he won the title. As a senior, he competed for ten seasons, collecting a total of two bronze and four gold medals at the European Championships. At the World Championships, in addition to three bronze medals, he won the World title in 1985, where his most inspired performance came in the free skating. A clean program featuring outstanding footwork and seven triple jumps, including a beautifully executed triple Lutz–triple toe loop combination, resulted in first-place votes from all nine judges. Silver and bronze medalists behind him with strong but not perfect programs were Orser and Boitano. Fadeev never defeated either of them again, but at that competition he won all three parts and was the best in the world.

The bronze medalist at Calgary was Viktor Petrenko (b. 1969) of Ukraine. He had been the World junior champion four years earlier. As a senior, his first medals, two bronze, were won at the Olympic Games and the World Championships in 1988. A groin injury sustained the following season resulted in a sixth-place finish at the World Championships, but for the next three years all medals were silver or gold. Hopes of capping his amateur career with the triple crown in 1992 disappeared early. Petr Barna of Czechoslovakia unexpectedly defeated him at the European Championships, but at the Olympic Games and the World Championships the gold medals belonged to Petrenko. Always a showman, Petrenko entered the world of professional skating, where he has presented many innovative programs. Like Boitano, Petrenko reinstated for the Lillehammer Olympics. He placed fourth, after which he, too, returned to his professional career.

THE BIELLMANN SPIN, THE ZAYAK RULE, AND SUMNER'S ARTISTRY

Denise Biellmann (b. 1962) is one of only two Swiss skaters to become a World champion, Hans Gerschwiler being the other.[5] Her relatively brief international career resulted in just three medals, bronze at the European Championships in 1979 and gold at the European and World Championships in 1981, but she had an unusually long professional career. Biellmann's nemesis as a competitor, more than almost any other World champion, was compulsory figures. She placed fourth in the compulsories at the European and World Championships in 1981, a significant improvement over previous years, and that allowed her to win with outstanding free skating. Previously, her best placement in figures had been eighth at the European Championships in 1979, the year of her bronze medal. Biellmann's one Olympic bid in 1980 began with twelfth place in the compulsory figures, but she placed second in the short program and first in the free skating for a final placement of fourth.

Biellmann's coach Otto Hügin, a disciple of Jacques Gerschwiler, had committed his teacher's system of figure skating to print, making it surprising that his most talented student suffered from weakness in compulsory figures. Biellmann's forte was free skating, particularly the more athletic aspects of it. Her programs included spectacular jumps and dazzling spins. She completed double Salchows at age seven and landed a triple Salchow at the Swiss Junior National Championships at age eleven. But it is not jumping that one associates with Biellmann; it is the spin she popularized that bears her name and is included in many free-skating programs. She reached back over her shoulder, grabbed the blade on her free foot, and raised it over her head, a move that requires much strength and extreme flexibility.

Elaine Zayak (b. 1965), like Biellmann, is remembered for athleticism, particularly her jumping prowess. She won both the U.S. and the World junior titles at age thirteen, and just three years later, in 1982, ascended the podium as the World champion. It was a great upset. She placed fourth in the compulsory figures and tenth in the short program but won the free skating decisively. None of the top skaters were consistent in all events, and those above her had major failures in their free skating. Zayak's rise to prominence was rapid. She astounded audiences and judges alike with multiple triple jumps not expected of women at that time. Six were included in her 1982 program. A relatively short amateur career ended two years later with a bronze medal at the World Championships. Zayak was an attractive skater who had dashing speed and youthful energy, but her artistry did not equal her athleticism. She presented exciting programs, and that continued through a five-year professional career with Stars on Ice and Symphony on Ice. Surprising many people, ten years after her amateur career, five after her professional career, she reinstated for the 1994 season. Shedding twenty pounds and training diligently, she entered the U.S. Nationals and at twenty-eight placed a respectable fourth. It was not enough to earn a place on the World or Olympic teams, but it demonstrated the tenacity that makes a great skater and that is associated with Elaine Zayak.

Zayak's six triple jumps at the World Championships included four toe loops and two Salchows. Most women at that time attempted no more than two. Established difficulty levels are employed in judging, and, for jumps, toe loops have the lowest value, with Salchows only slightly higher. Thus, while including more triple jumps than other skaters, Zayak was repeating the easiest ones rather than offering the variety seen today. The upshot was a rule adopted at the ISU Congress in 1983 prohibiting the repetition of triple jumps except once and only then when used in combination or sequence. It is commonly referred to as the "Zayak rule."

Denise Biellmann popular-
ized a spin that now bears her
name. (World Figure Skating
Museum and Hall of Fame)

Next in the roster of Ladies World Champions is Rosalynn Sumners (b. 1964), another
American but one who was the antithesis of her predecessor. She could do the jumps,
but her style rested on the emotion she could express through skating. Sumners, who
is remembered for her artistry, became the novice champion at age fourteen but had to
make a choice the following year between junior Nationals and junior Worlds, both of

which were scheduled for the third week of January. She became the third American to win the lady World junior title.[6] In her first year as a senior, 1981, Sumners placed fifth at the National Championships, and just a year later she won the first of three consecutive titles. She was the World champion in 1983 and the Olympic silver medalist in 1984. At the Olympic Games she won the compulsory figures, placed fifth in the short program owing to a missed double Axel Paulsen jump, and placed second in the free skating. Not proceeding to the World Championships, she turned professional and skated for two years with Disney on Ice. Finding that unrewarding and contrary to her artistic temperament, she seized the opportunity of joining the initial group of skaters for Scott Hamilton's American Tour, which became Stars on Ice. That afforded the opportunity of expanding artistic aspects of her skating, and she enjoyed a thirteen-year tenure with the company before retiring in 1999.

KATARINA WITT: TWO-TIME OLYMPIC CHAMPION

Not since Sonja Henie had any woman repeated as an Olympic champion when Katarina Witt (b. 1965) of the German Democratic Republic capped her amateur career with a second gold medal at Calgary in 1988. Her international career began in 1979, when at age thirteen she placed fourteenth at the European Championships. She placed fifth at the European and World Championships two years later and followed with silver medals in 1982. Witt became the European champion in 1983 and the World champion in 1984. Early in her career she was plagued by poor showings in the compulsories, but during the last five years of her amateur career noticeably improved figures coupled with consistently strong free skating made her a tough, hard-to-beat competitor. Witt's medal count in European, World, and Olympic competition is twelve gold and three silver.

Witt always presented an appealing and feminine persona on the ice. Her natural talent combined with a dedicated work ethic was enhanced by support from a strict communist sport system and a highly respected coach, Jutta Müller. In competition Witt displayed consistency, concentration, and an inner strength that overcame the problem with nerves that plagues so many skaters.

Witt seemed to thrive on the pressure of competition, and never was this clearer than at the Calgary Olympics. There were two battles that year. The most famous was the Battle of the Brians, but there was also a "Battle of the Carmens." Both Witt and former World champion Debi Thomas of the United States chose music from Bizet's opera *Carmen* for their free skating. Witt won the short program, but Thomas won the compulsory figures and was the leader entering the free skating. Witt presented a dramatic portrayal of the seductive Carmen. Although criticized by some for a rather slow middle section with a long pause in it, the dramatic effect resulted in artistic marks that included seven 5.9s. Thomas skated last and was not at her best. She bobbled her opening triple toe loop–triple toe loop combination jump and fell on a later jump. In addition, her non-literal interpretation of Carmen lacked the dramatic impact of Witt's portrayal. The result was a bronze medal. Elizabeth Manley (b. 1965), a dynamic competitor from Canada in perhaps her finest performance, jumped ahead of Thomas and claimed the silver medal. The much-anticipated Battle of the Carmens failed to provide the exciting conclusion and close finish of the Battle of the Brians.

Katarina Witt as Carmen in her second gold medal performance at the Winter Olympic Games, Calgary, 1988. (World Figure Skating Museum and Hall of Fame)

After the World Championships, Witt turned professional and in 1989 portrayed Carmen again in the film *Carmen on Ice*. It featured the Brians as well, Boitano as Don José and Orser as Escamillo. Witt has since appeared with touring companies and competed in many professional competitions. Her audience appeal never abated. Her many awards include the Jacques Favart Trophy and election into the World Figure Skating Hall of Fame.

Like Boitano and Petrenko, Witt elected to reinstate for the 1994 Olympic Games. She probably had no illusion of winning a medal, but given her vivacity, love of competing, and audience appeal, reinstatement seemed natural. It also provided a personal and human interest story. Her parents had been unable in the days of the cold war to attend her Olympic performances at Sarajevo and Calgary. With the reunification of Germany they could travel to Hamar.[7] Witt's free-skating program there, one of the most memorable and moving in the history of figure skating, was especially appropriate. Skating to the music "Where Have All the Flowers Gone?" she paid tribute to war-torn Sarajevo, the city where she had earned her first Olympic title. The program demonstrated an underlying aspect of what has made Witt one of the greatest performers of all times, the emotion she expresses through the subjects selected. Her most dramatic portrayal came a year later, when Sandra Bezic choreographed Witt's emotional *Schindler's List* program in which Witt became the "little girl in red," the only moment of color in Steven Spielberg's otherwise black-and-white, award-winning film of 1993.

THE ADVENT OF BLACK SKATERS

Witt's only silver medal in five years came at the 1986 World Championships. Defeating her was the American Debra (Debi) Thomas (b. 1967). It was a momentous event not because Witt was defeated but because for the first time a skater of African descent became a World champion. Thomas entered the National Championships in 1983 at age fifteen and placed thirteenth. Two years later she was the silver medalist. She placed fifth at her first World Championships that year and proceeded to collect medals of every color before turning professional in 1988. Thomas was an honor student in high school and during her final two years of competitive skating was pursuing a premedical curriculum at Stanford University. As a professional she appeared with Stars on Ice, skating primarily on weekends, while she completed her baccalaureate degree. Upon entering medical school she retired from skating. She is now a practicing physician.

No other black skater has become a World champion, although Surya Bonaly of France collected three consecutive silver medals during the early 1990s. Tai Babilonia, who with Randy Gardner won the 1979 World title in pairs, is of mixed Asian, American Indian, and African descent. There have been, however, several outstanding black skaters, primarily African Americans, who have collectively expanded the sport by being in it.

Debi Thomas is the first and only African American skater to win a World title. (World Figure Skating Museum and Hall of Fame)

The dean of black skaters is Mabel Fairbanks (1928–2002), who as a ten-year-old living in New York City received from her parents a pair of ice skates purchased in a pawn shop. In the 1930s and for three decades afterward, opportunities denied blacks in the United States included skating in public rinks regardless of their talent. Fairbanks was allowed to skate in one New York rink, primarily because she was a child. There Maribel Vinson reportedly recognized her talent and gave her a few lessons, presumably without charge. By the mid-1940s, her skating blossomed, but she could not compete because she did not belong to a skating club. Skating with professional touring companies was likewise not an option for an African American. Moving to California, Fairbanks ultimately became a respected teacher and coach. One is reminded of Gus Lussi's statement that if he could not be a champion himself he would create one.

Opportunities not open to Fairbanks would eventually be open to her students, and there have been many, the most famous of whom were Tai Babilonia and Randy Gardner. Although coached by John Nicks during their international career, they credit Fairbanks with pairing them and developing their fundamental technique. Many of Fairbanks's students were fine skaters. Atoy Wilson in 1966 was the first African American to become a U.S. novice champion. He had to join the USFSA as an individual member because, like his teacher, he was denied membership in skating clubs. After retiring from competitive skating in 1971 he toured with Ice Capades and Holiday on Ice. Other African American skaters taught by Fairbanks include Leslie Robinson, another Holiday on Ice star; Richard Ewell, the national junior champion in 1970; and Michelle McCladdie, who, skating with Ewell, won the 1972 junior pair title. For her groundbreaking work as a skater and coach Fairbanks was elected to the United States Figure Skating Hall of Fame in 1997.

MIDORI ITO, JILL TRENARY, AND KRISTI YAMAGUCHI

Media hype directed attention in Calgary to the battles of the Brians and the Carmens, but in the ladies event an eighteen-year-old jumping sensation from Japan provided another highlight of the Games. Midori Ito (b. 1969), less than five feet tall, included more and higher triple jumps than the other competitors. Jumping was her forte, compulsory figures her nemesis. At Calgary she placed tenth in figures, her best standing to date in international competition, but she placed third in the combined free skating, ahead of Debi Thomas. The result was a fifth-place finish. At the World Championships a month later, with the top six skaters from Calgary continuing, Ito slipped to sixth place. She again placed third in the free skating, but her compulsory figures dropped to fourteenth. Witt, Manley, and Thomas retired, positioning Ito to become the World champion a year later if she could improve her compulsory figures. Only Jill Trenary, fourth at the Olympic Games and the World Championships, seemed to stand in her way. Ito was quoted in *Skating* magazine after her Olympic effort, saying, "I want to make the compulsories better."[8] She did, and in 1989 she placed a career-best sixth in the compulsory figures. Coupled with outstanding free skating, she became Japan's first lady World Champion.[9]

Not only did Ito demonstrate more balanced skating but she also made history by being the first woman to complete a triple Axel Paulsen jump in competition. In two years, 1989 and 1990, Ito received ten perfect 6.0s at the World Championships, always in the technical marks, a record not matched by any singles skater. Janet Lynn is second with six, all granted for artistic presentation. Ito won the silver medal a year later, but in spite of the elimination of compulsory figures she slipped to fourth in 1991. Her second Olympic bid in 1992 produced a silver medal behind Kristi Yamaguchi. Ito did not proceed to the World Championships that year. Turning professional, she skated in shows, primarily in Japan, and served as a commentator for Japanese television.

Jill Trenary (b. 1968) of the United States was totally an opposite to Ito. She was strong in compulsory figures, and her free skating is remembered for artistry rather than athleticism. Trenary did not compete after the total elimination of compulsory figures, the result of a knee injury that required major surgery and a long recovery, but she is one of a relatively small number of contemporary skaters who voiced objection to their removal. As the reigning national champion and World bronze medalist, she said in 1989, "I don't like the way the sport is changing. I wish figures would stay in."[10] Trenary was a conservative at a time when the sport was changing. She became the World champion in 1990, the last year of compulsory figures, and the results are revealing. Ito, the silver medalist, was tenth in figures and first in the combined free skating. Trenary was first in figures and third in the combined free skating.

Fourth that year was America's next skating sensation. Kristi Yamaguchi (b. 1971) balanced artistry and athleticism to perfection, a talent apparent in 1990 when she placed second and third in the short program and free skating at the World Championships. She was ninth in the compulsory figures and benefited from their elimination a year later. With Trenary retired and figures eliminated, Yamaguchi was well positioned to become the World champion. At the United States Championships in 1991, she fell during a triple Salchow but completed six other triple jumps in an otherwise nearly flawless program. Tonya Harding, who skated later, delivered her finest competitive program, which included a clean triple Axel Paulsen jump. Harding won the national title, with Yamaguchi second and Nancy Kerrigan third. At the World Championships in Munich a month later the Americans swept the medals but in a different order. Yamaguchi became the World champion. The Olympic year followed, and Yamaguchi, as expected, won every competition. At the Olympic Games she entered the long program in first place. Skating to "Malagueña" she turned a planned triple Salchow into a double, a relatively easy jump that frequently caused her problems, and barely saved a triple loop jump, but it was otherwise a beautifully skated program that earned eight 5.9s for artistry. There were no totally clean programs that evening. Yamaguchi won her second World title and then retired. Her professional career centered on her role as a popular member of the Stars on Ice cast. She was inducted into the World Figure Skating Hall of Fame in 1998.

THE TOTAL ELIMINATION OF COMPULSORY FIGURES

George Anderson's *The Art of Skating,* published in 1852, contains a chapter entitled "Figure Skating." It covers specifically figures done on one foot. In a second edition published in 1868, sixteen years later, Anderson clarified his use of the term, saying that figure skating is "more frequently applied to those figures which are done on one foot." The words "more frequently" suggest that the use of the term was changing. H. E. Vandervell's *A System of Figure Skating,* published in 1869, just a year after Anderson's second edition, was the first to connect the words *figure* and *skating* as a defining title for the sport.[11]

Sometime during the late 1860s the sport became known as "figure skating," with the term understood to included all figures, simple and complex, then being drawn on the ice. Nearly a century and a quarter after that defining name evolved, the ISU eliminated compulsory figures from competition. The remnants of what originally defined the sport and fascinated skaters of the nineteenth century, the tracings left on the ice, were thereby removed, but the name *figure skating* remains.

It was not an abrupt decision to eliminate compulsory figures. A gradual diminishing of interest in them had occurred throughout the postwar era, including reductions in the number prepared for competition, the number skated in competition, the number of repetitions required, and the numerical value of them relative to the total score. But no single entity had greater influence on their ultimate discontinuance than television. The slow and meticulous tracing of compulsory figures, so difficult to perfect, does not provide the excitement of speed and athleticism demanded by television audiences. Appeasement to television interests seeking additional opportunities to provide the public with exciting programs skated by elite skaters ultimately accelerated the movement toward their total elimination. On March 7, 1990, at the World Championships in Halifax, Nova Scotia, Željka Čižmešija of Yugoslavia skated the historic last compulsory figure in international competition.[12] It was appropriate that she be last because her forte was compulsory figures.

Many skaters as we have seen suffered in competition from their inability to perfect compulsory figures, and not surprisingly, many members of the skating community strongly supported their elimination. There were others, coaches and skaters, who felt the technique gained from doing them more than compensated for the time spent learning and practicing them. Carlo Fassi predicted that "once figures were abolished, the sport would be dominated by fourteen and fifteen year old girls."[13] His statement was prophetic. Sonja Henie's first Olympic gold medal in 1928 was won at age fifteen, but not until the elimination of compulsory figures was that feat repeated. The Olympic gold medalist in 1994 was sixteen-year-old Oksana Baiul, in 1998 was fifteen-year-old Tara Lipinski, and in 2002 was sixteen-year-old Sarah Hughes.[14] All other Olympic gold medalists have been at least eighteen.

Scott Hamilton, writing nine years after the elimination of compulsory figures, expressed eloquently concerns he believes have been realized: "What I see out there today are a lot of pure jumpers, many of whom haven't learned to skate. And while this new generation of skaters should certainly feel proud of their technical achievements, it's sad that they'll never develop their edge skills in a more grounded and patient way nor feel the personal satisfaction of creating the perfect figure."[15]

CONTINUED SOVIET DOMINATION OF PAIR SKATING

From 1965 through 1981 only the Americans Tai Babilonia and Randy Gardner were able to unseat Soviet pairs at the World Championships, and that was the year Rodnina and Zaitsev did not compete. Soviet domination continued for the remainder of the century but not unabated. Twice in the 1980s and three times in the 1990s other countries fielded winning pairs, but from 1965 through 2002 the Soviets won an impressive thirty of the thirty-eight World titles, with successful challengers being held to one title each. Those in the 1980s were Sabine Baess and Tassilo Thierbach of the German Democratic Republic and Barbara Underhill and Paul Martini of Canada.

Baess (b. 1961) and Thierbach (b. 1956) competed at seven consecutive World Championships, beginning in 1978, and collected five medals. They became World champions in 1982. Their Olympic efforts resulted in sixth place in 1980 and fourth place in 1984. Underhill (b. 1963) and Martini (b. 1963) competed at six consecutive World Championships beginning in 1979, collecting two medals. They became World champions in 1984. Their Olympic efforts resulted in ninth place in 1980 and seventh place in 1984.

Irina Vorobieva (b. 1958) and Igor Lisovski (b. 1954) preceded Baess and Thierbach as World champions. Their relatively short international career began in 1979 with silver medals at the European Championships and a fourth-place finish at the World Championships. Not competing in 1980, they reappeared in 1981 and won both events. Continuing for one additional year, they won bronze medals at the European Championships and placed fifth at the World Championships.

Elena Valova (b. 1963) and Oleg Vasiliev (b. 1959) collected gold medals at Sarajevo in 1984, continuing the Soviet tradition of winning Olympic titles that had begun in 1964 and that would continue through 2002.[16] Valova and Vasiliev won the World title on their first try in 1983, but at the Championships following the Olympic Games in 1984 Underhill and Martini wrested the title away from them in a close competition. The

Soviets won the short program, but the Canadians won the free skating. Underhill and Martini retired, but Valova and Vasiliev continued and reclaimed the World title in 1985. Thus, during the six years from 1979 through 1984 new champions appeared annually: Babilonia and Gardner, Cherkasova and Shakhrai, Vorobieva and Lisovski, Baess and Thierbach, Valova and Vasiliev, and Underhill and Martini. For the next eight years, 1985 through 1992, Valova and Vasiliev and two other outstanding Soviet pairs, Gordeeva and Grinkov and Mishkutenok and Dmitriev, collectively claimed every World title.

Ekaterina Gordeeva (b. 1971) and Sergei Grinkov (1967–95), one of the most popular Soviet pairs, emerged in 1986 as the reigning World junior champions and in their first year as seniors climbed to the top of the World podium ahead of Valova and Vasiliev, a position they held for two years. They won Olympic gold at Calgary in 1988, but at the World Championships, Valova and Vasiliev triumphed over their younger rivals, concluding their amateur career as three-time World champions. Valova and Vasiliev's impressive six-year career includes a combined seven gold and six silver medals in European, World, and Olympic competition. They now reside and coach in the United States.

Gordeeva and Grinkov were paired in 1982. Gordeeva, a petite eleven-year-old, appeared small against her partner but not to the degree that Cherkasova had against Shakhrai three years earlier. As she grew, the height difference diminished. They won the World Junior title in 1985, and like their predecessors Valova and Vasiliev they never received less than a silver medal at the senior level. Their cumulative record in European, World, and Olympic competition includes an impressive nine gold and two silver medals.

An unfortunate incident occurred at the European Championships in 1987 when during the free skate Grinkov's trouser strap came undone and was dragging on the ice. Following the ISU rule regarding equipment failures adopted after the Rodnina and Zaitsev incident fourteen years earlier, the referee signaled for them to stop, which at the direction of their coach they chose to ignore. They were given the option of either reskating from the point of interruption or reskating the entire program at the end of their group, but neither choice was acceptable to their team leader. They were therefore declared to have withdrawn. Gordeeva and Grinkov turned professional in 1990 but reinstated for the Lillehammer Games in 1994 and succeeded in winning gold medals, the only reinstated skaters to do so. Election to the World Figure Skating Hall of Fame came in 1995.

While rehearsing at Lake Placid for a Stars on Ice tour in November 1995, Grinkov suddenly became dizzy and collapsed on the ice. He was still breathing upon arrival at the hospital but could not be revived. At twenty-eight one of the most popular skaters in the skating community and half of one of figure skating's most respected pair teams had died from a heart attack. After a short period in her native Russia, Gordeeva returned to the United States and rejoined Stars on Ice, where she developed a second career as a singles skater.

Four-time World champions Ekaterina Gordeeva and Sergei Grinkov, the only reinstated Olympic champions to win additional titles at the Lillehammer Games in 1994. (World Figure Skating Museum and Hall of Fame)

Following Gordeeva and Grinkov's retirement in 1990 their compatriots Natalia Mish-kutenok (b. 1970) and Artur Dmitriev (b. 1968), the reigning bronze medalists, became World champions. A year later they won the triple crown, European, Olympic, and World titles, after which they, too, retired. Surprisingly, Dmitriev reappeared in 1996 with a new partner, Oksana Kazakova, and won a second Olympic gold medal at Nagano in 1998.

THE INCOMPARABLE TORVILL AND DEAN

In 1970 Soviet ice dancers invaded territory that, with the exception of the era of the Czechs Romanová and Roman, had been the domain of British skaters, and for a decade they stood atop the World podium before being dethroned in 1980 by the Hungarians Krisztina Regöczy and András Sallay. For the next Olympic cycle the British regained their former prominence with the most famous ice dancers in the history of the disci-pline. Jayne Torvill (b. 1957) and Christopher Dean (b. 1958), from Nottingham, England, had competed for three years in European, World, and Olympic competition when in 1981 they stood atop the medal stand for the first of four times.

Torvill began her competitive career as a pair skater with Michael Hutchinson, win-ning the British Junior Championship when she was twelve and the Senior Champion-ship a year later. The partnership dissolved soon afterward, and for three years she tried singles' skating without significant success. In 1975 Janet Sawbridge, a former British ice dancing champion and World medalist, was coaching in Nottingham. She paired Torvill with Dean, an experienced ice dancer who had been the British junior champion with Sandra Elson. Torvill and Dean's development was not rapid, and the early results were not remarkable. In their first appearance at the European and World Championships in 1978 they placed ninth and eleventh. That same year, Sawbridge traded coaching for motherhood. Torvill and Dean selected Betty Callaway as their new coach. She had not had an international skating career but was coaching the current World bronze medal-ists, Regöczy and Sallay.

Callaway suddenly found herself coaching two future World champion couples. In the Olympic year, 1980, Torvill and Dean placed fourth at the World Championships and fifth at the Olympic Games. Regöczy and Sallay capped their career as World champions and Olympic silver medalists. Torvill and Dean entered the new Olympic cycle not having won a medal in international competition and were suddenly unbeatable. They retired four years later, never having won bronze or silver medals. Not until their reinstatement for the Lillehammer Games fourteen years later did they move down in the medal ranks.

Torvill and Dean's legacy lies in their influence through altering dramatically estab-lished concepts of ice dancing. Although their programs in 1981 were beautifully choreo-graphed, the innovations associated with them appeared most clearly in 1982 with two unique programs. For their original set pattern dance, which required a blues rhythm

Jayne Torvill and Christopher Dean, the greatest ice dancers in the history of the sport. (World Figure Skating Museum and Hall of Fame)

that year, they chose an extremely slow and haunting rendition of "Summertime" from George Gershwin's opera *Porgy and Bess* performed on harmonica. Offering a dance at such a slow tempo and with music played by an instrument offering little variety in timbre was a gamble, but the couple's strength was their ability to evoke and sustain specific moods while maintaining energy throughout programs. As conservative as ISU judges are perceived to be, "Summertime" earned six perfect 6.0s at the World Championships, five of them for artistic impression.

Their free-dance program "Mack and Mabel," one of their most popular routines, was set to music from a Broadway musical about the stormy relationship between Mack Sennett and Mabel Normand, and a conscious effort was made to portray those characters. Ballroom dancing carried to the ice was changed dramatically. "Up to then, we like other skaters, had created movements, pure and simple," but the concept of a storyline had further implications that they reported in their autobiography: "If there was a story, we were characters with roles to play."[17] The result was their greatest achievement to date, and it earned five 6.0s for artistic impression.

Having drawn so successfully on opera and musical comedy, Torvill and Dean continued in that vein for another year. Rock and roll was selected for the original dance rhythm in 1983, leading them to the musical *Song and Dance* by the popular British-born composer Andrew Lloyd Webber. For the free dance, they turned to the circus and to another popular musical, *Barnum,* the story of the American impresario P. T. Barnum. With those two programs Torvill and Dean accumulated an additional sixteen perfect 6.0s at the World Championships, seven for the original set pattern dance and nine for the free dance.

For the Olympic year Torvill and Dean abandoned musicals, for which emotions could easily be understood through familiarity with stage plays, and decided to link abstract orchestra music to devised storylines. They undertook bold interpretations of music, employing Spanish rhythms and culture and in doing so achieved their greatest successes. The original set pattern dance was skated to a paso doble, a Spanish dance that became popular about 1926.[18] The music selected was Nicolai Rimsky-Korsakov's "Capriccio Espagnol." Dean portrayed a matador, with Torvill being an inanimate object, his cape. The costumes as in previous years were designed by former World dance champion Courtney Jones. They were black and white with some color on the trim. Torvill's cape was black from the back, but with her arms outstretched the front became totally white. Brilliant choreography and inspired skating were rewarded with 6.0 marks from all judges for artistic impression for the first and only time in World competition.

The free dance was even more innovative. They selected Maurice Ravel's "Bolero," a setting of a late-eighteenth-century Spanish dance characterized by fast tempos and intricate rhythms. Musically, "Bolero" has little melodic or rhythmic development. It is not a piece that would readily be considered for a skating routine, but for Torvill and Dean the music became the background for a story of two lovers who, not able to stay together, climb a mountain and throw themselves from it. It was a perfect match between music and story, and one of the finest interpretive skating performances ever presented. The World judges awarded a total of thirteen 6.0s, which when added to nine for the original set pattern dance and seven for the compulsory dances gave them a total of twenty-nine. But that was almost anticlimatic. They had skated the same programs at the Sarajevo Games two weeks earlier and received a total of twenty perfect scores, including ones in all parts of the competition. In three years Torvill and Dean accumulated a total of seventy-eight 6.os in World and Olympic competition.

International tours, television specials, and professional competitions followed their amateur careers. Like other skaters from the era—Robin Cousins, Scott Hamilton, and Brian Boitano—they formed their own touring company but skated in established shows as well. Dean also served as a choreographer, primarily for the Canadians Isabelle and Paul Duchesnay.

Torvill and Dean elected to reinstate and compete at the 1994 Olympic Games. Although they were tied for first place entering the free dance, the judges placed them third. At nearly forty years of age they returned to their professional careers. Among their awards and accolades are being one of seven figure skating recipients of the Jacques Favart Trophy and induction into the World Figure Skating Hall of Fame.

THE RETURN OF SOVIET ICE DANCERS

The Soviet ice dancers Natalia Bestemianova (b. 1960) and Andrei Bukin (b. 1957) were for three years silver medalists behind Torvill and Dean, but when the champions retired they assumed that role. Like their predecessors, they were unbeatable for an entire Olympic cycle. Bestemianova and Bukin were sometimes criticized, primarily by skaters and writers in the West, for having unconventional posture and style and for theatrics sometimes employed in their characteristically avant-garde free-dance programs, but they consistently won the conservative and prescribed compulsory dances as well. They were dramatic in the sense of Torvill and Dean but in a less suave, more energetic vein. One commentator, in describing their exhibition number following the 1988 Olympic Games, said, "They loved and hated, ran and chased, captured and escaped, punished and forgave, using all the signature moves of their . . . free dances to make the audience shiver." Other ice dancers "skim across and float above the ice. Bestemianova and Bukin dig into it, wrenching from it . . . its frigidity, melting it with their stormy passion."[19]

Ice dancing had taken another major step forward, and the ISU at its 1988 Congress recognized and condoned that new direction by relaxing rules on technical content and reducing penalties for violations. Like their predecessors Torvill and Dean, Bestemianova and Bukin were recognized for the innovations they brought to ice dancing by being awarded the Jacques Favart Trophy.

Silver medalists behind Bestemianova and Bukin for four years were their teammates Marina Klimova (b. 1966) and Sergei Ponomarenko (b. 1960). Other than for a surprising upset at the 1991 World Championships, they, like their predecessors, won decisively every competition through an Olympic cycle, 1989 to 1992. Their style was initially neoclassic, but in 1991, sporting a new look, they skated to music from the 1962 film *Lawrence of Arabia* in a routine far removed from their usual style. Isabelle and Paul

Marina Klimova and Sergei Ponomarenko, three-time World ice dancing champions and the 1992 Olympic gold medalists. (Paul Harvath)

Duchesnay of France won the World title that year, but when the two couples met again at the Olympic Games in 1992 their roles were reversed. Klimova and Ponomarenko were the pursuers. Returning to a more classical program geared toward beauty and artistry, they skated to Bach's well-known Toccata and Fugue in D Minor and captivated the audience. After winning Olympic gold and reclaiming the World title they turned professional and toured for several seasons with Champions on Ice. In 2000 they were inducted into the World Figure Skating Hall of Fame.

Isabelle (b. 1963) and Paul (b. 1961) Duchesnay, a French Canadian sister and brother, represented France. He was born in Metz, France, and she in Quebec, Canada. They won bronze medals in 1989 and silver medals in 1990 before upsetting Klimova and Ponomarenko in 1991. Their Olympic effort in 1992 produced silver medals behind Klimova and Ponomarenko, and they chose not to defend their World title. Retiring from competitive skating, the siblings became coaches in the United States.

THE ISU AT A CENTURY

In 1992 the ISU turned one hundred. At thirty-nine nations strong, the union had endured two world wars and the geographic changes that resulted from them, had risen above politics and admitted into membership the divided countries of Germany and Korea, had dealt appropriately with the issue of apartheid in South Africa, and had most recently adjusted to the breakup of the Soviet Union. The Balkan States—Estonia, Latvia, and Lithuania—all of which had previously been members, rejoined the union in 1991. For one year only, 1992, former Soviet states, primarily Russia and Ukraine, were classified as the Commonwealth of Independent States and entered unified teams in ISU championships, but since 1993 all of the former Soviet countries have held separate membership. The union entered its second century as one of the most successful sports organizations in the world and continued to grow. By 2002 it numbered fifty-four members.[20]

To celebrate its hundredth anniversary, ISU historian Benjamin T. Wright, a long-time judge, referee, and past member and chair of the figure skating technical committee, wrote the comprehensive *Skating around the World, 1892–1992: The One Hundredth Anniversary History of the International Skating Union.*[21] Two additional books were published that year: *ISU Office Holders through the Years and ISU Congresses 1892–1992*, started by ISU honorary president James Koch and completed by Wright and Elemér Terták, and *Results: Figure Skating Championships, 1968–1991*, edited by Terták and Wright. Earlier competition records were published on the occasion of the ISU's seventy-fifth anniversary in *Seventy-five Years of European and World Championships in Figure Skating*. These four works are the most valuable primary sources on the history of figure skating since the founding of the ISU in 1892.

FOURTEEN

Albertville to Salt Lake City

TWO changes adopted in 1992 had major but short-term impacts on competitive figure skating. First, the IOC mandated a shift in the cycle of the Summer and Winter Olympic Games so they would alternate in biennial years. The Seventeenth Winter Games were then scheduled for Lillehammer, Norway, in 1994, just two years after the Albertville Games. Thus, the 1992 Olympians could remain eligible with just a two-year time commitment.[1]

Coupled with that permanent change was a more controversial decision by the ISU that permitted a one-time reinstatement of ineligible skaters to full eligibility and allowed them to compete at the European and World Championships and the Olympic Games in 1994. Several former Olympic champions reinstated and competed at the Lillehammer Games.[2] They included singles skaters Katarina Witt, Brian Boitano, and Viktor Petrenko; pair skaters Ekaterina Gordeeva and Sergei Grinkov; and ice dancers Jayne Torvill and Christopher Dean. Torvill and Dean had skated professionally for ten years, and Witt, Boitano, and Gordeeva and Grinkov for six years. Petrenko competed at Albertville in 1992 but had turned professional shortly afterward. Of the former champions, only Gordeeva and Grinkov won additional Olympic titles.[3] Torvill and Dean won bronze medals. Witt placed seventh, Boitano sixth, and Petrenko fourth. They competed against a new class of talented, athletic, and younger skaters who now dominated the sport.

The decade from Albertville in 1992 to Salt Lake City in 2002 proved to be one of figure skating's most dynamic as the sport changed with vertiginous speed. It endured the vicious attack on Nancy Kerrigan at the U.S. Championships in 1994 and suffered highly publicized judging controversies at the Olympic Games in 1998 and 2002. As a result of those events it enjoyed unprecedented popularity. Fueled by extensive media coverage and spurred by an ever-increasing number of popular and highly motivated skaters who sought the spotlight and its financial rewards, figure skating reached a much-expanded public that, for a short time, could not get enough of it.

THE GRAND PRIX SERIES AND THE FOUR CONTINENTS CHAMPIONSHIPS

The Grand Prix Series, implemented in the 1996 season, consists of six qualifying competitions plus the Grand Prix Finals for top point-winners from the qualifying competitions.[4] It provides skaters from throughout the skating world with opportunities to present and perfect their programs early in the competitive season and often to compete against those skaters with whom they may compete at the World Championships. Not incidentally, the series provided additional televised skating at a time when the public was demanding more.

The oldest of the Grand Prix events, Skate Canada, dates from 1973. At a planning meeting for the North American Championships held in April 1972 and attended by representatives from the USFSA and the CFSA, the Canadian delegation surprised the Americans by announcing Canada's immediate withdrawal from the long-established competition. Their intention, unknown to the Americans at the time, was to launch in 1973 an international invitational competition to be known as Skate Canada.

Nine countries were invited to participate at the first Skate Canada and to field one entry in each of three events: men's, ladies', and ice dancing, with the CFSA covering the cost of transportation and accommodations for competitors, team managers, referees, and judges. Canada, as the host country, would field three entries in each event.[5] Austria, Czechoslovakia, the Federal Republic of Germany, France, the German Democratic Republic, Great Britain, Japan, the Soviet Union, and the United States all sent competitors. Lynn Nightingale and Toller Cranston, both of Canada, won gold medals in the ladies' and men's events, and Hilary Green and Glyn Watts of Great Britain won the ice dancing.

Skate Canada became an annual event but was not held in 1979 owing to an agreement with the USFSA made to accommodate a pre-Olympic competition at Lake Placid, New York, site of the upcoming games. The skating venue at Lake Placid was new, and IOC regulations require that an international competition be previously held at venues employed for the games. Called the Flaming Leaves International Competition and sponsored by the USFSA, it provided Olympic contenders with the opportunity to compete at the venue where the games would be held three months later.[6] The Flaming Leaves success led the USFSA to continue the competition as an annual event called Skate America. Skate Canada and Skate America are the oldest of the Grand Prix events. Others include the NHK Trophy held in Japan since 1980; the Sparkassen Cup, originally called the Fuji Film Trophée; and the Nations Cup held in Gelsenkirchen, Germany, since 1986; the Trophée Lalique, originally called Grand Prix de Paris, held in France since 1987; and the Cup of Russia, held since 1996.[7]

Grand Prix events are held essentially for six consecutive weeks. Skaters, entered by their federations, are allowed to compete in no more than three. Points accumulated from placement in two of them, designated in advance, qualify competitors for the Grand Prix Finals.[8] There, the current best skaters compete against the same basic slate of skaters they will meet at the World Championships. Sixty-three percent of the medalists at the Grand Prix Finals have gone on to be medalists at the following World Championships.

A Junior Grand Prix Series was implemented in 1999. Member federations enter skaters in two of eight point-earning competitions. The top eight point-winners in each discipline qualify to compete in the Junior Grand Prix Finals. As in the senior series, prize money is awarded for each competition. The winners in 1999 were Song Gao of China, Deanna Stellato of the United States, pair skaters Aljana Savchenka and Stanislav Morozov of Ukraine, and ice dancers Emilie Nussear and Brandon Forsyth of the United States.

The North American Championships, before their demise in 1972, provided North American skaters with an opportunity parallel to that provided European skaters by the European Championships. At that time, medal contenders at the World Championships and the Olympic Games came from Europe and North America, but by the mid-1970s Asian skaters were competing successfully in international competition. Thus, European skaters had the advantage of an ISU championship event not available to all skaters.

To provide equal opportunities for skaters from throughout the skating world, in 1999 the ISU established the Four Continents Championships. It filled the void left by the demise of the North American Championships twenty-seven years earlier and provided skaters from North America as well as those from Africa, Asia, and Australia with ISU championships parallel to the European Championships. No South American country at that time held membership in the ISU, but in 2002 a historic milestone was reached when Brazil became the first South American member.

The Four Continents Championships were first held at Halifax, Nova Scotia, in February 1999. The winners, some of whom would become World champions, were singles' skaters Tatiana Malinina of Uzbekistan and Takeshi Honda of Japan, pair skaters Xue

Shen and Hongbo Zhao of China, and ice dancers Shae-Lynn Bourne and Victor Kraatz of Canada. Skaters from all four continents have competed annually.

MEN WORLD CHAMPIONS

Kurt Browning continued competing after the Albertville Games and in 1993 acquired a fourth World title, joining him to an elite group of men—Dick Button, Hayes Jenkins, and Scott Hamilton—who had done so in the postwar era. World champions since Browning's retirement include Elvis Stojko, Todd Eldredge, Alexei Yagudin, and Evgeny Plushenko, all of whom competed at the Salt Lake City Games in 2002. Stojko and Yagudin entered the Olympic season as three-time World champions with the potential to become the next four-time World champion. Yagudin prevailed and is the only man since World War II not from North America to become a four-time World champion.[9]

Winner of the silver medal behind Browning in 1993 and heir to the throne in World competition was a fellow Canadian, Elvis Stojko (b. 1972). When Stojko won his third and final World title five years later, Canada could boast of having won eight of the last eleven, an amazing statistic considering that earlier success among the men was limited to the back-to-back titles won by Donald Jackson and Donald McPherson in 1962 and 1963. Stojko's four Olympic bids produced a pair of silver medals.

Todd Eldredge (b. 1971), the only American man to win a World title during the period, boasts a longevity unusual for skaters at century's end. He competed internationally for sixteen years, from 1987 to 2002. Had he been included on the 1994 team he would have been, like Stojko, one of few skaters who have competed at four Olympic Games. Hailing from Chatham, Massachusetts, a small fishing village, Eldredge developed through a long career into one of America's favorite skaters. Only Dick Button's seven national titles surpass Eldredge's six in the postwar years. He won the World junior title at age sixteen and the World title ten years later at twenty-six. He won four Grand Prix events at least once but not the Grand Prix Finals. Eldredge skated into the era of quadruple jumps, a feat he was unable to accomplish but one in which his younger opponents excelled. His artistry made him popular with the American public, and after the Salt Lake City Games he joined Stars on Ice, where loyal fans continued rewarding him with standing ovations.

Two Russians, Alexei Yagudin (b. 1980) and Evgeny Plushenko (b. 1982), dominated men's skating during the 1999–2002 Olympic cycle, claiming all the gold and three of the silver medals at the European Championships, all of the gold and two of the silver medals at the World Championships, and all of the gold and two of the silver medals at the Grand Prix Finals. Yagudin is recognized for a level of artistry unusual among the men in recent years and has coupled that artistry with an accomplished jumping ability. He won the World junior title in 1995 and three consecutive World titles, beginning in

1998. A silver medal behind Plushenko in 2001 preceded his fourth World title in 2002. Grand Prix efforts have included wins at all except the NHK Trophy, a competition he has not entered. Yagudin trained through most of his senior career in the United States under the guidance of Russian coach Tatiana Tarasova.

Plushenko was born in Siberia, where his parents took him skating when he was four. His talent showed early, and he moved to St. Petersburg to train with Alexei Mishin. During the 1999–2002 Olympic cycle he won most of the competitions entered, and he holds the distinction of being the only man to win the Grand Prix Finals twice in succession. Plushenko was recognized early for his jumping prowess, but it was with notably improved artistry that he became the World champion in 2001.

The rivalry that developed between the two talented Russians was played out at the Salt Lake City Games. Plushenko won the short program and the first free skate, but Yagudin won the more heavily weighted second free skate and the gold medal.[10] Plushenko did not compete at the World Championships a month later, where Yagudin won his fourth title.

OLYMPIC GOLD WITHOUT WORLD TITLES

Only three times before 1994 did Olympic gold medalists retire from amateur skating without having won a World title. Magda Mauroy-Julin, the 1920 Olympic champion, retired before the World Championships were revived in 1922, and she remains the only woman to hold an Olympic title without a World title.[11] Two men, Wolfgang Schwarz and Robin Cousins, Olympic champions in 1968 and 1980, also lack World titles. During the fiercely competitive decade of the 1990s, however, two men and one pair, all Russians, won Olympic gold and retired without World titles: Alexei Urmanov in 1994, Ilia Kulik in 1998, and pair skaters Oksana Kazakova and Artur Dmitriev in 1998.[12]

Urmanov (b. 1973) first skated internationally in 1991. He won the European title in 1997, but his best effort at the World Championships produced a bronze medal in 1993. The Lillehammer Games in 1994 provided his day of glory. He retained his eligibility through the next Olympic cycle but did not defend his title at Nagano. During that period he won three Grand Prix events and was the first winner of the Grand Prix Finals.

Kulik (b. 1977), the World junior champion in 1995, competed at the European and World Championships for the next three years, outings that netted one medal of each color. The large number of outstanding skaters competing in the 1990s and attempting ever more difficult jumps has caused rankings to fluctuate as minor mistakes that proved disastrous for one competitor provided windows of opportunity for another. This is reflected in Kulik's record. Three World efforts resulted in ninth-, second-, and fifth-place finishes. After winning Olympic gold in Nagano, Kulik joined Stars on Ice.

Kazakova (b. 1975) enjoyed a short international career of just three years with Artur

Dmitriev, the former World and Olympic champion with Natalia Mishkutenok. Kazakova and Dmitriev won the European title in their first year together, 1996, but their best placement at the World Championships was third in 1997. Unfortunately, they had to withdraw in 1998 after winning the Olympic title because Dmitriev contracted food poisoning.

THE KERRIGAN-HARDING DEBACLE

Only once have lady competitors swept the medals in World or Olympic competition. Three Americans, Kristi Yamaguchi, Tonya Harding (b. 1970), and Nancy Kerrigan (b. 1969), carried home medals from the 1991 World Championships held in Munich. The results were decisive for Yamaguchi and Harding but not for Kerrigan. Midori Ito of Japan defeated her soundly in the short program before Kerrigan bested Ito in the free skating, causing a tie in the placements. Because the tie-breaker is the free skating, Kerrigan won the bronze medal and completed the American sweep.

Yamaguchi retired in 1992 as the reigning Olympic and World champion. With the Lillehammer Games just two years away, the stage was set for an exciting rivalry between the other two Americans who offered greatly contrasting styles, Harding's athleticism and Kerrigan's elegance. Both were viable candidates for Olympic gold. Harding was a more experienced skater, having appeared on the competitive scene three years before Kerrigan at both the junior and senior levels. They first competed against each other at the National Championships in 1988, Kerrigan's first appearance as a senior. Harding placed fifth, and Kerrigan twelfth. A year later they advanced in the standings to third and fifth. The year 1990 proved disastrous for Harding, who fell to seventh place as their roles reversed and Kerrigan advanced to fourth. But in 1991 the scrappy Harding returned and celebrated her greatest outing. She won the National title ahead of Yamaguchi and Kerrigan. Her clean triple Axel Paulsen jump ignited the audience, but she never rose to that level again. In 1992 Harding settled for the bronze medal behind Yamaguchi and Kerrigan, and in 1993 a dismal fourth place kept her off the World team. Kerrigan, in the meantime, had become America's newest "ice princess." Her elegant style, popularity, and competitive success weighed on Harding as she entered the 1994 season. Determined not to be excluded again from the World and Olympic teams, Harding became involved in figure skating's most sinister plot, one intended to ensure her position on those teams.

At the National Championships, following a practice session, a man approached Kerrigan, who had just exited the ice, and struck her above her landing knee with a collapsible metal baton. The attacker fled the scene, crashing through an acrylic exterior door and disappearing into a bitterly cold and snowy day in Detroit. Damage to Kerrigan's leg was severe but not permanent. Withdrawal from Nationals was necessary, but the

Kristi Yamaguchi, Tonya Harding, and Nancy Kerrigan swept the medals at the World Championships in 1991. (George Rossano)

victim was also a survivor who would compete at the Olympic Games. Two skaters could be sent to Lillehammer, and under USFSA rules competing at the National Championships is not a requirement for selection. Harding, skating without her chief rival, won the national title, and thirteen-year-old Michelle Kwan placed second. Harding and Kerrigan were subsequently named to the Olympic team, with Kwan as the alternate.

Initial speculation following the attack included the possibility that it was the work of a deranged fan. Just a year earlier the tennis star Monica Selles had been stabbed by a fan of number-two-ranked Steffi Graf. With Selles sidelined, Graf won. Perhaps a fan of some other skater wanted to sideline Kerrigan in the Olympic year, but attention soon turned to another scenario. Harding, the skater with so much raw talent but such an inconsistent record, had much to gain. The story unfolded publicly over the next several weeks as extensive media coverage and two quickly published paperback books reported on police and FBI investigations.[13]

At first Harding claimed innocence of wrongdoing as well as lack of knowledge regarding a plot against Kerrigan, but at a news conference three weeks after the attack she admitted learning after returning home to Portland, Oregon, that persons "close to me" might have been involved. Those persons included her husband, Jeff Gillooly; his friends, Shawn Eckardt and Derrick Smith; and the actual attacker, Shane Stant. All were soon implicated as the investigation continued and the plot unraveled. In a plea bargain that limited charges to one count of racketeering, Gillooly implicated Harding. She was not incarcerated but ultimately performed four hundred hours of public service, paid fines totaling $160,000, and was placed on probation. Her eligible skating career ended when the USFSA banned her for life and stripped her of the 1994 National title.[14]

The Lillehammer Games were held before the investigation was completed. Mounting evidence implicating Harding cast a shadow over her innocence, but she had not yet been found guilty of criminal wrongdoing and was allowed to compete. Media attention was overwhelming. Kerrigan and Harding shared the same practice ice, which increased the tension and added to the drama. In the short program Kerrigan skated brilliantly and won. Oksana Baiul of Ukraine and Surya Bonaly of France placed second and third. Harding placed tenth. Baiul won the free skating by a vote of five judges to four and claimed the gold medal. The silver and bronze medals went to Kerrigan and Lu Chen of China. Bonaly slipped to fourth place. Harding, in what was to be her final eligible performance, not as a result of turning professional but as a result of banishment by the USFSA, placed eighth.

Yamaguchi, Harding, and Kerrigan represented one of America's strongest ever pools of lady skaters. All became senior competitors between 1987 and 1990. Yamaguchi retired as the Olympic gold medalist in 1992, and Kerrigan as the Olympic silver medalist in 1994. Harding, the most gifted athletically of the three, departed the sport in disgrace. Her senior eligible career was the longest, from 1987 to 1994, and Yamaguchi's was the shortest, from 1989 to 1992. Each was a national champion once, Harding in 1991, Yamaguchi in 1992, and Kerrigan in 1993. Only Yamaguchi became a World champion, but Harding and Kerrigan both won silver medals. Although the three might be viewed as participants in another American rivalry, the results suggest otherwise. Harding defeated Yamaguchi only once. Kerrigan never defeated her. Harding defeated Kerrigan all but once before 1992, but after that Kerrigan always defeated Harding. Yamaguchi and Kerrigan were consistent skaters; Harding's career was a tale of ups and downs.

Nancy Kerrigan (b. 1969) was only once the national champion and never a World or Olympic champion, but she competed at a time when, in addition to Yamaguchi and Harding, other challengers included Oksana Baiul, Surya Bonaly, Lu Chen, and Yuka Sato. In that outstanding field she compiled an impressive record, medaling twice in three World Championships and twice at the Olympic Games. Kerrigan retired after the Lillehammer Games rather than proceed to the World Championships. She has undertaken some professional opportunities, skating in a few shows and competitions, but has chosen to devote herself primarily to a domestic life.

Narrowly defeating Kerrigan at the games was Oksana Baiul (b. 1977), an artistic fifteen-year-old from Odessa, Ukraine, who just a year earlier was virtually unknown outside her own country. She first appeared at the European Championships in 1993 and claimed the silver medal behind Surya Bonaly. At the World Championships eight weeks later she defeated Bonaly, the first of three skaters to deny her a World title. The Olympic year, 1994, began like the previous year with a silver medal behind Bonaly at the European Championships. Baiul then defeated both Bonaly and Kerrigan at the Olympic Games. Choosing not to defend her World title, she ended one of the shortest international careers in the history of figure skating. It was just thirteen months from her first European effort to her Olympic gold medal. Turning professional, she moved to the United States, where she toured with Champions on Ice and entered professional competitions.

THE ASIAN TRIUMPH: YUKA SATO AND LU CHEN

Japan, which joined the ISU in 1926, twice sent skaters to competitions before World War II. Two men competed at the World Championships and Olympic Games in 1932, held that year in North America, and four men and one woman competed at the World Championships and the Olympic Games in 1936. After the war Japanese men competed at the World Championships in 1951, but a quarter century passed before Minoru Sano claimed their first medal in 1977. Japanese women competed in 1957, but nearly a quarter century passed before Emi Watanabe claimed their first medal in 1979.[15] A decade later, in 1989, Midori Ito became Japan's first World champion. She retired after winning the silver medal at the Albertville Olympic Games in 1992, just as another popular Japanese skater, Yuka Sato (b. 1973) prepared to make her mark in international competition.[16]

Sato's relatively short career culminated with a World title in 1994. Baiul and Kerrigan had retired following the Lillehammer Games, and Lu Chen elected not to compete that year. Thus, none of the Olympic medalists proceeded to the World Championships. Sato, who had placed fifth at the Games, upset Surya Bonaly, who had placed fourth, to win the World Championship. She became the second skater in as many years to deny Bonaly a World title. Since retiring from eligible skating, Sato, known for her artistry, has enjoyed a successful professional career.

China, the second Asian country to make its presence felt on the international scene, joined the ISU in 1956, some thirty years after Japan, but did not compete in World or Olympic events until 1980. For three years China fielded one entry each in the men's, ladies', and pairs' events but with little success. Skipping two years, a team returned in 1985 with ice dancers added to its roster. China entered no skaters for the next five years, but in 1991 one of the most artistic skaters of the decade appeared. Lu Chen (b.

1976) won the bronze medal at the Junior World Championships that year and proceeded to the World Championships, where she placed twelfth. A year later she won the bronze medal ahead of the more experienced Harding and Bonaly, both of whom had placed ahead of her the previous month at the Albertville Games. Lu Chen won a second bronze medal in 1993, withdrew in 1994, and became the World champion in 1995. She was the third skater to deny Bonaly a World title.

One of the most exciting finishes in World Championship history came in 1996 as Lu Chen defended her title. Michelle Kwan of the United States skated immediately after Lu Chen had presented an artistically superb free skate and wrested away the World title with the impromptu inclusion of an extra triple jump at the end of an equally superb free skate. A disastrous year for Lu Chen followed. At the World Championships, she failed to survive the qualifying round. Then, in 1998, her final competitive season, she won a second Olympic bronze medal. Retiring after the games, she entered the world of professional skating, where her graceful style has served her well.

Other Asian countries holding membership in the ISU include Chinese Taipei; the Democratic People's Republic of Korea (North Korea); Hong Kong; Mongolia; the Republic of Korea (South Korea); and Thailand. Mongolia, which joined in 1960, has yet to enter figure skaters in World or Olympic competition. Thailand, which joined in 1988, was represented by one skater, Charuda Upatham, in 1989. The Democratic People's Republic of Korea, which joined in 1957, sent one skater, Kim Myo Sil, in 1979. Hong Kong, which joined in 1983, has sent skaters sporadically since 1985. Taipei, which also joined in 1983, has entered skaters every year less one since 1986. The Republic of Korea, which joined in 1948, maintains the longest, most active participation and has had entrants annually since 1972. None of these countries has enjoyed the success of Japan and China, but continuing participation by skaters from places such as Taipei and the Republic of Korea will undoubtedly lead to medal winners in the future.

SURYA BONALY

When Lu Chen won her World title in 1995, Surya Bonaly (b. 1973) of France suffered the disappointment of a third consecutive silver medal. She had finished behind Oksana Baiul in 1993 and Yuka Sato in 1994. Bonaly never won a World title or an Olympic medal of any color, but her free-spirited style throughout her eligible career, which spanned a decade, led to numerous successes and a few controversies. Praised and loved by loyal fans, she suffered criticism from others, including judges and coaches, for a perceived lack of artistry. Her athletic prowess was rarely doubted. She had won gymnastic competitions before becoming a teenager, and early successes there have been cited as a reason for her sometimes shallow edging. She was coached largely by her mother, a physical education teacher who lacked skating expertise.

Bonaly won her first national title in 1988, the year Debi Thomas completed her amateur career at the Calgary Olympics. She was born in Nice, France, of African parents but was adopted as an infant by Caucasian parents. At age sixteen Bonaly became the French national champion for the first of nine consecutive years, and beginning in 1991 she was the European champion for five years as well. During her most successful competitive years, 1989 through 1994, there were wins at many major competitions, including all the Grand Prix events: Trophée Lalique in 1989 and 1990, Skate Canada in 1991, Nations Cup in 1992, NHK Trophy in 1992 and 1993, and Skate America in 1994. Although she won the World junior title in 1991, the coveted World title always eluded her. From tenth place at age fifteen, she progressed to ninth and then fifth before falling to eleventh in 1992. A year later Bonaly leaped past all returning skaters to capture the silver medal behind Oksana Baiul. Included among those she defeated that year were Yuka Sato and Lu Chen, those skaters who would deny her the title in the ensuing two years.

Surya Bonaly's free-spirited approach to skating led to numerous successes and a few controversies. (Paul Harvath)

Bonaly competed at three Olympic Games but failed to medal. Her best placement was fourth in 1994. None of the medalists that year proceeded to the World Championships in Chiba, Japan, which set the stage for Bonaly to win the World title. Although she skated two clean programs, the graceful Yuka Sato, who had placed fifth at the games, skated flawlessly before a native audience and narrowly defeated her. At the award ceremony Bonaly refused at first to mount the medal stand and then removed the medal from around her neck after it was awarded. That manifestation of disappointment, viewed as poor sportsmanship, followed her throughout the remainder of her eligible career. Bonaly's third World silver medal in 1995 came with help from another skater. In fourth place after the short program, Bonaly would have placed third behind Nicole Bobek of the United States had Michelle Kwan not leaped past Bobek in the free skating, advancing Bonaly to second and dropping Bobek to third.

Bonaly's last international title was won at the European Championships in 1995. Her final three years of eligible skating proved to be disappointing. She collected just two international medals, silver at the European Championships in 1996 and bronze at Skate Canada in 1997. In addition, she lost her long-held national title. Most devastating was her final competitive season. She placed sixth at the European Championships and tenth at the Olympic Games. Her swan song as an eligible skater occurred at Nagano. In sixth place after the short program, she ended her Olympic free skate by defiantly executing her famous backflip directly in front of the judges, a move not allowed in competitive skating.[17]

A new generation of younger skaters had arrived. The medalists at Nagano were Tara Lipiniski, fifteen; Michelle Kwan, seventeen; and Lu Chen, twenty-one. Bonaly at age twenty-four was among the elder competitors. A professional career, where her free-spirited approach to skating could blossom to its fullest, was in the offing, and successes there reflect those of her early years as an eligible skater. She has been especially effective in team competitions. Side-by-side backflips with Kurt Browning to a cheering crowd at the conclusion of Ice Wars in 2000 demonstrated conclusively her strength and popularity.

MICHELLE KWAN AND HER RIVALRIES

Michelle Kwan (b. 1980), boasts a remarkable career that is partially the story of two rivalries, one short term and the other long term, one leading to the Nagano Olympics and the other to the Salt Lake City Olympics. The fifteen-year-old Kwan first competed against the thirteen-year-old Tara Lipinski, a tiny jumping sensation in her first year as a senior, at the 1996 National Championships. The medalists were Kwan, Tonia Kwiatkowski, and Lipinski, and it was a year in which the United States qualified to send three ladies to the World Championships. There, Lipinski had a disappointing first out-

Michelle Kwan presenting a beautiful forward outside spiral.

ing, placing twenty-second in the short program. But the resilient youngster bounced back. She placed eleventh in the free skating and finished fifteenth overall. Nothing that day suggested the success that would be hers during the next two years.

Tara Lipinski (b. 1982) began the new season by placing second behind Kwan at Skate America, but in three subsequent head-to-head battles—the Champions Series Finals, the United States Championships, and the World Championships—Lipinski held her senior rival to silver medals. One is reminded of Sonja Henie's sudden leap onto the world stage exactly seventy years earlier. Henie and Lipinski were the same age.

During the Olympic season, Lipinski's final year of eligible competition, the rivals met only twice. Kwan regained the national title. The rivalry reached its peak at Nagano, where Kwan won the short program and Lipinski was a close second. The winner of the more heavily weighted free skating would be the 1998 Olympic champion. Kwan skated conservatively. Lipinski skated aggressively. Her program was stronger athletically and included her famous triple loop–triple loop combination jump. It won the approval of the judges, and Lipinski became the youngest ever Olympic champion.[18]

The similarity with Henie ceased at that point. There would not be multiple Olympic gold medals or a long string of World championships. Professional opportunities in 1998 were plentiful and lucrative. In 1928 they were almost nonexistent. Lipinski elected to turn professional and in that arena has experienced a successful career. She joined Stars on Ice and became a senior member of the company.

Kwan continued to compete and by 2001 had become a four-time World champion, equaling the records of Lily Kronberger and Katarina Witt.[19] Perhaps more important, her grace and style have joined her to a remarkable group of Americans, including Peggy Fleming, Janet Lynn, and Dorothy Hamill, whose elegant style and unprecedented popularity have made them role models for young skaters.

Kwan's second rival came from Russia. Irina Slutskaya (b. 1979) was another youngster who began skating for health reasons. Her mother, a former skier, believed that fresh air would keep her daughter from frequent illnesses and took her skating at age four. By age ten she was training full time. Her rivalry with Kwan is best viewed in retrospect, as records for their first seven years of competing against each other, 1994 through 2000, show Kwan ahead of Slutskaya in sixteen of eighteen meetings. Slutskaya's two defeats of Kwan came at Centennial on Ice in 1996 and the Grand Prix Finals in 2000. Their acute rivalry occurred in the two seasons preceding the Salt Lake City Games.

Slutskaya first came to prominence as a youthful and vivacious skater at the European Championships in 1996. She had placed fifth the year before in her first season as a senior but now claimed the title, passing all those who had placed ahead of her the previous year: Surya Bonaly, Olga Markova of Russia, Elena Liashenko of Ukraine, and Tanja Szewczenko of Germany. Already that year she had won Skate Canada, Nations

Irina Slutskaya displayed newfound artistry at the World Championships in 2001. (Michelle Harvath)

Cup, and the Cup of Russia. In 1997 she repeated as the European champion and again won the Cup of Russia. Then for two years she regressed, winning only one competition, the Cup of Russia in 1999. Not yet having won the Russian national title, she briefly considered exiting the sport but returned for the 2001 season with newfound motivation and significantly improved artistry. With that transformation Slutskaya became the Russian national champion, reclaimed the European title, and won the Grand Prix Final for a second time, but at the World Championships she again placed second behind Kwan.

Maria Butyrskaya (b. 1972), Slutskaya's compatriot, was the Russian national champion every year except one from 1992 through the end of the decade. She won Skate Canada in 1992 and the Finlandia Trophy in 1996 as well as medals of other colors, but 1999 was her banner year. It resulted in twelve medals, eight gold and four silver, in as many competitions. In addition to winning three Grand Prix events she defeated Kwan to become Russia's first lady World champion. Butyrskaya was born and trained in Moscow, where she began skating at age five, and still resides there. As a professional she has undertaken tours in the United States, including ones with Champions on Ice.

At the beginning of the 2002 season Slutskaya, age twenty-two, Kwan twenty-one, and Butyrskaya twenty-nine, were ranked internationally in that order. Fourth in the rankings was a sixteen-year-old American, Sarah Hughes (b. 1985), who had defeated each of her older colleagues in Grand Prix events. Hughes became a senior skater in 1999. She placed fourth at the National Championships and seventh at the World Championships. In 2000 she won bronze medals at the National Championships and Trophée Lalique. In 2001 she won medals, silver or bronze, at every competition entered, including three Grand Prix events, the Grand Prix Finals, the National Championships, and the World Championships. Rapidly developing a reputation as a consistent skater, she was viewed as someone who with experience and maturity could become a World champion. Hughes's first major win came in the Olympic year at Skate Canada, where she defeated both Slutskaya and Kwan. That followed by a week a much-debated split decision at Skate America that placed Kwan first and Hughes second. The Grand Prix final was watched closely as Slutskaya, Kwan, and Hughes claimed the medals. It was Slutskaya's third consecutive Grand Prix title, a feat not duplicated in any discipline. Butyrskaya, who could never be ruled out, suffered medical problems just two weeks before the event and placed fourth.

The ladies' competition in Salt Lake City had become totally unpredictable. Kwan's primary competition was not limited to Slutskaya. It included the more senior Butyrskaya; the young sensation Hughes; and yet another young American, the petite, seventeen-year-old Sasha Cohen (b. 1984). Cohen, an athletically gifted and highly flexible skater, had not competed the previous season because of a back injury, but in 2002 she was skating well and considering raising the stakes by attempting a quadruple Salchow in her Olympic program. No woman had yet completed a quadruple jump in competition.

The ladies' competition provided the highlight of the Salt Lake City Games. The short program held no surprises. Kwan entered the free skating in first place, confidently poised to realize her dream of winning the title that had alluded her four years earlier. Slutskaya was solidly in second place and remained the primary challenger. Cohen, Hughes, and Butyrskaya were in third, fourth, and fifth. Few would have predicted the results of the free skating, which provided one of the most stunning upsets in figure skating history. Hughes presented a flawless program and became the Olympic champion. Slutskaya jumped ahead of Kwan and claimed the silver medal. Kwan settled for bronze. Cohen, who did not attempt the quadruple jump, placed fourth. Butyrskaya slipped to sixth.

Butyrskaya retired from eligible skating. Hughes remained eligible but chose not to proceed to the World Championships, where Slutskaya won both the short program and the free skating to ascend the podium as the 2002 World champion. Kwan placed second, with Cohen fourth. Fumie Suguri, a young artistic skater from Japan who placed fifth at the Olympic Games, jumped ahead of Cohen to claim her first World medal.

PAIR SKATING: THE RUSSIANS AND THEIR CHALLENGERS

It had been nine years since a non-Russian pair had won a World title when in 1993 the Canadians Isabelle Brasseur (b. 1970) and Lloyd Eisler (b. 1963), twice silver and once bronze medalists, skated brilliantly, won both programs, and stood atop the medal platform. They had won their national title in 1989, slipped to third in 1990, reclaimed the title in 1991, and held it for the remainder of their eligible career. Their Grand Prix titles include Skate Canada in 1988, Skate America in 1990, Nations Cup in 1991, and NHK Trophy in 1993. Since retiring as World champions, Brasseur and Eisler have enjoyed a highly successful professional career. Their legacy of unusually daring and exciting lifts offered as eligible competitors continued into their professional careers.

In fourth place at the World Championships in 1993 were Radka Kovaříková (b. 1975) and René Novotny (b. 1963) of the Czech Republic. They slipped to fifth place in 1994 but became in their final year of eligible competition, 1995, the first Czech pair to win a World title.[20]

Silver medalists at the World Championships in 1993 were Mandy Wötzel (b. 1973) and Ingo Steuer (b. 1966) of Germany, then in their first year of competing together. Both had previous international careers with other partners, Wötzel for five years with Axel Rauschenbach and Steuer for two years with Ines Müller. Wötzel and Steuer won the European title in 1995 and the World title in 1997. At their final competition, the Nagano Olympics in 1998, they placed third.

Thus, in odd-numbered years beginning in 1993 pairs from Canada, the Czech Republic, and Germany successively wrested World titles away from the Russians, but at the Olympic Games Russian pairs continued to prevail as they had since 1964. Elena Berezhnaya and Anton Sikharulidze were destined to continue that tradition in 2002, but a talented Canadian pair capable of seriously challenging them surfaced in 2000. Jamie Salé (b. 1977) and David Pelletier (b. 1974), competing at their first World Championships, placed fourth. Just a year later, skating before a Canadian crowd in Vancouver, they upset the more experienced and strongly favored Berezhnaya and Sikharulidze and entered the Olympic season as the reigning World champions. Confirming the legitimacy of their World title, two months before the games, again skating before a native audience, Salé and Pelletier defeated Berezhnaya and Sikharulidze at the Grand Prix Finals in Kitchener, Ontario. The stage was set for an exciting match-up between the two outstanding pairs in Salt Lake City.

Four Russian pairs claimed World titles during the decade preceding the Salt Lake City Games. Evgenia Shishkova (b. 1972) and Vadim Naumov (b. 1969) won bronze medals in 1993 on their way to becoming World champions in 1994. Although they placed fourth at the Lillehammer Games, the gold and silver medalists retired before the World Championships. Seizing the opportunity, Shishkova and Naumov leaped ahead of the defending World champions, Brasseur and Eisler, to win their only World title. Silver medals followed in 1995.

The career of Marina Eltsova (b. 1973) and Andrei Bushkov (b. 1969), World champions in 1996, parallels that of Shishkova and Naumov. Like their predecessors, they won bronze medals before becoming World champions and silver medals a year later. In their final year of eligible competition, 1998, they placed well down in the rankings, seventh at the Nagano Games and sixth at the World Championships.

Elena Berezhnaya (b. 1977) and Anton Sikharulidze (b. 1976) were reminiscent of the great Russian pairs of the past. Not since Mishkutenok and Dmitriev, who retired in 1992, has a Russian pair been as successful.[21] A bronze medal performance at the European Championships in 1997 was followed by a ninth-place finish at the World Championships, but in ensuing seasons they consistently medaled, and many were gold. As World champions twice, in 1998 and 1999, they are the only pair to repeat since Mishkutenok and Dmitriev. Unfortunately, they were not allowed to defend their title in 2000. Seven weeks earlier, during the European Championships, Berezhnaya inadvertently took a medication for bronchitis that contained a disallowed stimulant. It caused a positive reading of her doping test, leading to mandatory revocation of the European title.[22]

With Bereznaya and Sikharulidze, the expected winners, sidelined, the World title was open, and the stage was set for an exciting match-up between three less experienced pairs from as many countries, all of whom would eventually become World champions. After the short program, Xue Shen and Hongbo Zhao of China were in first place, with Maria Petrova and Alexei Tikhonov of Russia second and Jamie Salé and David Pelletier of Canada third. The gold medal was within reach of the pair who could win the free

Elena Berezhnaya and Anton Sikharulidze, two-time World champions from Russia, became unwittingly ensnared in a judging controversy at the 2002 Olympic Winter Games. (Paul Harvath)

skating, and the pressure was tremendous. None of the pairs skated cleanly, and all positions changed. The World champions were Petrova and Tikhonov, with Shen and Zhao second. Salé and Pelletier slipped to fourth as Sarah Abitbol and Stephane Bernadis of France advanced to third.

Maria Petrova (b. 1977) and Alexei Tikhonov (b. 1971) had won the European title and placed fourth at the World Championships in 1999. They placed second at the European Championships in 2000 but were awarded the title after Berezhnaya's failed doping test. With Bereznaya and Sikharulidze sidelined for the season, they became World champions.

Xue Shen (b. 1978) and Hongbo Zhao (b. 1973), China's first medal-winning pair, demonstrated consistent improvement throughout their career. At their first World Championships in 1994 they placed twenty-first. They did not compete in 1995, but upon returning placed fifteenth in 1996, eleventh in 1997, and fourth in 1998. Four medals followed, silver in 1999 and 2000, bronze in 2001, and gold in 2002. Their Olympic record includes a fifth-place finish at Nagano in 1998 and bronze medals at Salt Lake City in 2002. Coupled with Lu Chen's medals in 1994 and 1998, Chinese skaters have successfully medaled at three successive Olympic Games.

The Salt Lake City Olympics will long be remembered not only for the surprising upset in the ladies' competition but also, and infamously, for the unfortunate judging scandal in the pairs' competition that resulted in a flawed win for two pairs. The short program provided no surprises as Berezhnaya and Sikharulidze, Salé and Pelletier, and Shen and Zhao respectively placed first, second, and third. The winner of the free skating would be the gold medalist. By a five-to-four split of the judges, the Russians, Berezhnaya and Sikharulidze, defeated the Canadians, Salé and Pelletier. Shen and Zhao were third. The Russians and the Canadians both skated well, although Sikharu-lidze stepped out on the side-by-side double Axel Paulsen jumps, an obvious mistake. Salé and Pelletier skated a completely clean program. Not atypically, judges from East European countries placed the Russians first, whereas those from Western countries placed the Canadians first. The swing judge, who was from France, stated in the judges' meeting following the event that she had been "pressured" by the French Federation to give advantage to the Russians, presumably in exchange for a similar advantage for the French ice dancers, Marina Anissina and Gwendal Peizerat.

It was the kind of judging dishonesty that can, unfortunately, thrive in the environment of a subjectively evaluated sport. The situation at Salt Lake City was particularly blatant owing to the French judge's admission of impropriety. As a result of pressure applied by the media and a protest filed by the Canadian federation, the ISU subsequently awarded duplicate gold medals to Salé and Pelletier. There was precedence in other Olympic sports for awarding duplicate medals, but no such precedent existed in figure skating.

Neither Berezhnaya and Sikharulidze nor Salé and Pelletier competed in the following World Championships, where the Olympic bronze medalists Shen and Zhao stood atop the medal stand. Tatiana Totmianina and Maxim Marinin of Russia and Kyoko Ina and John Zimmerman of the United States were the silver and bronze medalists.

ICE DANCING

Russian domination of pair skating lessened slightly during the 1990s, but that was not the case for ice dancing. Isabelle and Paul Duchesnay, representing France, upset Marina Klimova and Sergei Ponomarenko to win the World title in 1991, but they are the only non-Russian champions between Torvill and Dean in 1984 and Anissina and Peizerat of France in 2000. Klimova and Ponomarenko won Olympic gold in 1992 and then reclaimed the World title. The Duchesnays, who placed second at the games, chose not to defend their World title.

Maia Usova (b. 1964) and Alexandr Zhulin (b. 1963), a husband and wife couple, won the European and World titles in 1993, their sixth year on the international scene. They had been thrice silver medalists and once bronze medalists at the European Championships and twice each silver and bronze medalists at the World Championships. In the Olympic year, 1994, the reinstated Jayne Torvill and Christopher Dean won the European Championships. Oksana Grishchuk and Evgeny Platov were the silver medalists, and Usova and Zhulin the bronze medalists. That set up a three-way challenge at the games that proved to be exciting and mildly controversial. Torvill and Dean placed third in the compulsory dances but won the original dance, creating at that point a tie for first place with Usova and Zhulin. Grishchuk and Platov were third. Placements for the free dance were the inverse of those for the original dance. Grishchuk and Platov became Olympic champions, with Usova and Zhulin second and Torvill and Dean third. Neither Usova and Zhulin, who turned professional, nor Torvill and Dean, who returned to the professional ranks, proceeded to the World Championships, where Grishchuk and Platov won their first World title.

Oksana Grishchuk (b. 1971) and Evgeni Platov (b. 1967), the most successful ice dancers of the 1990s, epitomize the expected slow development of ice dancers. They progressed incrementally from fifth place at the World Championships in 1990 to Olympic and World titles in 1994. Torvill and Dean had held them to silver medals at the European Championships that year in an extremely close competition, but Grishchuk and Platov were never again defeated. Their competitive record includes three European, four World, and two Olympic titles. They are the only ice dancers to win Olympic gold twice.

The win at Nagano in 1998 was not without controversy. There were accusations of "bloc judging," with the outcome predetermined by judges from former Eastern Bloc countries in collusion with those from Italy and France. Actionable evidence to substantiate the allegations was not available, although charges brought by the ice dancing technical committee did result in the suspension of two judges. Grishchuk and Platov won the compulsory dances and the original dance by split decisions, but they won the more heavily weighted free dance conclusively, with first-place ordinals from all nine judges.

The silver medalists at Nagano were Anjelika Krylova (b. 1973) and Oleg Ovsiannikov (b. 1970), who skated in the shadow of Grishchuk and Platov for three years, always to silver medals. Grishchuk and Platov retired following the Games, allowing Krylova and Ovsiannikov to ascend the podium as World champions that year. They announced their intention to remain eligible through the next Olympic cycle but retired a year later after winning the European title and successfully defending their World title.

Three experienced couples from as many countries surfaced as leading medal contenders heading into the 2002 games. They had first competed against each other at the World championships in 1994, the year Grishchuk and Platov won their first gold medals. Shae-Lynn Bourne and Victor Kraatz of Canada placed sixth, Marina Anissina and Gwendal Peizerat of France placed tenth, and Barbara Fusar-Poli and Maurizio Margaglio of Italy placed seventeenth.

Bourne (b. 1976) and Kraatz (b. 1971), in their second year on the international scene, placed a respectable tenth at the Lillehammer Games in 1994 and were fourth at the Nagano Games four years later. At the World Championships, four consecutive bronze medals were collected, beginning in 1996. Not competing in 2000, they reappeared a year later before a home audience in Vancouver and placed fourth. Returning in the Olympic season with rediscovered enthusiasm and significantly improved artistry, they won two Grand Prix events and the Grand Prix Finals.

Anissina (b. 1975) and Peizerat (b. 1972) became the second ice-dancing couple from France to win a World championship. The Duchesnays had done so nine years earlier. Anissina's career began in her native Russia, where she was twice the World junior champion with Ilia Averbukh before he began competing with his wife, Irina Lobacheva. In 1993 Anissina's search for a new partner took her to Lyon, France, and the home of the Peizerats, totally unable to converse in French. She learned the language rapidly and became a French citizen. Anissina and Peizerat first appeared on the world stage a year later and climbed steadily toward their first Olympic and World medals, bronze at the games and silver at the World Championships in 1998. Following an additional silver medal in 1999, they became World champions in 2000 and were considered to be strong candidates for Olympic gold in 2002, but a talented couple from Italy held them to silver medals at the Worlds Championships in 2001.

Barbara Fusar-Poli (b. 1972) and Maurizio Margaglio (b. 1974) had missed only one year since entering the World scene in 1993 as they, too, progressed steadily toward their first World medals, silver behind Anissina and Piezerat in 2000. It was a decisive upset when the following year they won both the original dance and the free dance to claim the World title. That set the stage for an exciting Olympic battle, one augmented by added pressure to become Italy's first Olympic figure skating medalists in any discipline, but the new season did not begin consistently. They won two Grand Prix events but settled for fourth place at the Grand Prix Finals.

The bronze medalists at the Grand Prix Finals were a beautifully matched, slightly older married couple who had first appeared internationally in 1993 as the Lithuanian national champions. Margarita Drobiazko (b. 1971) and Povilas Vanagas (b. 1970) competed annually thereafter, winning their first medals at the European and World Championships in 2000. They failed to medal in 2001 but entered the Olympic season prepared to challenge those couples favored to win.

Not competing in Grand Prix events during the Olympic season was the experienced Russian couple Irina Lobacheva (b. 1973) and Ilia Averbukh (b. 1973), who had first appeared internationally in 1994. They competed every year thereafter at the European and World Championships but entered the 2002 season having accumulated just three bronze medals.

Ice dancing at Salt Lake City provided a few surprises but no controversies. The top

Marina Anissina and Gwendal Peizerat in a dance lift at the 1996 World Championships. (Paul Harvath)

eight couples placed in the same order for all three events: compulsory dances, original dance, and free dance. Anissina and Peizerat became the first non-Russian Olympic champions since Torvill and Dean. Lobacheva and Averbukh were the surprise silver medalists. Fusar-Poli and Margaglio settled for the bronze. Bourne and Kraatz placed fourth, and Drobiazko and Vanagas fifth.

Neither Anissina and Peizerat nor Fusar-Poli and Margaglio proceeded to the World Championships, which Lobacheva and Averbukh won easily. Bourne and Kraatz were the silver medalists. The bronze medalists were decided by the free dance, and the result proved to be contentious. The Lithuanians were in third place entering the free dance, with an Israeli couple, Calait Chait and Sergei Sakhnovski, in fourth. By a split decision of the judges, the Israelis defeated the Lithuanians in the free dance and claimed the bronze medals. The Lithuanian Federation filed a protest supported by a petition signed by more than thirty skaters and coaches. It read, in part, "We would like to bring to your attention our discontent with the final results of the competition. We are particularly distressed with the awarding of the bronze medal. The Lithuanians skated a medal-worthy performance and were not justly rewarded."[23]

The protest was denied, but it demonstrated again problems stemming from subjective judging, especially in ice dancing. Bloc judging may have occurred. The judges from Hungary, Israel, Italy, Russia, and Ukraine placed the Israelis first; the judges from Britain, France, Germany, and the United States placed the Lithuanians first. Following on the heels of the judging scandal in the pairs' competition at Salt Lake City a month earlier, the Lithuanian protest underscored the need for reevaluation of figure skating's judging system. The subject provided a major topic of discussion at the following ISU Congress, one that resulted in substantial changes implemented on a trial basis in the 2003 season.

PART FOUR

Expanded Opportunities
at Century's End

FIFTEEN

New Disciplines

AN explosion in the popularity of figure skating as a spectator sport followed the sensationalized media coverage of the Kerrigan-Harding incident in 1994, but its popularity had been growing steadily for more than half a century. Since the 1960s, televised World and Olympic competition has taken the sport into the homes of millions who discovered and enjoyed the perfect balance between artistry and athleticism that figure skating offers. That could not help but develop an increasingly enthusiastic audience for the sport and lead inevitably to a participatory role as converts filled ice rinks.

Those new to skating discovered a recreational activity that persons of all ages could enjoy and that entire families could do together. Many, young and old, took lessons, and some became highly proficient. Not surprisingly, new competitive opportunities followed. Adult skating is the most recent and fastest-growing area of competitive figure skating; collegiate and intercollegiate skating has become an available part of the college experience; and synchronized skating has evolved from an unpretentious beginning into a World championship sport that may become an Olympic sport.

SYNCHRONIZED SKATING

In all sports, only a select few of the most gifted athletes can become competitors at an elite level. In figure skating, the potential for reaching that level is typically determined well before secondary school age, a time when young people often leave the sport as other interests and activities vie for their time and attention. Professional skating opportunities come much later and usually follow a successful competitive career. Talented skaters as young teenagers seek the challenge of competition and the thrill of performing in front of audiences, but few can proceed to the more advanced levels of competitive skating or to the professional world of show skating. Additional opportunities for them are needed.

Club carnivals since the mid-nineteenth century have provided opportunities for many skaters, children through adults and beginners through advanced, to perform for appreciative audiences. Presented traditionally as annual events produced in short periods of concentrated rehearsals, they were fun and exciting for all participants. By the 1930s they had become extremely spectacular and were, proportionally, more expensive to produce. Professional companies such as the Ice Follies and Ice Capades set high standards for skating shows, and after World War II they competed to some degree for the same audiences as the larger club carnivals. Fewer carnivals were presented as production costs increased, although more, not fewer, performance opportunities were needed to retain the interest of an ever-increasing number of young skaters.

In that environment, synchronized skating had its birth. Like carnivals, it provided performance opportunities for skaters, but unlike carnivals it had the advantage of being a year-round activity. Synchronized skating began specifically as a performance outlet, but it soon became a competitive discipline as well. The discipline was forty-four years old and well established when in 1998 the ISU adopted the term *synchronized skating* to replace a former term, *precision team skating*. The words *precision* and *team* are descriptive and central to understanding the discipline, its uniqueness, and its development.

Precision team skating, usually called "precision skating," was born in Ann Arbor, Michigan, in 1954. Richard Porter (1913–97) was concerned about teenaged girls who, unable to progress further in the fiercely competitive world of figure skating, lacked challenging opportunities and quit skating as other sports and educational pursuits competed for their time and interest. He organized sixteen girls into a team that trained regularly and performed throughout the year. Their routines were crisp and polished, similar to those done by drill teams, and that gave the discipline its name. Porter's team passed expectations and expanded rapidly. Soon it had doubled in size, and skaters were competing for spots on it. Selecting the name Hockettes, the team performed locally at first and nationally later.

The Hockettes remained unique but not unnoticed for more than a decade. Other skating clubs throughout the United States, recognizing Ann Arbor's success, began forming teams. Although the discipline was not yet widespread, in 1974, twenty years after Porter formed his team, a competitive event was held specifically for "drill teams," at the Central Pacific Regional Championships, possibly the earliest formal competition for precision team skating.[1]

In 1976 the Ann Arbor Figure Skating Club sponsored a precision skating competition, with invitations extended to teams throughout the United States and Canada. Seventeen novice-, junior-, and senior-level teams competed, including those from the Ilderton and Woodstock clubs in Canada. A year later the Ilderton Figure Skating Club sponsored a similar competition, with twenty-three teams from Canada and the United States participating. It became a highly successful annual event. Thirty-four teams participated in 1978, forty-three in 1979, sixty-seven in 1980, and eighty in 1981, demonstrating the rapidly increasing interest in precision skating.

Although precision skating was originally an American innovation, by the late 1970s Canadian teams had taken a leadership role in the discipline's further development. Teams from throughout Canada competed regularly against each other. Responding to this growing interest, the CFSA in 1982 established a committee to oversee precision skating and a year later sanctioned the first Canadian National Precision Skating Championships. Hosted by the Ilderton Figure Skating Club, sixty teams from throughout Canada participated at the novice, junior, and senior levels.

At the same time, the USFSA, at its Governing Council meeting in 1981, charged its competitions committee with proposing rules for precision skating. The resulting *Guidelines for Precision Team Skating* was adopted in 1982. Sectional championships were held in 1983 with forty-nine teams competing at five levels: juvenile, novice, junior, senior, and adult. The largest participation came from the Midwestern Section, the birthplace of precision skating. A year later, 1984, precision skating was contested at the national level, with thirty-eight teams competing. The champions were the Fraserettes from Fraser, Michigan, at the senior level and the Hot Fudge Sundaes from Buffalo, New York, at the junior level. By 1985 the number of competing teams had increased to fifty-two, with the Fraserettes and the Hot Fudge Sundaes successfully defending their titles. An increased number of entrants in 1986 necessitated implementing consolation rounds, and that year the East Coast teams excelled for the first time. Former medal-winners at the junior level, the Hot Fudge Sundaes and the Haydenettes from Lexington, Massachusetts, moved up and took top honors at the senior level.

The Fraserettes reclaimed the senior title in 1987 but relinquished it again a year later as the Haydenettes, soon to become an American dynasty, won their first of twelve senior national titles. They have won several international titles as well. Organized in the

1980s, the Haydenettes are all high school- and college-age skaters. During the 2002 season, in addition to placing fourth at the World Championships, they competed at the Cup of Russia in St. Petersburg and the Spring Cup in Milan, Italy.

The Lake Placid International Precision Skating Competition was first held in 1983, with seventy-one teams from Canada and the United States participating. The Canadians demonstrated their now-well-established competitive superiority by winning most of the titles. Only in the adult event, the Veteran Division, did Americans prevail. The Eis Fraus from Lexington, Massachusetts, won that event. Senior champions the London Supremes, junior champions the Ilderton Silver Jets, novice champions the London Ice Picks, and pre-novice champions Les Etincelles (the Sparklers) were all from Canada.

During the 1980s precision skating became truly international. Australian and Japanese teams, the first outside North America, were formed early in the decade. Fumi Omori of Tokyo Women's College of Physical Education, inspired by an article in *Skating* magazine, organized a team from members of the college figure skating club. In 1987 she took twenty-eight students to Lake Placid for the International Precision Skating Competition, and since 1989 her teams have competed abroad every year. European teams were being formed in the mid-1980s. Teams from Finland and Sweden developed rapidly and within a decade were successfully challenging Canada's leadership in the discipline.

Demonstrating precision skating's growing popularity, intermediate, juvenile, and adult events were added to the 1987 competition at Lake Placid, where more than 2,200 skaters representing ninety-two teams competed. Les Pirouettes de Laval from Quebec won the senior competition, with the Haydenettes placing second. Winners in the junior and novice competitions were the Ice Images from Burlington, Ontario, and the Hot Fudge Sundaes from Buffalo, New York. Top honors in the intermediate and juvenile competitions went to Canadian teams, Les Altesses (the Highnesses) and the Stepping Stones. In the adult competition two U.S. teams, Acton-Ups and Esprit de Corps, took top honors. The team from Tokyo Women's College was given a special award for traveling the greatest distance to compete.

At the ISU Congress in 1990, "group skating," including now the disciplines of fours and precision skating, was redefined, and an ad hoc committee with membership from Canada, Sweden, and the United States, countries most actively involved in the discipline, was appointed to propose rules and regulations for competition. The committee's recommendations were adopted in 1992, judges were appointed in 1993, and a technical committee was elected in 1994.

A major international event, the Snowflake Invitational Precision Competition, was first held in Boston in 1990, two years before the ISU rules were adopted. USFSA rules were followed. About nine hundred skaters from thirty-six teams representing six countries—Canada, Japan, Mexico, Norway, Sweden, and the United States—competed at

The Haydenettes have become a dynasty in American synchronized skating.

the juvenile, novice, junior, and senior levels. Canadian dominance continued as their teams won three of the four divisions. Les Pirouettes de Laval were the senior champions. Sweden's Team Surprise, soon to become a major contender at the senior level, lived up to its name by becoming the junior champions. The novice and juvenile champions and Les Pirouettes de Laval and Les Coccinelles (the Ladybirds) de Charlesbourg were from Canada.

The 1993 Snowflake International Precision Competition was the first held under ISU regulations, which require a technical program in addition to free skating. Twenty-four junior and senior level teams representing eight countries participated. Les Pirouettes de Laval continued their dominance, with the Rockettes from Finland and the Haydenettes placing second and third. Americans prevailed in the junior competition. The Crystalettes were followed by two Finnish teams, Step by Step and Team Fintastic.

By the end of the decade a regular season of international competitions had evolved, including the Finlandia Cup, formerly the Helsinki International Precision Competition; the Coupe Internationale, formerly the French Cup International in Rouen; the Neuchâtel Trophy in Neuchâtel, Switzerland; the Spring Cup in Milan, Italy; the North American Synchronized Skating International, formerly the Snowflake International Precision Competition, in the United States; and Precision Canada.

In anticipation of the first World championships for synchronized skating, four annual Synchronized Skating Challenge Cups were held, the first at Boston in 1996. Others followed in Turku, Finland; Bordeaux, France; and Gothenburg, Sweden. The results of the challenge cups, which included only senior events, demonstrate a phenomenon that has been seen in other disciplines throughout the history of figure skating. Countries surface as world leaders in specific disciplines during particular periods. Sweden and Canada have dominated competitive synchronized skating.

Boston, Mass., 1996:	Bordeaux, France, 1998:
1. Team Surprise SWE	1. Team Surprise SWE
2. Les Pirouettes CAN	2. black ice CAN
3. black ice CAN	3. Les Pirouettes CAN
Turku, Finland, 1997:	Gothenburg, Sweden, 1999:
1. black ice CAN	1. Team Surprise SWE
2. Les Pirouettes CAN	2. black ice CAN
3. Team Surprise SWE	3. Rockettes FIN

The first World Synchronized Skating Championship was held in Minneapolis in 2000, with twenty-one teams from sixteen countries competing. Countries whose teams had placed in the top five at the 1999 Challenge Cup in Gothenburg were permitted to enter two teams each. They included Canada, Finland, Germany, Sweden, and the United States.[2] Team Surprise of Sweden, winner of three of the Challenge Cups, became the first World champions; black ice, winner of the 1997 Challenge Cup, was second; and Marigold Ice Unity of Finland, which had twice placed fifth at the Challenge Cups, was third.

The second World Championship was held in Helsinki in 2001, again with twenty-one teams from sixteen countries competing. The team from the Netherlands did not return, but one from Estonia appeared for the first time. Team Surprise repeated as the winner. The Rockettes, a Finnish team that had placed fourth in 2000, was second; black ice slipped to third.

Participation increased at the third World Championship, held in Rouen, France, in 2002, with twenty-four teams from nineteen countries competing, including the Nether-

Team Surprise of Sweden, the most successful synchronized skating team. (Jyrki Kostermaa)

lands and Estonia. Croatia, Iceland, and Belgium sent teams for the first time. Marigold Ice Unity, the third-place-finisher in 2000 and fourth-place finisher in 2001, won, edging out the favored two-time champions, Team Surprise. Black ice was again third.

Team Surprise boasts the best overall record in synchronized skating, winning three of the four Challenge Cups and two of the three World Championships and medaling at those they did not win. Black ice has been equally consistent, winning the 1997 Challenge Cup and medaling at every Challenge Cup and World Championship. Marigold Ice Unity, winner of only one medal prior to winning the World championship in 2002, bolstered Scandinavian superiority by keeping the gold medals there. Not since the days of Ulrich Salchow, Gillis Grafström, and Sonja Henie have Scandinavian skaters dominated in any discipline.

Synchronized skating was initially an activity specifically for young women, and it has remained primarily but not exclusively a women's sport. Regulations do not prohibit men's participation, and some teams now include men, although the number on any team is always small. Owing to the importance of uniform appearance, a basic precept of the discipline, costuming presents a challenge for mixed-gender teams. ISU rules relating to costume color help but do not result in complete uniformity. One is always aware of men on synchronized teams. As one commentator noted following the 2000 World Championships, men can be "a distraction to the uniform look of the team."[3] Perhaps as synchronized skating continues to expand there will be all-male teams. The power and speed possible would provide exciting performances.

Synchronized skating competitions are for practical reasons held separately from those for singles, pairs, and ice dancing. They involve hundreds of skaters. A typical team includes twenty members as well as alternates, team managers, and coaches; for some competitions individual figure skating clubs enter teams in multiple divisions, juvenile through adult. More hotel rooms are required at synchronized competitions than at regular figure skating competitions. Logistics and costs associated with travel present major challenges, and sponsors are few in number.

Figure skating's newest international discipline is growing rapidly and is providing opportunities for a large number of dedicated skaters to participate in the sport. From its inception as an activity and performance outlet for local skaters who might otherwise have left the sport it has grown into a highly competitive discipline in which thousands of skaters compete nationally and internationally. The juvenile, intermediate, and adult divisions may retain some of their former recreational emphasis, but the higher divisions, novice, junior, and senior, have become extremely competitive. As early as 1991 an ISU official noted correctly that "precision is no longer a recreational sport. It is a very sophisticated competitive activity."[4] It is anticipated that synchronized skating will become an Olympic sport. That will bring even greater attention to it but move it further away from Richard Porter's original purpose.

SYNCHRONIZED SKATING MANEUVERS

Synchronized skating includes five basic maneuvers that constitute the required elements in competitive short programs. They are circles, lines, blocks, wheels, and intersections. A harmonious program requires continuity and continuous movement, with fluid transitions from one element to another while incorporating variety and complex changes within the individual elements. All maneuvers are subject to various transformations. Circles rotate in either direction. They include large single circles, circles within circles rotating in the same or opposite directions, and separate circles rotating around their own centers in the same or opposite directions.

Lines consist of either one or two rows of skaters. Long, straight lines are particularly impressive and difficult to maintain. Much variety can be achieved with a pair of lines parallel, perpendicular, or at any angle to each other as skaters move side by side or one behind the other. Blocks are maneuvers consisting of three or more lines that move as a unit in any direction. Wheels are rotating moves, usually spokelike patterns numbering from three to five. When two spokes are in the shape of a sine wave they are called "S wheels." Lines and parallel lines also rotate as wheels.

Intersections in which one group of skaters passes through another group are the most exciting maneuvers in synchronized skating. Varieties include one block or line passing through another, spokes rotating in opposite directions, circles that collapse on themselves, and V-shaped patterns passing through each other. More complex intersections include triangular and box intersections with skaters moving in multiple directions.

Maneuvers in synchronized skating are judged according to difficulty. It is more difficult, for example, to maintain a long, straight line or a large circle than to maintain two short parallel lines or two separate circles. Rotational maneuvers, circles and wheels, can be mobile, meaning that the entire formation travels across the ice while rotating, which increases the difficulty substantially. The length and size of lines and circles are affected not only by the number of skaters involved but also by the holds employed. When a hand-to-hand hold is employed and arms are outstretched fully a single line by a senior team extends nearly across the ice surface. As lines become shorter, with a shoulder-to-shoulder hold, for example, difficulty decreases although the number of skaters remains the same.

Other basic holds in addition to the hand-to-hand and shoulder-to-shoulder include elbow holds, "basket weave" holds, and hand-to-waist holds. Continual changes in holds are expected, and much variety is possible. Elbows can be hooked, or the elbow of one skater can be held by the hand of another. In basket weave holds, the hands of two skaters are joined in front of or behind a skater positioned between them. Basket weave holds can be employed with all skaters facing in the same direction or with every other skater facing in the opposite direction. In hand-to-waist or hand-to-shoulder holds, sometimes called "choo-choo holds," skaters follow each other and hold the waist or shoulders of the skater in front of them. Maneuvers are permitted without any hold or limitation on the time of separation, but a primary consideration in synchronized skating is maintaining equal distance between skaters, which is extremely difficult during separation.

Judging considerations include unison, difficulty, and presentation. Two programs are presented in international competition. The short program, of two-and-a-half minutes' duration, counts one-third of the total score. It requires inclusion of all five elements, with specified changes and transitions within those elements. The free-skating program, four-and-a-half minutes for seniors and four minutes for juniors, counts two-thirds of the total score. It has no specific required elements but must include an artistic balance of all basic maneuvers connected with intricate step sequences and constantly changing handholds. The music must include at least one change of tempo and cannot be vocal.

COLLEGIATE AND INTERCOLLEGIATE SKATING

Collegiate figure skating has a long history. The International Confederation of Students, organized in 1919, held Student World Championships for summer sports in 1924 and again in 1927 and 1928 before being named the International University Games. Five competitions were held before World War II. Beginning in 1928, winter sports were added, always at different times and locations but in the same years. Figure skating was one of those sports.

Competitions were reinstated after the war on a biennial basis from 1949 to 1957 under the name International University Sport Week, but they suffered from minimal participation by athletes from the West, clearly a reaction to the cold war. The Fédération Internationale de Sport Universitaire (FISU), established in 1948, had anticipated the problem and adopted a clause in its constitution which states that the "FISU pursues its objects without consideration or discrimination of a political, denominational, or racial nature." Under FISU leadership, the first Winter Universiade was held in 1958 at Zell-Am-See, Austria, and the first Summer Universiade, was held in 1959 at Torino, Italy. Winter and summer Universiades continue today. The FISU also sponsors the World University Championships, held since the early 1960s in even-numbered years. Contests are for specific sports, each at its own location. Twenty-five championships were held in 2002.

Figure skating events have been included in many international student competitions since the 1920s. Collegiate and intercollegiate competitions specifically for figure skating at the national level have also occurred from time to time in various countries. In Canada and the United States, competitions for college and university students, sanctioned by the national federations, were established in the 1980s and expanded in the 1990s. They have become an important part of figure skating.

Rooted in a history that spans nearly four decades, intercollegiate competitions following CFSA and USFSA rules date from the early 1960s. The Western Canadian Intercollegiate Figure Skating Championships provided team competitions beginning in 1961 for students from three institutions: the University of British Columbia in Vancouver, the University of Saskatchewan in Saskatoon, and the University of Alberta in Edmonton.[5] The 1967 competition, held at Alberta, included twelve-member teams from each of the participating universities. Singles' events consisted of compulsory figures and free skating, the pairs' event included only free skating, and the ice dancing event included only compulsory dances. CFSA judges officiated, and team point totals were determined by the simple addition of placement points. The winner that year was the University of British Columbia.

Similar competitions were held in eastern Canada, including ones among four institutions: McGill University in Montreal, the University of Toronto, the University of Montreal, and St. Lawrence University from just across the border in Canton, New York. Another was held in the United States between Bowling Green State University and the University of Michigan in 1968. But in Canada and the United States intercollegiate competitions were isolated events that resulted from a unique combination of available facilities, qualified competitors, and support from the universities involved. Figure skating as an established collegiate activity was not possible, particularly in the United States. Skating facilities were often not available; the number of qualified skaters, especially at small universities, did not justify competitive teams; and supporting arms of the regulatory bodies, the CFSA and USFSA, necessary for the encouragement of intercollegiate skating had not been established.

During the 1970s, primarily at the instigation of students themselves, figure skating clubs were formed at some universities, and by the 1980s the need for oversight and support was recognized. The CFSA and the USFSA established collegiate programs to support the established clubs and to encourage the formation of new ones. The number of collegiate clubs in the United States has remained small, numbering just forty-seven in 2002, while competitive opportunities were needed for all skaters attending all universities, not just those at schools with skating clubs. To meet this need, collegiate competitions were established for students at all universities, with or without skating clubs, who wanted to compete individually. Intercollegiate competitions were also established for students who attend universities with established skating clubs and want to compete in team competitions.

The U.S. National Collegiate Championships, inaugurated in 1985, provide competitive opportunities for all full-time university students who are members of the USFSA, whether through their home clubs or university clubs. Singles, pairs, and ice dancing events are offered at the junior and senior levels under USFSA rules for competition. Because the event is held annually in August, all competitors must be currently admitted students or have been students during the previous academic year. Gold medalists at the 1985 Championships, which included only events for senior men and ladies, were Kathaleen Kelly from Harvard University and Robert Rosenbluth from Emory University. Kelly, who won again in 1987 and 1989, proceeded to graduate school, earned a law degree, served on the board of directors of the USFSA, and became a national judge.

Because National Collegiate Championships are open to all full-time university students, members of Team USA, America's roster of elite skaters, who are matriculated students can compete. Many elite skaters, especially the ladies, are of high school age, and those of college age often do not matriculate while competing. Other competitive opportunities, often with substantial financial rewards, have become available to them. In the late 1980s, however, several elite and rising skaters competed and won National Collegiate titles. Among them were Paul Wylie from Harvard University in 1986; Todd Sand with Lori Blasco from California State University-Northridge in 1987; Nancy Kerrigan from Emmanuel College and Calla Urbanski with Mark Naylor from the University of Delaware in 1988; Urbanski and Naylor again in 1989; and Brian Wells with Laura Murphy from the University of Delaware in 1990.[6]

The National Collegiate Championships experienced a significant increase in participation through the 1980s, but that growth has not been sustained. Fourteen skaters from as many universities competed in singles' events at the first championships in

Kathaleen Kelly, three-time champion at the U.S. Collegiate Championships. (© J. Barry Mittan [www. jbmittan.com])

1985. Participation increased sixfold to eighty-eight as skaters from fifty-three universities competed in all four disciplines in 1990, but the numbers slipped to fifty-one as skaters from forty-two universities competed in singles and ice dancing events in 1995. Participation increased again in 2000, but not to the level of 1990. Sixty-eight skaters from fifty-eight universities competed in singles events. In 2002 the numbers were down again, when forty-eight skaters from forty-two universities entered only singles events.

The 2000 National Collegiate Championships provided the final, and for many sad, chapter in the long history of compulsory figures. Since their elimination by the ISU in 1990 they had continued as separate competitive events at USFSA-sanctioned competitions. But like special figures, which had continued as separate events after World War I, compulsory figures once removed from the mainstream of competition could not survive. On August 18, 2000, Brooke Pitman of Northern Arizona University skated the final figure, a forward outside–forward inside paragraph loop, at the last USFSA-sanctioned competition to include figures. She placed second in the senior ladies' event. The winners at the senior and junior levels were Jessica Koslow of Brandeis University and Angela Marquart of the University of North Dakota.

Miami University in Ohio and Western Michigan University have established figure skating as a varsity sport, which bodes well for its future. A sport's visibility and stature improve and its funding increases significantly when it becomes a designated sport in a department of athletics. Synchronized skating, which is almost exclusively a women's sport, can help athletic departments meet Title IX requirements and has the potential to become a National Collegiate Athletic Association (NCAA) sport.

Intercollegiate competitions have been held occasionally since the late 1960s. The early competition between Bowling Green State University and the University of Michigan has been mentioned. Among more recent competitions was one held in Cambridge, Massachusetts, in 1995. Largely a regional event, ten New England teams competed, six from Massachusetts, three from New York, and one from Vermont, but there was an eleventh team from Quincy University in Illinois. The winners were the University of Vermont, first; Boston University, second; and Colgate University, third. Intercollegiate competitions remained isolated events until April 2000, when the first USFSA-sponsored Intercollegiate Team Figure Skating Competition was held. Teams from seven universities that had qualified through conference competitions competed at Miami University of Ohio.[7] The winners at that inaugural event were Miami University, first; Dartmouth College, second; and the University of Delaware, third.

The United States is divided into three geographic conferences for intercollegiate skating, Eastern, Midwestern, and Pacific Coast, paralleling the sectional divisions employed in national competition. A minimum of three point-earning competitions are held annually in each conference, and the top three point-winning clubs or varsity teams from each conference proceed to the National Intercollegiate Team Figure Skating Championships. Events contested include free skating, solo dance, and "team maneuvers," an event specifically for three to five skaters. The 2002 Championships were hosted by the University of Michigan and included eight teams. Only the Pacific Coast Conference failed to send its full quota of three. The University of Delaware won the championship, with the University of Michigan second and Dartmouth College third.

ADULT SKATING

From thousands of skaters gliding across frozen ponds in nineteenth-century London, New York, and elsewhere to crowds of skaters circling indoor rinks throughout much of the world today, the magic of ice skating has excited all who participated, from beginners to skilled practitioners, from the very young to senior citizens, but not until recently have all skaters been served by established governing organizations. Synchronized skating and collegiate skating programs were developed in the 1980s, but adult skaters remained a largely unserved group.

Waltzing contests were held as early as the 1890s, and various events in which adults could participate have occurred sporadically throughout the twentieth century, but they have been locally sponsored, with little likelihood of sustainability. Structured adult skating is a product of the 1990s. Competitive events, primarily ladies' events, had been held in some regional competitions for about a decade when the USFSA program development committee was charged with establishing adult programs.[8]

The first Adult Championships were held at Wilmington, Delaware, in 1995, and participation surpassed all expectations. There, 421 skaters from thirty-seven states competed in singles', pairs', and ice dancing events. A year later at Lake Placid, New York, a 30 percent increase was realized as skaters from forty-three states competed. By the sixth annual Adult Championships in 2000, again at Lake Placid, a fourth ice surface had to be employed as 628 skaters, the largest number to date, competed. Adult skating entered the twenty-first century as the fastest-growing area of participation in the sport.

Adult Championships provide competitive opportunities for skaters of varied backgrounds and experiences. Some are former regional, sectional, and national competitors; others begin skating as adults and become competent practitioners. Adults of all ages and levels are accommodated. Four age groups, twenty-five to thirty-five, thirty-six to forty-five, forty-six to fifty-five, and fifty-six and older, are employed. Skaters are qualified to compete in specific events within their age groups based on test achievement.[9] "Masters" events in free skating and interpretive skating at senior, junior, and novice levels are based on the standard USFSA test structure, whereas "adult" events in free skating and interpretive skating at gold, silver, and bronze levels are based on a special set of tests established specifically for adult skaters. Similar divisions are employed for pair skating and ice dancing.

In adult skating one does not expect to see athletically difficult moves such as the multiple rotation jumps necessary for success in elite eligible skating but rather a level of artistry that results from maturity and sophistication.[10] Not surprisingly, interpretive events are especially popular for skaters as well as audiences. Rules regarding costumes

Barbara Sdandke of France, Rhea Schwartz of the United States, Chris Pascoe of Great Britain, and Carol Laws of the United States were the top finishers in the Bronze Ladies III event at the first Mountain Cup Championship in Villard de Lans, France. (Rhea Schwartz)

and music are nullified, which provides freedom and flexibility. After the first adult competition in Wilmington, John LeFevre, an international judge who became in 1998 the executive director of the USFSA, noted that "the adult skaters' interpretation of the music and their choreography is in many cases superior to that of younger skaters."[11]

Adult skating is not just an American phenomenon. It exists in other countries and in the international arena. Primarily through the effort of one woman, Barbara Standke, the now-well-established Mountain Cup International Competition was first held in 1999 at Villard de Lans, France. Because there were no international rules for adult competition, the USFSA's competition structure was followed. Ninety-four adults from eight countries, Australia, Belgium, Canada, Ecuador, France, Germany, Great Britain, and the United States, competed in ladies', men's, pairs', and interpretive events. The competition was successful beyond all expectations.

Standke participated and won a gold medal in the Bronze Ladies III event. Skating in that same event and placing second was the former USFSA adult skating committee chair, Rhea Schwartz, a leading proponent of adult skating. One other competitor, Karla Morales from Equador, deserves special mention. She won the Ladies Bronze Freestyle I event. No South American skater had competed since 1908, when Horatio Torromé, representing Argentina, did so at the London Olympic Games. Ninety-one years later, an Equadorian skater competed at the first Mountain Cup competition. Morales is from Quito, the capital of Ecuador, has no coach, and practices on a half-size rink. She reportedly learned to skate by watching video tapes and taking a few lessons while on vacation in the United States.

The Mountain Cup competition became an annual event, and others have followed. The ISU, recognizing the value and popularity of adult skating, has appointed a working committee, chaired by Rhea Schwartz, to develop the discipline and competitions for it.

The purpose, Schwartz explains, is "to encourage adult skating, to keep adults skating, to create a family of adult skating friends worldwide, and to provide the excitement of serious competition for those who want it."[12]

Adult skating is unique in that it is a lifetime sport and serves as a strong bond among people who have similar interests but different nationalities. As they compete against one another, they develop lifelong international friendships. One skater and writer succinctly noted that "it's an exciting time to be an adult figure skater."[13]

SIXTEEN

The World of Professional Skating

THE Ice Follies, Hollywood Ice Review, and Ice Capades were founded between 1936 and 1941, years immediately preceding U.S. entry into World War II. Holiday on Ice was founded during the war years. All survived the War and became increasingly spectacular as competition among them led to large casts, elaborate sets, and lavish costumes.[1]

The role of the amateur club carnival, a tradition dating from the nineteenth century, was challenged by these permanently established touring companies that operated with large budgets, professional production staffs, and many of the world's most decorated skaters. Carnivals, which had reached their peak in the 1930s, continued well into the postwar era, but their ability to compete with professional shows gradually declined. Clubs in major skating centers such as Boston and in developing skating centers such as Dallas continued to present carnivals for many years, but by the 1960s the number throughout the country had declined substantially.[2] Like combined skating, special figures, and compulsory figures, club carnivals have become largely relics of figure skating's storied past.

CONTINUATION OF THE PREWAR SHOWS

John Harris, the original president of Ice Capades, managed the company through twenty-four highly successful seasons as it expanded to include two casts, tours abroad, and performances in venues requiring use of the company's own ice-making equipment. Less than a year after the war, Ice Capades joined with its major competitor, the Ice Follies, to create an additional company, Ice Cycles, which debuted in Champaign, Illinois, in January 1946, but after three seasons Ice Capades purchased the Ice Follies' interest in Ice Cycles and created a division called Ice Capades International. Early trips abroad included performances at Empress Hall, Earl's Court in London during the summers of 1949 and 1950.

Through the 1950s and beyond, Ice Capades retained its original philosophy of presenting programs with "something for everyone."[3] Shows included scenes from operas such as Bizet's *Carmen,* Verdi's *Aida,* and Puccini's *La Bohème,* as well as from musicals such as Lerner and Loewe's *My Fair Lady* and Rogers and Hammerstein's *The King and I.* There were acts with Disney characters, comedy routines, and tricks such as skating on stilts. Former World and Olympic champions were featured, including Megan Taylor, Barbara Ann Scott, Dick Button, and Jacqueline du Bief as well as popular pairs including Barbara Wagner and Robert Paul.

Ice Capades was purchased in 1963 by Metromedia, a diversified company involved in entertainment and outdoor advertising, and subsequently by the International Broadcasting Corporation. Television at the time was viewed as threatening the survival of live shows, but Ice Capades continued to prosper. Still, the industry was changing, and the age of spectacular skating shows for general audiences gradually passed. By the early 1990s Ice Capades faced irreversible financial difficulties and could no longer compete with televised skating or smaller touring shows operating with less expensive formats. Hopelessly in debt and operating under Chapter 11 bankruptcy laws, the assets of Ice Capades were purchased in 1993 by Dorothy Hamill International. Hamill, a long-time headliner with the company, hoped to upgrade the shows while retaining the former emphasis on family entertainment at affordable ticket prices, a laudable but not reachable goal. The company's profitability could not be restored. Within a year it was sold to International Family Entertainment, resold soon afterward, and then disbanded.

The Ice Follies, the oldest skating show, had presented shows for more than forty years when in 1979 it was purchased by Feld Entertainment, a producer of rock concerts, musical productions, and Ringling Brothers and Barnum and Bailey's Circus. Feld Entertainment joined forces with the American Division of Holiday on Ice and for two seasons toured under the banner of Ice Follies and Holiday on Ice. Then, under an agreement with the Walt Disney Company, the Ice Follies revamped its show and marketed itself toward children. Disney on Ice undertook its first tour in 1981 and became international in 1986 with a trip to Japan. It has since toured the world, performing in forty-seven countries. From the humble beginnings of the Shipstads' first tour in 1936, skating's oldest show continues to prosper as Disney on Ice.

Sonja Henie's Hollywood Ice Review remained under the capable management of Arthur Wirtz through the 1950 season. He had managed Henie's shows since her arrival in the United States in 1936. Unlike the Ice Follies and Ice Capades, which over the years featured many former World and Olympic champions, Henie's shows revolved around her persona as the world's most decorated competitive skater and most successful show skater. As such, the Hollywood Ice Review was the original star show. Henie's talent and Wirtz's business connections guaranteed highly successful tours for fifteen years, but in 1951 Henie dissolved her business relationship with Wirtz, choosing to manage her own company.

The Sonja Henie Ice Review debuted in November 1951 in San Francisco.[4] Owing to exclusive arrangements with arena managers enjoyed by the Ice Follies, Ice Capades, and the Hollywood Ice Review, few large venues were open to Henie. In order to create additional venues, she purchased portable ice-making equipment, something Holiday on Ice was already using.[5] Because it took three days to set up the equipment and two days to dismantle it, a second portable rink was purchased, which allowed the company to perform almost continuously, but the cost of setting up, dismantling, and transporting equipment was prohibitive. Within months Henie's Ice Review suffered financial difficulties that threatened its survival.

Disaster struck on March 2, 1952. An accident involving collapsed temporary bleachers installed in Baltimore's Fifth Regiment Armory resulted in many injuries.[6] Subsequent liability concerns led to prohibitive bond requirements, necessitating the cancellation of performances scheduled in New York's Kingsbridge Armory. Shows continued in other cities through the remainder of the season, but Henie's company could not survive. Unwilling to accept defeat, she regrouped and continued producing ice shows for a short time, first in Canada and then in cooperation with Holiday on Ice in Europe.

HOLIDAY ON ICE

On Christmas Day 1943, an ice review entitled Holiday on Ice and named for the season opened and ran for eight days in Toledo, Ohio. In 1944 a second edition was produced. In 1945, under the leadership of Morris Chalfen, an entrepreneur who had a passion for figure skating and had previously managed a roller-skating show, the third edition was taken on the road. The company's ability to compete successfully with established shows resulted from using portable ice-making equipment. Holiday on Ice could perform in cities and venues not available to the other companies. In 1947 the company expanded its horizons with a tour to Central America, South America, and Cuba. In 1950 it crossed the Atlantic with even greater success, opening an eight-month season in Brussels, Belgium, and continuing with performances in Switzerland, France, Austria, and Germany.

Following the financial collapse of her Ice Review, Sonja Henie joined forces with Holiday on Ice in Europe and created the "Henie Show" that opened in Paris in 1953. Seventeen years had passed since Henie left Europe and sought her fortune in the United States. She was a legend there, but the postwar generation had not seen her skate. At forty-one, her effervescent style and presence on the ice thrilled European audiences, especially those in her native Oslo. A short lived division of Holiday on Ice called "Henie-Holiday" followed, but Henie's relationship with Holiday on Ice ended in 1956 after a tour to South America. She rarely skated afterward.

Holiday on Ice featured many World and Olympic champions, including Dick Button, Hayes Jenkins, Alain Giletti, Sjoukje Dijkstra, Donald McPherson, Emmerich Danzer, Tim Wood, Trixi Schuba, and Denise Biellmann, as the company toured the world and presented shows on five continents. Holiday on Ice represented the United States at the Brussels World Fair in 1958 and traveled to Russia under the newly established Cultural Exchange Program with the Soviet Union in 1959. The company was purchased in 1996 by Endemol Entertainment, a European conglomerate, and continues to produce shows, primarily in Europe.

INDIVIDUAL SKATERS' TOURS

From club carnivals to professional touring companies, ice shows had long provided entertainment to audiences that did not appreciate the technical aspects of figure skating. Then, during the 1960s, television began taking competitive skating into the homes of millions of viewers. The advent of World and Olympic events broadcast with expert commentary by former skaters such as Dick Button gradually led to a more savvy audience that could understand the sport's difficulty as well as appreciate its beauty. This more knowledgeable audience grew to expect technically difficult programs skated artistically by star performers, first as amateurs and later as professionals. As opera buffs attend operas to hear their favorite divas sing virtuosic arias, skating fans attend skating shows to see their favorite stars perform flashy free-skating routines. Shows led by and featuring skating's superstars would eventually supplant the traditional large-cast ice shows.

Disney on Ice, marketed toward children, continues to remain popular, but it is the exception. By the 1970s, the profitability of large and extravagant ice shows was diminishing. They could not survive without changes that would result in reduced production costs. By the 1980s, they were being challenged by star shows featuring one or a few former World and Olympic champions. Upon turning professional, some of the most popular skaters headlined their own companies. Their names usually defined the shows that typically included a few other champion-level skaters, but the casts were small in comparison to those of the traditional ice shows that had large choruses.

Most unusual and among the first were shows featuring the 1976 Olympic and World champion John Curry, one of the most balletic skaters of modern times. Upon retiring from competitive skating, Curry received offers from established ice shows but refused them, choosing to follow his own artistic ideals. He envisioned a skating company that would work together like a ballet company. Specifically, every skater would perform difficult artistic moves with all members of the cast in a true sense of ensemble. His first opportunity resulted in a small production billed as the John Curry Theatre of Skating, which opened at the Cambridge Theatre in London in December 1976. Its success led to an eight-week run with a larger cast the following summer at the London Palladium.

In November 1979, Curry's new company, now called Ice Dancing, opened in New York at the Felt Forum in Madison Square Garden. A four-week post-Christmas season at the Minskoff Theater followed. The venture was an unqualified success artistically and was aired on public television, but it was not successful financially. The company disbanded when financing for an additional tour was not forthcoming.

Curry studied dance, made guest skating appearances, and undertook a few acting roles until 1983, when new financial backing supported formation of the John Curry Skating Company. A cast of twelve, soon expanded to sixteen, began rehearsing in Vail, Colorado, as Curry realized his long-time dream of creating a skating company that would function like a corps de ballet. Its official debut, three performances accompanied by a full orchestra, was in Tokyo the following January. The European debut took place that spring at London's Royal Albert Hall and was followed in July with performances at the Metropolitan Opera House in New York. Additional performances were held at the Kennedy Center in Washington and the Wang Center in Boston.

Curry's company and remnants of it continued performing sporadically for several years, presenting some of the sports's most artistic skaters in the kind of ensemble skating so important to him. The ensemble included Peggy Fleming, Janet Lynn, JoJo Starbuck, Dorothy Hamill, and Lori Nichol, skaters who, like Curry, believed strongly in the concept of skating as a true art form. Their performances received audience approval and were rewarded with positive reviews as Curry's vision of ice skating as a balletic genre performed in theaters—not arenas—was realized.

The shows provided an artistic sophistication rarely seen but were never successful financially. Shows requiring many fewer hours of rehearsal and featuring a few high-profile skaters offering individual routines were more practical. In that format, ice dancers Jayne Torvill and Christopher Dean, two of the sport's most popular skaters, anchored shows under various titles. Less than a year after their World and Olympic victories in 1984, the Torvill and Dean World Tour opened at Wembley Arena in London. Later tours were entitled Torvill and Dean with the Russian Allstars (1988–90), the Best of Torvill and Dean (1992), Face the Music (1994–95), and Ice Adventures (1997–98). They also performed with permanently established companies, including Ice Capades in 1987 and Stars on Ice in 1996.

Shortly after their Olympic victory, Torvill and Dean accepted invitations to headline shows in Sydney and Melbourne, and while in Australia their own first world tour was planned, choreographed, and rehearsed. Included were four free-dance routines dating from their competitive days.[7] The innovative programs that had propelled them to success as amateurs remained in their repertoire, but they continued to experiment and stretch the boundaries of artistry with new programs. The finale of their 1984 show included an interpretation of Gustav Holst's suite *The Planets*. The second movement, "Venus," staged with Torvill portraying the goddess of love was particularly memorable. A large, lighted globe, a suspended prop, was gently thrown and recovered. In their final season as professionals, Carl Orff's oratorio *Carmina Burana,* a setting of medieval poetry, provided the background for another major achievement. More playful vaudeville-type numbers included the popular "Hat Trick," in which they continually snatched hats from each other's head, created for their tour with Ice Capades. Entering the world of modern music, Torvill and Dean selected music from Philip Glass's 1984 opera *Akhnaten,* about a pharaoh martyred for his monotheistic worship of the sun god. The program debuted on the Russian Allstars tour. From popular music for shows to classical music for opera, as amateurs and as professionals, Torvill and Dean explored continually the breadth of musical style more than other skaters.

Toller Cranston, Robin Cousins, Brian Boitano, Katarina Witt, and Elvis Stojko are among the stars who anchored their own shows, but the most successful of the star shows was conceived by Scott Hamilton. Stars on Ice, a favorite since its founding in 1986, features a small cast of skaters, primarily World and Olympic champions. In addition to solo numbers, the cast divides into small ensembles for simple skits. Joining Hamilton for the 1986 tour were World champion and Olympic silver medalist Rosalynn Sumners, who remained with the company through 1999, and World and Olympic bronze medalist Toller Cranston.[8]

Unlike the shows of Curry and Torvill and Dean, Stars on Ice has limited itself geographically to performances in North America. The first tour, called the "Scott Hamilton America Tour," included just five northeastern cities. Longer tours followed as the company, renamed Stars on Ice, gradually developed its position as one of two leading star shows still touring in the United States. Success has resulted partly from the significant number of former World and Olympic champions who have been mainstays with the company. In addition to Hamilton and Sumners, they have included Kristi Yamaguchi, Katarina Witt, Tara Lipinski, Kurt Browning, Ilia Kulik, and pair skaters Ekaterina Gordeeva and Sergei Grinkov.

TOM COLLINS AND HIS SHOWS

Skating shows through the 1970s continued featuring large choruses augmented by a few well-known stars. That format changed significantly during the 1980s, not only as the result of production costs but also a result of public interest in particular skaters whose amateur careers they had followed on television. Star shows such as those of Torvill and Dean successfully challenged the larger shows for their market share and remained successful well into the 1990s, but the wave of the future was shows that featured multiple stars in solo performances with group numbers relegated to opening and closing presentations of the entire company. The person most responsible for producing shows of this type is Tom Collins (b. 1931), a Canadian figure skater who competed in the 1940s. Upon turning professional, Collins toured with Henie's Hollywood Ice Review (1949–51) and Holiday on Ice (1951–62). Joining the management staff in 1962, he eventually became a vice president and remained with the company until 1971.

While employed by Holiday on Ice, Collins managed a tour of medalists from the 1969 World Championships held that year in Colorado Springs. The concept was a proven one, as similar tours had followed the championships held in Europe. Entitled the 1969 World Champions Figure Skating Exhibition, the tour included fifteen cities, seven in the United States and eight in Canada. The World Championships at that time were held triennially in North America, and tours under Collins's own management company followed championships at Calgary in 1972, Colorado Springs in 1975, Ottawa in 1978, and Hartford in 1981. The Winter Olympic Games at Lake Placid in 1980 also gave rise to a tour.

The World Championships in 1983 were held in Helsinki, Finland, but Collins's tours, now well established, became that year annual events in North America regardless of the site for the World Championships. Several name changes have occurred: the Tour of Champions in 1972, the World Figure Skating Tour from 1975 through 1983, the Tour of Olympic and World Figure Skating Champions from 1984 through 1988, the Tour of World Figure Skating Champions from 1989 through 1997, and Champions on Ice since 1998.

Nine women, six men, nine pairs, and three dance couples constituted the 1969 tour, all but two of whom had competed in Colorado Springs.[9] Collins's format evolved to include not only current World medalists but also those from previous years, both eligible and ineligible. Some have become frequent cast members. The Brians, Boitano and Orser, and the Carmens, Thomas and Witt, media favorites from the Calgary Olympics, all appeared on the tour that year and also in later years as professionals. Boitano became a mainstay with the company, appearing as recently as 2001. Remarkably, all but six of the seventy-nine World and Olympic champions from 1967 through 2002 have appeared on Collins's tours.

The 1994 tour following the Lillehammer Games was the most successful to date, clearly benefiting from the Kerrrigan-Harding incident at the U.S. Nationals in January. Forty-five shows were presented in forty-three cities the previous year. Seventy shows were presented in fifty-nine cities in 1994. Twelve more cities were added in 1995, and a two-tour season began in 1996 with seventy-six shows in seventy-four cities. The winter tour, primarily for ineligible skaters, occurred while eligible skaters were preparing for and competing in international events. The regular tour, primarily for eligible skaters, occurred after the World Championships. For the first winter tour, Collins recruited Dorothy Hamill, who just two years earlier had suffered the failure of Ice Capades.[10] Like Boitano, she became a mainstay with the company and has since skated on every winter tour. The number

The Champions on Ice cast, including Sasha Cohen, Sarah Hughes, Irina Slutskaya, and Michelle Kwan, acknowledges the audience following a performance. (Champions on Ice)

of shows presented annually has declined since 1996 as the publicity following the Kerrigan-Harding incident faded, but Champions on Ice successfully entered the new century at a level equal to that of the early 1990s and has remained the premier skating show.

THE CINEMA SINCE WORLD WAR II

Motion pictures since Sonja Henie's nine films released by Twentieth-Century Fox between 1937 and 1943 include her two later films *It's a Pleasure* (1945) and *The Countess of Monte Cristo* (1948), neither of which enjoyed the success of the earlier ones. Only a few films featuring figure skaters or stories about figure skating have since been released. The best are *Ice Castles* (1978), *Carmen on Ice* (1989), and *The Cutting Edge* (1991).

Exactly thirty years after Henie's last film, Columbia Pictures produced *Ice Castles,* a romantic tragedy about a young figure skater who is from a small midwestern town and has Olympic dreams and the talent to realize them. The film benefited from the current popularity of figure skating in the United States, where three of the nation's most beloved skaters, Peggy Fleming, Janet Lynn, and Dorothy Hamill, had generated great interest in the sport as they collectively won thirteen national, four World, and two Olympic titles immediately before the film's release. For *Ice Castles,* Lynn-Holly Johnson, the novice silver medalist at the U.S. Nationals in 1974 and a star of Ice Capades, was selected to portray the young Olympic hopeful Alexis Winston. Her dreams were not realized because of a freak accident that resulted in blindness, but "Lexie," in a personal triumph, does skate again, encouraged by her childhood sweetheart Nick Peterson

Lynn-Holly Johnson, star of the film *Ice Castles,* during her competitive career. (World Figure Skating Museum and Hall of Fame)

(Robby Benson, a teenage heartthrob of that era). Much of the intrigue and politics associated with figure skating is depicted or suggested in the story, including questionable judging, high-pressure coaching, and meddling "skating moms." *Ice Castles* was filmed in the Twin Cities, Minneapolis and St. Paul, and at the Broadmoor World Arena in Colorado Springs. Members of local skating clubs were employed for the skating scenes, an arrangement possible under ISU rules that allow member associations to enter into contractual agreements for their eligible skaters to perform with ineligible skaters.

A decade after the release of *Ice Castles,* media attention devoted to the Battle of the Carmens and the Battle of the Brians at the Calgary Olympic Games provided impetus for featuring three of those skaters, Katarina Witt, Brian Boitano, and Brian Orser, in a film based on Bizet's opera *Carmen.* Witt again portrayed Carmen, with the Brians, Boitano as Don José and Orser as Escamillo, her devoted suitors. *Carmen on Ice,* cast as an ice ballet and choreographed by Sandra Bezic, was filmed in Seville, Spain, where the story takes place, and in the German Democratic Republic. It was released in Europe in early 1990 and was broadcast on HBO in the United States shortly afterward.

The Cutting Edge, a Metro-Goldwyn-Mayer production based on an original script by Tony Gilroy, is a romantic comedy about a spoiled and obnoxious pair skater from a wealthy family. Desperate to obtain a partner, she reluctantly accepts an unsophisticated blue-collar former hockey player. Ultimately, they qualify to compete at the Albertville Olympic Games. Unlike *Carmen on Ice,* which featured well-known Olympic medalists in an ice ballet, or *Ice Castles,* which featured a successful national-level competitive skater in the lead role, *The Cutting Edge* starred Hollywood actors Moira Kelly and D. B. Sweeney. They learned to skate, but doubles were employed for the difficult skating scenes. Selected for their physical resemblance to Kelly and Sweeney were two former pair competitors, Sharon Carz and John Denton.[11] *The Cutting Edge* was filmed in Toronto, Ontario, with Robin Cousins serving as the choreographer and technical advisor.

PROFESSIONAL COMPETITIONS

Professional competitions in figure skating date from the years between the world wars, but not until the 1980s did they become a prominent part of skating. Public interest by that time justified the establishment of invitational events in which the current most popular professional skaters could compete in head-to-head battles and team competitions. The events were usually televised and supported by corporate sponsorship, appearance fees were paid to the skaters, and prize money was awarded.

The prototype, however, was the Open Professional Championships held in England under the auspices of the NSA from 1932 through 1956, missing the war years from 1939 to 1945.[12] Most of the competitors were show skaters, and the programs they presented were often those currently being performed in ice shows. Economically difficult times in the 1930s and 1940s forced many talented amateurs to turn professional early in their careers before securing international titles. Medaling at the Open Professional Championships enhanced a skater's reputation. The majority of the competitors were British; just seven of the fifty-three titles awarded were won by non-British skaters.[13] Cecilia Colledge was the only former World champion to win the competition.[14]

The championships continued to be held in England for another fourteen years, from 1957 to 1970, but under the auspices of the International Professional Skaters Association (IPSA). During that period, wider participation is evidenced by the number of former World champions who competed and won titles and the countries from which they came. They include Donald McPherson of Canada in 1965, Emmerich Danzer of Austria in 1968, Donald Jackson of Canada in 1970, and ice dancing champions Eva Romanová and Pavel Roman of Czechoslovakia in 1965. Although no former World champions won the ladies' or pairs' events, silver medalist Regine Heizer of Austria won in 1967, and pairs' silver medalists Margret Göbl and Franz Ningel of the Federal Republic of Germany won in 1963.

The Open Professional Championships continued for an additional three years, from 1971 to 1973, but no longer under the auspices of the IPSA. Owing to a lack of sponsorship in England they were moved in 1974 to Jaca, Spain, a village in the picturesque Pyrenees Mountains, where for seventeen years they prospered with local sponsorship as a popular competition that enjoyed broad international participation under the name World Professional Championships.

The championships in England remained the only major professional competition until Dick Button created the World Professional Figure Skating Championships, an invitational competition usually called the "World Pros," which were first held in Tokyo, Japan, in 1973, a year before the Open Professional Championships moved to Jaca.[15] Prize money was awarded in three disciplines, men's, ladies', and pairs. The winners were Janet Lynn, Ronald Robertson, and the Protopopovs. Seven years lapsed before the World Pros reappeared in Landover, Maryland, and became an annual event. In 1997 they were moved to Washington, D.C., where they continued for four more years before being discontinued. Candid Productions, Button's management company, was purchased in 1999 by SFX Entertainment with the expectation that the World Pros would continue. SFX, however, was subsequently purchased by Clear Channel Communications, which was primarily an operator of radio stations with little interest in figure skating. The World Pros were last held in 2000. Button has retained rights to the name *World Professional Figure Skating Championships,* which leaves open the potential for the once popular competition to be revived.

When the World Pros moved to Landover in 1980, skaters competed in a team format, with current Olympians challenging former Olympians. Linda Fratianne, Emi Watanabe, Robin Cousins, Charles Tickner, and ice dancers Krisztina Regöczy and András Sallay, all medalists at Lake Placid that year, defeated former Olympians Peggy Fleming, Dorothy Hamill, Toller Cranston, Gordon McKellen, and the pair of JoJo Starbuck and Kenneth Shelley. The team format was replaced in 1986 with head-to-head competitions. Winners that year were Dorothy Hamill, Robin Cousins, Tai Babilonia and Randy Gardner, and Jayne Torvill and Christopher Dean.

At the request of ABC, Button established a second professional competition to be held outside the United States with a change of location annually. The World Challenge of Champions, structured as a one-event competition with an exhibition following, debuted in Paris in 1985. Dorothy Hamill, Robin Cousins, and pair skaters Caitlin and Peter Carruthers claimed the first titles. Ice dancing was not included until 1989. Shortly after the Berlin Wall came down in 1990 the Challenge of Champions became the first professional competition to be held in the Soviet Union. The competition was held annually for fourteen years before being discontinued in 1998.

The World Pros and the Challenge of Champions were the longest-running and most important of the invitational professional competitions. In response to strong television ratings the number of other competitions burgeoned during figure skating's heyday from 1994 to 1998. Eight professional competitions were held in the United States and Canada within a two-month period during the fall of 1995.[16] Sponsors were readily available for any event in which the most popular skaters would compete, the result being that the same few skaters appeared in many competitions.

Lesser-known professionals were rarely invited to invitational events, and few competitive opportunities were available to them. The U.S. Open Professional Figure Skating Championships, produced by the Professional Skaters Guild of America and open to all professional skaters, was first held in 1981.[17] It served initially as a qualifying competition for the World Professional Championships at Jaca, with the top finishers being sent to Spain. In 1986 it was revamped to become a two-event competition. A challenge cup, open to all professional skaters, served as a qualifying event from which winners advanced to a master cup. The challenge cup served an important role, providing lesser-known professionals with exposure to agents and producers as well as the opportunity to advance to the master cup. The United States Open was last held in 1997.

PRO-AM COMPETITIONS

The rule change that allowed ineligible skaters to reinstate and compete against eligible skaters in ISU Championships gave rise to corporate-sponsored special competitions outside the established championships in which eligible skaters could compete against ineligible skaters while earning appearance fees and prize money. The "pro-ams" began in the United States at Hershey, Pennsylvania, in November 1992 with the Chrysler Concorde Pro-Am Figure Skating Challenge. Events for men and ladies were held, with four skaters, two eligible and two ineligible, in each event. All competitors were Americans and were judged by USFSA judges. They performed a short program and a free-skating program under slightly modified rules, primarily those relating to program length and the use of vocal music. In the ladies' competition, the eligible skaters, Nancy Kerrigan and Tonya Harding, placed first and second followed by the ineligible skaters, Caryn Kadavy and Rosalynn Sumners. In the men's competition, eligible and ineligible skaters alternated in the rankings. Paul Wylie, an ineligible skater, placed first followed by Mark Mitchell, Scott Hamilton, and Todd Eldredge.

Paul Wylie displayed a level of artistry unusual among men skaters of the 1990s. (World Figure Skating Museum and Hall of Fame)

Caryn Kadavy, a popular
professional skater of the
1990s. (World Figure Skating
Museum and Hall of Fame)

Less than five months later, in April 1993, a second and expanded pro-am competition was held in Los Angeles. The Hershey's Kisses Pro-Am Championships again included only singles' events but boasted a larger field of competitors. All who competed in Hershey except for Harding and Eldredge were scheduled to reappear, although Sumners withdrew owing to an injury. New competitors included Lisa Ervin, Tonia Kwiatkowski, Jill Trenary, Brian Boitano, Michael Chack, and Scott Davis. Top finishers in the men were Boitano, Hamilton, and Wylie, all ineligible skaters. Kadavy won the ladies' event followed by two eligible skaters, Kerrigan and Ervin.

Pairs' and ice dancing events were included at the AT&T U.S. Pro-Am Figure Skating Challenge held the following December in Philadelphia. The eligible competitors, pair skaters Jenni Meno and Todd Sand and ice dancers Renée Roca and Gorsha Sur, won their events. Winners in the singles events were Nancy Kerrigan and Brian Boitano.

The 1993 competitions were specifically for American skaters, but in November 1994 an international pro-am, the Thrifty Car Rental International Challenge, was held in Philadelphia. Although slightly more than half of the competitors were Americans, only Todd Eldredge managed to win. Surya Bonaly of France won the ladies' event, Evgenia Shishkova and Vadim Naumov of Russia won the pairs' event, and Anjelika Krylova and Oleg Ovsiannikov of Russia won the ice dancing event.

A team format was adopted for the U.S. Postal Service Skating Challenge a month later in Philadelphia. Teams of three eligible and two ineligible skaters were named for local hockey and basketball franchises. The winning Flyers included Michelle Kwan, Tara Lipinski, Dan Hollander, Caryn Kadavy, and Dorothy Hamill. The 76ers included Nicole Bobek, Tonia Kwiatkowski, Todd Eldredge, Rosalynn Sumners, and Paul Wylie.

All from that event except Dorothy Hamill and Tonia Kwiatkowski competed again at the Hershey's Kisses Challenge held in Greensboro, North Carolina, the following April. Entitled the "Battle of the Sexes," Nicole Bobek, Caryn Kadavy, Michelle Kwan, Tara Lipinski, Elizabeth Manley, and Rosalynn Sumners were pitted against Scott Davis, Todd Eldredge, Rudy Galindo, Dan Hollander, Michael Weiss, and Paul Wylie. The ladies won by a close margin in what was reported to have been the highest-rated televised skating event of the season.

EPILOGUE

Figure skating's popularity had grown steadily for more than half a century when the attack on Nancy Kerrigan and the unprecedented media coverage that followed thrust the sport into the limelight, if only briefly. Televised shows and competitions—professional, pro-am, and amateur—were in response to the public's demand for more skating and were offered at a level that could not be sustained. By century's end, television ratings had declined substantially, and except for major competitions, most televised events had disappeared. "For us and for everybody, the sport just got saturated," remarked Rob Correa, a senior vice president for CBS Sports.[1] In the mid-1990s CBS was airing as many as eight professional competitions annually. By the 2002 season, the termination year for this history, only Ice Wars, the most popular of the team competitions, was broadcast on CBS, and only the Hallmark Skater's Championships, a head-to-head competition and successor to Dick Button's World Professional Championships, was broadcast on NBC.

Most touring shows disappeared as well. The two well-established companies, Champions on Ice and Stars on Ice, still tour in the United States, although their attendance has declined from that of the mid-1990s. Holiday on Ice still tours in Europe. Champions on Ice, which maintains a balance of eligible and ineligible skaters, is continually bolstered by the infusion of new World and Olympic medalists. Its format, an evening of free-skating exhibitions, has proven durable and successful. Stars on Ice, which relies on the marketability of a small number of high-profile ineligible skaters, has experienced a greater decline in attendance.[2] The retirement of two of its original and most popular cast members, Rosalynn Sumners and Scott Hamilton, undoubtedly contributed to the declining attendance.[3]

Eligible skating has remained healthy because of the large

and stable number of children who enter the sport each year. As the most talented of them progress through the national ranks and advance to the international level of competition, they continue to raise the bar technically, and that maintains healthy public interest. When Timothy Goebel completed three clean quadruple jumps at Skate America in 1999, the public enthusiastically took notice.[4] When Sarah Hughes upset her competition with a phenomenal free-skating performance at the Olympic Games in 2002, the public cheered their new champion. When experienced skaters such as Michelle Kwan remain eligible and advance the beauty of figure skating as an art form with near perfection, the public retains its interest.

The balance of athleticism and artistry that defines figure skating has been retained as the sport has entered the twenty-first century, although there has been some eroding of artistry since the mid-1980s, a result of the ever-increasing emphasis on athleticism, especially jumping. Because exciting technical advances will continue, skaters, coaches, and officials should monitor carefully rule changes and judging criteria to assure retention of an appropriate balance between athleticism and artistry. Figure skating must not lose its unique identity.

Grand Prix events in the fall and the European, Four Continents, and World Championships in the early spring, all currently broadcast in the United States on ABC and its affiliated stations, provide adequate opportunities for eligible skaters to compete internationally and for the public to see the best of them perform in the world's most prestigious competitions. The saturation of televised skating in the mid to late 1990s led to boredom as the public watched the same few skaters present the same programs through entire seasons and beyond. That has given way to broadcasting only major competitions, and skating fans eagerly await each of them.

Opportunities afforded eligible skaters to earn prize money in Grand Prix events and to join the Champions on Ice tour provide earning potential that can surpass that of ineligible skaters, leading many elite skaters to remain eligible rather than join the professional ranks after winning a major title. Tara Lipinski and Ilia Kulik turned professional immediately after collecting their Olympic gold medals in 1998. Neither Sarah Hughes nor Alexei Yagudin elected to do so after collecting their Olympic gold medals in 2002.[5] Long-time rivals and World champions Michelle Kwan and Irina Slutskaya, already in their mid-twenties and veterans of two Olympics, retained their eligibility. Neither of them ruled out competing at the Olympic Games in 2006.

Major sponsors supported professional and pro-am skating events when television ratings were high but dropped them promptly when the bubble burst. The ISU, however, has had for more than a century only one raison d'etre, supporting amateur or eligible skating. The professional skating world, corporate interests, and the media will continue to wield influence and affect the manner in which the ISU operates, but the union's mission has always been, and should continue to be, one of service to the sport and its expansion as it promotes "organized development on the basis of friendship and mutual understanding between sportsmen."[6]

That having been said, the ISU has since 2002 been scrutinized by the skating community and the public more rigorously than ever before, a result of the judging scandal at the Salt Lake City Olympic Winter Games. The union's credibility has been brought into question, and it has undergone a time of crisis. Never before has the ISU needed to respond to attacks from so many fronts. Its responses and the resulting changes in how figure skating is judged will affect its ability to lead, at least in the short term, as well as the future of the sport itself.

As in previous scandals, the need to reevaluate the judging system in an effort to avoid similar problems in the future was clear. Unlike earlier scandals, the evaluation began almost immediately in reaction to the instantaneous outcry from the media and the challenge to the result of the pairs' competition filed by Skate Canada. An unprecedented result was the awarding of duplicate gold medals by the IOC at the recommendation of the ISU to the pair that placed second, in effect declaring a tie.

In April, two months after the games, the ISU Council convened at its headquarters in Lausanne, Switzerland, to hear the cases of Marie-Reine Le Gougne, the French judge in the pairs' event, who admitted to being "pressured" by her federation to favor the Russians Elena Berezhnaya and Anton Sikharulidze, and of Didier Gailhaguet, president of the Fédération Française des Sports de Glace, who allegedly did the pressuring. The verdict read, "Ms. Marie-Reine Le Gougne is suspended as ISU referee and judge and excluded from participation in any ISU event, e.g. ISU Championships, international competitions, exhibitions and all off-ice events, in any capacity for a period of three years," and "she is barred from participation in the 2006 Olympic Games."[7] The same suspension was given to Gailhaguet. The ISU appeals process requires written notification of that intention within twenty-eight days of the finding. Although La Gougne and Gailhaguet both threatened to appeal, such notification was not filed.

The punishment was broadly criticized within the skating community and by fans for its lack of severity, but proposals brought forward at the ISU Congress in June 2002 that would have mandated lifetime bans for judges found guilty of improprieties, national bias, or corruption lacked sufficient support for passage. Other actions resulting from or influenced by the scandal included the creation of a code of ethics and a resolution calling for the development of a proposal for a general restructuring of the union.

The sole spokesperson for the ISU in Salt Lake City following the revelation of Le Gougne's being "pressured" to favor the Russians and the resulting media outcry was ISU president Ottavio Cinquanta. Under ISU rules, referees and judges are not allowed to speak publicly until after the competition is completed. Cinquanta, a former speed skater, began promoting immediately a major change in figure skating's judging system that would replace the 6.0 mark and ordinal placement system with a point-earning system in which numerical values would be assigned to skating elements based on their degree of difficulty. The system could diminish subjectivity in judging but would not necessarily remove the threat of bloc judging, which was the root of the problem in Salt Lake City.

Various ideas designed to reduce the potential for bloc judging were discussed throughout the skating world following the Games, and specific proposals were presented to the 2002 Congress by the federations from Australia, the United States, and Canada. The Australians proposed eliminating the high and low marks, which would remove an inflated or deflated mark. The Americans proposed employing the median mark of the judges as a consensus vote of the panel, which would have a modifying affect on the scores. The Canadians proposed employing the results of a specified number of unidentified (anonymous) judges selected randomly by computer from an enlarged panel of judges and that would remove the potential for bloc judging.

The ISU voted to test on a trial basis the Canadian proposal. For championship events, nine judges were selected randomly from a panel of fourteen. The established 6.0 mark and ordinal placement system with separate scores for technical merit and presentation was retained. The system was first employed at Skate America in October. Scores for the entire panel of fourteen judges were posted in ascending numerical order, which meant that skaters could not determine which scores counted or which judges gave specific scores. It created confusion and frustration. Skaters at all levels of competition, juvenile to elite, had traditionally asked judges what they liked or disliked about their programs, especially those who marked them high or low. That suddenly became impossible. Because scores were posted in numerical order, those opposite each other in the technical merit and presentation columns were not from the same judge, and that caused further confusion. Michelle Kwan stated after her short program: "When I got my marks, I didn't look. It doesn't make any sense to me."[8] Similar responses came from other skaters.

The system's use throughout the 2002–3 season resulted in dissatisfaction from officials, coaches, skaters, and fans, primarily because of the judges' anonymity and perceived lack of accountability. The USFSA executive committee expressed opposition, and President Phyllis Howard stated that "the interim judging system has proven to be a failure where it counts most—public accountability." She continued, "The display of marks under the interim system provides no feedback to skaters or coaches and creates an environment of mistrust."[9] Kwan concurred: "Usually you know which judge gave you this. If you had a specific question after the event you could ask somebody and see what they thought about your program."[10]

The accountability issue resulted from the secrecy of judges' scores, which remain unknown even to the referees of the events. Only the ISU general secretary has access to that information until the end of the skating season. The encrypted data is then provided to the appropriate technical committees, but judges' names are withheld unless an "anomaly" is detected. The results are never open to public scrutiny. SkateFAIR (Skate

Fans for Accountability and ISU Reform), a grass-roots organization formed in the United States in the spring of 2003, carried its message of "no secret judging" to the 2003 World Championships in Washington. They picketed, wore lapel buttons, and posted signs in several languages throughout the arena.

One well-meaning group of officials and athletes formed the World Skating Federation (WSF) with the unrealistic goal of replacing the ISU as the IOC recognized international federation for figure skating. Efforts to obtain support from national federations proved fruitless because the WSF sponsored no international competitions in which skaters could be entered and had no authority to enter skaters in the Olympic Games. Thus, a country supporting the WSF in place of the ISU would have no international outlet for its skaters.

Concern was expressed within the skating community over the far-reaching proposal promoted by Cinquanta that if adopted would dramatically change the way figure skating is judged. It replaces the current 6.0 mark and ordinal placement system long employed to rank competitors with a point-earning system in which a basic value is assigned to every element employed in figure skating. As elements are included in programs, judges assign a grade relative to prescribed values by adding or subtracting up to three points to reflect the quality of execution. How well-centered was the spin? How clean was the jump?

Questions were raised about how artistry would be judged. Twenty-nine percent of the points awarded apply specifically to presentation or artistic results. At the end of each program, judges assign marks for five program components: skating skills, transitions, performance/execution, choreography, and interpretation.[11] Some coaches, judges, and referees expressed concern that the system would reward difficult elements done poorly, which would then be exacerbated by having just 29 percent of the score devoted to presentation, a value they considered too low. Presentation in the 6.0 and placement system is valued at 50 percent, at least theoretically. Technical merit and presentation marks are counted equally except in breaking ties in free skating and free dance.

Criticism was leveled at Cinquanta over the manner in which the proposed point-earning system was presented to the 2002 Congress. Historically, matters involving rules for figure skating or speed skating have been debated in separate sessions, thus being decided by delegates from the sport involved. For the new judging system, however, Cinquanta had it debated by the entire Congress. His justification was that the credibility of the ISU was at stake as a result of the Salt Lake City scandal. The proposal was presented by Cinquanta, who stated that "this is a project this is not a rule."[12]

The figure skating delegates presumed that the system would be tested and the results discussed at the next congress in 2004, but when the rules were published later that year, the figure skating delegates discovered that the "project" to which they had agreed was actually a "rule," which allowed the system to be employed officially at some events rather than just tested. The result of the misunderstanding was divisive. A few long-time respected officials who asked questions or raised objections resigned or were forced to resign from their positions in the ISU. Written protests came from six member federations, and the National Ice Skating Association of the United Kingdom filed a formal protest with the Court of Arbitration for Sport (CAS).[13]

The ISU Council, which included six members from speed skating and five from figure skating, voted at its meeting in March 2003 to employ the point-earning system at Grand Prix events in the fall of 2003. The system includes the posting of numerical scores for an entire panel of nine judges, with the two highest and two lowest scores eliminated, a double-trimmed mean in which just five scores count. The judges remain anonymous, thus ignoring the primary criticism of the system tested in the 2003 season.

In spite of these concerns, the system worked relatively well, and positive aspects of it outweighed the negative ones. Many competitors praised it. Although some federations, including the USFSA, would have preferred approving the system provisionally, allowing additional testing, many in the skating community, including coaches and skaters, felt the testing in 2003 demonstrated conclusively that strengths outweighed weaknesses. The system was approved at the 2004 Congress.

The point-earning system itself does not alleviate the potential for bloc judging, the root of the impropriety at Salt Lake City, but dropping high and low scores, as initially recommended by the Australian federation, reduces it dramatically. The system does address the inherent weakness of any performance judged subjectively by assigning numerical values to all skating elements, but reducing subjectivity substantially could change the character of the sport. Figure skating has evolved as both a sport and a performing art, which requires that it be judged both objectively and subjectively. The point-earning system appears to accomplish that. Although the anonymity of judges has been retained, Alexander Lakernik, chair of the ISU figure skating technical committee and one of the developers of the system, noted that "anonymity is not an essential part of the system." It is, he said, "a separate principle either accepted or not."[14]

The debate over figure skating's judging system lasted two years beyond the cut-off date for this book and provided all concerned with a sounding board for passionate discussion of the proposals considered. Judging was the major topic discussed at the biennial Congress in 2004 where the ISU adopted the point-earning system, perhaps the most important single issue brought forth in its 112–year history. The abolishment of compulsory figures fourteen years earlier affected only singles' skaters. The new judging system affects skaters in all disciplines, including synchronized skating.

Artistry is the sport's oldest dimension. Figure skating during the nineteenth century in the British Isles, on the Continent, and in North America developed distinctly different styles, but artistry was always the ultimate goal. As proficiency among skaters increased and competitions were established, the figures skated became more difficult and challenging, but until World War I emphasis remained primarily on artistry. Technical advances occurred between the wars, and during those years figure skating developed a unique balance between athleticism and artistry.

Jumping was not an important part of competitive figure skating until the 1930s, but more difficult jumps with more revolutions have been a continuum ever since. They are readily recognized by the skating public, and the success of a jump is usually made clear by the quality of its landing. Jumps are spectacular when done well, but attempts often result in poor landings or falls, which cause disruptions in the choreography. Audiences and commentators alike tend to count jumps and concern themselves more with whether a jump is completed than whether it represents good skating. Impressive fast footwork and complex spins require as much athletic ability as jumps, but falls are infrequent. Their quality is less easily recognized or understood by the casual viewing public. Those elements and others such as long, flowing spirals are innately more artistic than jumps and are necessary to maintain the balance between the athleticism and artistry that defines figure skating.

The ISU must continue to evaluate limitations and values placed on all elements to ensure that skaters retain an appropriate balance. If judging changes were to dilute the value of presentation, as some critics have feared, by rewarding disproportionally efforts at difficult athletic elements, specifically jumping, the public would be denied the opportunity of enjoying to its fullest the only sport that can boast of being equally an art form, but testing of the new system in 2003 suggests that will not be the case. Hopefully, the new judging system will foster continuing development of the world's most beautiful sport athletically and artistically.

PREFACE TO THE APPENDICES

COUNTRY ABBREVIATIONS FOR ISU MEMBERS

Before 1998 the country abbreviations used by the ISU were based on its official language, English since 1948. At its 1998 Congress the ISU adopted the country abbreviations used by the IOC, which are based on one of its official languages, French. Differences between them are reflected in the following listing. The appendices that follow employ the abbreviations in effect at the time of the event.

COUNTRY	JOINT	ISU	IOC
Andorra	AND		
Armenia	ARM		
Australia	AUS		
Austria	AUT		
Azerbaijan	AZE		
Belarus		BLR	BLS
Belgium	BEL		
Bosnia and Herzogovenia	BIH		
Brazil	BRA		
Bulgaria	BUL		
Canada	CAN		
China	CHN		
Chinese Taipei	TPE		
Croatia	CRO		
Cyprus	CYP		
Czech Republic	CZE		
Czechoslovakia	CZE		
Denmark	DEN		
Estonia	EST		
Finland	FIN		
France	FRA		
Georgia	GEO		
Germany	GER		
Federal Republic of Germany	FRG		
Democratic Republic of Germany	GDR		
Great Britain	GRB	GBR	
Greece	GRE		
Hong Kong	HKG		
Hungary	HUN		

COUNTRY	JOINT	ISU	IOC
Iceland	ICE		
Israel	ISR		
Italy	ITA		
Japan	JPN		
Kazakhstan	KAZ		
Korea			
Democratic Peoples Republic of Korea	DPK	PRK	
Republic of Korea	ROK	KOR	
Latvia	LAT		
Lithuania	LIT	LTU	
Luxembourg	LUX		
Mexico	MEX		
Mongolia	MGL		
Netherlands	NED		
New Zealand	NZL		
Norway	NOR		
Poland	POL		
Portugal	POR		
Romania	RUM	ROM	
Russia	RUS		
Slovak Republic	SVK		
Slovenia	SLO		
South Africa	SAF	RSA	
Soviet Union	URS		
Soviet Union (1992 only)	CIS	EUN	
Spain	SPN	ESP	
Sweden	SWE		
Switzerland	SWI	SUI	
Thailand	THA		
Turkey	TUR		
Ukraine	UKR		
United States	USA		
Uzbekistan	UZB		
Yugoslavia	YUG		

World Championships: Medalists in Figure Skating

Ladies

Location	Gold	Silver	Bronze
1906 Davos SWI	Madge Syers GRB	Jenny Herz AUT	Lily Kronberger HUN
1907 Vienna AUT	Madge Syers GRB	Jenny Herz AUT	Lily Kronberger HUN
1908 Troppau CSR	Lily Kronberger HUN	Elsa Rendschmidt GER	
1909 Budapest HUN	Lily Kronberger HUN		
1910 Berlin GER	Lily Kronberger HUN	Elsa Rendschmidt GER	
1911 Vienna AUT	Lily Kronberger HUN	Opika v. Méray Horváth HUN	Ludowika Eilers GER
1912 Davos SWI	Opika v. Méray Horváth HUN	D. Greenhough-Smith GRB	Phyllis Johnson GRB
1913 Stockholm SWE	Opika v. Méray Horváth HUN	Phyllis Johnson GRB	Svea Norén SWE
1914 St. Moritz SWI	Opika v. Méray Horváth HUN	Angela Hanka AUT	Phyllis Johnson GRB
1915–21 THE WORLD CHAMPIONSHIPS WERE NOT HELD.			
1922 Stockholm, SWE	Herma Szabo AUT	Svea Norén SWE	Margot Moe NOR
1923 Vienna AUT	Herma Szabo AUT	Gisela Reichmann AUT	Svea Norén SWE
1924 Oslo NOR	Herma Szabo AUT	Ellen Brockhöfft GER	Beatrix Loughran USA
1925 Davos SWI	Herma Szabo AUT	Ellen Brockhöfft GER	Elisabeth Böckel GER
1926 Stockholm SWE	Herma Szabo AUT	Sonja Henie NOR	Kathleen Shaw GRB
1927 Oslo NOR	Sonja Henie NOR	Herma Szabo AUT	Karen Simensen NOR
1928 London GRB	Sonja Henie NOR	Maribel Vinson USA	Fritzi Burger AUT
1929 Budapest HUN	Sonja Henie NOR	Fritzi Burger AUT	Melitta Brunner AUT
1930 New York USA	Sonja Henie NOR	Cecil Smith CAN	Maribel Vinson USA
1931 Berlin GER	Sonja Henie NOR	Hilde Holovsky AUT	Fritzi Burger AUT
1932 Montreal CAN	Sonja Henie NOR	Fritzi Burger AUT	Constance Samuel CAN
1933 Stockholm SWE	Sonja Henie NOR	Vivi-Anne Hultén SWE	Hilde Holovsky AUT
1934 Oslo NOR	Sonja Henie NOR	Megan Taylor GRB	Liselotte Landbeck AUT
1935 Vienna AUT	Sonja Henie NOR	Cecilia Colledge GRB	Vivi-Anne Hultén SWE
1936 Paris FRA	Sonja Henie NOR	Megan Taylor GRB	Vivi-Anne Hultén SWE
1937 London GRB	Cecilia Colledge GRB	Megan Taylor GRB	Vivi-Anne Hultén SWE
1938 Stockholm SWE	Megan Taylor GRB	Cecilia Colledge GRB	Hedy Stenuf USA
1939 Prague CSR	Megan Taylor GRB	Hedy Stenuf USA	Daphne Walker GRB
1940–46 THE WORLD CHAMPIONSHIPS WERE NOT HELD.			
1947 Stockholm SWE	Barbara Ann Scott CAN	Daphne Walker GRB	Gretchen Merrill USA
1948 Davos SWI	Barbara Ann Scott CAN	Eva Pawlik AUT	Jirina Nekolová CSR
1949 Paris FRA	Alena Vrzáňová CZE	Yvonne Sherman USA	Jeannette Altwegg GRB
1950 London GRB	Alena Vrzáňová CZE	Jeannette Altwegg GRB	Yvonne Sherman USA
1951 Milan ITA	Jeannette Altwegg GRB	Jacqueline du Bief FRA	Sonya Klopfer USA
1952 Paris FRA	Jacqueline du Bief FRA	Sonya Klopfer USA	Virginia Baxter USA
1953 Davos, SWI	Tenley Albright USA	Gundi Busch GER	Valda Osborn GRB
1954 Oslo NOR	Gundi Busch GER	Tenley Albright USA	Erica Batchelor GRB
1955 Vienna AUT	Tenley Albright USA	Carol Heiss USA	Hanna Eigel AUT
1956 Garmisch-Partenkirchen FRG	Carol Heiss USA	Tenley Albright USA	Ingrid Wendl AUT
1957 Colorado Springs USA	Carol Heiss USA	Hanna Eigel AUT	Ingrid Wendl AUT
1958 Paris FRA	Carol Heiss USA	Ingrid Wendl AUT	Hanna Walter AUT
1959 Colorado Springs USA	Carol Heiss USA	Hanna Walter AUT	Sjoukje Dijkstra NED
1960 Vancouver CAN	Carol Heiss USA	Sjoukje Dijkstra NED	Barbara Roles USA

1961   THE WORLD CHAMPIONSHIPS WERE NOT HELD.

1962 Prague CZE	Sjoukje Dijkstra NED	Wendy Griner CAN	Regine Heitzer AUT
1963 Cortina ITA	Sjoukje Dijkstra NED	Regine Heitzer AUT	Nicole Hassler FRA
1964 Dortmund FRG	Sjoukje Dijkstra NED	Regine Heitzer AUT	Petra Burka CAN
1965 Colorado Springs USA	Petra Burka CAN	Regine Heitzer AUT	Peggy Fleming USA
1966 Davos SWI	Peggy Fleming USA	Gabriele Seyfert GDR	Petra Burka CAN
1967 Vienna AUT	Peggy Fleming USA	Gabriele Seyfert GDR	Hana Mašková CZE
1968 Geneva SWI	Peggy Fleming USA	Gabriele Seyfert GDR	Hana Mašková CZE
1969 Colorado Springs USA	Gabriele Seyfert GDR	Beatrix Schuba AUT	Zsuzsa Almássy HUN
1970 Ljubljana YUG	Gabriele Seyfert GDR	Beatrix Schuba AUT	Julie Lynn Holmes USA
1971 Lyon FRA	Beatrix Schuba AUT	Julie Lynn Holmes USA	Karen Magnussen CAN
1972 Calgary CAN	Beatrix Schuba AUT	Karen Magnussen CAN	Janet Lynn USA
1973 Bratislava CZE	Karen Magnussen CAN	Janet Lynn USA	Christine Errath GDR
1974 Munich FRG	Christine Errath GDR	Dorothy Hamill USA	Dianne de Leeuw NED
1975 Colorado Springs USA	Dianne de Leeuw NED	Dorothy Hamill USA	Christine Errath GDR
1976 Gothenberg SWE	Dorothy Hamill USA	Christine Errath GDR	Dianne de Leeuw NED
1977 Tokyo JPN	Linda Fratianne USA	Anett Pötzsch GDR	Dagmar Lurz FRG
1978 Ottawa CAN	Anett Pötzsch GDR	Linda Fratianne USA	Susanna Driano ITA
1979 Vienna AUT	Linda Fratianne USA	Anett Pötzsch GDR	Emi Watanabe JPN
1980 Dortmund FRG	Anett Pötzsch GDR	Dagmar Lurz FRG	Linda Fratianne USA
1981 Hartford USA	Denise Biellmann SWI	Elaine Zayak USA	Claudia Kristofics-Binder AUT
1982 Copenhagen DEN	Elaine Zayak USA	Katarina Witt GDR	Claudia Kristofics-Binder AUT
1983 Helsinki FIN	Rosalynn Sumners USA	Claudia Leistner FRG	Elena Vodorezova URS
1984 Ottawa CAN	Katarina Witt GDR	Anna Kondrashova URS	Elaine Zayak USA
1985 Tokyo JPN	Katarina Witt GDR	Kira Ivanova URS	Tiffany Chin USA
1986 Geneva SWI	Debra Thomas USA	Katarina Witt GDR	Tiffany Chin USA
1987 Cincinnati USA	Katarina Witt GDR	Debra Thomas USA	Caryn Kadavy USA
1988 Budapest HUN	Katarina Witt GDR	Elizabeth Manley CAN	Debra Thomas USA
1989 Paris FRA	Midori Ito JPN	Claudia Leistner FRG	Jill Trenary USA
1990 Halifax CAN	Jill Trenary USA	Midori Ito JPN	Holly Cook USA
1991 Munich GER	Kristi Yamaguchi USA	Tonya Harding USA	Nancy Kerrigan USA
1992 Oakland USA	Kristi Yamaguchi USA	Nancy Kerrigan USA	Lu Chen CHN
1993 Prague CZE	Oksana Baiul UKR	Surya Bonaly FRA	Lu Chen CHN
1994 Chiba JPN	Yuka Sato JPN	Surya Bonaly FRA	Tanja Szewczenko GER
1995 Birmingham GRB	Lu Chen CHN	Surya Bonaly FRA	Nicole Bobek USA
1996 Edmonton CAN	Michelle Kwan USA	Lu Chen CHN	Irina Slutskaya RUS
1997 Lausanne SWI	Tara Lipinski USA	Michelle Kwan USA	Vanessa Gusmeroli FRA
1998 Minneapolis USA	Michelle Kwan USA	Irina Slutskaya RUS	Maria Butyrskay a RUS
1999 Helsinki FIN	Maria Butyrskaya RUS	Michelle Kwan USA	Julia Soldatova RUS
2000 Nice FRA	Michelle Kwan USA	Irina Slutskaya USA	Maria Butyrskaya RUS
2001 Vancouver CAN	Michelle Kwan USA	Irina Slutskaya RUS	Sarah Hughes USA
2002 Nagano JPN	Irina Slutskaya RUS	Michelle Kwan USA	Fumie Suguri JPN
2003 Washington USA	Michelle Kwan USA	Elena Sokolova RUS	Fumie Suguri JPN
2004 Dortmund GER	Shizuka Arakawa JPN	Sasha Cohen USA	Michelle Kwan USA
2005 Moscow RUS	Irina Slutskaya RUS	Sasha Cohen USA	Carolina Kostner ITA

Men

Location	Gold	Silver	Bronze
1896 St. Petersburg RUS	Gilbert Fuchs GER	Gustav Hügel AUT	Georg Sanders RUS
1897 Stockholm SWE	Gustav Hügel AUT	Ulrich Salchow SWE	Johan Lefstad NOR
1898 London GRB	Henning Grenander SWE	Gustav Hügel AUT	Gilbert Fuchs GER
1899 Davos SWI	Gustav Hügel AUT	Ulrich Salchow SWE	Edgar Syers GBR
1900 Davos SWI	Gustav Hügel AUT	Ulrich Salchow SWE	
1901 Stockholm SWE	Ulrich Salchow SWE	Gilbert Fuchs GER	

1902 London GRB	Ulrich Salchow SWE	Madge Syers GBR	Martin Gordan GER
1903 St. Petersburg RUS	Ulrich Salchow SWE	Nicolai Panin RUS	Max Bohatsch AUT
1904 Berlin GER	Ulrich Salchow SWE	Heinrich Burger AUT	Martin Gordan GER
1905 Stockholm SWI	Ulrich Salchow SWE	Max Bohatsch AUT	Per Thorén SWE
1906 Munich GER	Gilbert Fuchs GER	Heinrich Burger GER	Bror Meyer SWE
1907 Vienna AUT	Ulrich Salchow SWE	Max Bohatsch AUT	Gilbert Fuchs GER
1908 Troppau CSR	Ulrich Salchow SWE	Gilbert Fuchs GER	Heinrich Burger GER
1909 Stockholm SWE	Ulrich Salchow SWE	Per Thorén SWE	Ernst Herz AUT
1910 Davos SWI	Ulrich Salchow SWE	Werner Rittberger GER	Andor Szende HUN
1911 Berlin GER	Ulrich Salchow SWE	Werner Rittberger GER	Fritz Kachler AUT
1912 Manchester GRB	Fritz Kachler AUT	Werner Rittberger GER	Andor Szende HUN
1913 Vienna AUT	Fritz Kachler AUT	Wilhelm Böckl AUT	Andor Szende HUN
1914 Helsinki FIN	Gösta Sandahl SWE	Fritz Kachler AUT	Wilhelm Böckl AUT

1915–21 THE WORLD CHAMPIONSHIPS WERE NOT HELD.

1922 Stockholm SWE	Gillis Grafström SWE	Fritz Kachler AUT	Wilhelm Böckl AUT
1923 Vienna AUT	Fritz Kachler AUT	Wilhelm Böckl AUT	Gösta Sandahl SWE
1924 Manchester GRB	Gillis Grafström SWE	Wilhelm Böckl AUT	Ernst Oppacher AUT
1925 Vienna AUT	Wilhelm Böckl AUT	Fritz Kachler AUT	Otto Preissecker AUT
1926 Berlin GER	Wilhelm Böckl AUT	Otto Preissecker AUT	John Page GRB
1927 Davos SWI	Wilhelm Böckl AUT	Otto Preissecker AUT	Karl Schäfer AUT
1928 Berlin GER	Wilhelm Böckl AUT	Karl Schäfer AUT	Hugo Distler AUT
1929 London GRB	Gillis Grafström SWE	Karl Schäfer AUT	Ludwig Wrede AUT
1930 New York USA	Karl Schäfer AUT	Roger Turner USA	Georg Gautschi SWI
1931 Berlin GER	Karl Schäfer AUT	Roger Turner USA	Ernst Baier GER
1932 Montreal CAN	Karl Schäfer AUT	Montgomery Wilson CAN	Ernst Baier GER
1933 Zurich SWI	Karl Schäfer AUT	Ernst Baier GER	Markus Nikkanen FIN
1934 Stockholm SWE	Karl Schäfer AUT	Ernst Baier GER	Erich Erdös AUT
1935 Budapest HUN	Karl Schäfer AUT	Jack Dunn GRB	Dénes Pataky HUN
1936 Paris FRA	Karl Schäfer AUT	Graham Sharp GRB	Felix Kaspar AUT
1937 Vienna AUT	Felix Kaspar AUT	Graham Sharp GRB	Elemér Terták HUN
1938 Berlin GER	Felix Kaspar AUT	Graham Sharp GRB	Herbert Alward AUT
1939 Budapest HUN	Graham Sharp GRB	Freddie Tomlins GRB	Horst Faber GER

1940–46 THE WORLD CHAMPIONSHIPS WERE NOT HELD.

1947 Stockholm SWE	Hans Gerschwiler SWI	Richard Button USA	Arthur Apfel GRB
1948 Davos SWI	Richard Button USA	Hans Gerschwiler SWI	Ede Király HUN
1949 Paris FRA	Richard Button USA	Ede Király HUN	Edi Rada AUT
1950 London GRB	Richard Button USA	Ede Király HUN	Hayes Alan Jenkins USA
1951 Milan ITA	Richard Button USA	James Grogan USA	Helmut Seibt AUT
1952 Paris FRA	Richard Button USA	James Grogan USA	Hayes Alan Jenkins USA
1953 Davos SWI	Hayes Alan Jenkins USA	James Grogan USA	Carlo Fassi ITA
1954 Oslo NOR	Hayes Alan Jenkins USA	James Grogan USA	Alain Giletti FRA
1955 Vienna AUT	Hayes Alan Jenkins USA	Ronald Robertson USA	David Jenkins USA
1956 Garmisch-Partenkirchen FRG	Hayes Alan Jenkins USA	Ronald Robertson USA	David Jenkins USA
1957 Colorado Springs USA	David Jenkins USA	Tim Brown USA	Charles Snelling CAN
1958 Paris FRA	David Jenkins USA	Tim Brown USA	Alain Giletti FRA
1959 Colorado Springs USA	David Jenkins USA	Donald Jackson CAN	Tim Brown USA
1960 Vancouver CAN	Alain Giletti FRA	Donald Jackson CAN	Alain Calmat FRA

1961 THE WORLD CHAMPIONSHIPS WERE NOT HELD.

1962 Prague CZE	Donald Jackson CAN	Karol Divin CZE	Alain Calmat FRA
1963 Cortina ITA	Donald McPherson CAN	Alain Calmat FRA	Manfred Schnelldorfer FRG
1964 Dortmund FRG	Manfred Schnelldorfer FRG	Alain Calmat FRA	Karol Divin CZE
1965 Colorado Springs USA	Alain Calmat FRA	Scott Allen USA	Donald Knight CAN
1966 Davos SWI	Emmerich Danzer AUT	Wolfgang Schwarz AUT	Gary Visconti USA
1967 Vienna AUT	Emmerich Danzer AUT	Wolfgang Schwarz AUT	Gary Visconti USA
1968 Geneva SWI	Emmerich Danzer AUT	Tim Wood USA	Patrick Pera FRA

1969 Colorado Springs USA	Tim Wood USA	Ondrej Nepela CZE	Patrick Pera FRA
1970 Ljubljana YUG	Tim Wood USA	Ondrej Nepela CZE	Günter Zöller GDR
1971 Lyon FRA	Ondrej Nepela CZE	Patrick Pera FRA	Sergei Chetverukhin URS
1972 Calgary CAN	Ondrej Nepela CZE	Sergei Chetverukhin URS	Vladimir Kovalev URS
1973 Bratislava CZE	Ondrej Nepela CZE	Sergei Chetverukhin URS	Jan Hoffmann GDR
1974 Munich FRG	Jan Hoffmann GDR	Sergei Volkov URS	Toller Cranston CAN
1975 Colorado Springs USA	Sergei Volkov URS	Vladimir Kovalev URS	John Curry GRB
1976 Gothenberg SWE	John Curry GRB	Vladimir Kovalev URS	Jan Hoffmann GDR
1977 Tokyo JPN	Vladimir Kovalev URS	Jan Hoffmann GDR	Minoru Sano JPN
1978 Ottawa CAN	Charles Tickner USA	Jan Hoffmann GDR	Robin Cousins GRB
1979 Vienna AUT	Vladimir Kovalev URS	Robin Cousins GRB	Jan Hoffmann GDR
1980 Dortmund FRG	Jan Hoffmann GDR	Robin Cousins GRB	Charles Tickner USA
1981 Hartford USA	Scott Hamilton USA	David Santee USA	Igor Bobrin URS
1982 Copenhagen DEN	Scott Hamilton USA	Norbert Schramm FRG	Brian Pockar CAN
1983 Helsinki FIN	Scott Hamilton USA	Norbert Schramm FRG	Brian Orser CAN
1984 Ottawa CAN	Scott Hamilton USA	Brian Orser CAN	Alexandr Fadeev URS
1985 Tokyo JPN	Alexandr Fadeev URS	Brian Orser CAN	Brian Boitano USA
1986 Geneva SWI	Brian Boitano USA	Brian Orser CAN	Alexandr Fadeev URS
1987 Cincinnati USA	Brian Orser CAN	Brian Boitano USA	Alexandr Fadeev URS
1988 Budapest HUN	Brian Boitano USA	Brian Orser CAN	Viktor Petrenko URS
1989 Paris FRA	Kurt Browning CAN	Christopher Bowman USA	Grzegorz Filipowski POL
1990 Halifax CAN	Kurt Browning CAN	Viktor Petrenko URS	Christopher Bowman USA
1991 Munich GER	Kurt Browning CAN	Viktor Petrenko URS	Todd Eldredge USA
1992 Oakland USA	Viktor Petrenko CIS	Kurt Browning CAN	Elvis Stojko CAN
1993 Prague CZE	Kurt Browning CAN	Elvis Stojko CAN	Alexei Urmanov RUS
1994 Chiba JPN	Elvis Stojko CAN	Philippe Candeloro FRA	Viacheslav Zagorodniuk UKR
1995 Birmingham GRB	Elvis Stojko CAN	Todd Eldredge USA	Philippe Candeloro FRA
1996 Edmonton CAN	Todd Eldredge USA	Ilia Kulik RUS	Rudy Galindo USA
1997 Lausanne SWI	Elvis Stojko CAN	Todd Eldredge USA	Alexei Yagudin RUS
1998 Minneapolis USA	Alexei Yagudin RUS	Todd Eldredge USA	Evgeny Plushenko RUS
1999 Helsinki FIN	Alexei Yagudin RUS	Evgeny Plushenko RUS	Michael Weiss USA
2000 Nice FRA	Alexei Yagudin RUS	Elvis Stojko CAN	Michael Weiss USA
2001 Vancouver CAN	Evgeny Plushenko RUS	Alexei Yagudin RUS	Todd Eldredge USA
2002 Nagano JPN	Alexei Yagudin RUS	Timothy Goebel USA	Takeshi Honda JPN
2003 Washington USA	Evgeny Plushenko RUS	Timothy Goebel USA	Takeshi Honda JPN
2004 Dortmund GER	Evgeny Plushenko RUS	Brian Joubert FRA	Stefan Lindemann GER
2005 Moscow RUS	Stephane Lambiel SUI	Jeffrey Buttle CAN	Evan Lysacek USA

Pairs

Location	Gold	Silver	Bronze
1908 St. Petersburg RUS	Anna Hübler Heinrich Burger GER	Phyllis Johnson James Johnson GRB	A. L. Fischer L. P. Popowa RUS
1909 Stockholm SWE	Phyllis Johnson James Johnson GRB	Valborg Lindahl Nils Rosenius SWE	Gertrud Ström Richard Johansson SWE
1910 Berlin GER	Anna Hübler Heinrich Burger GER	Ludowika Eilers GER Walter Jakobsson FIN	Phyllis Johnson James Johnson GRB
1911 Vienna AUT	Ludowika Eilers GER Walter Jakobsson FIN		
1912 Manchester GRB	Phyllis Johnson James Johnson GRB	Ludowika Jakobsson Walter Jakobsson FIN	Alexia Bryn Yngvar Bryn NOR
1913 Stockholm SWE	Helene Engelmann Karl Mejstrik AUT	Ludowika Jakobsson Walter Jakobsson FIN	Christa von Szabo Leo Horwitz AUT
1914 St. Moritz SWI	Ludowika Jakobsson Walter Jakobsson FIN	Helene Engelmann Karl Mejstrik AUT	Christa von Szabo Leo Horwitz AUT

1915–21   THE WORLD CHAMPIONSHIPS WERE NOT HELD.

Year	Gold	Silver	Bronze
1922 Davos SWI	Helene Engelmann / Alfred Berger AUT	Ludowika Jakobsson / Walter Jakobsson FIN	Margaret Metzner / Paul Metzner GER
1923 Oslo NOR	Ludowika Jakobsson / Walter Jakobsson FIN	Alexia Bryn / Yngvar Bryn NOR	Elna Henrikson / Kaj af Ekström SWE
1924 Manchester GRB	Helene Engelmann / Alfred Berger AUT	Ethel Muckelt / John Page GRB	Elna Henrikson / Kaj af Ekström SWE
1925 Vienna AUT	Herma Szabo / Ludwig Wrede AUT	Andrée Joly / Pierre Brunet FRA	Lily Scholz / Otto Kaiser AUT
1926 Berlin GER	Andrée Joly / Pierre Brunet FRA	Lily Scholz / Otto Kaiser AUT	Herma Szabo / Ludwig Wrede AUT
1927 Vienna AUT	Herma Szabo / Ludwig Wrede AUT	Lily Scholz / Otto Kaiser AUT	Else Hoppe / Oscar Hoppe CSR
1928 London GRB	Andrée Brunet / Pierre Brunet FRA	Lily Scholz / Otto Kaiser AUT	Melitta Brunner / Ludwig Wrede AUT
1929 Budapest HUN	Lily Scholz / Otto Kaiser AUT	Melitta Brunner / Ludwig Wrede AUT	Olga Orgonista / Sándor Szalay HUN
1930 New York USA	Andrée Brunet / Pierre Brunet FRA	Melitta Brunner / Ludwig Wrede AUT	Beatrix Loughran / Sherwin Badger USA
1931 Berlin GER	Emília Rotter / László Szollás HUN	Olga Orgonista / Sándor Szalay HUN	Idi Papez / Karl Zwack AUT
1932 Montreal CAN	Andrée Brunet / Pierre Brunet FRA	Emilia Rotter / László Szollás HUN	Beatrix Loughran / Sherwin Badger USA
1933 Stockholm SWE	Emília Rotter / László Szollás HUN	Idi Papez / Karl Zwack AUT	Randi Bakke / Christen Christensen NOR
1934 Helsinki FIN	Emilia Rotter / László Szollás HUN	Idi Papez / Karl Zwack AUT	Maxi Herber / Ernst Baier GER
1935 Budapest HUN	Emília Rotter / László Szollás HUN	Ilse Pausin / Erich Pausin AUT	Lucy Galló / Rezsö Dillinger HUN
1936 Paris FRA	Maxi Herber / Ernst Baier GER	Ilse Pausin / Erich Pausin AUT	Violet Cliff / Leslie Cliff GRB
1937 London GRB	Maxi Herber / Ernst Baier GER	Ilse Pausin / Erich Pausin AUT	Violet Cliff / Leslie Cliff GRB
1938 Berlin GER	Maxi Herber / Ernst Baier GER	Ilse Pausin / Erich Pausin AUT	Inge Koch / Günther Noack GER
1939 Budapest HUN	Maxi Herber / Ernst Baier GER	Ilse Pausin / Erich Pausin GER	Inge Koch / Günther Noack GER

1940–46   THE WORLD CHAMPIONSHIPS WERE NOT HELD.

Year	Gold	Silver	Bronze
1947 Stockhom SWE	Micheline Lannoy / Pierre Baugniet BEL	Karol Kennedy / Peter Kennedy USA	Suzanne Diskeuve / Edmond Verbustel BEL
1948 Davos SWI	Micheline Lannoy / Pierre Baugniet BEL	Andrea Kekéssy / Ede Király HUN	Suzanne Morrow / Wallace Diestelmeyer CAN
1949 Paris FRA	Andrea Kekéssy / Ede Király HUN	Karol Kennedy / Peter Kennedy USA	Anne Davies / Carleton Hoffner Jr. USA
1950 London GRB	Karol Kennedy / Peter Kennedy USA	Jennifer Nicks / John Nicks GRB	Mariann Nagy / László Nagy HUN
1951 Milan ITA	Ria Baran / Paul Falk GER	Karol Kennedy / Peter Kennedy USA	Jennifer Nicks / John Nicks GRB
1952 Paris FRA	Ria Falk / Paul Falk GER	Karol Kennedy / Peter Kennedy USA	Jennifer Nicks / John Nicks GRB
1953 Davos SWI	Jennifer Nicks / John Nicks GRB	Frances Dafoe / Norris Bowden CAN	Mariann Nagy / László Nagy HUN
1954 Oslo NOR	Frances Dafoe / Norris Bowden CAN	Silvia Grandjean / Michel Grandjean SWI	Elisabeth Schwarz / Kurt Oppelt AUT
1955 Vienna AUT	Frances Dafoe / Norris Bowden CAN	Elisabeth Schwarz / Kurt Oppelt AUT	Mariann Nagy / László Nagy HUN

Year / Location	Gold	Silver	Bronze
1956 Garmisch-Partenkirchen GER	Elisabeth Schwarz / Kurt Oppelt AUT	Frances Dafoe / Norris Bowden CAN	Marika Kilius / Franz Ningel FRG
1957 Colorado Springs USA	Barbara Wagner / Robert Paul CAN	Marika Kilius / Franz Ningel FRG	Maria Jelinek / Otto Jelinek CAN
1958 Paris FRA	Barbara Wagner / Robert Paul CAN	Vera Suchánková / Zdenek Doležal CZE	Maria Jelinek / Otto Jelinek CAN
1959 Colorado Springs USA	Barbara Wagner / Robert Paul CAN	Marika Kilius / Hans Jürgen Bäumler FRG	Nancy Ludington / Ronald Ludington USA
1960 Vancouver CAN	Barbara Wagner / Robert Paul CAN	Maria Jelinek / Otto Jelinek CAN	Marika Kilius / Hans Jürgen Bäumler FRG
1961	THE WORLD CHAMPIONSHIPS WERE NOT HELD.		
1962 Prague CZE	Maria Jelinek / Otto Jelinek CAN	Liudmila Belousova / Oleg Protopopov URS	Margret Göbl / Franz Ningel FRG
1963 Cortina ITA	Marika Kilius / Hans Jürgen Bäumler FRG	Liudmila Belousova / Oleg Protopopov URS	Tatiana Zhuk / Alexandr Gavrilov URS
1964 Dortmund FRG	Marika Kilius / Hans Jürgen Bäumler FRG	Liudmila Belousova / Oleg Protopopov URS	Debbi Wilkes / Guy Revell CAN
1965 Colorado Springs USA	Liudmila Belousova / Oleg Protopopov URS	Vivian Joseph / Ronald Joseph USA	Tatiana Zhuk / Alexandr Gorelik URS
1966 Davos SWI	Liudmila Belousova / Oleg Protopopov URS	Tatiana Zhuk / Alexandr Gorelik URS	Cynthia Kauffman / Ronald Kauffman USA
1967 Vienna AUT	Liudmila Belousova / Oleg Protopopov URS	Margot Glockshuber / Wolfgang Danne FRG	Cynthia Kauffman / Ronald Kauffman USA
1968 Geneva SWI	Liudmila Belousova / Oleg Protopopov URS	Tatiana Zhuk / Alexandr Gorelik URS	Cynthia Kauffman / Ronald Kauffman USA
1969 Colorado Springs USA	Irina Rodnina / Alexei Ulanov URS	Tamara Moskvina / Alexei Mishin URS	Liudmila Belousova / Oleg Protopopov URS
1970 Ljubljana YUG	Irina Rodnina / Alexei Ulanov URS	Liudmila Smirnova / Andrei Suraikin URS	Heidemarie Steiner / Heinz-Ulrich Walther GDR
1971 Lyon FRA	Irina Rodnina / Alexei Ulanov URS	Liudmila Smirnova / Andrei Suraikin URS	Alicia Jo Starbuck / Kenneth Shelley USA
1972 Calgary CAN	Irina Rodnina / Alexei Ulanov URS	Liudmila Smirnova / Andrei Suraikin URS	Alicia Jo Starbuck / Kenneth Shelley USA
1973 Bratislava CZE	Irina Rodnina / Alexandr Zaitsev URS	Liudmila Smirnova / Alexei Ulanov URS	Manuela Gross / Uwe Kagelmann GDR
1974 Munich FRG	Irina Rodnina / Alexandr Zaitsev URS	Liudmila Smirnova / Alexei Ulanov URS	Romy Kermer / Rolf Österreich GDR
1975 Colorado Springs USA	Irina Rodnina / Alexandr Zaitsev URS	Romy Kermer / Rolf Österreich GDR	Manuela Gross / Uwe Kagelmann GDR
1976 Gothenberg SWE	Irina Rodnina / Alexandr Zaitsev URS	Romy Kermer / Rolf Österreich GDR	Irina Vorobieva / Alexandr Vlasov URS
1977 Tokyo JPN	Irina Rodnina / Alexandr Zaitsev URS	Irina Vorobieva / Alexandr Vlasov URS	Tai Babilonia / Randy Gardner USA
1978 Ottawa CAN	Irina Rodnina / Alexandr Zaitsev URS	Manuela Mager / Uwe Bewersdorff GDR	Tai Babilonia / Randy Gardner USA
1979 Vienna AUT	Tai Babilonia / Randy Gardner USA	Marina Cherkasova / Sergei Shakhrai URS	Sabine Baess / Tassilo Thierbach GDR
1980 Dortmund FRG	Marina Cherkasova / Sergei Shakhrai URS	Manuela Mager / Uwe Bewersdorff GDR	Marina Pestova / Stanislav Leonovich URS
1981 Hartford USA	Irina Vorobieva / Igor Lisovski URS	Sabine Baess / Tassilo Thierbach GDR	Christina Riegel / Andreas Nischwitz FRG
1982 Copenhagen DEN	Sabine Baess / Tassilo Thierbach GDR	Marina Pestova / Stanislav Leonovich	Caitlin Carruthers / Peter Carruthers USA
1983 Helsinki FIN	Elena Valova / Oleg Vasiliev URS	Sabine Baess / Tassilo Thierbach GDR	Barbara Underhill / Paul Martini CAN

1984 Ottawa CAN	Barbara Underhill	Elena Valova	Sabine Baess
	Paul Martini CAN	Oleg Vasiliev URS	Tassilo Thierbach GDR
1985 Tokyo JPN	Elena Valova	Larisa Selezneva	Katherina Matousek
	Oleg Vasiliev URS	Oleg Makarov URS	Lloyd Eisler CAN
1986 Geneva SWI	Ekaterina Gordeeva	Elena Valova	Cynthia Coull
	Sergei Grinkov URS	Oleg Vasiliev URS	Mark Rowsom CAN
1987 Cincinnati USA	Ekaterina Gordeeva	Elena Valova	Jill Watson
	Sergei Grinkov URS	Oleg Vasiliev URS	Peter Oppegard USA
1988 Budapest HUN	Elena Valova	Ekaterina Gordeeva	Larisa Selezneva
	Oleg Vasiliev URS	Sergei Grinkov URS	Oleg Makarov URS
1989 Paris FRA	Ekaterina Gordeeva	Cindy Landry	Elena Bechke
	Sergei Grinkov URS	Lyndon Johnston CAN	Denis Petrov URS
1990 Halifax CAN	Ekaterina Gordeeva	Isabelle Brasseur	Natalia Mishkutenok
	Sergei Grinkov URS	Lloyd Eisler CAN	Artur Dmitriev URS
1991 Munich GER	Natalia Mishkutenok	Isabelle Brasseur	Natasha Kuchiki
	Artur Dmitriev URS	Lloyd Eisler CAN	Todd Sand USA
1992 Oakland USA	Natalia Mishkutenok	Radka Kovaříková	Isabelle Brasseur
	Artur Dmitriev EUN	René Novotny CZE	Lloyd Eisler CAN
1993 Prague CZE	Isabelle Brasseur	Mandy Wötzel	Evgenia Shishkova
	Lloyd Eisler CAN	Ingo Steuer GER	Vadim Naumov RUS
1994 Chiba JPN	Evgenia Shishkova	Isabelle Brasseur	Marina Eltsova
	Vadim Naumov RUS	Lloyd Eisler CAN	Andrei Bushkov RUS
1995 Birmingham GRB	Radka Kovaříková	Evgenia Shishkova	Jenni Meno
	René Novotny CZE	Vadim Naumov RUS	Todd Sand USA
1996 Edmonton CAN	Marina Eltsova	Mandy Wötzel	Jenni Meno
	Andrei Bushkov RUS	Ingo Steuer GER	Todd Sand USA
1997 Lausanne SWI	Mandy Wötzel	Marina Eltsova	Oksana Kazakova
	Ingo Steuer GER	Andrei Bushkov RUS	Artur Dmitriev RUS
1998 Minneapolis USA	Elena Berezhnaya	Jenni Meno	Peggy Schwarz
	Anton Sikharulidze RUS	Todd Sand USA	Mirko Müller GER
1999 Helsinki FIN	Elena Berezhnaya	Xue Shen	Dorota Zagorska
	Anton Sikharulidze RUS	Hongbo Zhao CHN	Mariusz Siudek POL
2000 Nice FRA	Maria Petrova	Xue Shen	Sarah Abitbol
	Alexei Tikhonov RUS	Hongbo Zhao CHN	Stephane Bernadis FRA
2001 Vancouver CAN	Jamie Salé	Elena Berezhnaya	Xue Shen
	David Pelletier CAN	Anton Sikharulidze RUS	Hongbo Zhao CHN
2002 Nagano JPN	Xue Shen	Tatiana Totmianina	Kyoko Ina
	Hongbo Zhao CHN	Maxim Marinin RUS	John Zimmerman USA
2003 Washington USA	Xue Shen	Tatiana Totmianina	Maria Petrova
	Hongbo Zhao CHN	Maxim Marinin RUS	Alexei Tikhonov RUS
2004 Dortmund GER	Tatiana Totmianina	Xue Shen	Quing Pang
	Maxim Marinin RUS	Hongbo Zhao CHN	Jian Tong CHN
2005 Moscow RUS	Tatiana Totmianina	Maria Petrova	Dan Zhang
	Maxim Marinin RUS	Alexei Tikhonov RUS	Hao Zhang CHN

Ice Dancing

Location	Gold	Silver	Bronze
1952 Paris FRA	Jean Westwood	Joan Dewhirst	Carol Peters
	Lawrence Demmy GRB	John Slater GRB	Daniel Ryan USA
1953 Davos SWI	Jean Westwood	Joan Dewhirst	Carol Peters
	Lawrence Demmy GRB	John Slater GRB	Daniel Ryan USA
1954 Oslo NOR	Jean Westwood	Nesta Davies	Carmel Bodel
	Lawrence Demmy GRB	Paul Thomas GRB	Edward Bodel USA

Year / Location	First	Second	Third
1955 Vienna AUT	Jean Westwood / Lawrence Demmy GRB	Pamela Weight / Paul Thomas GRB	Barbara Radford / Raymond Lockwood GRB
1956 Garmisch-Partenkirchen FRG	Pamela Weight / Paul Thomas GRB	June Markham / Courtney Jones GRB	Barbara Thompson / Gerard Rigby GRB
1957 Colorado Springs USA	June Markham / Courtney Jones GRB	Geraldine Fenton / William McLachlan CAN	Sharon McKenzie / Bert Wright USA
1958 Paris FRA	June Markham / Courtney Jones GRB	Geraldine Fenton / William McLachlan CAN	Andrée Anderson / Donald Jacoby USA
1959 Colorado Springs USA	Doreen Denny / Courtney Jones GRB	Andrée Jacoby-Anderson / Donald Jacoby USA	Geraldine Fenton / William McLachlan CAN
1960 Vancouver CAN	Doreen Denny / Courtney Jones GRB	Virginia Thompson / William McLachlan CAN	Christiane Guhel / Jean Paul Guhel FRA
1961	THE WORLD CHAMPIONSHIPS WERE NOT HELD.		
1962 Prague CZE	Eva Romanová / Pavel Roman CZE	Christiane Guhel / Jean Paul Guhel FRA	Virginia Thompson / William McLachlan CAN
1963 Cortina ITA	Eva Romanová / Pavel Roman CZE	Linda Shearman / Michael Phillips GRB	Paulette Doan / Kenneth Ormsby CAN
1964 Dortmund FRG	Eva Romanová / Pavel Roman CZE	Paulette Doan / Kenneth Ormsby CAN	Janet Sawbridge / David Hickinbottom GRB
1965 Colorado Springs USA	Eva Romanová / Pavel Roman CZE	Janet Sawbridge / David Hickinbottom GRB	Lorna Dyer / John Carrell USA
1966 Davos SWI	Diane Towler / Bernard Ford GRB	Kristin Fortune / Dennis Sveum USA	Lorna Dyer / John Carrell USA
1967 Vienna AUT	Diane Towler / Bernard Ford GRB	Lorna Dyer / John Carrell USA	Yvonne Suddick / Malcolm Cannon GRB
1968 Geneva SWI	Diane Towler / Bernard Ford GRB	Yvonne Suddick / Malcolm Cannon GRB	Janet Sawbridge / Jon Lane GRB
1969 Colorado Springs USA	Diane Towler / Bernard Ford GRB	Liudmila Pakhomova / Alexandr Gorshkov URS	Judy Schwomeyer / James Sladky USA
1970 Ljubljana YUG	Liudmila Pakhomova / Alexandr Gorshkov URS	Judy Schwomeyer / James Sladky USA	Angelika Buck / Erich Buck FRG
1971 Lyon FRA	Liudmila Pakhomova / Alexandr Gorshkov URS	Angelika Buck / Erich Buck FRG	Judy Schwomeyer / James Sladky USA
1972 Calgary CAN	Liudmila Pakhomova / Alexandr Gorshkov URS	Angelika Buck / Erich Buck FRG	Judy Schwomeyer / James Sladky USA
1973 Bratislava CZE	Liudmila Pakhomova / Alexandr Gorshkov URS	Angelika Buck / Erich Buck FRG	Hilary Green / Glyn Watts GRB
1974 Munich FRG	Liudmila Pakhomova / Alexandr Gorshkov URS	Hilary Green / Glyn Watts GRB	Natalia Linichuk / Gennadi Karponosov URS
1975 Colorado Springs USA	Irina Moiseeva / Andrei Minenkov URS	Colleen O'Connor / Jim Millns USA	Hilary Green / Glyn Watts GRB
1976 Gothenberg SWE	Liudmila Pakhomova / Alexandr Gorshkov URS	Irina Moiseeva / Andrei Minenkov URS	Colleen O'Connor / Jim Millns USA
1977 Tokyo JPN	Irina Moiseeva / Andrei Minenkov URS	Janet Thompson / Warren Maxwell GRB	Natalia Linichuk / Gennadi Karponosov URS
1978 Ottawa CAN	Natalia Linichuk / Gennadi Karponosov URS	Irina Moiseeva / Andrei Minenkov URS	Krisztina Regöczy / András Sallay HUN
1979 Vienna AUT	Natalia Linichuk / Gennadi Karponosov URS	Krisztina Regöczy / András Sallay HUN	Irina Moiseeva / Andrei Minenkov URS
1980 Dortmund FRG	Krisztina Regöczy / András Sallay HUN	Natalia Linichuk / Gennadi Karponosov URS	Irina Moiseeva / Andrei Minenkov URS
1981 Hartford USA	Jayne Torvill / Christopher Dean GRB	Irina Moiseeva / Andrei Minenkov URS	Natalia Bestemianova / Andrei Bukin URS
1982 Copenhagen DEN	Jayne Torvill / Christopher Dean GRB	Natalia Bestemianova / Andrei Bukin URS	Irina Moiseeva / Andrei Minenkov URS

	Gold	Silver	Bronze
1983 Helsinki FIN	Jayne Torvill / Christopher Dean GRB	Natalia Bestemianova / Andrei Bukin URS	Judy Blumberg / Michael Seibert USA
1984 Ottawa CAN	Jayne Torvill / Christopher Dean GRB	Natalia Bestemianova / Andrei Bukin URS	Judy Blumberg / Michael Seibert USA
1985 Tokyo JPN	Natalia Bestemianova / Andrei Bukin URS	Marina Klimova / Sergei Ponomarenko URS	Judy Blumberg / Michael Seibert USA
1986 Geneva SWI	Natalia Bestemianova / Andrei Bukin URS	Marina Klimova / Sergei Ponomarenko URS	Tracy Wilson / Robert McCall CAN
1987 Cincinnati USA	Natalia Bestemianova / Andrei Bukin URS	Marina Klimova / Sergei Ponomarenko URS	Tracy Wilson / Robert McCall CAN
1988 Budapest HUN	Natalia Bestemianova / Andrei Bukin URS	Marina Klimova / Sergei Ponomarenko URS	Tracy Wilson / Robert McCall CAN
1989 Paris FRA	Marina Klimova / Sergei Ponomarenko URS	Maia Usova / Alexandr Zhulin URS	Isabelle Duchesnay / Paul Duchesnay FRA
1990 Halifax CAN	Marina Klimova / Sergei Ponomarenko URS	Isabelle Duchesnay / Paul Duchesnay FRA	Maia Usova / Alexandr Zhulin URS
1991 Munich GER	Isabelle Duchesnay / Paul Duchesnay FRA	Marina Klimova / Sergei Ponomarenko URS	Maia Usova / Alexandr Zhulin URS
1992 Oakland USA	Marina Klimova / Sergei Ponomarenko CIS	Maia Usova / Alexandr Zhulin CIS	Oksana Grishchuk / Evgeny Platov CIS
1993 Prague CZE	Maia Usova / Alexandr Zhulin RUS	Oksana Grishchuk / Evgeny Platov RUS	Anjelika Krylova / Vladimir Fedorov RUS
1994 Chiba JPN	Oksana Grishchuk / Evgeny Platov RUS	Sophie Moniotte / Pascal Lavanchy FRA	Susanna Rahkamo / Petri Kokko FIN
1995 Birmingham GRB	Oksana Grishchuk / Evgeny Platov RUS	Susanna Rahkamo / Petri Kokko FIN	Sophie Moniotte / Pascal Lavanchy FRA
1996 Edmonton CAN	Oksana Grishchuk / Evgeny Platov RUS	Anjelika Krylova / Oleg Ovsiannikov RUS	Shae-Lynn Bourne / Victor Kraatz CAN
1997 Lausanne SWI	Oksana Grishchuk / Evgeny Platov RUS	Anjelika Krylova / Oleg Ovsiannikov RUS	Shae-Lynn Bourne / Victor Kraatz CAN
1998 Minneapolis USA	Anjelika Krylova / Oleg Ovsiannikov RUS	Marina Anissina / Gwendal Peizerat FRA	Shae-Lynn Bourne / Victor Kraatz CAN
1999 Helsinki FIN	Anjelika Krylova / Oleg Ovsiannikov RUS	Marina Anissina / Gwendal Peizerat FRA	Shae-Lynn Bourne / Victor Kraatz CAN
2000 Nice FRA	Marina Anissina / Gwendal Peizerat FRA	Barbara Fusar-Poli / Maurizio Margaglio ITA	Margarita Drobiazko / Povilas Vanagas LIT
2001 Vancouver CAN	Barbara Fusar-Poli / Maurizio Margaglio ITA	Marina Anissina / Gwendal Peizerat FRA	Irina Lobacheva / Ilia Averbukh RUS
2002 Nagano JPN	Irina Lobacheva / Ilia Averbukh RUS	Shae-Lynn Bourne / Victor Kraatz CAN	Galit Chait / Sergei Sakhnovski ISR
2003 Washington USA	Shae-Lynn Bourne / Victor Kraatz CAN	Irina Lobacheva / Ilia Averbukh RUS	Albena Denkova / Maxim Staviyski BUL
2004 Dortmund GER	Tatiana Navka / Roman Kostomarov RUS	Albena Denkova / Maxim Staviyski BUL	Kati Winkler / Rene Lohse GER
2005 Moscow RUS	Tatiana Navka / Roman Kostomarov RUS	Tanith Belbin / Benjamin Agosto USA	Elena Grushina / Ruslan Goncharov UKR

Synchronized Skating

Location	Gold	Silver	Bronze
2000 Minneapolis USA	Team Surprise SWE	black ice CAN	Marigold Ice Unity FIN
2001 Helsinki FIN	Team Surprise SWE	Rockettes FIN	black ice CAN
2002 Rouen FRA	Marigold Ice Unity FIN	Team Surprise SWE	black ice CAN
2003 Ottawa CAN	Team Surprise SWE	Marigold Ice Unity FIN	Les Supremes CAN
2004 Zagreb CRO	Marigold Ice Unity FIN	Team Surprise SWE	Rockettes FIN
2005 Götborg SWE	Team Surprise SWE	Rockettes FIN	Marigold Ice Unity FIN

APPENDIX B

European Championships: Medalists in Figure Skating

Ladies

Location	Gold	Silver	Bronze
1930 Vienna AUT	Fritzi Burger AUT	Ilse Hornung AUT	Vivi-Anne Hultén SWE
1931 St. Moritz SWI	Sonja Henie NOR	Fritzi Burger AUT	Hilde Holovsky AUT
1932 Paris FRA	Sonja Henie NOR	Fritzi Burger AUT	Vivi-Anne Hultén SWE
1933 London GRB	Sonja Henie NOR	Cecilia Colledge GRB	Fritzi Burger AUT
1934 Prague CZE	Sonja Henie NOR	Liselotte Landbeck AUT	Maribel Vinson USA
1935 St. Moritz SWI	Sonja Henie NOR	Liselotte Landbeck AUT	Cecilia Colledge GRB
1936 Berlin GER	Sonja Henie NOR	Cecilia Colledge GRB	Megan Taylor GRB
1937 Prague CSR	Cecilia Colledge GRB	Megan Taylor GRB	Emmy Puzinger AUT
1938 St. Moritz SWI	Cecilia Colledge GRB	Megan Taylor GRB	Emmy Puzinger AUT
1939 London GRB	Cecilia Colledge GRB	Megan Taylor GRB	Daphne Walker GBR
1940–46 THE EUROPEAN CHAMPIONSHIPS WERE NOT HELD.			
1947 Davos SWI	Barbara Ann Scott CAN	Gretchen Merrill USA	Daphne Walker GRB
1948 Prague CSR	Barbara Ann Scott CAN	Eva Pawlik AUT	Alena Vrzáňová CZE
1949 Milan ITA	Eva Pawlik AUT	Alena Vrzáňová CZE	Jeannette Altwegg GBR
1950 Oslo NOR	Alena Vrzáňová CZE	Jeannette Altwegg GRB	Jacqueline du Bief FRA
1951 Zurich SWI	Jeannette Altwegg GBR	Jacqueline du Bief FRA	Barbara Wyatt GBR
1952 Vienna AUT	Jeannette Altwegg GBR	Jacqueline du Bief FRA	Barbara Wyatt GBR
1953 Dortmund FRG	Valda Osborn GBR	Gundi Busch GER	Erica Batchelor GBR
1954 Bolzano ITA	Gundi Busch GER	Erica Batchelor GBR	Yvonne Sugden GBR
1955 Budapest HUN	Hanna Eigel AUT	Yvonne Sugden GBR	Erica Batchelor GBR
1956 Paris FRA	Ingrid Wendl AUT	Yvonne Sugden GBR	Erica Batchelor GBR
1957 Vienna AUT	Hanna Eigel AUT	Ingrid Wendl AUT	Hanna Walter AUT
1958 Bratislava CZE	Ingrid Wendl AUT	Hanna Walter AUT	Joan Haanappel NET
1959 Davos SWI	Hanna Walter AUT	Sjoukje Dijkstra NET	Joan Haanappel NET
1960 Garmisch-Partenkirchen GER	Sjoukje Dijkstra NET	Regine Heitzer AUT	Joan Haanappel NET
1961 Berlin GER	Sjoukje Dijkstra NET	Regine Heitzer AUT	Jana Mrázková CZE
1962 Geneva SWI	Sjoukje Dijkstra NET	Regine Heitzer AUT	Karin Frohner AUT
1963 Budapest HUN	Sjoukje Djikstra NET	Nicole Hassler FRA	Regine Heitzer AUT
1964 Grenoble FRA	Sjoukje Dijkstra NET	Regine Heitzer AUT	Nicole Hassler FRA
1965 Moscow URS	Regine Heitzer AUT	Sally-Anne Stapleford GRB	Nicole Hassler FRA
1966 Bratislava CZE	Regine Heitzer AUT	Gabriele Seyfert GDR	Nicole Hassler FRA
1967 Ljubljana YUG	Gabriele Seyfert GDR	Hana Mašková CZE	Zsuzsa Almássy HUN
1968 Västerås SWE	Hana Mašková CZE	Gabriele Seyfert GDR	Beatrix Schuba AUT
1969 Garmisch-Partenkirchen GER	Gabriele Seyfert GDR	Hana Mašková CZE	Beatrix Schuba AUT
1970 Leningrad URS	Gabriele Seyfert GDR	Beatrix Schuba AUT	Zsuzsa Almássy HUN
1971 Zurich SWI	Beatrix Schuba AUT	Zsuzsa Almássy HUN	Rita Trapanese ITA
1972 Gothenburg SWE	Beatrix Schuba AUT	Rita Trapanese ITA	Sonja Morgenstern GDR
1973 Cologne FRG	Christine Errath GDR	Jean Scott GRB	Karin Iten SWI
1974 Zagreb YUG	Christine Errath GDR	Dianne de Leeuw NED	Liana Drahová CZE
1975 Copenhagen DEN	Christine Errath GDR	Dianne de Leeuw NED	Anett Pötzsch GDR
1976 Geneva SWI	Dianne de Leeuw NED	Anett Pötzsch GDR	Christine Errath GDR
1977 Helsinki FIN	Anett Pötzsch GDR	Dagmar Lurz FRG	Susanna Driano ITA

1978 Strasbourg FRA	Anett Pötzsch GDR	Dagmar Lurz FRG	Elena Vodorezova URS
1979 Zagreb YUG	Anett Pötzsch GDR	Dagmar Lurz FRG	Denise Biellmann SWI
1980 Gothenburg SWE	Anett Pötzsch GDR	Dagmar Lurz FRG	Susanna Driano ITA
1981 Innsbruck AUT	Denise Biellmann SWI	Sanda Dubravčić YUG	Claudia Kristofics-Binder AUT
1982 Lyon FRA	Claudia Kristofics-Binder AUT	Katarina Witt GDR	Elena Vodorezova URS
1983 Dortmund FRG	Katarina Witt GDR	Elena Vodorezova URS	Claudia Leistner FRG
1984 Budapest HUN	Katarina Witt GDR	Manuela Ruben FRG	Anna Kondrashova URS
1985 Gothenburg SWE	Katarina Witt GDR	Kira Ivanova URS	Claudia Leistner FRG
1986 Copenhagen DEN	Katarina Witt GDR	Kira Ivanova URS	Anna Kondrashova URS
1987 Sarajevo YUG	Katarina Witt GDR	Kira Ivanova URS	Anna Kondrashova URS
1988 Prague CZE	Katarina Witt GDR	Kira Ivanova URS	Patricia Neske FRG
1989 Birmingham GRB	Claudia Leistner FRG	Natalia Lebedeva URS	Marina Kielmann FRG
1990 Leningrad URS	Evelyn Grossmann GDR	Natalia Lebedeva URS	Marina Kielmann FRG
1991 Sofia BUL	Surya Bonaly FRA	Evelyn Grossmann GDR	Patricia Neske FRG
1992 Lausanne SWI	Surya Bonaly FRA	Marina Kielmann FRG	Marina Kielmann GER
1993 Helsinki FIN	Surya Bonaly FRA	Oksana Baiul UKR	Olga Markova RUS
1994 Copenhagen DEN	Surya Bonaly FRA	Oksana Baiul UKR	Elena Liashenko UKR
1995 Dortmund GER	Surya Bonaly FRA	Olga Markova RUS	Maria Butyrskaya RUS
1996 Sofia BUL	Irina Slutskaya RUS	Surya Bonaly FRA	Yulia Lavrenchuk UKR
1997 Paris FRA	Irina Slutskaya RUS	Krisztina Czako HUN	Tanja Szewczenko GER
1998 Milan ITA	Maria Butyrskaya RUS	Irina Slutskaya RUS	Viktoria Volchkova RUS
1999 Prague CZE	Maria Butyrskaya RUS	Julia Soldatova RUS	Viktoria Volchkova RUS
2000 Vienna AUT	Irina Slutskaya RUS	Maria Butyrskaya RUS	Viktoria Volchkova RUS
2001 Bratislava CZE	Irina Slutskaya RUS	Maria Butyrskaya RUS	Viktoria Volchkova RUS
2002 Lausanne SUI	Maria Butyrskaya RUS	Irina Slutskaya RUS	Victoria Volchkova RUS
2003 Malmö SWE	Irina Slutskaya RUS	Elena Sokolova RUS	Julia Sebestyen HUN
2004 Budapest HUN	Julia Sebestyen HUN	Elena Liashenko UKR	Elena Sokolova RUS
2005 Torino ITA	Irina Slutskaya RUS	Susanna Pöykiö FIN	Elena Liashenko UKR

Men

Location	Gold	Silver	Bronze
1891 Hamburg GER	Oskar Uhlig GER	A. Schmitson GER	Franz Zilly GER
1892 Vienna AUT	Eduard Engelmann AUT	Tibor von Földváry HUN	Georg Zachariades AUT
1893 Berlin GER	Eduard Engelmann AUT	Henning Grenander AUT	Georg Zachariades AUT
1894 Vienna AUT	Eduard Engelmann AUT	Gustav Hügel AUT	Tibor von Földváry HUN
1895 Budapest HUN	Tibor von Földváry HUN	Gustav Hügel AUT	Gilbert Fuchs GER
1896–97 THE EUROPEAN CHAMPIONSHIPS WERE NOT HELD.			
1898 Trondheim NOR	Ulrich Salchow SWE	Johan Lefstad NOR	Oscar Holthe NOR
1899 Davos SWI	Ulrich Salchow SWE	Gustav Hügel AUT	Ernst Fellner AUT
1900 Berlin GER	Ulrich Salchow SWE	Gustav Hügel AUT	Oscar Holthe NOR
1901 Vienna AUT	Gustav Hügel AUT	Gilbert Fuchs GER	Ulrich Salchow SWE
1902–3 THE EUROPEAN CHAMPIONSHIPS WERE NOT HELD.			
1904 Davos SWI	Ulrich Salchow SWE	Max Bohatsch AUT	Nicolai Panin RUS
1905 Bonn GER	Max Bohatsch AUT	Heinrich Burger GER	Karl Zenger GER
1906 Davos SWI	Ulrich Salchow SWE	Ernst Herz AUT	Per Thorén SWE
1907 Berlin GER	Ulrich Salchow SWE	Gilbert Fuchs GER	Ernst Herz AUT
1908 Warsaw POL	Ernst Herz AUT	Nicolai Panin RUS	S. Predrzymirski AUT
1909 Budapest HUN	Ulrich Salchow SWE	Gilbert Fuchs GER	Per Thorén SWE
1910 Berlin GER	Ulrich Salchow SWE	Werner Rittberger GER	Per Thorén SWE
1911 Leningrad RUS	Per Thorén SWE	Karl Ollow RUS	Werner Rittberger GER
1912 Stockholm SWE	Gösta Sandahl SWE	Ivan Malinin RUS	Martin Stixrud NOR
1913 Oslo NOR	Ulrich Salchow SWE	Andor Szende HUN	Wilhelm Böckl AUT
1914 Vienna AUT	Fritz Kachler AUT	Alexander Krogh NOR	Wilhelm Böckl AUT
1915–21 THE EUROPEAN CHAMPIONSHIPS WERE NOT HELD.			

1922 Davos SWI	Wilhelm Böckl AUT	Fritz Kachler AUT	Ernst Oppacher AUT
1923 Oslo NOR	Wilhelm Böckl AUT	Martin Stixrud NOR	Gunnar Jakobsson FIN
1924 Davos SWI	Fritz Kachler AUT	Ludwig Wrede AUT	Werner Rittberger GER
1925 Triberg GER	Wilhelm Böckl AUT	Werner Rittberger GER	Otto Preissecker AUT
1926 Davos SWI	Wilhelm Böckl AUT	Otto Preissecker AUT	Georg Gautschi SWI
1927 Vienna AUT	Wilhelm Böckl AUT	Hugo Distler AUT	Karl Schäfer AUT
1928 Troppau CSR	Wilhelm Böckl AUT	Karl Schäfer AUT	Otto Preissecker AUT
1929 Davos SWI	Karl Schäfer AUT	Georg Gautschi SWI	Ludwig Wrede AUT
1930 Berlin GER	Karl Schäfer AUT	Otto Gold CSR	Markus Nikkanen FIN
1931 Vienna AUT	Karl Schäfer AUT	Ernst Baier GER	Hugo Distler AUT
1932 Paris FRA	Karl Schäfer AUT	Ernst Baier GER	Erich Erdös AUT
1933 London GBR	Karl Schäfer AUT	Ernst Baier GER	Erich Erdös AUT
1934 Seefeld GER	Karl Schäfer AUT	Dénes Pataky HUN	Elemér Terták HUN
1935 St. Moritz SWI	Karl Schäfer AUT	Felix Kaspar AUT	Ernst Baier GER
1936 Berlin GER	Karl Schäfer AUT	Graham Sharp GBR	Ernst Baier GER
1937 Prague CZE	Felix Kaspar AUT	Graham Sharp GBR	Elemér Terták HUN
1938 St. Moritz SWI	Felix Kaspar AUT	Graham Sharp GBR	Herbert Alward AUT
1939 London GRB	Graham Sharp GBR	Freddie Tomlins GBR	Horst Faber GER

1940–46 THE EUROPEAN CHAMPIONSHIPS WERE NOT HELD.

1947 Davos SWI	Hans Gerschwiler SWI	Vladislav Čáp CZE	Fernand Leemans BEL
1948 Prague CSR	Richard Button USA	Hans Gerschwiler SWI	Edi Rada AUT
1949 Milan ITA	Edi Rada AUT	Ede Király HUN	Helmut Seibt AUT
1950 Oslo NOR	Ede Király HUN	Helmut Seibt AUT	Carlo Fassi ITA
1951 Zurich SWI	Helmut Seibt AUT	Horst Faber GER	Carlo Fassi ITA
1952 Vienna AUT	Helmut Seibt AUT	Carlo Fassi ITA	Michael Carrington GRB
1953 Dortmund FRG	Carlo Fassi ITA	Alain Giletti FRA	Freimut Stein GER
1954 Bolzano ITA	Carlo Fassi ITA	Alain Giletti FRA	Karol Divin CZE
1955 Budapest HUN	Alain Giletti FRA	Michael Booker GRB	Karol Divin CZE
1956 Paris FRA	Alain Giletti FRA	Michael Booker GRB	Karol Divin CZE
1957 Vienna AUT	Alain Giletti FRA	Karol Divin CZE	Michael Booker GRB
1958 Bratislava CZE	Karol Divin CZE	Alain Giletti FRA	Alain Calmat FRA
1959 Davos SWI	Karol Divin CZE	Alain Giletti FRA	Norbert Felsinger AUT
1960 Garmisch-Partenkirchen GDR	Alain Giletti FRA	Norbert Felsinger AUT	Manfred Schnelldorfer FRG
1961 Berlin FRG	Alain Giletti FRA	Alain Calmat FRA	Manfred Schnelldorfer FRG
1962 Geneva SWI	Alain Calmat FRA	Karol Divin CZE	Manfred Schnelldorfer FRG
1963 Budapest HUN	Alain Calmat FRA	Manfred Schnelldorfer FRG	Emmerich Danzer AUT
1964 Grenoble FRA	Alain Calmat FRA	Manfred Schnelldorfer FRG	Karol Divin CZE
1965 Moscow URS	Emmerich Danzer AUT	Alain Calmat FRA	Peter Jonas AUT
1966 Bratislava CZE	Emmerich Danzer AUT	Wolfgang Schwarz AUT	Ondrej Nepela CZE
1967 Ljubljana YUG	Emmerich Danzer AUT	Wolfgang Schwarz AUT	Ondrej Nepela CZE
1968 Västerås SWE	Emmerich Danzer AUT	Wolfgang Schwarz AUT	Ondrej Nepela CZE
1969 Garmisch-Partenkirchen FRG	Ondrej Nepela CZE	Patrick Pera FRA	Sergei Chetverukhin URS
1970 Leningrad URS	Ondrej Nepela CZE	Patrick Pera FRA	Günter Zöller GDR
1971 Zurich SWI	Ondrej Nepela CZE	Sergei Chetverukhin URS	Haig Oundjian GRB
1972 Gothenburg SWE	Ondrej Nepela CZE	Sergei Chetverukhin URS	Patrick Pera FRA
1973 Cologne FRG	Ondrej Nepela CZE	Sergei Chetverukhin URS	Jan Hoffmann GDR
1974 Zagreb YUG	Jan Hoffmann GDR	Sergei Volkov URS	John Curry GRB
1975 Copenhagen DEN	Vladimir Kovalev URS	John Curry GRB	Yuri Ovchinnikov URS
1976 Geneva SWI	John Curry GRB	Vladimir Kovalev URS	Jan Hoffmann GDR
1977 Helsinki FIN	Jan Hoffmann GDR	Vladimir Kovalev URS	Robin Cousins GRB
1978 Strasbourg FRA	Jan Hoffmann GDR	Vladimir Kovalev URS	Robin Cousins GBR
1979 Zagreb YUG	Jan Hoffmann GDR	Vladimir Kovalev URS	Robin Cousins GRB
1980 Gothenburg SWE	Robin Cousins GRB	Jan Hoffmann GDR	Vladimir Kovalev URS
1981 Innsbruck AUT	Igor Bobrin URS	Jean-Christophe Simond FRA	Norbert Schramm FRG

1982 Lyon FRA	Norbert Schramm FRG	Jean-Christophe Simond FRA	Igor Bobrin URS
1983 Dortmund FRG	Nobert Schramm FRG	Jozef Sabovčik CZE	Alexandr Fadeev URS
1984 Budapest HUN	Alexandr Fadeev URS	Rudi Cerne FRG	Norbert Schramm FRG
1985 Gothenburg SWE	Jozef Sabovčik CZE	Vladimir Kotin URS	Grzegorz Filpowski POL
1986 Copenhagen DEN	Jozef Sabovčik CZE	Vladimir Kotin URS	Alexandr Fadeev URS
1987 Sarajevo YUG	Alexandr Fadeev URS	Vladimir Kotin URS	Viktor Petrenko URS
1988 Prague CZE	Alexandr Fadeev URS	Vladimir Kotin URS	Viktor Petrenko URS
1989 Birmingham GRB	Alexandr Fadeev URS	Grzegorz Filpowski POL	Petr Barna CZE
1990 Leningrad URS	Viktor Petrenko URS	Petr Barna CZE	Viacheslav Zegorodniuk URS
1991 Sofia BUL	Viktor Petrenko URS	Petr Barna CZE	Viacheslav Zegorodniuk URS
1992 Lausanne SWI	Petr Barna CZE	Viktor Petrenko EUN	Alexei Urmanov EUN
1993 Helsinki FIN	Dmitri Dmitrenko UKR	Philippe Candeloro FRA	Eric Millot FRA
1994 Copenhagen DEN	Viktor Petrenko UKR	Viacheslav Zagorodniuk UKR	Alexei Urmanov RUS
1995 Dortmund GER	Ilia Kulik RUS	Alexei Urmanov RUS	Viacheslav Zagorodniuk UKR
1996 Sofia BUL	Viacheslav Zagorodniuk UKR	Igor Pashkevich RUS	Ilia Kulik RUS
1997 Paris FRA	Alexei Urmanov RUS	Philippe Candeloro FRA	Viacheslav Zagorodniuk UKR
1998 Milan ITA	Alexei Yagudin RUS	Evgeny Plushenko RUS	Alexandr Abt RUS
1999 Prague CZE	Alexei Yagudin RUS	Evgeny Plushenko RUS	Alexei Urmanov RUS
2000 Vienna AUT	Evgeny Plushenko RUS	Alexei Yagudin RUS	Dmitri Dmitrenko UKR
2001 Bratislava CZE	Evgeny Plushenko RUS	Alexei Yagudin RUS	Stanick Jeannette FRA
2002 Lausanne SWI	Alexei Yagudin RUS	Alexandr Abt RUS	Brian Joubert FRA
2003 Malmö SWE	Evgeny Plushenko RUS	Brian Joubert FRA	Stanick Jeannette FRA
2004 Budapest HUN	Brian Joubert FRA	Evgeny Plushenko RUS	Ilia Klimkin RUS
2005 Torino ITA	Evgeny Plushenko RUS	Brian Joubert FRA	Stefan Lindemann GER

Pairs

Location	Gold	Silver	Bronze
1930 Vienna AUT	Olga Orgonista	Emilia Rotter	Gisela Hochhaltinger
	Sándor Szalay HUN	László Szollás HUN	Otto Preissecker AUT
1931 St. Moritz SWI	Olga Orgonista	Emilia Rotter	Lilly Gaillard
	Sándor Szalay HUN	László Szollás HUN	Willy Petter AUT
1932 Paris FRA	Andrée Brunet	Lilly Gaillard	Idi Papez
	Pierre Brunet FRA	Willy Petter AUT	Karl Zwack AUT
1933 London GRB	Idi Papez	Lilly Scholz-Gaillard	Mollie Phillips
	Karl Zwack AUT	Willy Petter AUT	Rodney Murdoch GRB
1934 Prague CSR	Emilia Rotter	Idi Papez	Zofja Bilorowna
	László Szollás HUN	Karl Zwack AUT	Tadeusz Kowalski POL
1935 St. Moritz SWI	Maxi Herber	Idi Papez	Lucy Galló
	Ernst Baier GER	Karl Zwack AUT	Rezsö Dillinger HUN
1936 Berlin GER	Maxi Herber	Violet Cliff	Piroska Szekrényessy
	Ernst Baier GER	Leslie Cliff GRB	Attila Szekrényessy HUN
1937 Prague CZE	Maxi Herber	Ilse Pausin	Piroska Szekrényessy
	Ernst Baier GER	Erich Pausin AUT	Attila Szekrényessy HUN
1938 Troppau CZE	Maxi Herber	Ilse Pausin	Inge Koch
	Ernst Baier GER	Erich Pausin AUT	Günther Noack GER
1939 Zakopane POL	Maxi Herber	Ilse Pausin	Inge Koch
	Ernst Baier GER	Erich Pausin AUT	Günther Noack GER
1940–46 THE EUROPEAN CHAMPIONSHIPS WERE NOT HELD.			
1947 Davos SWI	Micheline Lannoy	Winifred Silverthorne	Suzanne Diskeuve
	Pierre Baugniet BEL	Dennis Silverthorne GBR	Edmond Verbustel BEL
1948 Prague CSR	Andrea Kekéssy	Blazena Knittlová	Herta Ratzenhofer
	Ede Király HUN	Karel Vosatka CZE	Emil Ratzenhofer AUT
1949 Milan ITA	Andrea Kekéssy	Mariann Nagy	Herta Ratzenhofer
	Ede Király HUN	László Nagy HUN	Emil Ratzenhofer AUT

1950 Oslo NOR	Mariann Nagy	Eliane Steinemann	Jennifer Nicks
	László Nagy HUN	André Calame SWI	John Nicks GRB
1951 Zurich SWI	Ria Baran	Eliane Steinemann	Silvia Grandjean
	Paul Falk GER	André Calame SWI	Michel Grandjean SWI
1952 Vienna AUT	Ria Falk	Jennifer Nicks	Marianne Nagy
	Paul Falk GER	John Nicks GRB	László Nagy HUN
1953 Dortmund FRG	Jennifer Nicks	Mariann Nagy	Elisabeth Schwarz
	John Nicks GBR	László Nagy HUN	Kurt Oppelt AUT
1954 Bolzano ITA	Silvia Grandjean	Elisabeth Schwarz	Sonja Balunová
	Michel Grandjean SWI	Kurt Oppelt AUT	Miroslav Balun CZE
1955 Budapest HUN	Mariann Nagy	Vera Suchánková	Marika Kilius
	László Nagy HUN	Zdenek Doležal CZE	Franz Ningel GER
1956 Paris FRA	Elisabeth Schwarz	Mariann Nagy	Marika Kilius
	Kurt Oppelt AUT	László Nagy HUN	Franz Ningel FRG
1957 Vienna AUT	Vera Suchánková	Mariann Nagy	Marika Kilius
	Zdenek Doležal CZE	László Nagy HUN	Franz Ningel FRG
1958 Bratislava CZE	Vera Suchánková	Nina Zhuk	Joyce Coates
	Zdenek Doležal CZE	Stanislav Zhuk URS	Anthony Holles GBR
1959 Davos SWI	Marika Kilius	Nina Zhuk	Joyce Coats
	Hans Jürgen Bäumler FRG	Stanislav Zhuk URS	Anthony Holles GBR
1960 Garmisch-	Marika Kilius	Nina Zhuk	Margret Göbl
Partenkirchen FRG	Hans Jürgen Bäumler FRG	Stanislav Zhuk URS	Franz Ningel FRG
1961 Berlin FRG	Marika Kilius	Margret Göbl	Margrit Senf
	Hans Jürgen Bäumler FRG	Franz Ningel FRG	Peter Göbel GDR
1962 Geneva SWI	Marika Kilius	Liudmila Belousova	Margret Göbl
	Hans Jürgen Bäumler FRG	Oleg Protopopov URS	Franz Ningel FRG
1963 Budapest HUN	Marika Kilius	Liudmila Belousova	Tatiana Zhuk
	Hans Jürgen Bäumler FRG	Oleg Protopopov URS	Alexandr Gavrilov URS
1964 Grenoble FRA	Marika Kilius	Liudmila Belousova	Tatiana Zhuk
	Hans Jürgen Bäumler FRG	Oleg Protopopov URS	Alexandr Gavrilov URS
1965 Moscow URS	Liudmila Belousova	Gerda Johner	Tatiana Zhuk
	Oleg Protopopov URS	Ruedi Johner SWI	Alexandr Gavrilov URS
1966 Bratislava CZE	Liudmila Belousova	Tatiana Zhuk	Margot Glockshuber
	Oleg Protopopov URS	Alexandr Gavrilov URS	Wolfgang Danne FRG
1967 Ljubljana YUG	Liudmila Belousova	Margot Glockshuber	Heidemarie Steiner
	Oleg Protopopov URS	Wolfgang Danne FRG	Heinz-Ulrich Walther GDR
1968 Västerås SWE	Liudmila Belousova	Tamara Moskvina	Hiedemarie Steiner
	Oleg Protopopov URS	Alexei Mishin URS	Heinz-Ulrich Walther GDR
1969 Garmisch-	Irina Rodnina	Liudmila Belousova	Tamara Moskvina
Partenkirchen FRG	Alexei Ulanov URS	Oleg Protopopov URS	Alexei Mishin URS
1970 Leningrad URS	Irina Rodnina	Liudmila Smirnova	Heidemarie Steiner
	Alexei Ulanov URS	Andrei Suraikin URS	Heinz-Ulrich Walther GDR
1971 Zurich SWI	Irina Rodnina	Liudmila Smirnova	Galina Karelina
	Alexei Ulanov URS	Andrei Suraikin URS	Georgi Proskurin URS
1972 Gothenburg SWE	Irina Rodnina	Liudmila Smirnova	Manuela Gross
	Alexei Ulanov URS	Andrei Suraikin URS	Uwe Kagelmann GDR
1973 Cologne FRG	Irina Rodnina	Liudmila Smirnova	Almut Lehmann
	Alexandr Zaitsev URS	Alexei Ulanov URS	Herbert Wiesinger FRG
1974 Zagreb YUG	Irina Rodnina	Romy Kermer	Liudmila Smirnova
	Alexandr Zaitsev URS	Rolf Österreich GDR	Alexei Ulanov URS
1975 Copenhagen DEN	Irina Rodnina	Romy Kermer	Manuela Gross
	Alexandr Zaitsev URS	Rolf Österreich GDR	Uwe Kagelmann GDR
1976 Geneva SWI	Irina Rodnina	Romy Kermer	Irina Vorobieva
	Alexandr Zaitsev URS	Rolf Österreich GDR	Alexandr Vlasov URS
1977 Helsinki FIN	Irina Rodnina	Irina Vorobieva	Marina Cherkasova
	Alexandr Zaitsev URS	Alexandr Vlasov URS	Sergei Shakhrai URS

1978 Strasbourg FRA	Irina Rodnina Alexandr Zaitsev URS	Marina Cherkasova Sergei Shakhrai URS	Manuela Mager Uwe Bewersdorff GDR
1979 Zagreb YUG	Marina Cherkasova Sergei Shakhrai URS	Irina Vorobieva Igor Lisovski URS	Sabine Baess Tassilo Thierbach GDR
1980 Gothenburg SWE	Irina Rodnina Alexandr Zaitsev URS	Marina Cherkasova Sergei Shakhrai URS	Marina Pestova Stanislav Leonovich URS
1981 Innsbruck AUT	Irina Vorobieva Igor Lisovski URS	Christina Riegel Andreas Nischwitz FRG	Marina Cherkasova Sergei Shakhrai URS
1982 Lyon FRA	Sabine Baess Tassilo Thierbach GDR	Marina Pestova Stanislav Leonovich URS	Irina Vorobieva Igor Lisovski URS
1983 Dortmund FRG	Sabine Baess Tassilo Thierbach GDR	Elena Valova Oleg Vasiliev URS	Birgit Lorenz Knut Schubert GDR
1984 Budapest HUN	Elena Valova Oleg Vasiliev URS	Sabine Baess Tassilo Thierbach GDR	Birgit Lorenz Knut Schubert GDR
1985 Gothenburg SWE	Elena Valova Oleg Vasiliev URS	Larisa Selezneva Oleg Makarov URS	Veronika Pershina Marat Akbarov URS
1986 Copenhagen DEN	Elena Valova Oleg Vasiliev URS	Ekaterina Gordeeva Sergei Grinkov URS	Elena Bechke Valeri Kornienko URS
1987 Sarajevo YUG	Larisa Selezneva Oleg Makarov URS	Elena Valova Oleg Vasiliev URS	Katrin Kanitz Tobias Schröter GDR
1988 Prague CZE	Ekaterina Gordeeva Sergei Grinkov URS	Larisa Selezneva Oleg Makarov URS	Peggy Schwarz Alexander König GDR
1989 Birmingham GRB	Larisa Selezneva Oleg Makarov URS	Mandy Wötzel Axel Rauschenbach GDR	Natalia Mishkutenok Artur Dmitriev URS
1990 Leningrad URS	Ekaterina Gordeeva Sergei Grinkov URS	Larisa Selezneva Oleg Makarov URS	Natalia Mishkutenok Artur Dmitriev URS
1991 Sofia BUL	Natalia Mishkutenok Artur Dmitriev URS	Elena Bechke Denis Petrov URS	Evgenia Shishkova Vadim Naumov URS
1992 Lausanne SWI	Natalia Mishkutenok Artur Dmitriev CIS	Elena Bechke Denis Petrov CIS	Evgenia Shishkova Vadim Naumov CIS
1993 Helsinki FIN	Marina Eltsova Andrei Bushkov RUS	Mandy Wötzel Ingo Steuer GER	Evgenia Shishkova Vadim Naumov RUS
1994 Copenhagen DEN	Ekaterina Gordeeva Sergei Grinkov RUS	Evgenia Shishkova Vadim Naumov RUS	Natalia Mishkutenok Artur Dmitriev RUS
1995 Dortmund GER	Mandy Wötzel Ingo Steuer GER	Radka Kovaříková René Novotny CZE	Evgenia Shishkova Vadim Naumov RUS
1996 Sofia BUL	Oksana Kazakova Artur Dmitriev RUS	Mandy Wötzel Ingo Steuer GER	Sarah Abitbol Stephane Bernadis FRA
1997 Paris FRA	Marina Eltsova Andrei Bushkov RUS	Mandy Wötzel Ingo Steuer GER	Elena Berezhnaya Anton Sikharulidze RUS
1998 Milan ITA	Elena Berezhnaya Anton Sikharulidze RUS	Oksana Kazakova Artur Dmitriev RUS	Sarah Abitbol Stephane Bernadis FRA
1999 Prague CZE	Maria Petrova Alexei Tikhonov RUS	Dorota Zagorska Mariusz Siudek POL	Sarah Abitbol Stephane Bernadis FRA
2000 Vienna AUT	Elena Berezhnaya Anton Sikharulidze RUS	Maria Petrova Alexei Tikhonov RUS	Dorota Zagorska Mariusz Siudek POL
2001 Bratislava CZE	Elena Berezhnaya Anton Sikharulidze RUS	Tatiana Totmianina Maxim Marinin RUS	Sarah Abitbol Stephane Bernadis FRA
2002 Lausanne SWI	Tatiana Totmianina Maxim Marinin RUS	Sarah Abitbol Stephane Bernadis FRA	Maria Petrova Alexei Tikhonov RUS
2003 Malmö SWE	Tatiana Totmianina Maxim Marinin RUS	Sarah Abitbol Stephane Bernadis FRA	Maria Petrova Alexei Tikhonov RUS
2004 Budapest HUN	Tatiana Totmianina Maxim Marinin RUS	Maria Petrova Alexei Tikhonov RUS	Dorota Zagorska Mariusz Siudek POL
2005 Torino ITA	Tatiana Totmianina Maxim Marinin RUS	Julia Obertas Sergei Slavnov RUS	Maria Petrova Alexei Tikhonov RUS

Ice Dancing

Location	Gold	Silver	Bronze
1954 Bolzano ITA	Jean Westwood	Nesta Davies	Barbara Radford
	Lawrence Demmy GRB	Paul Thomas GRB	Raymond Lockwood GRB
1955 Budapest HUN	Jean Westwood	Pamela Weight	Barbara Radford
	Lawrence Demmy GRB	Paul Thomas GRB	Raymond Lockwood GRB
1956 Paris FRA	Pamela Weight	June Markham	Barbara Thompson
	Paul Thomas GRB	Courtney Jones GRB	Gerard Rigby GRB
1957 Vienna AUT	June Markham	Barbara Thompson	Catherine Morris
	Courtney Jones GRB	Gerard Rigby GRB	Michael Robinson GRB
1958 Brtatislava CZE	June Markham	Catherine Morris	Barbara Thompson
	Courtney Jones GRB	Michael Robinson GRB	Gerard Rigby GRB
1959 Davos SWI	Doreen Denny	Catherine Morris	Christiane Guhel
	Courtney Jones GRB	Michael Robinson GRB	Jean Paul Guhel FRA
1960 Garmisch-Partenkirchen FGR	Doreen Denny	Christiane Guhel	Mary Parry
	Courtney Jones GRB	Jean Paul Guhel FRA	Roy Mason GRB
1961 Berlin FRG	Doreen Denny	Christiane Guhel	Linda Shearman
	Courtney Jones GRB	Jean Paul Guhel FRA	Michael Phillips GRB
1962 Geneva SWI	Christiane Guhel	Linda Shearman	Eva Romanová
	Jean Paul Guhel FRA	Michael Phillips GRB	Pavel Roman CZE
1963 Budapest HUN	Linda Shearman	Eva Romanová	Janet Sawbridge
	Michael Philipps GRB	Pavel Roman CZE	David Hickinbottom GRB
1964 Grenoble FRA	Eva Romanová	Janet Sawbridge	Yvonne Suddick
	Pavel Roman CZE	David Hickinbottom GRB	Roger Kennerson GRB
1965 Moscow URS	Eva Romanová	Janet Sawbridge	Yvonne Suddick
	Pavel Roman CZE	David Hickinbottom GRB	Roger Kennerson GRB
1966 Bratislava CZE	Diane Towler	Yvonne Suddick	Jitka Babická
	Bernard Ford GRB	Roger Kennerson GRB	Jaromir Holan CZE
1967 Ljubljana YUG	Diane Towler	Yvonne Suddick	Brigitte Martin
	Bernard Ford GRB	Malcolm Cannon GRB	Francis Gamichon FRA
1968 Västerås SWE	Diane Towler	Yvonne Suddick	Janet Sawbridge
	Bernard Ford GRB	Malcolm Cannon GRB	Jon Lane GRB
1969 Garmisch-Partenkirchen GER	Diane Towler	Janet Sawbridge	Liudmila Pakhomova
	Bernard Ford GRB	Jon Lane GRB	Alexandr Gorshkov URS
1970 Leningrad URS	Liudmila Pakhomova	Angelika Buck	Tatiana Voitiuk
	Alexandr Gorshkov URS	Erich Buck FRG	Viacheslav Zhigalin URS
1971 Zurich SWI	Liudmila Pakhomova	Angelika Buck	Susan Getty
	Alexandr Gorshkov URS	Erich Buck FRG	Roy Bradshaw GRB
1972 Gothenburg SWE	Angelika Buck	Liudmila Pakhomova	Janet Sawbridge
	Erich Buck FRG	Alexandr Gorshkov URS	Peter Dalby GRB
1973 Cologne FRG	Liudmila Pakhomova	Angelika Buck	Hilary Green
	Alexandr Gorshkov URS	Erich Buck FRG	Glyn Watts GRB
1974 Zagreb YUG	Liudmila Pakhomova	Hilary Green	Natalia Linichuk
	Alexandr Gorshkov URS	Glyn Watts GRB	Gennadi Karponosov URS
1975 Copenhagen DEN	Liudmila Pakhomova	Hilary Green	Natalia Linichuk
	Alexandr Gorshkov URS	Glyn Watts GRB	Gennadi Karponosov URS
1976 Geneva SWI	Liudmila Pakhomova	Irina Moiseeva	Natalia Linichuk
	Alexandr Gorshkov URS	Andrei Minenkov URS	Gennadi Karponosov URS
1977 Helsinki FIN	Irina Moiseeva	Krisztina Regöczy	Natalia Linichuk
	Andrei Minenkov URS	András Sallay HUN	Gennadi Karponosov URS
1978 Strasbourg FRA	Irina Moiseeva	Natalia Linichuk	Krisztina Regöczy
	Andrei Minenkov URS	Gennadi Karponosov URS	András Sallay HUN
1979 Zagreb YUG	Natalia Linichuk	Irina Moiseeva	Krisztina Regöczy
	Gennadi Karponosov URS	Andrei Minenkov URS	András Sallay HUN

1980 Gothenburg SWE	Natalia Linichuk	Krisztina Regöczy	Irina Moiseeva
	Gennadi Karponosov URS	András Sallay HUN	Andrei Minenkov URS
1981 Innsbruck AUT	Jayne Torvill	Irina Moiseeva	Natalia Linichuk
	Christopher Dean GRB	Andrei Minenkov URS	Gennadi Karponosov URS
1982 Lyon FRA	Jayne Torvill	Natalia Bestemianova	Irina Moiseeva
	Christopher Dean GRB	Andrei Bukin URS	Andrei Minenkov URS
1983 Dortmund FRG	Natalia Bestemianova	Olga Volozhinskaia	Karen Barber
	Andrei Bukin URS	Alexandr Svinin URS	Nicholas Slater GBR
1984 Budapest HUN	Jayne Torvill	Natalia Bestemianova	Marina Klimova
	Christopher Dean GRB	Andrei Bukin URS	Sergei Ponomarenko URS
1985 Gothenburg SWE	Natalia Bestemianova	Marina Klimova	Petra Born
	Andrei Bukin URS	Sergei Ponomarenko URS	Rainer Schönborn FRG
1986 Copenhagen DEN	Natalia Bestemianova	Marina Klimova	Natalia Annenko
	Andrei Bukin URS	Sergei Ponomarenko URS	Genrikh Sretenski URS
1987 Sarajevo YUG	Natalia Bestemianova	Marina Klimova	Natalia Annenko
	Andrei Bukin URS	Sergei Ponomarenko URS	Genrikh Sretenski URS
1988 Prague CZE	Netalia Bestemianova	Natalia Annenko	Isabelle Duchesnay
	Andrei Bukin URS	Genrikh Sretenski URS	Paul Duchesnay FRA
1989 Birmingham GRB	Marina Klimova	Maia Usova	Natalia Annenko
	Sergei Ponomarenko URS	Alexandr Zhulin URS	Genrikh Sretenski URS
1990 Leningrad URS	Marina Klimova	Maia Usova	Isabelle Duchesnay
	Sergei Ponomarenko URS	Alexandr Zhulin URS	Paul Duchesnay FRA
1991 Sofia BUL	Marina Klimova	Isabelle Duchesnay	Maia Usova
	Sergei Ponomarenko URS	Paul Duchesnay FRA	Alexandr Zhulin URS
1992 Lausanne SWI	Marina Klimova	Maia Usova	Oksana Grishchuk
	Sergei Ponomarenko CIS	Alexandr Zhulin CIS	Evgeny Platov CIS
1993 Helsinki FIN	Maia Usova	Oksana Grishchuk	Susanna Rahkamo
	Alexandr Zhulin RUS	Evgeny Platov RUS	Petri Kokko FIN
1994 Copenhagen DEN	Jayne Torvill	Oksana Grishchuk	Maia Usova
	Christopher Dean GRB	Evgeny Platov RUS	Alexandr Zhulin RUS
1995 Dortmund GER	Susanna Rahkamo	Sophie Moniotte	Anjelika Krylova
	Petri Kokko FIN	Pascal Lavanchy FRA	Oleg Ovsiannikov RUS
1996 Sofia BUL	Oksana Grishchuk	Anjelika Krylova	Irina Romanova
	Evgeny Platov RUS	Oleg Ovsiannikov RUS	Igor Yaroshenko UKR
1997 Paris FRA	Oksana Grishchuk	Anjelika Krylova	Sophie Moniotte
	Evgeny Platov RUS	Oleg Ovsiannikov RUS	Pascal Lavanchy FRA
1998 Milan ITA	Oksana Grishchuk	Anjelika Krylova	Marina Anissina
	Evgeny Platov RUS	Oleg Ovsiannikov RUS	Gwendal Peizerat FRA
1999 Prague CZE	Anjelika Krylova	Marina Anissina	Irina Lobacheva
	Oleg Ovsiannikov RUS	Gwendal Peizerat FRA	Ilia Averbukh RUS
2000 Vienna AUT	Marina Anissina	Barbara Fusar-Poli	Margarita Drobiazko
	Gwendal Peizerat FRA	Maurizio Margaglio ITA	Povilas Vanagas LIT
2001 Bratislava CZE	Barbara Fusar-Poli	Marina Anissina	Irina Lobacheva
	Maurizio Margaglio ITA	Gwendal Peizerat FRA	Ilia Averbukh RUS
2002 Lausanne SWI	Marina Anissina	Barbara Fusar-Poli	Irina Lobacheva
	Gwendal Peizerat FRA	Maurizio Margaglio ITA	Ilia Averbukh RUS
2003 Malmö SWE	Irina Lobacheva	Albena Denkova	Tatiana Navka
	Ilia Averbukh RUS	Maxim Staviyski BUL	Roman Kostomarov RUS
2004 Budapest HUN	Tatiana Navka	Albena Denkova	Elena Grushina
	Roman Kostomarov RUS	Maxim Staviyski BUL	Ruslan Goncharov UKR
2005 Torino ITA	Tatiana Navka	Elena Grushina	Isabelle Delobel
	Roman Kostomarov RUS	Ruslan Goncharov UKR	Olivier Schoenfelder FRA

Four Continents Championships: Medalists in Figure Skating

Ladies

Location	Gold	Silver	Bronze
1999 Halifax CAN	Tatiana Malinina UZB	Amber Corwin USA	Angela Nikodinov USA
2000 Osaka JPN	Angela Nikodinov USA	Stacey Pensgen USA	Annie Bellemare CAN
2001 Salt Lake City USA	Fumie Suguri JPN	Angela Nikodinov USA	Yoshie Onda JPN
2002 Jeonju KOR	Jennifer Kirk USA	Shizuka Arakawa JPN	Yoshie Onda JPN
2003 Beijing CHN	Fumie Suguri JPN	Shizuka Arakawa JPN	Yukari Nakano JPN
2004 Hamilton CAN	Yukina Ota JPN	Cynthia Phaneuf CAN	Amber Corwin USA
2005 Gangreung KOR	Fumie Suguri JPN	Yoshie Onda JPN	Jennifer Kirk USA

Men

Location	Gold	Silver	Bronze
1999 Halifax CAN	Takeshi Honda JPN	Chengjiang Li CHN	Elvis Stojko CAN
2000 Osaka JPN	Elvis Stojko CAN	Chengjiang Li CHN	Min Zhang CHN
2001 Salt Lake City USA	Chengjiang Li CHN	Takeshi Honda JPN	Michael Weiss USA
2002 Jeonju ROK	Jeffrey Buttle CAN	Takeshi Honda JPN	Song Gao CHN
2003 Beijing CHN	Takeshi Honda JPN	Min Zhang CHN	Chengjiang Li CHN
2004 Hamilton CAN	Jeffrey Buttle CAN	Emanuel Sandhu CAN	Evan Lysacek USA
2005 Gangreung KOR	Evan Lysacek USA	Chengjiang Li CHN	Daisuka Takahashi JPN

Pairs

Location	Gold	Silver	Bronze
1999 Halifax CAN	Xue Shen Hongbo Zhao CHN	Kristy Sargeant Kris Wirtz CAN	Danielle Hartsell Steve Hartsell USA
2000 Osaka JPN	Jamie Salé David Pelletier CAN	Kyoko Ina John Zimmerman USA	Tiffany Scott Philip Dulebohn USA
2001 Salt Lake City USA	Jamie Salé David Pelletier CAN	Xue Shen Hongbo Zhao CHN	Kyoko Ina John Zimmerman USA
2002 Jeonju ROK	Qing Pang Jian Tong CHN	Anabelle Langlois Patrice Archetto CAN	Dan Zhang Hao Zhang CHN
2003 Beijing CHN	Xue Shen Hongbo Zhao CHN	Qing Pang Jian Tong CHN	Dan Zhang Hao Zhang CHN
2004 Hamilton CAN	Qing Pang Jian Tong CHN	Dan Zhang Hao Zhang CHN	Valerie Marcoux Craig Buntin CAN
2005 Gangreung KOR	Dan Zhang Hao Zhang CHN	Qing Pang Jian Tong CHN	Katheryn Orscher Garrett Lucash USA

Ice Dancing

Location	Gold	Silver	Bronze
1999 Halifax CAN	Shae-Lynn Bourne Victor Kraatz CAN	Chantal Lefebvre Michel Brunet CAN	Naomi Lang Peter Tchernyshev USA
2000 Osaka JPN	Naomi Lang Peter Tchernyshev USA	Marie-France Dubreuil Patrice Lauzon CAN	Jamie Silverstein Justin Pekarek USA
2001 Salt Lake City USA	Shae-Lynn Bourne Victor Kraatz CAN	Naomi Lang Peter Tchernyshev USA	Marie-France Dubreuil Patrice Lauzon CAN
2002 Jeonju KOR	Naomi Lang Peter Tchernyshev USA	Tanith Belbin Benjamin Agosto USA	Megan Wing Aaron Lowe CAN
2003 Beijing CHN	Shae-Lynn Bourne Victor Kraatz CAN	Tanith Belbin Benjamin Agosto USA	Naomi Lang Peter Tchernyshev USA
2004 Hamilton CAN	Tanith Belbin Benjamin Agosto USA	Marie-France Dubreuil Patrice Lauzon CAN	Megan Wing Aaron Lowe CAN
2005 Gangreung KOR	Tanith Belbin Benjamin Agosto USA	Melissa Gregory Denis Petukhov USA	Lydia Manon Ryan O'Meara USA

APPENDIX D

North American Championships: Medalists in Figure Skating

Ladies

Location	Gold	Silver	Bronze
1923 Ottawa CAN	Theresa Blanchard USA	Beatrix Loughran USA	Dorothy Jenkins CAN
1925 Boston USA	Beatrix Loughran USA	Cecil Smith CAN	Theresa Blanchard USA
1927 Toronto CAN	Beatrix Loughran USA	Constance Wilson CAN	Cecil Smith CAN
1929 Boston USA	Constance Wilson USA	Maribel Vinson USA	Suzanne Davis USA
1931 Ottawa CAN	Constance W. Samuel CAN	Elizabeth Fisher CAN	Edith Secord USA
1933 New York USA	Constance W. Samuel CAN	Cecil S. Gooderham CAN	Suzanne Davis USA
1935 Montreal CAN	Constance W. Samuel CAN	Maribel Vinson USA	Suzanne Davis USA
1937 Boston USA	Maribel Vinson USA	Veronica Clarke CAN	Eleanor O'Meara CAN
1939 Toronto CAN	Mary Rose Thacker CAN	Joan Tozzer USA	Norah McCarthy CAN
1941 Ardmore USA	Mary Rose Thacker CAN	Eleanor O'Meara CAN	Norah McCarthy CAN
1943 THE NORTH AMERICAN CHAMPIONSHIPS WERE NOT HELD.			
1945 New York USA	Barbara Ann Scott CAN	Gretchen Merrill USA	Janette Ahrens USA
1947 Ottawa CAN	Barbara Ann Scott CAN	Janette Ahrens USA	Yvonne Sherman USA
1949 Ardmore USA	Yvonne Sherman USA	Marlene Smith CAN	Virginia Baxter USA
1951 Calgary CAN	Sonya Klopfer USA	Suzanne Morrow CAN	Tenley Albright USA
1953 Cleveland USA	Tenley Albright USA	Carol Heiss USA	Barbara Gratton CAN
1955 Regina CAN	Tenley Albright USA	Carol Heiss USA	Patricia Firth USA
1957 Rochester USA	Carol Heiss USA	Carole Jane Pachl CAN	Joan Schenke USA
1959 Toronto CAN	Carol Heiss USA	Lynn Finnegan USA	Nancy Heiss USA
1961 Philadelphia USA	Laurence Owen USA	Wendy Griner CAN	Sonia Snelling CAN
1963 Vancouver CAN	Wendy Griner CAN	Petra Burka CAN	Shirra Kenworthy CAN
1965 Rochester USA	Petra Burka CAN	Peggy Fleming USA	Valerie Jones CAN
1967 Montreal CAN	Peggy Fleming USA	Valerie Jones CAN	Albertina Noyes USA
1969 Oakland USA	Janet Lynn USA	Karen Magnussen CAN	Linda Carbonetto CAN
1971 Peterborough CAN	Karen Magnussen CAN	Janet Lynn USA	Suna Murray USA

Men

Location	Gold	Silver	Bronze
1923 Ottawa CAN	Sherwin Badger USA	Melville Rogers CAN	
1925 Boston USA	Melville Rogers CAN	Nathaniel Niles USA	
1927 Toronto CAN	Melville Rogers CAN	Sherwin Badger USA	Roger Turner USA
1929 Boston USA	Montgomery Wilson CAN	Roger Turner USA	Frederick Goodridge USA
1931 Ottawa CAN	Montgomery Wilson CAN	James Madden USA	Gail Borden II USA
1933 New York USA	Montgomery Wilson CAN	James Madden USA	Robin Lee USA
1935 Montreal CAN	Montgomery Wilson CAN	Robin Lee USA	James Madden USA
1937 Boston USA	Montgomery Wilson CAN	Roger Turner USA	Ralph McCreath CAN
1939 Toronto CAN	Montgomery Wilson CAN	Robin Lee USA	Ralph McCreath CAN
1941 Ardmore USA	Ralph McCreath CAN	Eugene Turner USA	William Grimditch Jr. USA
1943 THE NORTH AMERICAN CHAMPIONSHIPS WERE NOT HELD.			
1945 THE MEN'S EVENTS WERE NOT HELD.			
1947 Ottawa CAN	Richard Button USA	James Grogan USA	Wallace Diestelmeyer CAN
1949 Ardmore USA	Richard Button USA	James Grogan USA	Hayes Alan Jenkins USA
1951 Calgary CAN	Richard Button USA	James Grogan USA	Hayes Alan Jenkins USA
1953 Cleveland USA	Hayes Alan Jenkins USA	Peter Firstbrook CAN	Ronald Robertson USA

1955 Regina CAN	Hayes Alan Jenkins USA	David Jenkins USA	Charles Snelling CAN
1957 Rochester USA	David Jenkins USA	Charles Snelling CAN	Tim Brown USA
1959 Toronto CAN	Donald Jackson CAN	Tim Brown USA	Robert Brewer USA
1961 Philadelphia USA	Donald Jackson CAN	Bradley Lord USA	Gregory Kelley USA
1963 Vancouver CAN	Donald McPherson CAN	Tommy Litz USA	Scott Allen USA
1965 Rochester USA	Gary Visconti USA	Scott Allen USA	Donald Knight CAN
1967 Montreal CAN	Donald Knight CAN	Scott Allen USA	Gary Visconti USA
1969 Oakland USA	Tim Wood USA	Jay Humphry CAN	John Petkevich USA
1971 Peterborough CAN	John Petkevich USA	Toller Cranston CAN	Kenneth Shelley USA

Pairs

Location	Gold	Silver	Bronze
1923 Ottawa CAN	Dorothy Jenkins Gordon McLennan CAN	Theresa Blanchard Nathaniel Niles USA	Clara Frothingham Charles Rotch USA
1925 Boston USA	Theresa Blanchard Nathaniel Niles USA	Gladys Rogers Melville Rogers CAN	
1927 Toronto CAN	Marion MacDougall Chauncey Bangs CAN	Theresa Blanchard Nathaniel Niles USA	Constance Wilson Montgomery Wilson CAN
1929 Boston USA	Constance Wilson Montgomery Wilson CAN	Theresa Blanchard Nathaniel Niles USA	Maribel Vinson Thornton Coolidge USA
1931 Ottawa, Ont. CAN	Constance W. Samuel Montgomery Wilson CAN	Frances Claudet Chauncey Bangs CAN	Beatrix Loughran Sherwin Badger USA
1933 New York USA	Constance W. Samuel Montgomery Wilson CAN	Maud Smith Jack Eastwood CAN	Kathleen Lopdell Donald Cruikshank CAN
1935 Montreal CAN	Maribel Vinson George Hill USA	Constance W. Samuel Montgomery Wilson CAN	Louise Bertram Stewart Reburn CAN
1937 Boston USA	Veronica Clarke Ralph McCreath CAN	Maribel Vinson George Hill USA	Grace Madden James Madden USA
1939 Toronto CAN	Joan Tozzer Bernard Fox USA	Norah McCarthy Ralph McCreath CAN	Aidrie Cruikshank Donald Cruikshank CAN
1941 Ardmore USA	Eleanor O'Meara Ralph McCreath CAN	Donna Atwood Eugene Turner USA	Patricia Vaeth Jack Might USA
1943	THE NORTH AMERICAN CHAMPIONSHIPS WERE NOT HELD.		
1945	THE PAIRS EVENT WAS NOT HELD.		
1947 Ottawa CAN	Suzanne Morrow Wallace Diestelmeyer CAN	Yvonne Sherman Robert Swenning USA	Karol Kennedy Peter Kennedy USA
1949 Ardmore USA	Karol Kennedy Peter Kennedy USA	Marlene Smith Donald Gilchrist CAN	Irene Maguire Walter Muehlbronner USA
1951 Calgary CAN	Karol Kennedy Peter Kennedy USA	Janet Gerhauser John Nightingale USA	Jane Kirby Donald Tobin CAN
1953 Cleveland USA	Frances Dafoe Norris Bowden CAN	Carole Ormaca Robin Greiner USA	Margaret Anne Graham Hugh Graham Jr. USA
1955 Regina CAN	Frances Dafoe Norris Bowden CAN	Carole Ormaca Robin Greiner USA	Barbara Wagner Robert Paul CAN
1957 Rochester USA	Barbara Wagner Robert Paul CAN	Maria Jelinek Otto Jelinek CAN	Nancy Rouillard Ronald Ludington USA
1959 Toronto CAN	Barbara Wagner Robert Paul CAN	Nancy Ludington Ronald Ludington USA	Maribel Owen Dudley Richards USA
1961 Philadelphia USA	Maria Jelinek Otto Jelinek CAN	Maribel Owen Dudley Richards USA	Debbi Wilkes Guy Revell CAN
1963 Vancouver CAN	Debbi Wilkes Guy Revell CAN	Gertrude Desjardins Maurice Lafrance CAN	Vivian Joseph Ronald Joseph USA
1965 Rochester USA	Vivian Joseph Ronald Joseph USA	Cynthia Kauffman Ronald Kauffman USA	Susan Huehnergard Paul Huehnergard CAN

1967 Montreal CAN	Cynthia Kauffman	Susan Berens	Betty Lewis
	Ronald Kauffman USA	Roy Wagelein USA	Richard Gilbert USA
1969 Oakland USA	Cynthia Kauffman	Alicia Jo Starbuck	Mary Petrie
	Ronald Kauffman USA	Kenneth Shelley USA	Robert McAvoy CAN
1971 Peterborough CAN	Alicia Jo Starbuck	Melissa Militano	Sandra Bezic
	Kenneth Shelley USA	Mark Militano USA	Val Bezic CAN

Ice Dancing

Location	Gold	Silver	Bronze
1947 Ottawa, Ont. CAN	Lois Waring	Anne Davies	Marcella Willis
	Walter Bainbridge Jr. USA	Carleton Hoffner Jr. USA	Frank Davenport USA
1949 Ardmore USA	Lois Waring	Irene Maguire	Anne Davies
	Walter Bainbridge Jr. USA	Walter Muehlbronner USA	Carleton Hoffner Jr. USA
1951 Calgary CAN	Carmel Bodel	Carol Peters	Pierrette Paquin
	Edward Bodel USA	Daniel Ryan USA	Donald Tobin CAN
1953 Cleveland USA	Carol Peters	Virginia Hoyns	Carmel Bodel
	Daniel Ryan USA	Donald Jacoby USA	Edward Bodel USA
1955 Regina CAN	Carmel Bodel	Joan Zamboni	Virginia Hoyns
	Edward Bodel USA	Roland Junso USA	William Kipp USA
1957 Rochester USA	Geraldine Fenton	Joan Zamboni	Sharon McKenzie
	William McLachlan CAN	Roland Junso USA	Bert Wright USA
1959 Toronto CAN	Geraldine Fenton	Andrée Jacoby	Ann Martin
	William McLachlan CAN	Donald Jacoby USA	Edward Collins CAN
1961 Philadelphia USA	Virginia Thompson	Donna Lee Carrier	Paulette Doan
	William McLachlan	Roger Campbell USA	Kenneth Ormsby CAN
1963 Vancouver, B.C. CAN	Paulette Doan	Donna Lee Mitchell	Sally Schantz
	Kenneth Ormsby CAN	John Mitchell CAN	Stanley Urban USA
1965 Rochester USA	Lorna Dyer	Kristin Fortune	Carole Forrest
	John Carrell USA	Dennis Sveum USA	Kevin Lethbridge CAN
1967 Montreal CAN	Lorna Dyer	Joni Graham	Judy Schwomeyer
	John Carrell USA	Donald Phillips CAN	James Sladky USA
1969 Oakland USA	Donna Taylor	Judy Schwomeyer	Debbie Gerken
	Bruce Lennie CAN	James Sladky USA	Raymond Tiedemann USA
1971 Peterborough CAN	Judy Schwomeyer	Ann Millier	Mary Campbell
	James Sladky USA	Harvey Millier USA	Johnny Johns USA

Fours

Location	Gold	Silver	Bronze
1923 Ottawa CAN	Elizabeth Blair	Clara Hartmann	Clara Frothingham
	Florence Wilson	Grace Munstock	Theresa Blanchard
	Philip Chrysler	Paul Armitage	Charles Rotch
	C. R. Morphy CAN	Joel Liberman USA	Sherwin Badger USA
1925–31 FOURS EVENTS WERE NOT HELD AS PART OF THE NORTH AMERICAN CHAMPIONSHIPS.			
1933 New York USA	Margaret Davis	Constance Wilson Samuel	Theresa Blanchard
	Prudence Holbrook	Elizabeth Fisher	Suzanne Davis
	Melville Rogers	Montgomery Wilson	Richard Hapgood
	Guy Owen CAN	Hubert Sprott	Fred Parmenter USA
1935 Montreal CAN	Margaret Davis	Nettie Prantel	Suzanne Davis
	Prudence Holbrook	Ardelle Kloss	Grace Madden
	Melville Rogers	Joseph Savage	Frederick Goodridge
	Guy Owen CAN	Roy Hunt USA	George Hill USA

1937 Boston USA	Margaret Davis	Naomi Slater	Nettie Prantel
	Prudence Holbook	Aidrie Cruikshank	Ardelle Kloss
	Melville Rogers	Jack Hose	Joseph Savage
	Guy Owen CAN	Donald Cruikshank CAN	George Boltres USA
1939 Toronto CAN	Hazel Caley	Ruth Hall	Marjorie Parker
	Dorothy Caley	Gillian Watson	Nettie Prantel
	Montgomery Wilson	Donald Gilchrist	Joseph Savage
	Ralph McCreath CAN	Sandy McKechnie CAN	George Boltres USA
1941 Ardmore USA	Janette Ahrens	Therese McCarthy	
	Mary Louise Premer	Virginia Wilson	
	Lyman Wakefield Jr.	Donald Gilchrist	
	Robert Uppgren USA	Michael Kirby CAN	

1943   THE NORTH AMERICAN CHAMPIONSHIPS WERE NOT HELD.

1945–47   THE FOURS EVENTS WERE NOT HELD.

1949 Ardmore USA	Marilyn Thomsen	Mary Spence Kenner	Jean Matze
	Janet Gerhauser	Vera Smith	Elizabeth Royer
	Marlyn Thomsen	Peter Dunfield	Henry Mayer IV
	John Nightingale USA	Peter Firstbrook CAN	Newbold Black IV USA

1951–71   THE FOURS EVENTS WERE NOT HELD.

Olympic Games: Medalists in Figure Skating

Ladies

Location	Gold	Silver	Bronze
1908 London GBR	Madge Syers GBR	Elsa Rendschmidt GER	Dorothy Greenhough-Smith GBR
1912 FIGURE SKATING EVENTS WERE NOT HELD.			
1916 THE OLYMPIC GAMES WERE NOT HELD.			
1920 Antwerp BEL	Magda Mauroy-Julin SWE	Svea Norén SWE	Theresa Weld USA
1924 Chamonix FRA	Herma Szabo AUT	Beatrix Loughran USA	Ethel Muckelt GBR
1928 St. Moritz SWI	Sonja Henie NOR	Fritzi Burger AUT	Beatrix Loughran USA
1932 Lake Placid USA	Sonja Henie NOR	Fritzi Burger AUT	Maribel Vinson USA
1936 Garmisch-Partenkirchen GER	Sonja Henie NOR	Cecilia Colledge GBR	Vivi-Anne Hultén SWE
1940 THE OLYMPIC WINTER GAMES WERE NOT HELD.			
1944 THE OLYMPIC WINTER GAMES WERE NOT HELD.			
1948 St. Moritz SWI	Barbara Ann Scott CAN	Eva Pawlik AUT	Jeannette Altwegg GBR
1952 Oslo NOR	Jeannette Altwegg GBR	Tenley Albright USA	Jacqueline du Bief FRA
1956 Cortina ITA	Tenley Albright USA	Carol Heiss USA	Ingrid Wendl AUT
1960 Squaw Valley USA	Carol Heiss USA	Sjoukje Dijkstra NED	Barbara Roles USA
1964 Innsbruck AUT	Sjoukje Dijkstra NED	Regine Heitzer AUT	Petra Burka CAN
1968 Grenoble FRA	Peggy Fleming USA	Gabriele Seyfert GDR	Hana Mašková CZE
1972 Sapporo JPN	Beatrix Schuba AUT	Karen Magnussen CAN	Janet Lynn USA
1976 Innsbruck AUT	Dorothy Hamill USA	Dianne de Leeuw NED	Christine Errath GDR
1980 Lake Placid USA	Anett Pötzsch GDR	Linda Fratianne USA	Dagmar Lurz FRG
1984 Sarajevo YUG	Katarina Witt GDR	Rosalynn Sumners USA	Kira Ivanova URS
1988 Calgary CAN	Katarina Witt GDR	Elizabeth Manley CAN	Debra Thomas USA
1992 Albertville FRA	Kristi Yamaguchi USA	Midori Ito JPN	Nancy Kerrigan USA
1994 Hamar NOR	Oksana Baiul UKR	Nancy Kerrigan USA	Lu Chen CHN
1998 Nagano JPN	Tara Lipiniski USA	Michelle Kwan USA	Lu Chen CHN
2002 Salt Lake City USA	Sarah Hughes USA	Irina Slutskaya RUS	Michelle Kwan USA

Men

Location	Gold	Silver	Bronze
1908 London GBR	Ulrich Salchow SWE	Richard Johansson SWE	Per Thorén SWE
1912 FIGURE SKATING EVENTS WERE NOT HELD.			
1916 THE OLYMPIC GAMES WERE NOT HELD.			
1920 Antwerp BEL	Gillis Grafström SWE	Andreas Krogh NOR	Martin Stixrud NOR
1924 Chamonix FRA	Gillis Grafström SWE	Wilhelm Böckl AUT	Georg Gautschi SWI
1928 St. Moritz SWI	Gillis Grafström SWE	Wilhelm Böckl AUT	Robert van Zeebroeck BEL
1932 Lake Placid USA	Karl Schäfer AUT	Gillis Grafström SWE	Montgomery Wilson CAN
1936 Garmisch-Partenkurchen GER	Karl Schäfer AUT	Ernst Baier GER	Felix Kaspar AUT
1940 THE OLYMPIC WINTER GAMES WERE NOT HELD.			
1944 THE OLYMPIC WINTER GAMES WERE NOT HELD.			
1948 St. Moritz SWI	Richard Button USA	Hans Gerschwiler SWI	Edi Rada AUT
1952 Oslo NOR	Richard Button USA	Helmut Seibt AUT	James Grogan USA

1956 Cortina ITA	Hayes Alan Jenkins USA	Ronald Robertson USA	David Jenkins USA
1960 Squaw Valley USA	David Jenkins USA	Karol Divin CZE	Donald Jackson CAN
1964 Innsbruck AUT	Manfred Schnelldorfer FRG	Alain Calmat FRA	Scott Allen USA
1968 Grenoble FRA	Wolfgang Schwarz AUT	Tim Wood USA	Patrick Pera FRA
1972 Sapporo JPN	Ondrej Nepela CZE	Sergei Chetverukhin URS	Patrick Pera FRA
1976 Innsbruck AUT	John Curry GBR	Vladimir Kovalev URS	Toller Cranston CAN
1980 Lake Placid USA	Robin Cousins GBR	Jan Hoffmann GDR	Charles Tickner USA
1984 Sarajevo YUG	Scott Hamilton USA	Brian Orser CAN	Jozef Sabovčik CZE
1988 Calgary CAN	Brian Boitano USA	Brian Orser CAN	Viktor Petrenko URS
1992 Albertville FRA	Viktor Petrenko EUN	Paul Wylie USA	Christopher Bowman USA
1994 Hamar NOR	Alexei Urmanov RUS	Elvis Stojko CAN	Philippe Candeloro FRA
1998 Nagano JPN	Ilia Kulik RUS	Elvis Stojko CAN	Philippe Candeloro FRA
2002 Salt Lake City USA	Alexei Yagudin RUS	Evgeny Plushenko RUS	Timothy Goebel USA

Pairs

Location	Gold	Silver	Bronze
1908 London GBR	Anna Hübler	Phyllis Johnson	Madge Syers
	Heinrich Burger GER	James Johnson GBR	Edgar Syers GBR
1912 FIGURE SKATING EVENTS WERE NOT HELD.			
1916 THE OLYMPIC GAMES WERE NOT HELD.			
1920 Antwerp BEL	Ludowika Jakobsson	Alexia Bryn	Phyllis Johnson
	Walter Jakobsson FIN	Yngvar Bryn NOR	James Johnson GBR
1924 Chamonix FRA	Helene Engelmann	Ludowika Jakobsson	Andrée Joly
	Alfred Berger AUT	Walter Jakobsson FIN	Pierre Brunet FRA
1928 St. Moritz SWI	Andrée Brunet	Lily Scholz	Melitta Brunner
	Pierre Brunet FRA	Otto Kaiser AUT	Ludwig Wrede AUT
1932 Lake Placid USA	Andrée Brunet	Beatrix Loughran	Emilia Rotter
	Pierre Brunet FRA	Sherwin Badger USA	László Szollás HUN
1936 Garmisch-Partenkirchen GER	Maxi Herber	Ilse Pausin	Emilia Rotter
	Ernst Baier GER	Erich Pausin AUT	László Szollás HUN
1940 THE OLYMPIC WINTER GAMES WERE NOT HELD.			
1944 THE OLYMPIC WINTER GAMES WERE NOT HELD.			
1948 St. Moritz SWI	Micheline Lannoy	Andrea Kekéssy	Suzanne Morrow
	Pierre Baugniet BEL	Ede Király HUN	Wallace Diestelmeyer CAN
1952 Oslo NOR	Ria Falk	Karol Kennedy	Mariann Nagy
	Paul Falk GER	Peter Kennedy USA	László Nagy HUN
1956 Cortina ITA	Elisabeth Schwarz	Frances Dafoe	Mariann Nagy
	Kurt Oppelt AUT	Norris Bowden CAN	László Nagy HUN
1960 Squaw Valley USA	Barbara Wagner	Marika Kilius	Nancy Ludington
	Robert Paul CAN	Hans-Jürgen Bäumler GER	Ronald Ludington USA
1964 Innsbruck AUT	Liudmila Belousova	Marika Kilius	Debbi Wilkes
	Oleg Protopopov URS	Hans-Jürgen Bäumler GER	Guy Revell CAN
1968 Grenoble FRA	Liudmila Belousova	Tatiana Zhuk	Margot Glockshuber
	Oleg Protopopov URS	Alexandr Gorelik URS	Wolfgang Danne FRG
1972 Sapporo JPN	Irina Rodnina	Liudmila Smirnova	Manuela Gross
	Alexei Ulanov URS	Andrei Suraikin URS	Uwe Kagelmann GDR
1976 Innsbruck AUT	Irina Rodnina	Romy Kermer	Manuela Gross
	Alexandr Zaitsev URS	Rolf Österreich GDR	Uwe Kagelmann GDR
1980 Lake Placid USA	Irina Rodnina	Marina Cherkasova	Manuela Mager
	Alexandr Zaitsev URS	Sergei Shakhrai URS	Uwe Bewersdorff GDR
1984 Sarajevo YUG	Elena Valova	Caitlin Carruthers	Larisa Selezneva
	Oleg Vasiliev URS	Peter Carruthers USA	Oleg Makarov URS
1988 Calgary CAN	Ekaterina Gordeeva	Elena Valova	Jill Watson
	Sergei Grinkov URS	Oleg Vasiliev URS	Peter Oppegard USA

1992 Albertville FRA	Natalia Mishkutenok	Elena Bechke	Isabelle Brasseur
	Artur Dmitriev EUN	Denis Petrov EUN	Lloyd Eisler CAN
1994 Hamar NOR	Ekaterina Gordeeva	Natalia Mishkutenok	Isabelle Brasseur
	Sergei Grinkov RUS	Artur Dmitriev RUS	Lloyd Eisler CAN
1998 Nagano JPN	Oksana Kazakova	Elena Berezhnaya	Mandy Wötzel
	Artur Dmitriev RUS	Anton Sikharulidze RUS	Ingo Steuer GER
2002 Salt Lake City USA	Elena Berezhnaya	*Jamie Salé	Xue Shen
	Anton Sikharulidze RUS	David Pelletier CAN	Hongbo Zhao CHN

*Salé and Pelletier were subsequently awarded duplicate gold medals by the IOC at the request of the ISU.

Ice Dancing

Location	Gold	Silver	Bronze
1976 Innsbruck AUT	Liudmila Pakhomova	Irina Moiseeva	Colleen O'Connor
	Alexandr Gorshkov URS	Andrei Minenkov URS	Jim Millns USA
1980 Lake Placid USA	Natalia Linichuk	Krisztina Regöczy	Irina Moiseeva
	Gennadi Karponosov URS	András Sallay HUN	Andrei Minenkov URS
1984 Sarajevo YUG	Jayne Torvill	Natalia Bestemianova	Marina Klimova
	Christopher Dean GBR	Andrei Bukin URS	Sergei Ponomarenko URS
1988 Calgary CAN	Natalia Bestemianova	Marina Klimova	Tracy Wilson
	Andrei Bukin URS	Sergei Ponomarenko URS	Robert McCall CAN
1992 Albertville FRA	Marina Klimova	Isabelle Duchesnay	Maia Usova
	Sergei Ponomarenko EUN	Paul Duchesnay FRA	Alexandr Zhulin EUN
1994 Hamar NOR	Oksana Grishchuk	Maia Usova	Jayne Torvill
	Evgeny Platov RUS	Alexandr Zhulin RUS	Christopher Dean GBR
1998 Nagano JPN	Oksana Grishchuk	Anjelika Krylova	Marina Anissina
	Evgeny Platov RUS	Oleg Ovsiannikov RUS	Gwendal Peizerat FRA
2002 Salt Lake City	Marina Anissina	Irina Lobacheva	Barbara Fusar-Poli
	Gwendal Peizerat FRA	Ilia Averbukh RUS	Maurizio Margaglio ITA

Special Figures

Location	Gold	Silver	Bronze
1908 London GBR	Nicolai Panin RUS	Arthur Cumming GBR	George Hall-Say GBR

Picture Gallery of World and Olympic Figure Skating Champions

From the beginning of the World Figure Skating Championships in 1896 and of figure skating events at the Olympic Games in 1908 through the 2005 season, there have been 153 World and Olympic champions. Emphasis in this book has been on those remarkable skaters. They are the athlete/artists who as competitors shaped figure skating and made it the magnificent sport it has become. It is appropriate to honor them individually and collectively in this gallery.

Each skater's picture is included, along with the world and Olympic titles they hold and the years they won them. The pictures are arranged chronologically by disciplines: ladies', men, pairs', ice dancing, special figures, and synchronized skating. Most of the skaters won medals of other colors in world and Olympic competition as well as titles and medals in other important competitions. Much of that information is provided in the preceding text.

It was not an easy task to locate pictures of every world and Olympic champion, but it has been accomplished. Pictures of a few early skaters came from books that have been out of print and out of copyright for more than seventy-five years. For all others, the sources are here given. As stated in the Acknowledgments, I am deeply indebted to those who have made this possible. They include the World Figure Skating Museum, Paul and Michelle Harvath, other photographers, and the skaters themselves. Collectively, they have made this unique record possible.

The World Figure Skating Museum and Hall of Fame in Colorado Springs, Colorado, provided the pictures of Madge Syers, Lily Kronberger, Magda Mauroy-Julin, Herma Szabo, Sonja Henie, Cecilia Colledge, Megan Taylor, Barbara Ann Scott, Alena Vrzanova, Jeannette Altwegg, Jacqueline du Bief, Tenley Albright, Gundi Busch, Carol Heiss, Sjoukje Dijkstra, Petra Burka, Peggy Fleming, Gabriele Seyfert, Beatrix Schuba, Karen Magnussen, Christine Errath, Dianne de Leeuw, Dorothy Hamill, Linda Fratianne, Anett Pötzsch, Elaine Zayak, Rosalynn Sumners, Katarina Witt, Debra Thomas, Midori Ito, Jill Trenary, Kristi Yamaguchi, Lu Chen, Michelle Kwan, Gilbert Fuchs, Gustav Hügel, Henning Grenander, Ulrich Salchow, Gösta Sandahl, Gillis Grafström, Wilhelm Böckl, Karl Schäfer, Felix Kaspar, Graham Sharp, Hans Gerschwiler, Richard Button, Hayes Alan Jenkins, David Jenkins, Alain Giletti, Donald Jackson, Donald McPherson, Manfred Schnelldorfer, Alain Calmat, Emmerich Danzer, Wolfgang Schwarz, Tim Wood, Ondrej Nepela, Jan Hoffmann, Sergei Volkov, John Curry, Vladimir Kovalev, Charles Tickner, Robin Cousins, Scott Hamilton, Brian Boitano, Brian Orser, Kurt Browning, Viktor Petrenko, Elvis Stojko, Todd Eldredge, Anna Hübler and Heinrich Burger, Phyllis Johnson and James Johnson, Ludowika Eilers and Walter Jakobsson, Helene Engelmann and Alfred Berger, Andrée Joly and Pierre Brunet, Lilly Scholz and Otto Kaiser, Emilie Rotter and László Szollás, Maxi Herber and Ernst Baier, Micheline Lannoy and Pierre Baugniet, Andrea Kekéssy and Ede Király, Karol Kennedy and Peter Kennedy, Ria Baron and Paul Falk, Jennifer Nicks and John Nicks, Frances Dafoe and Norris Bowden, Elisabeth Schwarz and Kurt Oppelt, Maria Jelinek and Otto Jelinek, Marika Kilius and Hans Jürgen Bäumler, Liudmila Belousova and Oleg Protopopov, Irina Rodnina and Alexei Ulanov,

Irina Rodnina and Alexandr Zaitzev, Tai Babilonia and Randy Gardner, Marina Cherkasova and Sergei Shakhrai, Irina Vorobieva and Igor Lisovski, Sabine Baess and Tassilo Thierbach, Elena Valova and Oleg Vasiliev, Barbara Underhill and Paul Martini, Natalia Mishkutenok and Artur Dmitriev, Isabelle Brasseur and Lloyd Eisler, Jean Westwood and Lawrence Demmy, Doreen Denny and Courtney Jones, Eva Romanová and Pavel Roman, Diane Towler and Bernard Ford, Liudmila Pakhomova and Alexandr Gorshkov, Irina Moiseeva and Andrei Minenkov, Natalia Linichuk and Gennadi Karponosov, Krisztina Regöczy and András Sallay, Jayne Torvill and Christopher Dean, Natalia Bestemianova and Andrei Bukin, Isabelle Duchesnay and Paul Duchesnay, Oksana Grishchuk and Evgeni Platov, Nikolai Panin, and Marigold Ice Unity.

Photographer Paul Harvath provided pictures of Yuka Sato, Tara Lipinski, Irina Slutskaya, Alexei Urmanov, Alexei Yagudin, Evgeny Plushenko, Evgenia Shishkova and Vadim Naumov, Radka Kovaříková and René Novotny, Marina Eltsova and Andrei Bushkov, Elena Berezhnaya and Anton Sikharulidze, Oksana Kazakova and Artur Dmitriev, Maria Petrova and Alexei Tikhonov, Marina Klimova and Sergei Ponomarenko, Anjelika Krylova and Oleg Ovsiannikov, Marina Anissina and Gwendal Peizerat, and Shae-Lynn Bourne and Victor Kraatz.

Photographer Michelle Harvath provided pictures of Maria Butyrskaya, Sarah Hughes, Ilia Kulik, Mandy Wötzel and Ingo Steuer, Jamie Salé and David Pelletier, Xue Shen and Hongbo Zhao, Barbara Fusar-Poli and Maurizio Margaglio, and Irina Lobacheva and Ilia Averbukh.

Other photographers include Lois Yuen, who provided pictures of Denise Biellmann, Ekaterina Gordeeva and Sergei Grinkov, and Maia Usova and Alexandr Zhulin; J. Barry Mittan, who provided pictures of Shizuka Arakawa, Tatiana Marinina and Maxim Marinin, and Tatiana Navka and Roman Kostomarov; Michelle Wojdyla, who provided the picture of Stephane Lambiel; and Jyrki Kostermaa, who provided the picture of Team Surprise. Skaters who provided pictures include Alexandr Fadeev, Barbara Wagner (Barbara Wagner and Robert Paul), Paul Thomas (Pamela Weight and Paul Thomas), and Courtney Jones (June Markham and Courtney Jones).

World and Olympic Champions
THE LADIES

Madge Syers
World champion, 1906, 1907; Olympic champion, 1908. (Unless noted otherwise, this and all other illustrations in the gallery are courtesy of the World Figure Skating Museum and Hall of Fame, Colorado Springs, Colo.)

Lily Kronberger
World champion, 1908–11

Opika von Méray Horváth
World champion, 1912–14

Magda Mauroy-Julin
Olympic champion, 1920 (Louis Magnus, *Le patinage artistique* [1913])

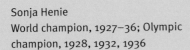

Herma Szabo
World champion, 1922–26; Olympic
champion, 1924

Sonja Henie
World champion, 1927–36; Olympic
champion, 1928, 1932, 1936

Cecilia Colledge
World champion, 1937

Megan Taylor
World champion, 1938, 1939

Barbara Ann Scott
World champion, 1947, 1948;
Olympic champion, 1948

Alena Vrzáňová
World champion, 1949, 1950

Jeannette Altwegg
World champion, 1951; Olympic champion, 1952

Jaqueline du Bief
World champion, 1952

Tenley Albright
World champion, 1953, 1955;
Olympic champion, 1956

Gundi Busch
World champion, 1954

Carol Heiss
World champion, 1956–60; Olympic champion, 1960

Sjoukje Dijkstra
World champion, 1962–64; Olympic champion, 1964

Petra Burka
World champion, 1965

Peggy Fleming
World champion, 1966–68; Olympic champion,
1968

Gabriele Seyfert
World champion, 1969–70

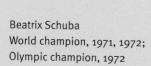

Beatrix Schuba
World champion, 1971, 1972;
Olympic champion, 1972

Karen Magnussen World champion, 1973

Christine Errath
World champion, 1974

Dianne de Leeuw
World champion, 1975

Dorothy Hamill
World champion, 1976;
Olympic champion, 1976

Linda Fratianne
World champion, 1977, 1979

Anett Pötzsch
World champion, 1978, 1980; Olympic
champion, 1980

Denise Biellmann
World champion, 1981 (Lois Yuen)

Elaine Zayak
World champion, 1982

Rosalynn Sumners
World champion, 1983

Katarina Witt
World champion, 1984, 1985, 1987, 1988;
Olympic champion, 1984, 1988

Debra Thomas
World champion, 1986

Midori Ito
World champion, 1989

Jill Trenary
World champion, 1990

Kristi Yamaguchi
World champion, 1991, 1992; Olympic
champion, 1992

Oksana Baiul
World champion, 1993; Olympic
champion, 1994 (Paul Harvath)

Yuka Sato
World champion, 1994

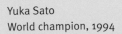

Lu Chen
World champion, 1995

Michelle Kwan
World champion, 1996, 1998,
2000, 2001, 2003 (Paul Harvath)

Tara Lipinski
World champion, 1997;
Olympic champion, 1998
(Michelle Harvath)

Maria Butyrskaya
World champion, 1999 (Paul
Harvath)

Irina Slutskaya
World champion, 2002, 2005 (Michelle Harvath)

Sarah Hughes
Olympic champion, 2002
(Michelle Harvath)

Shizuka Arakawa
World champion, 2004
(J. Barry Mittan)

World and Olympic Champions

THE MEN

Gilbert Fuchs
World champion, 1896, 1906

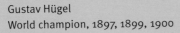

Gustav Hügel
World champion, 1897, 1899, 1900

Henning Grenander
World champion, 1898

Ulrich Salchow
World champion, 1901–5,
1907–11; Olympic champion,
1908

Fritz Kachler
World champion, 1912, 1913, 1923

Gösta Sandahl
World champion, 1914

Gillis Grafström
World champion 1922, 1924, 1929; Olympic
champion, 1920, 1924, 1928

Wilhelm Böckl
World champion,
1925–28

Karl Schäfer
World champion, 1930–36; Olympic champion, 1932, 1936

Felix Kaspar
World champion, 1937, 1938

Graham Sharp
World champion, 1939

Hans Gerschwiler
World champion, 1947

Richard Button
World champion, 1948–52; Olympic champion,
1948, 1952

Hayes Alan Jenkins
World champion,
1953–56; Olympic
champion, 1956

David Jenkins
World champion, 1957–59; Olympic champion, 1960

Alain Giletti
World champion, 1960

Donald Jackson
World champion, 1962

Donald McPherson
World champion, 1963

Manfred Schnelldorfer
World champion, 1964; Olympic champion, 1964

Alain Calmat
World champion, 1965

Emmerich Danzer
World champion, 1966–68

Wolfgang Schwarz
Olympic champion, 1968

Tim Wood
World champion, 1969, 1970

Ondrej Nepela
World champion, 1971–73;
Olympic champion 1972

Jan Hoffmann
World champion, 1974, 1980

Sergei Volkov
World champion, 1975

John Curry
World champion, 1976; Olympic champion, 1976

Vladimir Kovalev
World champion, 1977, 1979

Charles Tickner
World champion, 1978

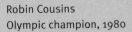

Robin Cousins
Olympic champion, 1980

Scott Hamilton
World champion, 1981–84;
Olympic champion, 1984

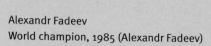

Alexandr Fadeev
World champion, 1985 (Alexandr Fadeev)

Brian Boitano
World champion, 1986, 1988;
Olympic champion, 1988

Brian Orser
World champion, 1987

Kurt Browning
World champion, 1989, 1990, 1991, 1993

Viktor Petrenko
World champion, 1992; Olympic
champion, 1992

Elvis Stojko
World champion, 1994, 1995, 1997

Alexei Urmanov
Olympic champion, 1994
(Paul Harvath)

Todd Eldredge
World champion, 1996

Alexei Yagudin
World champion, 1998–2000,
2002; Olympic champion
2002 (Paul Harvath)

Ilia Kulik
Olympic champion, 1998 (Michelle Harvath)

Evgeny Plushenko
World champion, 2001, 2003, 2004
(Paul Harvath)

Stephane Lambiel
World Champion 2005
(Michelle Wojdyla)

World and Olympic Champions
PAIRS

Anna Hübler and Heinrich Burger
World champions, 1908, 1910; Olympic champions, 1908

Phyllis Johnson and
James Johnson
World champions, 1909, 1912

Ludowika Eilers and
Walter Jakobsson
World champions, 1911, 1914,
1923; Olympic champions,
1920

Helene Engelmann and
Karl Mejstrik
World champions, 1913 (Louis
Magnus, *Le patinage artis-
tique* [1913])

Helene Engelmann and
Alfred Berger
World champions, 1922,
1924; Olympic champions,
1924

Herma Szabo and Ludwig Wrede
World champions, 1925, 1927 (Irving Brokaw, *The Art of Skating* [1926])

Andrée Joly and Pierre Brunet
World champions, 1926, 1928, 1930, 1932; Olympic champions, 1928, 1932

Lily Scholz and Otto Kaiser
World champions, 1929

Emilia Rotter and
Lászlò Szollás
World champions, 1931,
1933–35

Maxi Herber and Ernst Baier
World champions, 1936–39;
Olympic champions, 1936

Micheline Lannoy and Pierre Baugniet
World champions, 1947, 1948; Olympic champions, 1948

Andrea Kekéssy and Ede Király
World champions, 1949

Karol Kennedy and Peter Kennedy
World champions, 1950

Ria Baran and Paul Falk
World champions, 1951, 1952; Olympic champions, 1952

Jennifer Nicks amd John Nicks
World champions, 1953

Frances Dafoe and
Norris Bowden
World champions, 1954, 1955

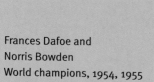

Elisabeth Schwarz and Kurt Oppelt
World champions, 1956; Olympic
champions, 1956

Barbara Wagner and Robert Paul
World champions, 1957–60; Olym-
pic champions, 1960 (Barbara
Wagner)

Maria Jelinek and Otto Jelinek
World champions, 1962

Marika Kilius and
Hans Jürgen Bäumler
World champions, 1963, 1964

Liudmila Belousova and Oleg Protopopov
World champions, 1965–68; Olympic champions, 1964, 1968

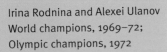

Irina Rodnina and Alexei Ulanov
World champions, 1969–72;
Olympic champions, 1972

Irina Rodnina and
Alexandr Zaitsev
World champions, 1973–78;
Olympic champions, 1976,
1980

Tai Babilonia and
Randy Gardner
World champions, 1979

Marina Cherkasova and
Sergei Shakhrai
World champions, 1980

Irina Vorobieva and
Igor Lisovski
World champions, 1981

Sabine Baess and
Tassilo Thierbach
World champions, 1982

Elena Valova and
Oleg Vasiliev
World champions, 1983, 1985,
1988; Olympic champions,
1984

Barbara Underhill and Paul Martini
World champions, 1984

Ekatarina Gordeeva and
Sergei Grinkov
World champions, 1986, 1987,
1989, 1990; Olympic champions,
1988, 1994 (Lois Yuen)

Natalia Mishkutenok and
Artur Dmitriev
World champions, 1991, 1992;
Olympic champions, 1992

Isabelle Brasseur and
Lloyd Eisler
World champions, 1993

Evgenia Shishkova and Vadim Naumov
World champions, 1994 (Paul Harvath)

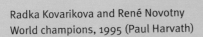

Radka Kovarikova and René Novotny
World champions, 1995 (Paul Harvath)

Marina Eltsova and Andrei Bushkov
World champions, 1996 (Paul Harvath)

Mandy Wötzel and Ingo Steuer
World champions 1997 (Michelle Harvath)

Elena Berezhnaya and
Anton Sikharulidze
World champions, 1998, 1999; Olympic champions, 2002 (Paul Harvath)

Oksana Kazakova and
Artur Dmitriev
Olympic champions, 1998 (Paul Harvath)

Maria Petrova and Alexei Tikhonov
World champions, 2000 (Paul Harvath)

Jamie Salé and David Pelletier
World champions, 2001; Olympic champions, 2002 (Michelle Harvath)

Xue Shen and Hongbo Zhao
World champions, 2002, 2003 (Michelle
Harvath)

Tatiana Totmianina and
Maxim Marinin
World champions, 2004, 2005

Champions of Ice Dancing

Jean Westwood and
Lawrence Demmy
World champions, 1952–55

Pamela Weight and
Paul Thomas
World champions, 1956
(Paul Thomas)

Doreen Denny and Courtney Jones
World champions 1959, 1960

June Markham and
Courtney Jones
World champions, 1957, 1958
(Courtney Jones)

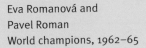

Eva Romanová and
Pavel Roman
World champions, 1962–65

Diane Towler and Bernard Ford
World champions, 1966–69

Liudmila Pakhomova and
Alexandr Gorshkov
World champions, 1970–74,
1976; Olympic champions,
1976

Irina Moiseeva and
Andrei Minenkov
World champions, 1975,
1977

Natalia Linichuk and Gennadi Karponosov
World champions, 1978, 1979; Olympic
champions, 1980

Krisztina Regöczy and András Sallay
World champions, 1980

Jayne Torvill and Christopher Dean
World champions, 1981–84; Olympic
champions, 1984

Natalia Bestemianova and
Andrei Bukin
World champions, 1985–88;
Olympic champions, 1988

Marina Klimova and
Sergei Ponomarenko
World champions, 1989,
1990, 1992; Olympic champions, 1992 (Paul Harvath)

Isabelle Duchesnay and
Paul Duchesnay
World champions, 1991

Maia Usova and
Alexandr Zhulin
World champions, 1993
(Lois Yuen)

Oksana Grishchuk and
Evgeny Platov
World champions, 1994–97;
Olympic champions, 1994,
1998

Anjelika Krylova and Oleg Ovsiannikov
World champions, 1998, 1999 (Paul Harvath)

Marina Anissina and
Gwendal Peizerat
World champions, 2000;
Olympic champions, 2002
(Paul Harvath)

Barbara Fusar-Poli and
Maurizio Margaglio
World champions, 2001 (Michelle
Harvath)

Irina Lobacheva and Ilia Averbukh
World champions, 2002 (Michelle
Harvath)

Shae-Lynn Bourne and
Victor Kraatz
World champions, 2003
(Paul Harvath)

Tatiana Navka and Roman Kostomarov
World champions, 2004, 2005

Olympic Champion of Special Figures

Nicolai Panin
Olympic champion,
1908

World Champions of Synchronized Skating

Team Surprise
World champions, 2000, 2001, 2003, 2005 (Jyrki Kostermaa)

Marigold Ice Unity
World champions, 2002, 2004

NOTES

CHAPTER 1: SKATING BEFORE FIGURES

1. Quoted from the videocassette *Magic Memories on Ice 2*.

2. This was by an ISU regulation, however, by special dispensation; the free-skating portion of the World Championships the following year in Vienna was held on the outdoor rink of the Wiener Eislauf-Verein (Vienna Skating Club).

3. Quoted from the videocassette *Magic Memories on Ice*.

4. Brown, *Figure Skating: A History*, 18.

5. Fitz Stephen, *Norman London*, 58–59.

6. The woodcut is by the Dutch artist Johannes Brugman (1400–1473).

CHAPTER 2: ENGLAND: THE BIRTHPLACE OF FIGURE SKATING

1. Brown, *Ice Skating: A History*, 33.

2. Ibid., 35.

3. Jones, *The Art of Skating*, vi.

4. Jones does not use the term *clamp*, but he wrote that "there is another method practised by many, which is, the having a piece of plate iron fixed across the stock at the heel, and a piece of the same sort on the tread; these pieces of iron have their ends turned up; that on the tread, to fit over the edges of the shoe-soles; and the other over the heel, to which the iron is screwed on both sides."

5. Jones died in 1772, the year his treatise first appeared. Thus, revisions that appear in later editions are by other writers.

6. Although we have little information on skating in Ireland, there is evidence of its practice there. Anderson in his preface to *The Art of Skating* refers to a small treatise published there many years ago.

7. *The Edinburgh Skating Club*, 15.

8. Ibid., 20.

9. Ibid., 18, 33.

10. A second edition published sixteen years later under his own name precedes by just one year the more extensive *Figure Skating* by Vandervell and Witham. Anderson omits in the second edition his valuable description of skating in England at mid-century but adds new figures being skated by members of the London Skating Club.

11. Anderson, *The Art of Skating*, v.

12. Ibid., 15.

13. Ibid., 24–25. This is the earliest discovered use of the term *fancy skating*.

14. Ibid., 26.

15. Ibid., 28–33. Modern figure skates have blades with a radius ranging from seven to eight and a half feet.

16. Ibid., 42.

17. Nigel Brown stated that the club "is often erroneously referred to as the London Skating Club, but no such designation was ever given it by its members" (*Ice Skating: A History,* 66). Many writers of the period, including Vandervell and Witham, referred to themselves as members of the London Skating Club.

18. Vandervell and Witham, *A System of Figure Skating,* 31.

19. Ibid., 30.

20. Ibid., 231.

21. Ibid., 233.

22. Ibid., 160–61.

23. Adams, *Skating,* 28.

24. Vandervell and Witham, *A System of Figure Skating,* 219–229.

25. "Intricate Figure Skating."

26. Monier-Williams, *Figure Skating Simple and Combined,* 60–62.

27. Vandervell and Witham, *A System of Figure Skating,* 186.

28. Ibid., 255.

29. For a more detailed description of simultaneous skating, see Lowther, *Combined Figure Skating,* 7–11.

30. Ibid., 57.

31. Thompson, *Hand-in-Hand Figure Skating,* 1.

32. Ibid., 3.

33. Bird, *Our Skating Heritage,* 8.

34. Ibid., 10.

35. In 1990 the organization was made a public limited company under Acts of Parliament, and the name became the National Ice Skating Association of Great Britain, Ltd. It then went through a second change to become the National Ice Skating Association of the United Kingdom, Ltd., reflecting increasing interest in skating in Northern Ireland.

36. Bird, *Our Skating Heritage,* 16.

37. Ibid., 18.

38. Ibid., 21.

CHAPTER 3: SKATING IN THE NEW WORLD

1. Alberts, *Benjamin West,* 60. There is no Serpentine River; the reference is to an artificial lake usually called the Serpentine.

2. Ibid., 61.

3. *Maryland Gazette,* February 7, 1765.

4. *Boston Gazette,* February 1, 1731.

5. *Pennsylvania Gazette,* July 28, 1748.

6. The term *pond* was often used generically for any skating surface.

7. Lindsay, "A History of Sport in Canada, 1807–1867," 51.

8. *Charter and By-Laws of the Philadelphia Skating Club and Humane Society,* 4.

9. Ibid., 6.

10. Swift and Clark, *The Skaters Text Book.* 102.

11. "The Skating Scene."

12. According to William H. Brown (*Handbook of Figure Skating,* 14), "Swift" was William H. Bishop, champion of America in 1868, and *The Skaters Text Book* was written by Clark.

13. Swift and Clark, *The Skaters Text Book,* 41–42.

14. Ibid., 54. The "German Waltz" was probably just the simple waltz, for which there were many variations. It was likely not "The German," in which waltz steps were employed. For the basic steps of the waltz, see Ferraro, *The Art of Dancing,* 67.

15. Meagher, *Lessons in Skating,* 72.

16. Combined skating was not gender-specific in England. Swift and Clark use the words *skaters* and *persons* throughout their combined skating section except in their discussion of the rose.

17. Swift and Clark, *The Skaters Text Book,* 73.

18. Ibid., 77.

19. "Skating—Progress of Our People in the Accomplishment."

20. Ibid.

21. Yglesias, *Figure Skating,* 1.

22. Swift and Clark, *The Skaters Text Book,* 24.

23. "Feats on Skates."

24. Most reliable is an early article on Haines by Andreas Bundtzen dating from 1881 and entitled "Jackson Haines, den Fantastique." It is included in Bang, *Konståkingens 100–åriga historia.* Also valuable is an article by Winfield A. Hird entitled "The Father of Figure Skating" and in *Skating* magazine in January 1941, which includes family information provided by relatives.

25. Moore, *Reflections on the CFSA,* 8.

26. Ibid.,16.

27. Ibid., 30.

28. For a complete list see Swift and Clark, *The Skaters Text Book,* 107.

29. "Acrobatic Skaters."

30. The presumption here is that the word *amateur* was added for the indicated reason. Another possible reason is to avoid using the same name as the British association.

31. "Canadian Skating Events."

32. The name was changed to U.S. Figure Skating in 2002.

33. Charter members include Beaver Dam Winter Sports Club (Mill Neck, N.Y.), the Skating Club of Boston, the Chicago Figure Skating Club, the New York Skating Club, the Philadelphia Skating Club and Humane Society, the Sno Birds of Lake Placid, and the Twin City (now Minneapolis) Figure Skating Club. All except the Sno Birds are still members.

34. Meagher, *Lessons in Skating,* 50.

35. Ibid., 9–10.

36. Ibid., 8.

37. Ibid., 63.

CHAPTER 4: SKATING ON THE CONTINENT

1. The Duke of York became King James II (1685–88), and William of Orange became King William III (1689–1702). The Duke of Monmouth was the illegitimate son of Charles II.

2. Brown, *Ice Skating: A History,* 30.

3. Garcin, *Le vrai patineur,* title page.

4. Ibid., 41–42.

5. Ibid., 37.

6. Ibid., 55.

7. Ibid., 61.

8. Ibid., 80.

9. Diamantidi, Korper, and Wirth, *Spuren auf dem Eise* (1881), 1.

10. In England the international style, known first as the continental style, continued well into the postwar era. Duff-Taylor, writing in 1930, observes, "Even now one hears the expression 'Continental Style.' There is no such thing" (*Skating*, 11).

11. Most writers refer to the competition only as an international event. Nigel Brown uses the title "Great International Skating Tournament" with quotation marks but without documentation for its source. Brown, *Ice Skating: A History*, 89.

12. Moore, *Reflections on the CFSA*, 13–16.

13. "Panin" was a pseudonym of Nicolai Kolomenkin. Russian aristocrats often used pseudonyms when participating in activities such as sporting events.

14. Syers, *The Art of Skating (International Style)*, 33.

15. Monier-Williams, *Figure Skating Simple and Combined*, 66.

16. The Internationale Eislauf-Vereingung (IEV) became the International Skating Union (ISU) in 1947, when English replaced German as the official language of the union. Although the title *IEV* is correct through that date, to avoid confusion ISU is used in this volume.

CHAPTER 5: THE END OF AN ERA

1. *Seventy-five Years of European and World's Championships in Figure Skating*, 148.

2. Kachler became World champion again in 1923 and later served as an ISU Council member.

3. World championships for ladies, which began in 1906, and pairs, which began in 1908, were called initially championships of the ISU, a practice that continued through 1923. They are, in fact, World Championships and are so called in this book.

4. Adams, *Skating*, 88.

5. Brokaw's first book, published in 1910, was updated significantly for the 1926 edition; shorter editions almost identical to each other were published in 1915 and 1917.

6. Brokaw, *The Art of Skating* (1910), xi.

7. The school was founded in 1883 and continues today under the name Buckingham Browne and Nichols School, following a merger with the Buckingham Girls' School in 1974.

8. Karl Zenger, a champion of Germany, placed third in the European championships of 1905 and fourth in the World Championships of 1906.

9. Meyer, *Skating with Bror Meyer*, 73.

10. In the strictest English style, the free leg touches the skating leg, but that practice was not necessarily followed. This was called the "Flick and Jam School." Browne, *Handbook of Figure Skating*, 11.

11. Swift and Clark, *The Skaters Textbook*, 41; Browne, *Handbook of Figure Skating*, 14.

12. Meagher, *Lessons in Skating*, 15.

13. Browne, *Handbook of Figure Skating*, 28, translated from *Wettlauf-Ordung der Internationalen Eislauf-Vereinigung, festgesetz vom III ordentlichen Congress zu Stockholm, 1897.*

14. British writers still refer to the "English style," long after combined skating had all but disappeared in England. As T. D. Richardson wrote in 1930, "The critic may ask what place a chapter on the English style may find in a book on Modern Figure Skating. In a biography a place is found for

ancestry!—so I excuse myself" (*Modern Figure Skating* [1930], 197). English-style skating is still practiced in a few places.

15. Syers was not the first woman to skate against men. There is reference to a Miss A. Malmgren, a Russian, competing against men at an international competition in St. Petersburg in 1890 (Brown, *Ice Skating: A History,* 147).

16. Alexander, "Lili Kronberger Szent-Györgyi," 28.

17. Ice hockey became an Olympic sport in 1920, and men's speed skating in 1924.

CHAPTER 6: COMPETITIVE SKATING BETWEEN THE WARS

1. The first international competition after the war was the Nordic Games, held in Oslo in 1919.

2. The Chamonix Games were part of the eighth Olympic Games held in Paris that year, but two years later the IOC officially designated them the first Winter Games.

3. Wright, *Skating around the World,* 37.

4. Included in addition to Italy, the United States, and Japan were Czechoslovakia, Estonia, Latvia, Poland, and Yugoslavia.

5. Although "compulsory figures" is officially the correct term, the leading writers of the period between the wars, Brokaw, Meyer, and Böckl, are all consistent in using the term *school figures.* In 1910 Brokaw labeled his chart "compulsory or school figures."

6. The USFSA abolished all tests in compulsory figures effective in 2003, a year after the cut-off date for this book.

7. Böeckl, *Willy Boeckl on Figure Skating,* 120.

8. Straight legs were not employed for spread eagles in England or France at the time Jones and Garcin wrote their books. The straight leg position came much later.

9. Entitled *System in Jumping* by T. P. C. Low, it is printed in Richardson, *Modern Figure Skating* (1938), 161–68.

10. The ISU *Judges Handbook* does not describe the jump. The USFSA *Rulebook* describes it as the "three jump (waltz jump)." A waltz jump and a three-jump are different. A waltz jump is a half-revolution jump from a forward outside edge to a backward outside edge on the opposite foot. A three-jump is a half-revolution jump from a forward outside edge to a backward inside edge on the same foot. The description in the USFSA *Rulebook* is that of a waltz jump.

11. The Lutz jump takes its name from its inventor, an obscure skater named Alois Lutz who was a member of the Vienna Skating Club. Because the rotation in the air is opposite to the takeoff edge it is the most difficult jump other than the Axel Paulsen jump. It is often cheated in performance by a quick change of edge before the point of takeoff, which then makes it a flip jump with a Lutz approach. The unofficial name for this is a "flutz jump."

12. Wright, *Skating in America,* 67.

13. Brokaw, *The Art of Skating* (1910), 72.

14. Sit spins in both directions can be seen in Curry's "Scheherazade" program recorded on the video *Magic Memories on Ice 2.*

15. Boeckl, *Willy Boeckl on Figure Skating,* 125.

16. The performance can be seen on the video *Magic Memories on Ice 2.*

17. Wright, *Skating in America,* 67.

18. For further detail see Wright, *Skating around the World,* 57. Silva's fifth-place finishes came at the World Championships in 1925 and 1926 and at the Olympic Games in 1928. There were no other appearances at the European Championships.

19. Ladies and pairs were still named "ISU champions" through 1923; beginning in 1924, the designation was changed to "World champions."

20. *100 Jahre Wiener Eislauf-Verein,* 39.

21. Wright, *Reader's Guide to Figure Skating's Hall of Fame,* no page. The competitor was Mrs. T. D. Richardson, who skated the pairs event with her husband.

22. Gisela Reichmann was the silver medalist at the World Championships in 1923, Ilse Hornung was the silver medalist at the European Championships in 1930, and Emmy Puzinger was the bronze medalist at the European Championships in 1937 and 1938.

23. Landbeck also competed successfully in speed skating, representing Austria and Belgium.

24. Bird, *Our Skating Heritage,* 55.

25. Ibid., 57.

26. Michelle Kwan won her ninth national title at the U.S. Championships in 2005.

27. Strait and Henie, *Queen of Ice, Queen of Shadows,* 76.

CHAPTER 7: SKATING WITH A PARTNER

1. Diamantidi, Korper, and Wirth, *Spuren auf dem Eise* (1892), 275.

2. Brokaw, *The Art of Skating* (1910), 116.

3. Col. H. Vaughan Kent, a former skater and NSA champion in 1897, reported much later that "from enquiries I made in Canada there is little doubt that the waltz step was skated there in the sixties of the last century, and it is identically the same step skated today to valse music." Kent, *Combined Figures and Ice-Valsing,* 128.

4. Law, *Valsing on Ice,* 9.

5. Quoted in Law, *Valsing on Ice,* 5.

6. Magnus, *Le patinage artistique,* 77.

7. Law, *Valsing on Ice,* 10.

8. Rules included in Law, *Valsing on Ice,* 39–51.

9. Ibid., 12.

10. This could have been another Austrian skater Otto Bohatsch, who skated with his wife, Mizzi.

11. Brokaw, *The Art of Skating* (1915), 163.

12. Yglesias, *Figure Skating,* 89.

13. Canada held a waltzing competition at their Nationals in 1910 but not again until 1935, when it became an annual event. The United States held a competition for the waltz and the fourteen-step in 1914, and there was an original dance competition in 1929, but dance was not a regular offering until 1936.

14. Richardson, *Modern Figure Skating* (1938), 180.

15. The article is included in Brokaw, *The Art of Skating* (1910), 122–29.

16. Meagher, *A Guide to Artistic Skating,* 112.

17. Brokaw, *The Art of Skating* (1910), 122.

18. Richardson (1887–1971) played field hockey for England. While at Cambridge University he was a successful boxer and also wrestled in two weight divisions. He was later the Swiss Open golf champion twice. Actively involved in skating throughout his life, he was a World Champion and Olympic competitor, an NSA office-holder, and a World referee as well as the author of several books on skating.

19. Quoted in Richardson, *Modern Figure Skating* (1938), 169 but not in Yglesias's books.

20. Richardson, *Modern Figure Skating* (1938), 169.

21. Meyer, *Skating with Bror Meyer,* 122.

22. Boeckl, *Willy Boeckl on Figure Skating,* 159.

23. Ibid., 161.

24. Ibid., 159.

25. Donna Atwood and Eugene Turner both entered the 1941 U.S. Nationals as singles skaters. Atwood won the junior ladies' event, and Turner won the senior men's event. Together they won the senior pair event.

26. The only French competitors in any discipline before the Brunets were pair skaters Mrs. Del Monte and Louis Magnus, who placed fifth at the World Championships in 1912. Magnus wrote an important book on skating (*Le patinage artistique,* 1914).

27. Jean Pierre Brunet was a fine pair skater with his partner Donna Jean Pospisil. They won the United States National Championship in 1945 and 1946. Brunet gave up competitive skating in 1946 to pursue his college education and was accepted for admission to the Massachusetts Institute of Technology in 1948. One month before matriculating he was killed in an automobile accident.

28. Boeckl, *Willy Boeckl on Figure Skating,* 170.

29. Ronald Ludington, a former pair skater and ice dancer as well as a highly successful coach, formed the two teams from skaters at the training center where he coached. The winning four included Elaine Asanakis, Calla Urbanski, Rocky Marval, and Joel McKeever.

30. Information furnished via e-mail by Karen Cover, archivist at the World Figure Skating Museum, Oct. 5, 2000.

31. Canadian fours were winners in both years. Christine Hough, Cindy Landry, Lyndon Johnston, and Doug Ladret won in 1989, and Stacy Ball, Isabelle Brasseur, Jean-Michelle Bombardier, and Lloyd Eisler in 1990. Two Canadian and one American fours competed each year, and a four from the Federal Republic of Germany did so in 1990.

32. Robertson, "Skate Canada," 50.

CHAPTER 8: SKATING FOR AN AUDIENCE

1. I was a member of an active skating club at Mercury Roller Rink in Norfolk, Virginia, that presented highly successful shows as late as the mid-1950s, with proceeds going to benefit polio research.

2. From an article by Paul Armitage of the New York Skating Club included in Brokaw, *The Art of Skating* (1926), 188.

3. The New York Hippodrome opened originally on April 12, 1905, as America's National Theater. Huge by standards of the day, it seated 5,200 people and featured a stage that could accommodate casts of a thousand. Over the years it provided a venue for musicals, operas, concerts, vaudeville shows, sporting events, religious services, pageants, and conventions. The last performance there was on June 27, 1939, and it was demolished later that year.

4. Brown, *Ice Skating: A History,* 151.

5. Mitsuko Funakashi is pictured doing the Charlotte stop during an Ice Capades performance in 1970. Hamilton, *Ice Capades, Years of Entertainment,* 110.

6. *Hip-Hip-Hooray!* opened on September 30, 1915, and closed on May 15, 1916, a run of 425 performances. *Get Together* opened on September 3, 1921, and closed on April 22, 1922, for a run of 397 performances.

7. For a complete synopsis of the story see "The World's First Ice Skating Movie." Nigel Brown gives the year of the film as 1915 (*Ice Skating: A History,* 151).

8. Cruikshank, *Figure Skating for Women*, 18.

9. Ibid., 14.

10. Stephenson, "The Hall of Fame," 5.

11. Strait and Henie, *Queen of Ice, Queen of Shadows*, 52.

12. Rodnina has more European titles than Henie. The lady's competition was not held at the European Championships until 1930. Henie won from 1931 through 1936.

13. Dunn, who won the silver medal at the World Championships in 1935, was Henie's constant companion during her final competitive year, a relationship that continued as she began her career in the United States. Although they never skated together competitively, Dunn was her skating partner for two years after arriving in America. He died prematurely in 1939 of tularemia (rabbit fever). Henie, *Wings on My Feet*, 54; Bird, *Our Skating Heritage*, 60.

14. Henie, *Wings on My Feet*, 84.

15. Ibid., 86.

16. Langdon, *Earls Court*, 114.

17. Strait and Henie, *Queen of Ice, Queen of Shadows*, 306.

18. She is also known, especially in England, by her married name, Mrs. Joel Riordan.

19. Brown, *Ice Skating: A History*, 173.

CHAPTER 9: THE GOLDEN AGE OF AMERICAN SKATING

1. At the Olympic Games in 1908, Horatio Torromé, an English expatriate from Argentina, competed and placed last. He is the only South American to ever compete in an ISU or an Olympic competition. No South American country has ever been a member of the union, and thus membership statistics provided do not include Argentina.

2. No senior events for men were held in Canada in 1943 and 1944 or in the United States in 1944 and 1945.

3. There are three records in the prewar years that should be noted. Roger Turner won seven consecutive titles from 1928 through 1934; Maribel Vinson won nine titles between 1928 and 1937, but owing to her being in Europe in 1934 they were not consecutive; and Theresa Weld and Nathaniel Niles won nine consecutive pair titles from 1918 to 1927. No competition was held in 1919. In 2005, three years after the cut-off date for this book, Michelle Kwan won her ninth national title.

4. Brown, *Ice Skating: A History*, 180.

5. The communist takeover creating Czechoslovakia as a satellite occurred just as the 1948 European Championships ended. Button and Scott as well as other Western skaters managed to return home safely.

6. Between Olympic events Button introduced other new jumps, including the consecutive double loop: the double-loop combination in 1949, the triple-double loop in 1950 (a sequence of three double loops), and the double Axel Paulsen–double loop combination in 1951.

7. Haponski, "Gus Lussi Speaks," 10.

8. Button, *Dick Button on Skates*, 82.

9. The only returning lady competitor other than Daphne Walker was Britta Rahlem of Sweden, who placed ninth at the World Championships in 1947.

10. Young, *The Golden Age of Canadian Figure Skating*, 87.

11. The placement in the free-skating event was, first, Virginia Baxter of the United States; second, Jacqueline du Bief; third, Tenley Albright; and, fourth, Jeannette Altwegg.

12. Fassi, *Figure Skating with Carlo Fassi*, ix.

13. Altwegg was the gold medalist twice at the European Championships (1951 and 1952); she did not compete at the World Championships in 1952.

14. Langdon, *Earls Court*, 116.

CHAPTER 10: RECOVERY IN EUROPE, PAIR SKATING, AND ICE DANCING

1. Much of this information is taken from Du Bief, *Thin Ice*, chapter 5.

2. The European and World Championships were not, however, the first postwar winter sports competitions. The Nordic Championships were held at Stockholm a full year earlier, and that same winter an international event was held in Helsinki, Finland, a country Germany marched through during its drive eastward in June 1941.

3. Wright, *Skating around the World*, 83.

4. Countries represented in 1947 but not 1948 include Australia, Finland, Norway, and Sweden.

5. In addition to Wilkie, other appointees included Marcel Nicaise of Belgium, who would later serve as a council member and vice president, and Larry Parker of the United States. Owing to illness, Parker was replaced by William O. Hickok of the United States, who would later serve on the ice dancing technical committee.

6. Fifty years later, in 1997, the ISU's headquarters was moved to Lausanne.

7. Tai Babilonia and Randy Gardner of the United States were the World champions in 1979.

8. A photographer continued taking pictures of Karol after he was asked to stop. Their father was also involved in the incident.

9. Ethel Muckelt and John Page won silver medals in 1924, and Violet and Leslie Cliff won bronze medals in 1936 and 1937.

10. Morrow was the Canadian junior champion with Norris Bowden in 1945. Diestelmeyer was the Canadian junior champion with Floriane Ducharmey in 1942, and the Canadian senior champion with Joyce Perkins in 1946.

11. The bronze medalists, Mariann and László Nagy of Hungary, were placed first by one judge, and the Nicks and the Nagys were tied by one judge.

12. The short program for pair skating was first required at the European Championships in 1963, at the World Championships in 1964, and at the Olympic Games in 1968.

13. Owing to the controversy following the pair skating at the Salt Lake City Olympics in 2002, the Canadians Jamie Salé and David Pelletier, who had been placed second to the Russians Elena Berezhnaya and Anton Sikharulidze, were awarded duplicate gold medals by the IOC on the recommendation of the ISU.

14. Group one (easy dances) are the fourteen-step and rocker foxtrot; group two (waltzes) are the European waltz, American waltz, Westminster waltz, and Viennese waltz; group three (quick dances) are the kilian, quickstep, and paso doble; and group four (slow dances) are the tango, Argentine tango, and blues.

15. *Regulations of the International Skating Union 1949*, 85.

16. Brown, *Ice Skating: A History*, 186.

17. The North American championships were not held in 1943.

18. For discussions of the dissolution of the North American Championships, see Moore, *Reflections on the CFSA*, 133–41, and Wright, *Skating in America*, 236–37.

19. ZAMBONI® is a registered trademark of the Frank J. Zamboni Company, Inc. There are other manufacturers of ice surfacing machines, but, as in many cases, the name of the primary manufacturer is often employed generically for all such machines.

20. Frank Zamboni's original machine was the Model A, and only one was built. Henie's two machines and Ice Capades' machine were the Model B, only four of which were built. The first Model B went to an ice rink in Pasadena, California.

21. Zane, *The Great Zamboni.*

22. Mitch, "A Tragedy Remembered," 37.

CHAPTER 11: THE ARTISTIC SIXTIES

1. Scott Allen competed at the World Championships through 1968. His one medal, won in 1965, was silver. None of the other skaters competed in World competition past 1964.

2. Gross, *Donald Jackson, King of Blades,* quoted on the dust jacket.

3. Young, *The Golden Age of Canadian Figure Skating,* 151–53.

4. Schnelldorfer is one of only two European men to compete at the European Championships who has won an Olympic title but not a European title. His successor, Wolfgang Schwarz, was the other.

5. Dianne de Leeuw was World champion in 1975 and the Olympic silver medalist in 1976. Although she skated for the Netherlands, the home country of her parents, she was born, trained, and lived in the United States.

6. Jutta Müller was the German Democratic Republic's junior ladies' champion in 1952 and placed second in the Senior Ladies' Championships from 1953 through 1955.

7. Young, *The Golden Age of Canadian Figure Skating,* 131.

8. The other pair was Maia Balenkaia and Igor Moskvin, who placed eleventh. Moskvin later coached the Protopopovs and is married to another highly successful Russian coach, Tamara Moskvina.

9. Wright, *Skating around the World,* 149.

10. They were married in 1957, but she used her surname, Belousova, throughout their skating career. Shelukhin, *Symphony on Ice.*

11. Ibid., 17.

12. Zhuk and Gorelik did not compete internationally in 1967 or at the European Championships in 1968.

13. Their medals include silver in 1968 and bronze in 1969 at the European Championships and silver in 1969 at the World Championships.

14. Chaikovsky, *Figures on Ice,* 61.

15. Eva used the feminine ending in the Czech language for her surname.

16. Silver medalists at the 1962 European Championships were Linda Shearman and Michael Phillips of Great Britain. They defeated Romanová and Roman again in 1963 when they became the European champions. Their only medal at the World Championships was silver in 1963.

17. Bird, *Our Skating Heritage,* 78.

18. Wright, *Skating around the World,* 146.

19. Article 3, paragraph 3, of the constitution, as printed in 1998 (earlier designated as Article 2, paragraph 2).

20. Russia's early medalists at the World Championships were Georg Sanders (bronze, 1896); Nicolai Panin (silver, 1903); and pair skaters A. L. Fischer and L. P. Popowa (bronze, 1908). At the Olympic Games in 1908, Nicolai Panin was the gold medalist in special figures.

21. Wright, *Skating around the World,* 158.

22. Five handbooks were eventually written: *Compulsory Figures, Single Free Skating, Pair Skating, Ice Dancing,* and *Synchronized Skating.* The one for compulsory figures was discontinued after they were eliminated from competition.

23. The change went into effect in the 1969 season.

24. Wright, *Skating around the World*, 144.

25. The silver samba and the starlight waltz were added in 1965; the rhumba was added in 1969; and the tango romantica, Yankee polka, and Ravensburger waltz were added in 1975. Later additions included the Austrian waltz, golden waltz, and cha cha congelado.

26. Avery Brundage (1888–1975), who participated in the decathlon and pentathlon at the 1912 Olympics at Stockholm, served as president of the U.S. Olympic Committee from 1929 through 1952. He became a member of the IOC in 1936 and was vice chair from 1945 through 1952 and president from 1952 through 1972.

CHAPTER 12: THE DYNAMIC SEVENTIES

1. Quoted from the videocassette *Magic Memories on Ice*.

2. La Chance, "Trixi Schuba, A Champion Revisited," 37.

3. Bass, *Skating, Elegance on Ice*, 33.

4. Quoted from the videocassette *Magic Memories on Ice*.

5. Milton, *Skate, One Hundred Years of Figure Skating*, 27.

6. Lynn, *Peace + Love*, 86.

7. Lynn and Fleming have five each; Merrill, who competed during the war years and beyond, has six. The only lady since Lynn to join this group is Michelle Kwan, who through 2002 has a total of six, of which five are consecutive. From the prewar era, Theresa Weld Blanchard had a total of six, of which five are consecutive, and Maribel Vinson had a total of nine, of which six are consecutive.

8. Midori Ito holds the record for perfect scores by a singles skater in technical merit, with ten at the World Championships—five in 1989 and five in 1990.

9. Bird, "Christine, Charm and Wit," 40.

10. In 1975 an ISU rule change affecting skaters who hold dual citizenship required that the choice made for their first international competition be continued throughout their amateur career. The rule was later dropped.

11. A short program was not employed at the European Championships until a year later, 1974.

12. Non-Russian World pair champions since 1965 are Tai Babilonia and Randy Gardner of the United States (1979), Sabine Baess and Tassilo Thierbach of the German Democratic Republic (1982), Barbara Underhill and Paul Martini of Canada (1984), Isabelle Brasseur and Lloyd Eisler of Canada (1993), Radka Kovaříková and René Novotny of the Czech Republic (1995), Mandy Wötzel and Ingo Steuer of Germany (1997), Jamie Salé and David Pelletier of Canada (2001), and Xue Shen and Hongbo Zhao of China (2002). At the Olympic Games in 2002, Elena Berezhnaya and Anton Sikharulidze of Russia won the competition, but duplicate gold medals were awarded afterward to Jamie Salé and David Pelletier of Canada (chapter 14).

13. Yelensky, "Acrobatics on Ice," 25.

14. Ibid., 24.

15. Ibid., 57.

16. No other pair has achieved six World titles, but seven have achieved four titles. Four did so consecutively: Herber and Baier (1936–39), Wagner and Paul (1957–60), the Protopopovs (1965–68), and Rodnina and Ulanov (1969–72). Three did not: the Brunets (1926, 1928, 1930, and 1932), Rotter and Szöllas (1931 and 1933–35), and Gordeeva and Grinkov (1986, 1987, 1989, and 1990).

17. Angelika and Erich Buck of the Federal Republic of Germany upset Pakhomova and Gorshkov at the European Championships in 1972, winning both the compulsory dances and the free dance. The results were reversed decisively eight weeks later at the World Championships.

18. Only Torvill and Dean have more perfect 6.0s, a total of fifty-six. Klimova and Ponomarenko have fifteen, and Bestemianova and Bukin have fourteen. The most for a singles skater is ten by Midori Ito. The most for a pairs' skater is nine by Irina Rodnina, collectively with her two partners.

19. Wright, *Skating around the World,* 183.

20. Article 3, section 3, states: "The ISU does not approve of interference in its sports based on political or any other grounds and will make every effort to avoid such interference."

21. Rule 134, 3b, states: "The national anthem of the country of the champion(s) shall be played and the flags of the countries of the three medal winners shall be hoisted, whenever possible (except when prevented by government or law)."

22. It was first raised to eighteen for singles skaters and eighteen and twenty for women and men in pair skating and ice dancing.

23. Wright, *Skating around the World,* 189.

CHAPTER 13: SKATING REDIRECTED: LAKE PLACID TO ALBERTVILLE

1. Although the jump was declared completed by ISU officials present, the landing was not checked, resulting in three (3) three turns on the landing edge. Thus the question of whether the jump was actually completed has long been debated.

2. Hamilton's disease was never definitively diagnosed, and after various false diagnoses he was taken to Children's Hospital in Boston and examined by Dr. Henry Shwachman, who suspected but could not confirm that it was Shwachman's Syndrom, a pancreatic enzyme deficiency Shwachman is credited with identifying.

3. Hamilton is one of several skaters who have supported humanitarian causes through their fame and wealth. Following his cure from cancer he formed the Scott Hamilton Cares Initiative, which supports cancer research and education.

4. Montgomery Wilson won the Canadian championship nine times but not consecutively (1929–35, 1938–39).

5. Stephane Lambiel of Switzerland won the World title in 2005.

6. The first four World junior ladies' champions, all from the United States, were Jill Sawyer (1978), Elaine Zayak (1979), Rosalynn Sumners (1980), and Tiffany Chin (1981). The winners of the ISU Junior Championships, which preceded the World Junior Championships, were Suzie Brasher of the United States in 1976 and Carolyn Skoczen of Canada in 1977.

7. The figure skating events were held at Hamar, Norway, which is about 120 km south of Lillehammer.

8. Vestal, "Midori Ito," 48.

9. Emi Watanabe, bronze medalist in 1979, is Japan's only ladies' medalist before Ito.

10. Walbert, "Jill Trenary, Facing the End of and Era," 31.

11. Terms for figure skating in most languages do not include reference to figures. In French the term is *patinage artistique;* in German, it is *Eiskunstlauf.*

12. David Liu of Taiwan was the last man to skate figures. Both Čižmešija and Liu received certificates.

13. Hamilton, *Landing It,* 213.

14. Baiul was the World champion at age fifteen, and Lipinski was the World champion at age fourteen. Henie was the World champion at age fourteen.

15. Hamilton, *Landing It,* 171.

16. Elena Berezhnaya and Anton Sikharulidze of Russia won gold medals in 2002, but owing to a

judging controversy, duplicate gold medals were awarded to Jamie Salé and David Pelletier of Canada (chapter 14).

17. Torvill and Dean, *Torvill and Dean: The Autobiography of Ice Dancing's Greatest Stars,* 82.

18. Although its name means "double step" in Spanish, the paso doble is a kind of one-step in duple compound meter.

19. Copley-Graves, *Figure Skating History,* 352.

20. Nations joining after 1992, the anniversary year, include Andorra, Armenia, Azerbaijan, Belarus, Bosnia/Herzegovina, Croatia, Cypress, Georgia, Iceland, Israel, Kazakhstan, Portugal, the Slovak Republic, Slovenia, Ukraine, and Uzbekistan.

21. Wright is also the author of *Skating in America* and numerous articles published in *Skating* magazine. He served as president of the USFSA from 1973 through 1976 and was honored for his service to skating through election into the World Figure Skating Hall of Fame in 1997.

CHAPTER 14: ALBERTVILLE TO SALT LAKE CITY

1. At the 1986 Congress, the ISU officially eliminated the terms *amateur* and *professional,* replacing them with *eligible* and *ineligible* to bring the General Regulations in conformity with those of the IOC.

2. The figure skating events were actually held at Hamar, Norway, which is about 120 kilometers south of Lillehammer.

3. It is noteworthy that all three medal winners in the pairs' competition were reinstated skaters. The silver medalists were Mishkutenok and Dmitriev, and the bronze medalists were Brasseur and Eisler.

4. The Grand Prix Series was called the Champions Series for its first three years, from 1996 to 1998.

5. A pairs' event was added to Skate Canada in 1984.

6. The event was originally to be called Norton Skate, and references are still made to that name, including the results published in *Skating* magazine in October 1979. The name "Flaming Leaves International Competition" was adopted to reflect the foliage in the Adirondack Mountains in late September.

7. An additional Grand Prix event, the Cup of China, was added for the 2003–4 season, which is after the cut-off date for this history.

8. Twelve points are awarded for first place, nine points for second place, seven points for third place, five points for fourth place, four points for fifth place, and so on.

9. Three prewar men won four or more World Championships: Ulrich Salchow won ten (1901–5 and 1907–11), Willy Böckl won four (1925–28), and Karl Schäfer won seven (1930–36).

10. The short program was by a five-to-two split of the judges; both free-skating programs were by four-to-three splits.

11. Sarah Hughes, who upset the field in Salt Lake City, did not proceed to the World Championships and thus has no World title. She did not retire, and it was presumed that she would retain her eligiblity and compete in future World Championships. In 2005 she joined Stars on Ice.

12. Artur Dmitriev, with his previous partner Natalia Mishkutenok, won World titles in 1991 and 1992.

13. One paperback book on each skater appeared in February: Coffee and Layden, *Thin Ice* (Harding) and Reisfeld, *Kerrigan Courage.* A second paperback book on each skater appeared later that year: Haight and Varder, *Fire on Ice* (Harding) and Coffey and Bondy, *Dreams of Gold* (Kerrigan).

14. A USFSA hearing panel stripped Harding of her title in June 1994, and the USFSA Executive Committee subsequently voted to leave the title vacant. Michelle Kwan, therefore, remains the silver medalist, and Nicole Bobek is the bronze medalist.

15. Japan has not been so successful in the pairs and dance disciplines, first competing in 1962 but not again until 1970. Since 1970 Japanese skaters have competed every year, not necessarily in both disciplines. Placements have consistently been low in the rankings.

16. Sato's mother, Kumiko Okawa, had competed at the World Championships four times, beginning in 1964; her father, Nobuo Sato, competed six times, beginning in 1960.

17. Bonaly's backflip is landed on one foot. She is the only skater to do so, and it is her signature move. She had done it six years earlier in a practice session at the Albertville Games and was warned at that time against doing it.

18. Lipinski was fifteen years and eight months old, Sonja Henie was fifteen years and ten months old, and Oksana Baiul was sixteen years and three months. The same three skaters are also the youngest World ladies' champions in the same order and approximately eleven months younger.

19. Kronberger was the World champion consecutively from 1908 to 1911. Witt was the World champion in 1984, 1985, 1987, and 1988. There have been two five-time World champions: Herma Szabo (1922–26) and Carol Heiss (1956–60). Sonja Henie was the World champion ten times, from 1927 to 1936. Kwan became a five-time World champion in 2003.

20. Czech skaters have produced World champions once in each discipline. In addition to Kavařiková and Novotny, Alena Vrzáňová was the World ladies' champion from 1949 to 1950; Eva Romanová and Pavel Roman were the World ice dancing champions from 1962 to 1965; and Ondrej Nepela was the World champion from 1971 to 1973. Nepela is the only Czech to become an Olympic champion.

21. Ekatarina Gordeeva and Sergei Grinkov, one of the Soviet Union's most successful pairs, reinstated in 1994 and won additional European and Olympic titles. They did not proceed to the World Championships that year.

22. This is the only ISU Championship title lost as the result of a doping violation.

23. Zanca, "World Triumphs," 20.

CHAPTER 15: NEW DISCIPLINES

1. The term *drill teams* was employed for only a short time and almost exclusively in the Pacific Coast section of the United States.

2. Synchronized teams in international competition are referred to and announced by the name of their country, not by the name of their team. When two teams from the same country participate, they are numbered one and two. For clarity in this book, including Appendix A, "World Championships," the team names are employed and their countries indicated.

3. Shulman, "On Balance," 26.

4. Charles DeMore, an ISU Council member and USFSA past president, is quoted in *Skating* magazine. Chyet, "Hey Precision, You've Come a Long Way Baby," 74.

5. Competitions between the University of Saskatchewan and the University of Alberta date to 1949.

6. For collegiate pairs and ice dancing, only one partner is required to be a full-time student. Laura Murphy was just thirteen when she competed.

7. Boston University, Dartmouth College, Miami University, Pennsylvania State University, University of Delaware, University of Michigan, and Western Michigan University competed in 2000.

8. The first Adult National Championships were held under the auspices of the program develop-

ment committee, which then formed an adult skating subcommittee. A separate adult skating committee was formed after the Governing Council meeting in 1998.

9. For practical reasons, the groups can be combined or subdivided at the discretion of the referee at any competition.

10. The envelope, however, is widening. At the 2002 championships held in Ann Arbor, Larry Holliday, the Championship Masters gold medalist, successfully included a triple Salchow (a double toe–loop combination jump) in his program. It is the only triple jump yet landed in the Adult National Championships.

11. Anderson, "Adult Skaters Turn Out in Force," 30.

12. E-mail from Schwartz, Feb. 20, 2004.

13. Cooper, "Foreign Exchange," 17.

CHAPTER 16: THE WORLD OF PROFESSIONAL SKATING

1. For the genesis of the three prewar shows see chapter 8.

2. The Skating Club of Boston continues to offer its annual Ice Chips, advertised as the longest-running, club-sponsored ice carnival.

3. Hamilton, *Ice Capades, Years of Entertainment,* 56.

4. Wirtz owned the name Hollywood Ice Review and continued presenting ice shows under that name for five years.

5. Ice Capades also purchased ice-making equipment in the early 1950s.

6. Fortunately there were no deaths. Blame for the disaster was placed on construction workers who failed to install adequate bracing on the temporary bleachers.

7. The four numbers were entitled "Paso Doble," "Barnum," "Mack and Mabel," and "Bolero."

8. Other early cast members included Sandy Lenz, Brian Pockar, the dance couple of Judy Blumberg and Michael Seibert, and the pair team of Lisa Carey and Chris Harrison.

9. Seventeen women, seventeen men, thirteen pairs, and fifteen dance couples competed in Colorado Springs. The two members of the 1969 tour who did not compete were Hana Masková of Czechoslovakia who had withdrawn and Karen Magnussen of Canada who had sustained an injury before the competition but who had competed at the World Championships the previous year.

10. Hamill had skated on Collins' tours as early as 1975.

11. Sharon Carz and Doug Williams placed fourth at the U.S. Nationals in 1991. Angela Deneweth and John Denton placed fifth at the U. S. Nationals in 1990.

12. An ice dancing event was held in 1939, but other events were not held.

13. Two Americans, Howard Nicholson and Nathan Walley each successively won two men's titles, 1932 through 1935. One title each was won by Reginald E. Park of Australia in 1953, Melitta Brunner of Austria in 1932, and the pair of Ferdinand Leemans and Elvire Collin of Belgium in 1949.

14. Cecilia Colledge won in 1947 and 1948. Jennifer Nicks who with her brother John won the 1953 World Championship in pairs won the Open Professional Championship as a singles skater in 1955 and 1956.

15. There was unresolved conflict involving the similarity of the names employed for the two championships: "World Professional Championships" for the Jaca competitions and "World Professional Figure Skating Championships" for Button's competitions.

16. The Legends in Huntington, West Virginia, October 10–11; Northwestern Mutual Life World Team Skating Championships in Milwaukee, Wisconsin, October 20; Riders Ladies Skating Championships in Mankato, Minnesota, and Rosemont, Illinois, October 25 and 28; Starlight Championships

in New York, New York, October 30; Gold Championships in Vancouver, British Columbia, November 18; Canadian Professional Figure Skating Championships in Hamilton, Ontario, December 1–2; and World Professional Figure Skating Championships in Landover, Maryland, December 9.

17. The championships were called the U.S. Professional Figure Skating Championships through 1984. They were renamed the U.S. Open Professional Figure Skating Championships.

EPILOGUE

1. Lund, *Frozen Assets,* 116.

2. Ibid., 89. The decline in attendance is reported to have been 40 to 50 percent in 2002.

3. Kristi Yamaguchi, another of the company's long-time and most popular members, retired at the end of the 2002 season.

4. The three jumps were a quadruple Salchow done in combination with a triple toe loop, a quadruple toe loop, and a solo quadruple Salchow.

5. Alexei Yagudin retired from competitive skating in 2004 owing to injuries.

6. Taken from Article 3 of the *ISU Constitution and General Regulations.*

7. Elfman and Lund, "The Beef Goes On," 39–40.

8. Elfman, "Judging Faces the Jury," 24.

9. Elfman, "Imperialist Union," 44.

10. Ibid., 42.

11. For detailed information on points awarded for elements as well as for the program components, see "New Judging System Figure Skating/Ice Dancing," International Skating Union Communication no. 1207.

12. Ibid., 40.

13. CAS determined "that the 2002 Congress had been conducted properly and that unless violation of the ISU Constitution or Swiss law is proved, the CAS cannot review Congress decisions." ISU Circular Letter 589.

14. Elfman, "To the Point," 44.

SELECTED BIBLIOGRAPHY

"Acrobatic Skaters." *New York Times,* Feb. 23, 1886.

Adams, Douglas. *Skating.* London: George Bell and Sons, 1890.

Alberts, Robert C. *Benjamin West: A Biography.* Boston: Houghton Mifflin, 1978.

Alexander, Freda. "Lili Kronberger Szent-Györgyi." *Skating* 42 (April 1965): 28.

Anderson, William H. "Adult Skaters Turn Out in Force." *Skating* 72 (June 1995): 30–32.

Bang, Gunnar. *Konståkingens 100–åriga historia.* Malmö: Absalons Forlag, 1966.

Bass, Howard. *Skating: Elegance on Ice.* London: Chartwell Books, 1980.

Bird, Dennis. "Christine, Charm and Wit." *Skating* 51 (May 1974): 40–41, 59.

——. *Our Skating Heritage: A Centenary History of the National Skating Association of Great Britain, 1879–1979.* London: National Skating Association of Great Britain, 1979.

Boeckl, Wilhelm Richard. *Willy Boeckl on Figure Skating.* New York: Moore Press, 1937.

Brokaw, Irving. *The Art of Skating.* New York: Charles Schribner's Sons, 1910.

——. *The Art of Skating.* New York: American Sports Publishing, 1915.

Browne, George H. *Figure Skating with Seventy-four Illustrations and Diagrams.* Boston: Perry Mason, 1892.

——. *A Handbook of Figure Skating.* Springfield, Mass.: Barney and Berry, 1900, 1910, 1913.

Brown, Nigel. *Ice Skating: A History.* New York: A. S. Barnes, 1959.

Button, Dick. *Dick Button on Skates.* Englewood Cliffs: Prentice-Hall, 1955.

"Canadian Skating Events." *New York Times,* Feb. 1, 1888.

Chaikovsky, Anatoly. *Figures on Ice.* Moscow: Progress Publishers, 1978.

Charter and By-laws of the Philadelphia Skating Club and Humane Society. Philadelphia: J. B. Chandler, Printer, 1864.

Chyet, Jennifer. "Hey Precision, You've Come a Long Way Baby." *Skating* 68 (April 1991): 70–74.

Coffey, Frank, and Joe Layden. *Thin Ice: The Complete Uncensored Story of Tonya Harding, America's Bad Girl of Ice Skating.* New York: Pinnacle Books, 1994.

Coffey, Wayne, and Filip Bondy. *Dreams of Gold: The Nancy Kerrigan Story.* New York: St. Martin's Paperbacks, 1994.

Constitution and General Regulations, 1998–2000. Lausanne: International Skating Union, 1998.

Cooper, Michelle. "Foreign Exchange." *Skating* 78 (Feb. 2001): 17–18, 64, 70.

Copley-Graves, Lynn. *Figure Skating History: The Evolution of Dance on Ice.* Columbus: Platoro Press, 1992.

Cruikshank, James A. *Figure Skating for Women.* New York: American Sports Publishing, 1922.

Cyclos [George Anderson]. *The Art of Skating; with Plain Directions for the Acquirement of the Most Difficult and Elegant Moves.* Glasgow: Thomas Murray and Son, 1852.

Dědič, Josef. *Single Figure Skating for Beginners and Champions.* Prague: Olympia, 1974.

Dench, Robert, and Rosemarie Stewart. *Pair Skating and Dancing on Ice.* New York: Prentice-Hall, 1943.

Diamantidi, Demeter, Carl von Korper, and Max Wirth. *Spuren auf dem Eise.* Vienna: Alfred Hölder, 1881.

———. *Spuren auf dem Eise.* Vienna: Alfred Hölder, 1892.

Du Bief, Jacqueline. *Thin Ice.* London: Cassell, 1956.

Duff-Taylor, Squire. *Skating.* London: Seeley, Service, 1930.

The Edinburgh Skating Club with Diagrams of Figures and a List of Members. Edinburgh: N.p., 1865.

Elfman, Lois. "Imperialist Union, Blind Judgements of the ISU Put In Crisis." *International Figure Skating* 9 (May–June 2003): 40–44.

———. "Judging Faces the Jury." *International Figure Skating* 8 (Jan.–Feb. 2003): 24–25.

———. "To the Point: The Skating World Tries Out a New Judging System." *International Figure Skating* 10 (March–April 2004): 40–44.

———, and Mark A. Lund. "The Beef Goes On." *International Figure Skating* 8 (July–Aug. 2002): 39–41.

Fassi, Carlo. *Figure Skating with Carlo Fassi.* New York: Charles Schribner's Sons, 1980.

"Feats on Skates." *New York Times,* March 2, 1875.

Ferraro, Edward. *The Art of Dancing.* New York: N.p., 1859.

Fitz Stephen, William. *Norman London.* New York: Italica Press, 1990.

Fuchs, Gilbert. *Theorie und Praxis des Kunstlaufes am Eise.* Laibach: Selbstverlag, 1926.

Garcin, Jean. *Le vrai patineur.* Paris: J. Gillé Fils, 1813.

Gill, Edward L. *The Skater's Manual: A Complete Guide to the Art of Skating.* New York: Andrew Peck, Publishers, 1867.

Gross, George. *Donald Jackson, King of Blades.* Toronto: Queen City Publishing, 1977.

Haight, Abby, and J. E. Vader. *Fire on Ice: The Exclusive Inside Story of Tonya Harding.* New York: Times Books, 1994.

Hamilton, F. F., Jr. *Ice Capades "Years of Entertainment."* Washington: Penchant Publishing, 1974.

Hamilton, Scott, with Lorenzo Benet. *Landing It: My Life On and Off the Ice.* New York: Kensington Books, 1999.

Haponski, William. "Gus Lussi Speaks." *Skating* 47 (June 1970): 10–11, 42–43.

Henie, Sonja. *Wings on My Feet.* New York: Prentice-Hall, 1940.

Hird, Winfield A. "The Father of Figure Skating." *Skating* 28 (Jan. 1941): 5–7.

Hügin, Otto, and Jack Gerschwiler. *The Technique of Skating.* London: Cassell, 1977.

100 Jahre Wiener Eislauf-Verein. Vienna: N.p., 1967.

"Intricate Figure Skating." *New York Times,* Feb. 22, 1880.

Jones, Robert. *The Art of Skating.* London: William Cole, 1772.

Judges' Handbook 1: Compulsory Figures. Davos Platz: International Skating Union, 1984.

Judges' Handbook 2: Single Free Skating and the Technical Program. Davos Platz: International Skating Union, 1993.

Judges' Handbook 3: Pair Skating. Davos Platz: International Skating Union, 1993.

Judges' Handbook 4: Ice Dancing. Davos Platz: International Skating Union, 1988.

Judges' Handbook 5: Synchronized Skating. Lausanne: International Skating Union, 1999.

Kent, Herbert Vaughan. *Combined Figures and Ice-Valsing.* London: Hutchinson, 1930.

La Chance, Leo E. "Trixi Schuba: A Champion Revisited." *Skating* 70 (Jan. 1993): 36–38, 41.

Langdon, Claude. *Earls Court.* London: Stanley Paul, 1953.

Law, Ernest. *Valsing on Ice Described and Analysed with Hints for Attaining Proficiency in the Art.* London: Hugh Rees, 1908.

Lindsay, Peter Leslie. "A History of Sport in Canada, 1807–1867." Ph.D. diss., University of Alberta, Edmonton, 1969.

Lowther, Henry Cecil, *Combined Figure Skating.* London: Horace Cox, 1902.

Lund, Mark A. *Frozen Assets.* Worcester: Ashton International Media, 2002.

Lussi, Gustave, and Maurice Richards. *Championship Figure Skating.* New York: A. S. Barnes, 1951.

Lynn, Janet, with Dean Merrill. *Peace + Love.* Carol Stream: Creation House, 1973.

Magic Memories on Ice. Videocassette. ABC Sports, 1990.

Magic Memories on Ice 2. Videocassette. ABC Sports, 1993.

Magnus, Louis. *Le patinage artistique.* Paris: Bibliothèque Larousse, 1914.

Meagher, George A. *A Guide to Artistic Skating.* London: T. C. and E. C. Jack, 1919.

———. *Lessons in Skating.* New York: Dodd, Mead, 1900.

Meyer, Bror. *Skating with Bror Meyer.* New York: Doubleday, Page, 1921.

Milton, Steve. *Skate: One Hundred Years of Figure Skating.* North Pomfret, Vt.: Trafalgar Square Publishing, 1996.

Mitch, Dale. "A Tragedy Remembered." *Skating* 63 (Feb. 1986): 34–41, 67.

Monier-Williams, Montagu, Winter Randall Pidgeon, and Arthur Dryden. *Figure Skating Simple and Combined.* New York: Macmillan, 1892.

Moore, Teresa. *Reflections on the CFSA, 1887–1990.* Gloucester, Ont.: Canadian Figure Skating Hall of Fame, 1993.

Moskvina, Tamara, and Igor Moskvin. *Pair Skating as Sport and Art.* Davos Platz: International Skating Union, 1993.

"New Judging System Figure Skating/Ice Dancing." International Skating Union Communication 1207, April 16, 2003.

Hundert Jahre Wiener Eislauf-Verein. Vienna: N.p., 1967.

Owen, Maribel Vinson. *The Fun of Figure Skating.* New York: Harper and Row, 1960.

Regulations of the International Skating Union 1949. Davos Platz: International Skating Union, 1949.

Reisfeld, Randi. *The Kerrigan Courage: Nancy's Story.* New York: Ballentine Books, 1994.

Richardson, T. D. *Modern Figure Skating.* Rev. ed. London: Bethune, 1938.

Robertson, Peter K. "Skate Canada." *Skating* 66 (Dec. 1989): 42–50.

Seventy-five Years of European and World's Championships in Figure Skating: Results in Figure Skating. N.p.: International Skating Union, 1967.

Shelukhin, Anatoly A. *Symphony on Ice: The Protopopovs.* Columbus, Ohio: Platoro Press, 1993.

Shulman, Carole. "One Balance." *Professional Skater Magazine* 31 (May–June 2000): 26–27, 32–33.

"Skating: Progress of Our People in the Accomplishment." *New York Times,* Dec. 31, 1865.

"The Skating Scene." *New York Times,* Dec. 8, 1867.

Stephenson, Richard. "The Hall of Fame." *Skating* 63 (March 1986): 68–69.

Strait, Raymond, and Leif Henie. *Queen of Ice, Queen of Shadows: The Unsuspected Life of Sonja Henie.* Lanham: Scarborough House, 1985.

Swift, Frank, and Marvin R. Clark. *The Skaters Text Book.* New York: John A. Gray and Green, 1868.

Syers, Edgar, and Madge Syers. *The Art of Skating (International Style).* London: Horace Cox, 1913.

Terták, Elemér, and Benjamin T. Wright, eds. *Results: Figure Skating Championships, 1968–1991.* Davos Platz: International Skating Union, 1992.

Thompson, Norcliffe G., and F. Laura Cannan. *Hand-in-Hand Figure-Skating.* London: Longmans, Green, 1896.

Torvill, Jayne, and Christopher Dean, with John Man. *Torvill and Dean: The Autobiography of Ice Dancing's Greatest Stars.* Secaucus: Carol Publishing Group, 1998.

United States Figure Skating Association Rulebook. Colorado Springs: U.S. Figure Skating Association (published annually).

Vandervell, H. E., and T. Maxwell Witham. *A System of Figure Skating, Being the Theory and Practice of the Art as Developed in England, with a Glance at its Origin and History.* London: McMillan, 1869.

Vestal, Deb. "Midori Ito." *Skating* 65 (Oct. 1988): 46–48.

Vinson, Maribel Y. *Advanced Figure Skating.* New York: McGraw-Hill, 1940.

——. *Primer of Figure Skating.* New York: McGraw-Hill, 1938.

Walbert, Gerri. "Jill Trenary, Facing the End of an Era." *Skating* 66 (Dec. 1989): 28–31.

Weyden, Erik Van Der. *Dancing on Ice.* London: C. Arthur Pearson, 1951.

Witham, T. Maxwell. *A System of Figure Skating, Being the Theory and Practice of the Art as Developed in England, with a Glance at Its Origin and History.* London: Horace Cox, 1897.

"The World's First Ice Skating Movie." *Skating* 68 (July 1991): 21.

Wright, Benjamin T. *Reader's Guide to Figure Skating's Hall of Fame.* Boston: United States Figure Skating Association, 1981.

——. *Skating around the World, 1892–1992: The One-Hundredth Anniversary History of the International Skating Union.* Davos Platz: International Skating Union, 1992.

——. *Skating in America: The Seventy-fifth Anniversary History of the United States Figure Skating Association.* Colorado Springs: U.S. Figure Skating Association, 1996.

——, and Elemér Terták. *Office Holders through the Years and ISU Congresses 1892–1990.* Davos Platz: International Skating Union, 1992.

Yglesias, Herbert Ramon. *Figure Skating.* London: George Routledge and Sons, Limited, n.d.

Young, David. *The Golden Age of Canadian Figure Skating.* Toronto: Summerhill Press, 1984.

Zanca, Salvatore. "World Triumphs." *Skating* 79 (May 2002): 12–21.

Zane, D. B. *The Great Zamboni.* Cypress, Calif.: Dizon Publishing, 1998.

INDEX

JAMES R. HINES "lived on skates" during his teen years. Following that came more than ten years of college, resulting in degrees through the Ph.D. from Old Dominion University, Virginia Commonwealth University, and the University of North Carolina-Chapel Hill in music theory and music history. A long career as an educator resulted, but his love of skating never ceased. He is a professor of music at Christopher Newport University in Newport News, Virginia.

The University of Illinois Press
is a founding member of the
Association of American University Presses.

———————————————————————

Composed in 10/14.5 Meta Normal
with Meta and Trajan display
by Jim Proefrock
at the University of Illinois Press
Designed by Paula Newcomb
Manufactured by Four Colour Imports

University of Illinois Press
1325 South Oak Street
Champaign, IL 61820-6903
www.press.uillinois.edu